American Building

American Building

The Environmental Forces That Shape It

James Marston Fitch
with William Bobenhausen

New York / Oxford / Oxford University Press / 1999

This new edition of *American Building: The Environmental Forces That Shape It* is
dedicated to the American Institute of Architects Committee on the Environment (COTE).

Oxford University Press

Oxford   New York
Athens   Auckland   Bangkok   Bogotá   Buenos Aires   Calcutta
Cape Town   Chennai   Dar es Salaam   Delhi   Florence   Hong Kong   Istanbul   Karachi
Kuala Lumpur   Madrid   Melbourne   Mexico City   Mumbai
Nairobi   Paris   São Paulo   Singapore   Taipei   Tokyo   Toronto   Warsaw

and associated companies in
Berlin   Ibadan

This book was designed and set in Apollo and Rotis by Jeff Hoffman.

Cataloging-in-Publication Data
Fitch, James Marston.
American building : the environmental forces that shape it / by
James Marston Fitch, William Bobenhausen.
p.   cm.   Includes bibliographical references and index.
ISBN 0-19-511040-4
1. Architecture and society—United States.
I. Bobenhausen, William, 1949– .
II. Title.
NA2543.S6F54   1999
720'.973—dc21   98-15670

1 3 5 7 9 8 6 4 2
Printed in the United States of America
on acid-free paper

Contents

Foreword by Richard Blinder   vii

Preface   ix

1   Experiential Bases for Esthetic Decisions   3

2   The Social Consequences of Architectural Intervention   24

3   Fair and Warmer   37
Control of the Thermal Environment

4   Pure as the Air You Breathe   68
Control of the Atmospheric Environment

5   "Oh, Say, Can You See . . ."   102
Control of the Luminous Environment

6   Silence—Men At Work   147
Control of the Sonic Environment

7   The Architectural Manipulation of Space, Time, and Gravity   182

8   Skeleton and Skin   221
The Morphological Development of Structural Systems

9   The Integration of Environmental Control Systems   257

10   Plan: The Instrument of Policy   299

11   Toward Sustainability   329

12   Prospects for the Democratic Esthetic   349

Notes   361

Credits for Illustrations   373

Index   379

Foreword

Richard Blinder

In a world where considerations of style have overshadowed those of substance and in a profession whose loudest voices have promoted fashionable rather than meaningful form in architecture, there has been one clear consistent voice of reason concerned with the built world and the forces that shape it: the voice of James Marston Fitch. In his role as educator, author, critic, and design practitioner for more than six decades now, Fitch has both pioneered and continually defined and redefined the goals of a viable architecture, old and new.

When American architectural historiography was still in its infancy, Fitch's *American Building: The Forces That Shape It* (1948) helped to formulate the social and structural goals of his generation of architects and historians. When, in the decade of the 1950s, modernism in architecture began to show signs of degenerating into a sterile formalism, Fitch—then architectural editor at *House Beautiful*—proposed an architecture based upon microclimatic analysis, a concept definitively presented in his *American Building: The Environmental Forces That Shape It* (1972). As "urban renewal" began to lay waste to America's vital city centers, Fitch created the nation's first academic program in historic preservation at Columbia University in 1964—its purpose to train young architects, planners, and historians to preserve and restore the historic buildings and districts then threatened with destruction. In turn, when preservationists, caught up in zealous fervor, began to see cities as museums, it was Fitch who prodded his colleagues, reminding them that the city is an ever-changing, rather than static, organism. In his seminal book, *Historic Preservation: Curatorial Management of the Built World* (1982), Fitch reminded us that the built world is a functional whole, one in which buildings of past and present must coexist as the foundation for the future.

Fitch's pioneering and provocative work, aimed at preserving America's built legacy while making it a better place in which to live, is fully documented in his formidable bibliography of books and articles, published both in the United States and abroad. From his first essay to appear in print in 1933, a discussion of the reasons why the forces of modernism were bound to triumph over the historicizing eclecticism of the day, to his more recent arguments against the vapidity of post-modernist theory, Fitch's voice has retained one clear principle: architecture, indeed design in general, should respect the forces inherent in nature while both serving and expressing the values basic to modern American society.

Few people have so fundamentally transformed the conscience of our profession. For his reasoned yet compassionate work, his publications, his lectures, his key positions as educator, consultant and practitioner, and his foreign missions (to India, Japan, Italy, Central Europe, and Lebanon, among others), Fitch has received numerous awards and diplomas, including five honorary doctorates, the AIA Gold Medal (1976), the ACSA Distinguished Professorship (1986), and the Louise du Pont Crowninshield Award (1985). Although he entered the field as a traditional *beaux arts* architect, the Depression years forced him to work in areas that provided a broadening experience, first with the Tennessee Valley Authority and then with the newly founded Federal Housing Authority in Washington. The offer of a job as an editor at the *Architectural Record* brought him to New York in 1936 and put him in contact with the exciting new developments in modern architecture then beginning to take hold in the United States.

Possibly the most crucial experience in his formation was the U.S. Army's assigning him to training in meteorology during his World War II service. The study of weather led him to the perception that people's experiences of their own local microclimates were the realities that determined architecture. He gradually came to see that people, buildings, and the environment all modified each other, with the ultimate result that human capacities were able to blossom as never before.

"I began to see all this functioning on three scales," he says. "Micro, mezzo, and macro, if you will. Starting with clothing and extending to buildings, with cities as the scale that extends beyond buildings. Obviously I didn't invent any of this. But I think I was the first to give it an holistic formation for architects, and slowly it began to organize my thinking about what I wanted to tell people about how any building that is worthy of the name building works in their favor."

This is ultimately the subject of the book at hand: how architecture can modify the environment in man's favor, which is, after all, what has made possible the great preponderance of human accomplishment. In chapter after chapter Fitch details with scientific precision the various ways architecture can intervene to allow the warm-blooded mammals we call "humans" to function at their maximum potential. Diagrams supplement the text to demonstrate how light, sound, and temperature can be architecturally manipulated to provide the maximum comfort, along with a minimum of environmental depletion. Generations of architects have by now had their consciousness raised by the contents of this book. Updated with the latest technical information by architect William Bobenhausen, this new edition will continue to impact beneficially on the architectural profession and the architectural consumer alike.

Preface

This book is the second edition of my study that was first published in 1972 under the identical title, *American Building: The Environmental Forces That Shape It*. That book was in turn the reappearance of the second half of a still earlier version with almost the same title, *American Building: The Forces That Shape It* (Houghton Mifflin, 1948). Thus the substance of the present volume has been in print for just on fifty years. And the response those earlier versions have continued to generate would seem to justify a new, updated edition. I am therefore reprinting substantially in its entirety the general text, which explicates my broad concepts of man-environment relations. The original text was richly documented by case histories, support information, and statistics, most of which remain valid. However, because of advances in the field, some of this information required updating and augmentation to encompass new developments. To this end I enlisted the assistance of William Bobenhausen, an architect who specializes in environmentally responsible design and who has served on the faculties of The City College of New York, Pratt Institute, and New Jersey Institute of Technology. He undertook the exacting task of updating the case studies and supporting text to reflect the most recent advances in both theory and practice in the field. He thus becomes co-author of this book.

James Marston Fitch
November 1998

The last time this volume was published was the year before the first world energy crisis. I was just completing architectural studies and entering the profession. Since then, I have taught upwards of three thousand university students and thousands of architects on environmentally sensitive and responsible design. The lessons came not from school, but from personal effort, study, and application of fundamental principles—as I was profoundly inspired early on by the writings of Fitch and the Olgyays. When invited to collaborate on this edition, I was honored, and gladly agreed. With this revised edition, including the new chapter, "Toward Sustainability," we hope to inform, motivate, and impassion yet a new generation of architects.

William Bobenhausen
November 1998

We are grateful for the contributions of the following specialists who have made it possible to bring the book up to the minute as far as technical information is concerned. Engineer Horst Berger provided an incisive review of the material on structures and generously contributed photographs from his own recently published work. Catherine Coombs Bobenhausen, a certified industrial hygienist, assisted throughout the research and updating process, particularly in the area of air quality. Gary Siebein, an acoustical consultant, contributed his expertise on the subject. Dr. John Kinney checked selected medical references in the text for their accuracy and relevance. Manny Halpern reviewed the section on ergonomics, a science that was in its infancy when this book was last published. Architect William McDonough granted permission to include the "Hannover Principles" and a case study of his work. We greatly appreciate the contributions of Donald Prowler, including his insightful review of the manuscript as it was nearing completion. We would like to also express our appreciation to the Lincoln Center for the Performing Arts, Fay Jones, Steven Strong, Joyce Lee, Diane Serber, and Dori Clarke for providing photographs for this edition.

A generous grant from Furthermore, the publication program of The J. M. Kaplan Fund, supported the publication of this book. Our special gratitude goes to Joyce Berry, Art and Architecture Editor at Oxford University Press, for her guidance and support during the lengthy process of revision. And we greatly appreciate the superlative copy editing of Madeline Gutin Perri and the management of the production effort directed by Joellyn Ausanka at Oxford.

The environmental forces that we must take into consideration when shaping our buildings have not greatly changed in the decades since the book was first written. What has changed is the degree to which these forces are understood, especially on a local or meso-climatic level, and it is gratifying to see that the quality of the design response continues to improve. However, with increasing evidence of profound climatic changes being triggered by the combustion gases generated by worldwide industrialization, the challenges of creating an environmentally benign architecture are more urgent than ever.

The Authors
November 1998

American Building

Experiential Bases for Esthetic Decisions

The fundamental thesis of this book is that the ultimate task of architecture is to act in favor of human beings — to interpose itself between people and the natural environment in which they find themselves in such a way as to remove the gross environmental load from their shoulders. The central function of architecture is thus to lighten the very stress of life. Its purpose is to maximize our capacities by permitting us to focus our limited energies upon those tasks and activities that are the essence of the human experience.

This successful interposition between people and their natural environment furnishes the material basis of all great architecture. To wrest the objective conditions for our optimal development and well-being from a Nature that only seldom provides them, to satisfy our physiological and psychological requirements at optimal levels — this, beyond question, is the objective basis of any architecture that is both beautiful and good. To design such buildings, as Gropius once so movingly put it, is an authentic act of love.

It goes without saying that all architects aspire to the creation of beautiful buildings. But a fundamental weakness in most discussions of architectural esthetics is a failure to relate it to its matrix of experiential reality. Our whole literature suffers from this conceptual limitation in that it tends to divorce the esthetic process from the rest of experience, as though it were an abstract problem in pure logic. Thus we persist in discussing buildings as though their esthetic impact upon us were an exclusively visual phenomenon. And this leads immediately to serious misconceptions as to the actual relationship between the building and its human occupants. Our very terminology reveals this misapprehension: we speak of having *seen* such and such a building, of liking or not liking its *looks*, of its *seeming* too large or too small in scale. These are all useful terms, of course, insofar as they convey a part of the whole truth about our relationship to our buildings. But they are also extremely misleading in suggesting that we exist in some dimension quite separate and apart from our buildings—that our only relationship with them is that of passive exposure, that this exposure occurs only along the narrow channel of vision, and that the whole experience is unaffected by the environment in which it occurs.

The facts are of course quite otherwise, and our modes of thought must be revised to correspond to them. For architecture—like human beings themselves—is totally submerged in the natural external environment. It can never be felt, perceived, experienced, in anything less than multidimensional totality. A change in one aspect or quality of this environment inevitably affects our perception of and response to all the rest. Recognition of this fact is crucial for esthetic theory, above all for architectural esthetics. Far from being narrowly based upon any single sense of perception such as vision, our response to a building derives from our body's *total* response to and perception of the environmental conditions the building affords. It is literally impossible to experience architecture in any "simpler" way. *In architecture there are no spectators: there are only protagonists, participants.* The body of critical literature that pretends otherwise is based largely upon photographs of buildings rather than the experience of the actual building. (It seldom occurs to us to remember that even when we study the pictures of one building in a book or magazine, we usually do so while sheltered by another. We could no more enjoy photographs of a beautiful building while seated on a bench in the pouring rain than we could respond favorably to a concert in a storm-tossed lifeboat at sea. Most such esthetic experiences occur in the controlled environment of architecture.)

Analogies between architecture and the other forms of art are common in esthetic literature. Obviously, architecture shares many formal characteristics with them. Like a painting or a sculpture, a ballet or a symphony, a building may be analyzed from the point of view of proportion, balance, rhythm, color, texture, and so on. But such analogies will be misleading unless we constantly bear in mind that our experiential relationship with architecture is fundamentally of a different order from that of the other arts. With architecture, we are *submerged* in the experience, whereas the relationship between us and a painting or a symphony is much more one of simple *exposure*. (Even here, however, we must be careful not to oversimplify reality. The primary significance of a painting may indeed be visual, or of a concert, aural, but perception of these art forms occurs always in a situation of experiential totality.)

Leonardo da Vinci claimed for painting a great advantage over the other forms of art—namely, that the painter had the unique power of fixing, once and for all, not only the vantage point from which his or her painting was to be viewed but also the internal environment (illumination, atmospheric effects, spatial organization) under which the painted action took place. Such a claim is only partly true for any art form, as we have just seen—for architecture it is preposterous. Nevertheless, architects since the Renaissance have accepted without challenge this proposition, thereby obscuring another fundamental difference between architecture and the other arts. The other arts involve a unilinear exposure,* a one-way and irreversible sequence of events, while the experience of architecture, on the contrary, is polydirectional.

This Davincian restriction has been perpetuated, ironically enough, by the development of still photography. The photographer can capture only the visual facsimile of the building, being by definition unable to present a facsimile of all sensory aspects—that is, how it smells, feels, and sounds. But even as a purely visual facsimile, the photograph has invisible limitations of great consequence. The photographer, like Leonardo's painter, is limited by both choice and necessity to delineating only a few aspects (among the infinity of possible ones) of the building's behavior: *time* (day or night, winter or summer); *space* (front or back, living room or kitchen, aerial or worm's-eye view); *condition* (empty or furnished, occupied or vacant, clean or dirty, sunshine or rain).

All of these inherent limitations of photography make it in the highest degree unlikely that, upon such doubly limited sensory data, we could arrive at a viable estimate of the experiential reality of the building. And yet the fame of most of the monuments of modern architecture often rests upon exactly such a narrow factual base. In some cases this is inevitable, the photographic facsimile having long outlived the original (e.g., Mies van der Rohe's Barcelona Exposition building of 1929, which has only recently been rebuilt—Fig. 1−1).

* This linearity is most obvious in novel or play, ballet or symphony, where esthetic satisfaction is dependent upon the orderly unrolling of a fused line of narrative or musical development.

Figure 1–1 / German Pavilion, Barcelona Exposition, Spain, 1929. Ludwig Mies van der Rohe, architect. The fame of the building is based largely on this photograph, yet little data is given on actual environmental conditions the pavilion afforded at the hot Spanish noon.

In this case and in others (e.g., the view from below the falls of the Frank Lloyd Wright house at Bear Run, Pennsylvania—Fig. 1–2) the photograph has become more famous than the building or structure itself! These photographs are not mendacious. Such aspects of these buildings do (or did), of course, exist, and what these facsimiles bring us of their (vanished) presence is important. But they represent at best only the merest fraction of the total, polydimensional experiential reality of the actual building. And we must constantly bear this in mind if we are to comprehend the full complexity of architectural design.

Then there is the Haj Terminal at Jeddah International Airport, which is widely admired for its structural virtuosity yet rarely appreciated for satisfying its primary design intention: to mediate the intense heat of the Saudi desert (see Fig. 1–3). Each year hundreds of thousands of pilgrims arrive by air during the Holy Month of the Haj on their way to Mecca. After deplaning from one of the hundred Boeing 747s that might arrive on a given day during the Holy Month, the pilgrims are shaded by the vast tented structure as they await buses for Mecca. This structure gives the whole complex a noticeably gentler microclimate than the desert outside.

It should be mentioned that today's architects can study the three-dimensional qualities of buildings during the design process by using computer programs that allow them to virtually walk through the various spaces of the building. In some sense, this type of

Figure 1–2 / House at Bear Run, Pennsylvania, 1935. Frank Lloyd Wright, architect. Taken from an improbable vantage point in midwinter, this photograph tells us nothing about inside conditions where the cascade is invisible, perceivable only as noise, humidity, and chill.

A

B

Figure 1–3 / Haj Terminal, Jeddah
International Airport, Saudi Arabia,
1981. Skidmore Owings & Merrill, architects. The ambient air temperature on a
typical Jeddah day is about 95°F. Had the
terminal been covered in a more conventional manner with a concrete or metal
roof, the air temperature within the open
air terminal would approach 150°F.
Instead, the Teflon-coated fiberglass fabric structure protects the pilgrims from
the searing desert sun while limiting air
temperatures to about 104°F. Views are
(A) Exterior view showing scale compared to a 747 aircraft; (B) Interior view
of pilgrims awaiting bus transport to
Mecca beneath fabric structure.

simulation has revolutionized design, allowing architects to "experience" potential solutions for the proposed building. In reality, this is yet another way of limiting our observations to the sense of vision. Fundamentally, there has been no great leap forward from photography; architects are still prone to focus on the visual at the expense of polydimensional reality.

Building Regulates the Body's Transactions

As completely as fish in water, people are submerged in their own environment, the limits of which appear to be fixed in both a temporal and a spatial sense. But, unlike fish, people act upon their environment as well as being acted upon by it. Conscious attempts at manipulating it are at least as old as the human species. And the cumulative results of such attempts have been — especially in recent times — to give contemporary men and women a much wider knowledge of their environment, and much greater control over it, than ever before. It lies within neither the scope of this study nor the competence of its authors to delineate more than a small portion of the complex relationship between people and their natural environment. Nevertheless, as a result of the rapid expansion of both the earth and life sciences, it is imperative for architects to understand the essential nature of this relationship, as building is the most important instrument used to modify it.

Our physical environment must be thought of as a composite structure formed of many distinct, coexistent, yet interacting elements that may actually be viewed as complete microenvironments in themselves. (Indeed, for the purpose of analysis, they must be so regarded in order to resolve the contradictions they pose for the architect.) In this book we are concerned only with those factors that act directly upon the human body and that can be immediately and directly modified by buildings. These may be listed as (1) thermal; (2) atmospheric; (3) aqueous; (4) luminous; (5) sonic; (6) world of objects; and (7) spatio-gravitational forces.

Evolving in this external matrix, the human body developed an analogous specialization of function; in a sense, this can be compared to a system of channels designed to carry the two-way, highly specialized commerce between the body and the outside world. These channels are likewise distinct, coexistent, and interdependent. For example, the main task of the skin is to maintain the critically important "balance of trade" between the body's internal and external thermal environments. The respiratory system handles the essential exchange between the body and its atmospheric environment, importing the oxygen required for combustion and exhaling the waste product, carbon dioxide. Similarly, the digestive system handles the fuel supply by ingesting food and water and excreting body wastes. These are fundamentally metabolic functions that are locked together in a complex feedback system of controls. They exist independently of our perception of them; indeed, they precede consciousness itself and are its indispensable basis.

The above is, of course, a necessary oversimplification, for, with the marvelous economy of the body, all these systems for *responding* to the environment are integrated with mechanisms for *perceiving* changes in its qualities and dimensions. Thus the skin provides the sense of touch for perceiving the texture, form, resistance, and temperature of the world of objects. The respiratory system includes provisions for our sense of smell, while the digestive system yields the closely allied sense of taste. Even the musculature, which contains, supports, and moves the body in space, provides that synoptic sense of orientation known as proprioception. And superimposed upon these are the most wonderful senses of all, those of sight and hearing. (These last, ironically, are so completely independent of the rest that life is possible without either or even both of them, as the life of writer and lecturer Helen Keller proved.)

The external physical environment into which the human organism is projected at birth differs profoundly from that in which its fetal development occurred. Instead of a habitat designed specifically for its optimal development, it now finds itself in one where many environmental properties are hostile to survival and all of whose properties, friendly and hostile alike, are in continuous and often violent fluctuation across time and space. The metabolic requirements of the individual organism are constant. Its capacity for adaptation to external change, though fairly broad, is strictly limited. Thus arises the fundamental paradox of human existence.

Immersed in its physical environment, the animal body is never for a moment free of paradox because its existence depends upon the *maintenance of an internal equilibrium that external nature does not afford*. The higher the form of life, the more complex is the function and the more intricate the structure of the body—hence the more important its internal equilibrium. The body's dependence upon external nature is absolute—in the fullest sense of the word, *uterine*. And yet, unlike the womb, this external environment never affords optimum conditions for the development of the individual. The contradictions between internal requirements and external conditions are normally stressful. Hence, as Pavlov put it, "the animal organism as a system exists in surrounding nature only by means of a constant balancing [between] this system and its environment." By means of this balancing, the body maintains a private internal environment whose most extraordinary feature is its constancy. Walter B. Cannon, the great Harvard physiologist, described it thus:

So characteristic is this constancy and so peculiar are the processes which maintain it that it has been given a special name, *homeostasis* . . . there is the steadiness of our body temperature, a trait which we share with most other mammals and with birds. The development of a nearly thermostable state in higher vertebrates should be regarded as one of the most valuable advances in biological evolution.[1]

Thanks to the flexibility of its metabolic and perceptual mechanisms, the body is able to accommodate itself to a fairly wide range of fluctuations in the external environment. Thus the skin, with its sweat glands and capillaries, can greatly speed up or slow down the rate of heat transfer to the thermal environment. The heart and lungs can acclimatize themselves to fairly wide variations in oxygen content and atmospheric pressure. The range of physical intensities that the eye perceives is enormous, while for the ear a sound so intense as to be painful is on the order of *ten trillion* times the minimum audible intensity. But the limits of such accommodations are sharp and obdurate and occur only within the overall limits established by the body as a whole. Beyond these limits, an ameliorating element, a "third environment," is required.

Because the external environment seldom affords the human body the precise mix that it requires at any given moment, we have perfected two ameliorating devices: clothing and building. Both act as interfaces between the internal microenvironment of the body and the macroenvironment of external nature. Both modulate the play of raw environmental forces on the body's surfaces. Simultaneously they create a third and intermediate mesoenvironment whose characteristics can be tailored to meet human requirements (Fig. 1–6). The principal difference between clothing and building is, of course, that one protects the individual only while the other shelters social process as well. Traditionally the function of clothing (aside from conventions of modesty and display) has been to manipulate the thermal environment.

Indeed, it has been shown that the clothing typically worn in the Arctic keeps the subclothing temperature near a comfortable 93°F, or virtually the same as that recorded for people living in temperate and tropical environments.[2] In essence, more than adapting to the cold, we use clothing to shield us and supply us with a tropical "climate" to which we are better adapted. Many physiologists believe that humans are of tropical origin, observing that we are almost hairless, have more sweat glands than any other mammal, and, like other tropical animals, our metabolic rate (unclothed, at rest) begins to rise when the environmental temperature drops below 82°F. As a result, we must accommodate to thermal extremes, either through use of clothing, buildings, or behavior (such as avoiding cooling from the wind by sheltering from it). As people increasingly enter new environmental circumstances (submarine, outer space) their clothing comes more and more to resemble buildings, with life-support systems for manipulating temperature, air pressure, and chemical composition, even body waste disposal.

Because of the continuous fluctuation of all environmental factors across time, the building wall must be visualized not as a simple barrier but rather as a selectively permeable membrane with the capacity to admit, reject, or filter any of these environmental factors (Fig. 8–5). All building walls have always acted in this fashion, of course, as we shall see in Chapter 8. Modern scientific knowledge and technical competence merely make possible much higher, more elegant and precise levels of performance.

Before birth, the womb affords an optimal environment for development of the fetus. But once born into the world, it enters into a much more complex relationship with its environment, for existence is now on two levels, not one: the metabolic and the perceptual. The two are inseparable, as we have seen, the metabolic being the material basis of consciousness. Many of life's fundamental processes transpire at this level: heartbeat, respiration, digestion, hypothalamic heat-exchange controls, etc. Metabolic disturbance occurs only when external environmental conditions begin to drop below the minimal or rise above the maximal limits of existence. And sensual perception of the environment can come into play only *after* these limiting requirements are met. Loss of consciousness (fainting) is one of the body's characteristic responses to extreme environmental stress, e.g., loss of oxygen, extremes of pressure, acceleration, heat, and cold.

One might in all justice say of each of these systems, metabolic and perceptual, that each has its own native habitat in the external world — that is, a general set of environmental conditions under which it operates and an inner zone in which it operates most effectively. The topologies of these habitats can be described by:

1. the magnitude of support or the intensity of stimulation offered the system
2. the spatial organization and physical dimensions of that relationship
3. the temporal limits or duration of the experience

The Habitats of Metabolism and the Senses

The habitat of our metabolic system extends across four environmental components: thermal, atmospheric, aqueous, and nutritive. For the average, well-nourished adult, at rest and lightly clothed, this metabolic habitat has a well-known shape and location on the bioclimatic chart (Fig. 3–1). But any change in the metabolic rate of the body due to activity or other causes immediately requires a change in its habitat. By contrast, any radical change in the external environment requires a complementary modification in the protection offered the body by building and clothing.

The systems of sensory perception also have their respective "habitats" whose topologies can be described systematically, as we see in the following chapters. Vision, hearing, and olfaction are fundamentally processes for scanning the middle and far reaches of the environment; being distance receptors, they occupy habitats that are spatially three-dimensional. The boundary of vision (Fig. 5–5) extends across the wave band from ultraviolet (around 400 nanometers [nm]) to infrared (720 nm); vertically, it extends from a lower threshold of perception to an upper threshold of pain; axially, it extends out to infinity. The habitat of hearing (Fig. 6–1) has comparable boundaries of width (wave bands of energy), height (from the lower threshold of audibility to the upper one of blast and pain), and axial orientation (echo, reverberation). Although the mechanism of olfaction is only partially understood, its habitat is known to cover a horizontal spectrum of seven stereochemical categories of odor and to extend vertically from the lowest level of perceptible odor to an upper one of intolerable stench or asphyxiation. The nose's fantastic capacity to perceive odors in dilutions of one to one billion, or to discriminate between compounds of great chemical complexity, make it a scanning sense of the highest order, though we are seldom conscious of employing it.

The senses of taste and touch are means of exploring the near environment. That of touch comes from a complex system of sensors in the skin and muscles that give us the tactile, haptic, and kinesthetic capacities to perceive the temperature, humidity, pressure, shape, texture, and weight of objects. Though the subject is enormously complex, it is apparent that the habitat of this sense has limits analogous to the others. The thermal sensors have upper and lower limits of tolerance to heat and cold. Those of pressure can register a range of stimuli all the way from the gentlest breeze to the stab or the blow, those of texture from that of butter to that of tree bark. And of course the entire kinesthetic-proprioceptive capacity is completely wedded to its own special habitat of terrestrial gravity.

But all of these perceptual habitats occur in space. To move through this space, we must overcome the inertia of gravity and the friction of motion. Thus our path or trajectory through space is actually the resolution of a system of forces—environmental, mechanical, and psychological—that act upon an individual at any given moment. For this reason, the way in which space is organized, architecturally and urbanistically, is a factor in the esthetic aspects of experiencing it. All this may be obvious, yet the malfunction of most of our urban constructs shows how inadequately we understand the consequences of ignoring it. Zoologists, anthropologists, and psychologists have become increasingly interested in the impact of various spatial organizations upon animal communities. These investigations have important implications for the design of human communities. They suggest that there are minimal and maximal spatial dimensions for all of our activities and relationships; an *optimal* scale should therefore be established for each of them.

The noted anthropologist Edward Hall approached this problem from the opposite point of view, that of trying to establish optimal physical dimensions for various types of contacts and relationships.[3] Partly, the scale of such relationships is a quantification of our powers of perception—how well we can hear the words of the actor, how clearly we can see the face of a friend, whether or not we can touch the person we love. The spatial requirements of such relationships are real and are satisfied only when space is organized to facilitate them. But the problem is not simply one of acuity of perception. We want contact with the actor, the friend, the lover, but we do not want to be as close to the actor as to the friend, nor as close to the friend as to the lover. Investigations of this sort throw new light on some of the thorniest problems of architecture and urbanism. They point to the underlying reason for the failure in real life of so many designs that seemed attractive in drawings and photographs: that the spaces had been organized according to abstract principles of formal composition—that is, to *look* good—rather than to facilitate specific experiential requirements. This complex aspect of design, involving ergonomics, anthropometrics, and proxemics, is treated at some length in chapter 7.

A Spectrum of Stress

Clearly the precondition to sensory perception is metabolic process, just as sensory perception constitutes the material basis for the esthetic process. But this process only begins to operate maximally—that is, as a uniquely human faculty—when the impact upon the body of all environmental forces is held within comfortable limits (limits that are established by the body as a whole). Thus we can construct a kind of experiential spectrum of stress extending from too much work to none at all, from sensory overload to

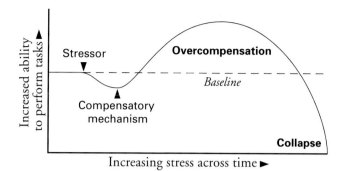

Figure 1–4 / The individual's capacity to accomplish assigned tasks drops under stress. Although, with adequate motivation, a person can compensate, recovery is limited across time. Continued overload leads to decline and ends in collapse.

no sensory stimulation whatever. Both extremes are hostile to the animal body's survival. History affords an ample record of the disastrous consequences of too much stress—overwork, exposure, exhaustion—and current scientific investigations fully confirm it. The work of aerospace physiologists and psychiatrists establishes this end of the experiential spectrum (Fig. 1–4): sensory overloading is destructive, first of effective performance, then of balanced judgment, finally of rationality itself.[4]

There has been less research on the other extreme, that of *too little* stress, even at the laboratory level. Just as we cannot conceive of the animal body removed from its environmental matrix, we cannot imagine its being literally at rest—free of the stimulation that comes from the very processes of living. Investigations of the effects of sensory deprivation indicate that too little stress is as deleterious to the body as too much. Volunteer subjects for such experiments were reduced to gibbering incoherence in a matter of hours by being isolated from all visual, sonic, haptic, and thermal stimulation[5] (Fig. 1–5). One pioneering investigator of the effects of sensory deprivation, Woodburn Heron, concludes:

Prolonged exposure to a monotonous environment, then, definitely has deleterious effects. The individual's thinking is impaired; he shows childish emotional responses; his visual perception becomes disturbed; he suffers from hallucination; his brain-pattern changes.[6]

Psychic satisfaction with a given situation is thus directly related to physiologic well-being, just as dissatisfaction must be related to discomfort. A condition of neither too great nor too little sensory stimulation permits the fullest exercise of the critical faculties upon that situation or any aspect of it. But even this proposition is not indefinitely extensible in time. As the above-quoted Heron concluded (in a paper significantly entitled "The Pathology of Boredom"):

. . . a changing sensory environment seems essential for human beings. Without it, the brain ceases to function in an adequate way, and abnormalities of behavior develop. In fact . . . "variety is not the spice of life: it is the very stuff of it."[7]

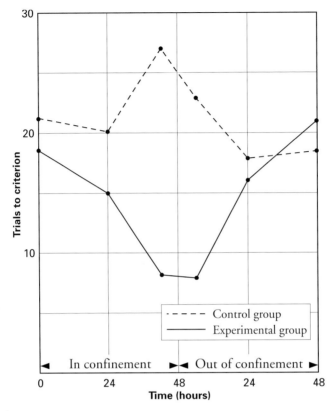

Figure 1–5 / The effect of sensory deprivation on the individual, expressed in terms of capability to learn; note rapidity and depth of decline, slowness of recovery. (Each point is mean value of four subjects.)

The psychosomatic equilibrium sought by the body is dynamic, a continuing resolution of opposites. Every experience has built-in time limits. Perception itself has upper and lower thresholds. One set is purely quantitative: the ear cannot perceive sounds of very high pitch (above 20,000 cycles per second); the eye does not perceive radiation below 400 nanometers. But other thresholds are functions of time; constant exposure to a steady stimulation at some fixed level ultimately deadens our capacity to perceive it.

However, physical comfort cannot be mechanically equated with esthetic satisfaction. All standards of beauty and ugliness stand ultimately upon the bedrock of material existence, though the standards themselves vary astonishingly. Human beings have always had the same sensory apparatus for perceiving changes in the qualities and dimensions of their environment. Human beings have always had the same central nervous system for analyzing and responding to the stimuli thus perceived. Moreover, the physiological limits of this experience are absolute and intractable. Ultimately, physiology, and not culture, establishes the levels at which sensory stimuli become traumatic. With such extremes—high temperatures, blinding lights, cutting edges and heavy blows, noise at blast level, intense concentrations of odor—experience goes beyond mere perception; outrage and insult to the organism become somatic stress. Excessive loading of any one of these senses can prevent a balanced assessment of the total experiential situation. (A temperature of 120°F or a sound level of 120 decibels can render the most beautiful room uninhabitable.) Only as long as these stimuli do not reach stressful levels of intensity, rational assessment and hence esthetic judgments are possible. Then, and only then, formal criteria derived from personal idiosyncrasy and socially conditioned value judgments come into play.

The value judgments that people apply to these stimuli, the evaluation they make of the total experience as being either beautiful or ugly — these vary, measurably with the individual, enormously with culture. This is so clearly the case in the history of art that it should not need repeating. Yet we constantly forget it. Today, anthropology, ethnology, and archaeology alike show us the immense range of esthetically satisfactory standards that the race has evolved in its history — from cannibalism to vegetarianism in food; from the pyramid to the curtain wall in architecture; from polygamy and polyandry to monogamy and celibacy in sex; from sari to bikini in dress. Yet we often act, even today, as if our own esthetic criteria were absolutely valid instead of being, as is indeed the case, absolutely relative for all cultures except our own.

Our esthetic judgments are substantially modified by non-sensual data derived from social experience. This again can be easily confirmed in daily life. It is ultimately our faith in antiseptic measures that makes the immaculate white nurses' uniforms and spotless sheets of the hospital so reassuring. It is our knowledge of their cost which exaggerates the visual difference between diamonds and crystal, or the gustatory difference between the flavor of pheasant and chicken. It was our knowledge of Hitler's Germany that converted the swastika from the good luck sign of many North, Central, and South American Indians to the hated symbol of Nazi terror. All sensory perception is modified by consciousness. Consciousness applies to received stimuli the criteria of digested experience, whether acquired by individuals or received by them from their culture. The esthetic process cannot be isolated from this matrix of experiential reality. It constitutes, rather, a quintessential evaluation of and judgment on it.

Simply as animals, human beings might have survived without the capacity to construct a third environment. Theoretically, at least, people might have migrated like birds or hibernated like bears. There are even a few favored spots on earth, like Hawaii, in which biological survival might have been possible without any architectural modification at all. But, on the base of sheer biological existence, human beings construct the vast superstructure of institutions, processes, and activities that is civilization — and these could not survive exposure to the natural environment even in those climates in which, biologically, people could survive year-round without protection from the elements (Fig. 1−6).

Architecture: The "Third Environment"

Thus human beings were compelled to invent architecture in order, ultimately, to become fully human. By means of it we surrounded ourselves with a new environment tailored to our specifications, interposed between ourselves and the world. The building, in even its

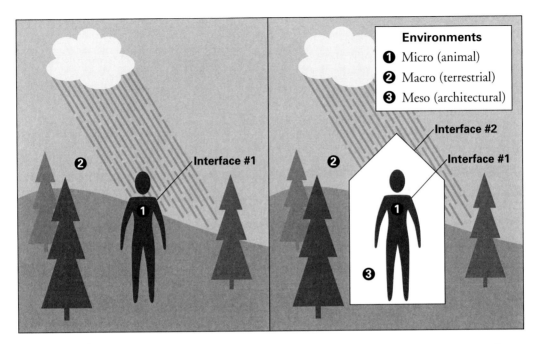

Figure 1–6 / Interaction between animal organism and its environment occurs across one interface—that of the animal epidermis. But civilization introduces two artificial membranes to modify
this relationship: clothing and architecture. Clothing lifts the environmental load off the individual. Architecture, by creating a third built environment, takes the environmental load off both
individuals and their institutions and processes, freeing a greater portion of human energies for
socially productive activity.

simplest form, invests us, surrounds and encapsulates us at every level of our existence,
metabolically and perceptually. Thus it must be regarded as a special container whose
central function is to intervene in our favor. The building—and, by extension, the
city—has the task of lightening the stress of life, of shielding us from raw environmental
stresses, of permitting us as *homo fabricans* to focus our energies upon productive work.
Again, the uterine analogy—and not accidentally, for the building permits us to modulate the play of environmental forces upon ourselves and our processes, to guarantee their
uninterrupted development, in very much the same way as the womb protects the
embryo (see chapter 8).

The matter by no means ends here, however. The architect does not build for an individual, alone and at rest. Typically, he or she builds for social action, people at work.
This confronts the architect with another set of contradictions. Work, as the writer Hannah Arendt reminds us, is not a "natural" activity.[8] According to this definition, only
labor is "natural"—that is, those activities we share with the entire animal world where
the whole body is used to meet its biological needs, to feed it, bathe it, dress it, protect it
from attack. Work, on the other hand, is "unnatural"—that is, the uniquely human use
of the hand and the brain to produce the artificial, nonbiological world of human artifice

(skyscrapers, textbooks, computer programs, paintings, spaceships, highways, symphonies, and pharmaceuticals). Both levels of human activity are, of course, fundamental to civilization; the world of work can only exist as a superstructure on the world of labor. But insofar as we share the world of labor with beasts, it can fairly be described as at once natural and subhuman. Only the world of work, of human thought and artifice, is uniquely human.

This distinction between "work" and "labor," by no means as fine as it might at first appear, has important consequences for architectural design. If the architect ever builds for the wholly "natural" person, it will be in a house, to accommodate biological activities of resting, eating, lovemaking, and play. Most other modern building types involve people at work, engaged in a wide spectrum of "unnatural" processes. Each of these involves stress. Stress, as we have seen, comes either from too much or too little stimulation, from sensory overloading and underloading alike. Biologically, human beings require a dynamic environmental balance, a golden mean between extremes. But modern work knows no such requirements—on the contrary, for maximum output and optimum quality, it usually implies environments of absolute constancy (e.g., pharmaceuticals, printing) and often requires extreme conditions never met in nature (e.g., high-temperature metallurgy, cobalt radiation therapy, etc.). When plotted, these two sets of requirements—those of the worker and those of the work—seldom lie along the same curve. From this it follows that architecture must meet two distinctly different sets of environmental criteria: those of people at some "unnatural" task, and those of the "unnatural" process itself.

Variety may indeed be the very stuff of our natural life. But most of our human activities are, to a greater or lesser extent, "unnatural." From the moment we place young children in kindergarten, we are imposing "unnatural" tasks upon them—placing their eyesight, their posture, their capacity for attention under quite abnormal stress. This situation grows more acute throughout their education and normal working lives. As adults, their biological existence will be linked to processes that are never completely congruent with their own. Often these involve work that is fractionalized, repetitive, and hence often unintelligible to the individual; often, the processes are actually dangerous. Only in agrarian circumstances do people confront work whose "natural" environment, rhythms, and wholeness correspond to their own; but few American workers are nowadays involved in this type of work.

Each kind of work, each social process or activity in which people find themselves engaged, represents a different level of commitment or participation. We have said that there are no spectators in architecture, only protagonists and participants, but the *levels* of participation vary immensely, from being largely passive to being totally active or engaged. Participation may be largely emotional (like that of the theatergoer), primarily intellectual (like that of the child learning to read), largely manual (like the worker in the assembly line), or total (like the surgeon and patient in the operating room). We go to the theater for what we call *entertainment*—that is, for an experience that, however important, is not central to animal existence. In surgery, on the other hand, we are involved in a process where the issues are literally those of life and death. Yet this does not mean, as architects often seem to think, that the theater is less "real" than the surgery or that the experiential needs of the theatergoer are more simply met than those of the surgical patient.

Hierarchy of Commitment: Theater, Classroom, Factory, Hospital

It is in the theater that we find people engaged in one of the most complex of all their esthetic acts. And for this reason, the performance is very sensitive to the spatial and environmental qualities of the architectural container in which it is projected.

Here the requirements of the eye and ear must indeed be well met. Optimal satisfaction with the theater must subsume optimal acuity of perception. This is a function of the size and shape of the container, no less than its luminous, acoustical, and thermal response. The notorious malfunction of the buildings at New York's Lincoln Center when first built (see chapter 6) is a reflection of how little we sometimes understand the subtleties of this problem. In the first place, it seems quite probable that the physical dimensions of theaters are not really susceptible to the sort of unlimited expansion so common today. No matter how plausible electronic amplification of sound and light may make that expansion seem, the unaided sweep of the eye and the ear together establish an optimal range of perception. Beyond this radius is a progressive lowering of the esthetic impact of the experience, no matter what technological means of amplification are available. For this reason, the form and size of the classic Greek theater (Fig. 6–3), based upon its understanding of the habitat of eye and ear, is probably still the paradigm.

But there is unquestionably another and more subtle explanation for these imperfectly functioning theaters: our tendency to regard the process of design as primarily a matter of visual selection and organization (see chapter 5). By their very appearance—the forms, colors, patterns, and decorative motifs they employ—these theaters establish the fact that they are conceived *primarily to delight the eye and only incidentally to satisfy the requirements of the ear*. No ear ever asked for these gold-leafed hexagons, plaster pinwheels, enormous chandeliers of chrome and crystal. Such forms are not, *a priori*, hostile to good acoustics; they are merely irrelevant. The ear has a habitat that may or may not be pleasing to the eye; it cannot in any case be discovered or mapped by the eye alone. The ear is indifferent to the color that is so important to the eye, but it is highly sensitive to the form and texture beneath it. It does not object if the balcony fascia is decorated in baroque swags; it merely requires that they offer the acoustically proper profile and molecular structure. Under such circumstances, architects err when they try to work backward from a visually pleasing to an acoustically satisfactory form, and acoustical engineers err when accepting the task of trying to convert the architect's visual cliché into aurally satisfactory experience.

While the child's physical relation to teacher and blackboard is nominally the same as that of audience to actor, the actual involvement is much more profound. The child is being asked to work, and a whole series of rewards and punishments are set up to enforce this demand. Under ideal circumstances, physical growth and intellectual development should be steady and parallel throughout the year. In theory, the child's learning capacity should be as high at the end of the school day as at the beginning. In reality, of course, this is impossible. Energies flag as the day advances and nothing but rest, food, and play restores them. The question for architects is: How can the building intervene in the child's favor? How shall we manipulate the external environment so that the "unnatural" task of becoming literate advances with optimum speed and with minimum stress?

It should be immediately apparent that the child's requirements are dynamic and imply a dynamic relationship with the classroom. No classroom should confront the child with a fixed set of daylong environmental norms (e.g., 72°F air, 50 percent humidity, 60 foot-candles of light at desktop, 30 decibels of noise, etc.). The probability is that, far from being held at some fixed level, environmental conditions should be continually changing. *But this change cannot be casual or statistically indeterminate;* if change alone were all that was required, the class could be held in a nearby meadow. It must be a *designed* response to the child's changing requirements. The child may well need less heat at 2 P.M. than at 9 A.M. At day's end the child may need less humidity and more oxygen; more light, of a different color; a chair that permits a different posture; or sound levels higher or lower than in the morning. Whatever the requirements are, they could only derive from children themselves, in the experiential circumstances of study. They cannot be met by mechanistic engineers who may perpetuate windowless classrooms and steady state controls nor by formalistic architects who design as though visual perception is the whole of experience.

For adults at their place of work, the problem is yet more intricate. The functional task of the building is to shift the environmental load from their shoulders, permitting them to focus their energies upon the work to be performed. This proposition is most obviously valid for the factory, where the stress of manual labor is clear and conditions of work often hazardous, but it applies with equal force to the office, the shop, and the kitchen. This aspect of building design carries the architect into the very center of an extremely complex problem involving questions of physiology and psychology upon which even specialists in these fields find it hard to agree. The level of commitment or participation required of the worker varies immensely—from the constant alertness and discrimination required of the cook or the mechanic to the stupefying monotony of the assembly line. The connection between work and environment, on the one hand, and fatigue, on the other, is umbilical, but the mechanism of fatigue itself is by no means entirely understood.

Fatigue is a perfectly "natural" phenomenon, part of the basic metabolic cycle of impairment and recovery in the living organism. One of the most puzzling aspects of fatigue is its duality; it is at once objective and subjective, physiological and psychological. No two people respond in exactly the same way to the same task, and the same people respond quite differently to the same task under varying emotional or environmental circumstances. In recent years much research has focused on the malady known as chronic fatigue syndrome, which affects many working persons.

Four factors whose values can be objectively measured are involved in fatigue: (1) the time spent at work, (2) the character of the work itself, (3) the environmental conditions under which the work is performed, and (4) the condition of the worker (i.e., age, health, nutrition, emotional state). In this complicated field, which is discussed in more detail in chapter 7, the architect seldom controls more than the third of these factors. But to accomplish even this effectively, the architect needs to know much more about the others than commonly is known. Only thus can formal solutions be avoided that violate the experiential situations upon which they are imposed.

The symbiotic relationship between the architectural container and the people and processes contained is nowhere clearer than in the modern hospital. Here we find every degree of biological stress, including those of birth and death; a wide range of highly specialized technologies, each with its own environmental requirements; and the narrowest margins for error of any building type—success and failure are literally matters of life and death. Here, if anywhere, we can observe the integral connection between metabolic function and esthetic response.

The seriously ill patient—above all, the major surgery case—traverses the full experiential spectrum during a stay at the hospital. Stress is greatest under surgery. Patients' relationship with their environment can be almost wholly defined in somatic terms. Under total anesthesia, there is no esthetic aspect to the experience. (It is significant, in this connection, to note that the words *anesthesia* and *esthetic* have a common origin in the Greek word meaning "to feel" or "to perceive.")

Patients' process of convalescence—through the recovery room, intensive nursing, regular nursing, and ambulatory state, on up to discharge—takes them through every level of stress. Precisely as the metabolic crisis diminishes does their esthetic response rise to the front of consciousness. Colors, lights, noises, and odors that they were too ill to notice can now become major factors of experience. Satisfactory manipulation of these elements becomes a part of active therapy.

The surgeon and the hospital staff, too, meet a period of thermal stress during operative procedures. At this juncture, requirements for the surgeon oppose those of the patient. Where the latter requires warm, moist air (and anti-explosive measures demand even higher humidities), the staff—under variable nervous tension—should ideally be submerged in dry, cool air. The room's thermo-atmospheric environment is usually designed to favor the surgical staff. Likewise, the luminous environment of the operating room must be wholly designed in the surgeon's favor. The color of the walls, of the uniforms, even of the towels is quite as important to the visual acuity of the surgeon as the lighting fixtures themselves.

Thus, every decision made in the design of the operating room is based upon functional considerations objectively evaluated. The very nature of the intervention fundamentally prohibits abstractly esthetic considerations. The margin of safety is too narrow to allow the architect the luxury of formalistic decisions based upon subjective preferences. In varying degrees, this situation obtains in other specialized areas of the hospital, and it will increase as the hospital comes to be regarded not merely as a container for peo-

Peter Mauss/Esto

Figure 1 – 7 / Hospital for Special Surgery, Major Modernization Project, New York, 1996. Architecture for Health Science & Commerce, PC, architects. To create a more comforting environment at this world-renowned orthopedics/rheumatology special teaching hospital, the new addition features a dramatic five-story atrium that provides daylight and panoramic views of the East River from the patient unit lounges.

ple and processes but as being itself an actual instrument of therapy. There is much evidence of this tendency already: the hyperbaric chamber where barometric pressure and oxygen content are manipulated in the treatment of both circulatory disorders and gas gangrene; the metabolic surgery suites where body temperatures are reduced to slow the metabolic rate before difficult surgery; the use of heated atmospheres for serious burn cases; the use of artificially cooled dry air to lighten the thermal stress on cardiac cases; the use of electrostatic precipitation and ultraviolet radiation to produce disinfected atmospheres for difficult respiratory ailments or to prevent cross-infection from contagious disease. Here the building designer does not merely manipulate the natural environment in the patient's favor but actually creates totally new environments with no precedent in nature as specific instruments of therapy.

The exact point in hospitalization at which these environmental manipulations cease to be purely therapeutic and become merely questions of comfort or satisfaction — that is, the point at which they cease to be functional and become esthetic problems — is not easy to isolate. Objectionable odors, disturbing noises and lights, uncomfortable beds, lack of privacy, hot, humid atmosphere—all these work against "beauty" in the hospital room. They may also delay convalescence. We cannot hope to make modern medical procedures pretty and the well-adjusted patient will probably want to leave the hospital as soon as possible under any circumstances. All the more reason, then, that every external factor be analyzed as objectively as possible with a view to expediting recovery.

All of this suggests the possibility of establishing, much more precisely than ever before, an objective basis for esthetic decision. It cannot, in any case, be avoided. Everything the architect does, every form adopted or material specified, has esthetic repercussions. The problem is thus not Hamlet's: to act or not to act. It is rather to act wisely, understanding the total consequences of many decisions. If architects' esthetic standards are to be placed on a firmer factual basis than that on which they now stand, they will need the help of physiologists, psychologists, and anthropologists to do it. A much more systematic and detailed investigation of humanity's actual psychosomatic relationship with the environment is needed than has yet been attempted, at least in architecture. It is not at all accidental that we can find the broad lines of such research appearing in the field of aerospace medicine, for people can penetrate space only by encapsulating themselves in a container of terrestrial environment. To accomplish this we must ask fundamental questions. What, actually, is this environment? What specifically is its effect upon us? What is its relation to human pleasure and delight?

In the design of space vehicles, for example, it is no longer possible to say where problems of simple biological survival leave off and more complex questions of human satisfaction begin. Clearly, they constitute *different ends of one uninterrupted spectrum of human experience*. It is very probable that the upper end of this spectrum, involving as it does our innermost subjective existence, can never be fully explored or understood. But it can certainly be far better understood than it is today, especially among architects.

American society today employs approximately 300 distinct building types to provide the specialized environments required by its multiform activities.[9] Most of them embody contradictions that must be resolved at two different levels: first between the persons and processes contained and then between their container and the natural environment. Respect for these two conditions is essential if the building is to be operationally successful. And yet, respect for these two conditions often leaves the architect with little room to manipulate the building for purely formal—that is, esthetic—ends. If we examine the specifications for these various building types, we see that they can be classified according to the degree of participation they subsume on the part of the users of the building. From such a classification it becomes apparent that, as participation becomes more total, the architect's opportunities for subjective expression steadily diminish. The fundamental contradiction in architecture is always between the requirements of functional and formal criteria. The more complex or vital the process to be housed, the more critical this contradiction becomes. Hence the architect's freedom to create necessarily diminishes in inverse proportion to the criticalness of the task.

Most contemporary failures in architecture stem either from a failure to understand this situation or else from a refusal to come to terms with it. Of course, no building can

Figure 1 – 8 / The Arnold Center for Radiation Oncology, The New York Hospital Medical Center of Queens, 1995. Architecture for Health Science & Commerce, PC, architects. The use of modern medical examination and treatment technologies (e.g., CAT scans, MRIs) can be extremely disquieting and stressful for patients and their families. The design challenge with this project was to convert a dark parking garage into a bright, cheerful, and functionally efficient radiation oncology center to treat over 1,200 patients a year and to support research activities.

grow like an organism. Architects do not work with living tissue, with its powers of cellular division and genetic memory. In this sense, buildings must always be designed by people, and these people always bring to the task preconceived ideas of what forms they ought to assume. As Ernst Fischer, the Austrian philosopher, has said, a good honeybee will often put a bad architect to shame. "But what from the very first distinguishes the most incompetent of architects from the best of bees is that the architect has built a cell in his head before he constructs it in wax."[10] Good or bad, beautiful or ugly, the building is always the expression of somebody's creative ambitions. Today, more than ever in history, these ambitions must be contained, structured, and disciplined by objectively verifiable terms of reference.

The Social Consequences of Architectural Intervention

If, as we have seen, the central function of building is to lift the raw load of the physical environment from our backs and to create that third meso-environment required by civilization, then we must judge building as we do any other instrument or tool—that is, by its performance. And the central criterion for judging building performance must necessarily be amenity, well-being, ultimately health. Does the building regulate the relations between the individual and the environment in such a way as to guarantee optimal well-being? From the standpoint of society as a whole, does the total stock of building provide that control of environmental factors which guarantees maximum productivity in all its manifold processes and activities?

Clearly, these are questions easier to ask than to answer. A bewildering variety of forces play upon the life of the individual or the activities of the group, and only a limited portion of them are subject to manipulation by architectural means. It must also be remembered that, in human society, each level of cultural development establishes its own internal standards of health, amenity, efficiency. Its architecture can thus be measured only against its own potential. The Eskimo igloo would offer few of the amenities required by middle-class American families. But, relative to the material resources and technological potentials of the Eskimo culture of the time, it represents an instrument of architectural intervention of astonishing precision and refinement.

The very word *health* may describe a real state of being but it nevertheless has ambiguous parameters. Medically, it implies a state of normal function

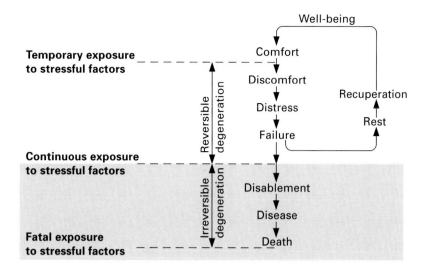

Figure 2 – 1 / The biological phenomenon of work-fatigue-rest-recovery is cyclical. Any exogenous factor that distorts or disrupts this rhythm is inimical to the well-being of the individual. All experience occurs in situations in which the environment itself is one exogenous factor; architecture intervenes to optimize its effect on the cycle.

that can vary with age, sex, and genetic stock. Here we do not confront two separate states of being — healthful and unhealthful — with a stark division between the two. Rather we face a spectrum of conditions that progresses, often by slow and imperceptible degrees, from health through discomfort, distress, disease, and disablement, to end in death. For the individual, of course, the progression is not necessarily even or direct. For the victims of Hiroshima near the blast site or on TWA flight 800, it was telescoped into a split second; for those afflicted with AIDS, an agonizing progress of disease may drag out for years. In one way or the other, it is the characteristic spectrum through which we all pass on the journey from the cradle to the grave. The object of medical and public health endeavor is to extend the period of health over as long a time and as broad a base as possible by systematically isolating and eliminating those factors that contribute to discomfort, disease, and disablement (Fig. 2–1). With modern nutrition and medical care, in 1996 the average life expectancy in the United States was 76 years; lacking equivalent services, the average citizen of Zambia died at 49.[1]

The whole subject is extremely complex and it would be dangerous to overestimate the role of architecture as a contributing factor, but it would be equal folly to underestimate it. For, clearly, health, disease, and death always occur in real experiential situations. The environment is always a factor (whether large or small) in the progression and it is the task of architects and city planners to examine their responsibilities here much more clearly than they have done in the past.

This examination must proceed at two distinctly different levels: that of individual buildings and that of the assemblage of buildings that constitutes a communal fabric —

the city, town, or village as a whole. There is a qualitative difference between the performance of the individual unit and that of a group of units, even when they are internally identical. One of the paradoxes of modern technology is that it makes possible an unprecedentedly high order of performance in the individual building and yet organizes them into cities whose environmental conditions are more dangerous, hazardous, or less comfortable than ever before.

One way in which individual buildings affect our health is exemplified in that type with which we are most familiar: the home. In addition to being most familiar, it now appears that the home is also the most hazardous, accounting for more disabling injuries than those occurring in the workplace and on the road combined. In 1995 there were 7.3 million injuries in the home, or an average of one person in 36 suffered disabling injuries that limited their activities one full day or more, at a total national cost of about $95 billion. In 1994 approximately 190 million days of restricted activity and 50 million days of bed disability resulted from injuries in and around the house.[2]

Outright deaths from injuries in the home have trended downward over the years from 28 per 100,000 population in 1912 to only 10 per 100,000 in 1995. Accidents in the home annually kill about 26,000 Americans, about the same number as in 1912; but in 1912 there were only 21 million households, as opposed to over 97 million households today. It remains true, however, that as a cause of disability and death, the home-induced accident still ranks much higher than is necessary. Why is this? Falling (from one level to another, around the house and on the premises) was the most common cause of accidental death in the home through 1994.[3]

How can the statistics be further reduced? Their cause lies in deficiencies in the building rather than in the building's occupants. Their cure, therefore, is primarily a problem of redesign of the dwelling. No home can be 100 percent accident-proof, of course; the factor of human fallibility enters into the use of a house just as it does that of an automobile. Education of the occupant must parallel redesign for safety. But in a statistical sense, the main burden of blame lies on the house, not its user. This is clearly established by census surveys that show that home accidents do not occur at random. On the contrary, accidents of a given type happen only to persons of a given age and sex while occupied at given tasks at given places within the house. If the accident were the fault of the person and not the tool, there would be no such pattern to the distribution.

In 1995 the incidence rate for falls increased with age (e.g., from 6 per 100,000 for those 65–74 years of age to 34 per 100,000 for those aged 75 and older). At first glance this might seem a most difficult thing to pin on the building itself. However, over 200,000 of such injuries were linked to bathroom structures or fixtures in 1994.[4] This suggests that the design of today's bathroom equipment—tubs, showers, grab bars, soap dispensers, etc.—should be modified to a much greater degree than it is already. In recent years, improved products have begun to enter the marketplace (Fig. 2–2). Such products incorporate ergonomic design to accommodate a wider anthropometric range. Although many improved products now exist, it is still the rare home that is so equipped even if an occupant requires them.

Figure 2–2 / Application of the relatively new concept of *universal design*—creating spaces that are safe, comfortable, and convenient for people of all ages and sizes—often produces subtle but important changes such as those depicted in this brightly daylit bathroom. The integral can-tilevered seat not only eases entry into the whirlpool tub but is also useful for parents sitting close to their children while bathing them. Safety rails make it easier to get out of the tub and prevent slipping. An offset faucet with anti-scald valve is an added safety feature.

A person preparing and serving a meal has to make many movements around the kitchen—up to overhead shelves, down to the oven, across elements on the stove, into the freezer, etc. There is much lifting, chopping, blending, and stirring connected with the whole chemistry of cooking, and much of it is hazardous. Yet, unlike the industrial worker, the cook has been the subject of few really fundamental time and motion studies. Much of the equipment—cabinets, stoves, dishes, pots, and pans—is poorly designed and poorly organized with reference to physical and psychic requirements; often it is worn out. No wonder, then, that somebody falls from a bad ladder while trying to reach an archaic utensil on a shelf that should never have been there in the first place.

Today the architectural profession is beginning to yield to a more universal approach that seeks to provide design solutions that are safe and accessible for all people regardless of their abilities. Indeed, an Association of Safe and Accessible Products (ASAP) now exists and has offices in Washington, D.C., to promote the development and use of such products. Kitchens are being equipped with multiple counter heights to enhance accessibility. Multiple counter heights have other benefits, including the option to install a dishwasher higher to minimize bending for those with back problems.

Some companies, such as General Electric (GE) have begun to take a proactive approach to accessible design. GE designed (with Mary Jo Peterson) and built a "Real Life" demonstration kitchen for the 1995 convention of the National Association of Home Builders. Some of its features included counters at multiple heights to support specific tasks, including heights above 36 inches; areas adaptable for seated work; access for wheelchairs; a door-mounted step stool to help reach items in upper cabinets; roll-out shelves and cart; and a counter with a raised insert in a contrasting color to contain spills and clarify the edge for people with poor vision. Universal design incorporates design features that improve access for everyone, not just the elderly and those with disabilities.

Buildings should be designed for optimum ease, speed and safety of movement. This movement usually resolves itself into two characteristic patterns: people moving toward things and things moving toward people. In the case of the house, movement is almost exclusively of the first sort, while in the factory the opposite is the case. In both of these cases, however, attention to the design of entrances to buildings can prevent avoidable injuries (Fig 2−3).

The faulty design of buildings, furnishings, and equipment also accounts for many of the burns, asphyxiations, cuts, suffocations, poisonings, electrocutions, and other accidental injuries that occur in the home. Thorough investigation of the causal relations of burns (which accounted for 3,600 deaths in 1995[5]) and asphyxiations (400 deaths in 1995, including that of tennis champion Vitas Gerulaitis) would indicate how cooking and heating units should be redesigned. There has been recent progress in this area. All currently manufactured vented gas heaters are required by industry safety standards to have safety shutoff devices to protect against carbon monoxide poisoning and all new unvented heaters have a pilot light safety system called an oxygen depletion sensor (ODS), which shuts off the heater when there is not enough fresh air.

Many danger points in our houses are unconsciously avoided without our being aware of them, but many others are accidents just waiting to happen. Accidents in the home are the result of characteristic movements and processes that require the closest scrutiny if they are to be reduced or eliminated. This does not always imply that the house is structurally bad. An interior stairway may be inherently dangerous because it is steep, slippery, badly lighted, or winding — but it may be none of these and still be a source of accidents because the only telephone is at its bottom and someone is always in a hurry when running down to answer it. The first instance implies redesign of the stair; the latter indicates need for two telephones — one at the top and one at the bottom, or one of the cordless or cellular phones so commonly used today.

This problem arises in many forms throughout the building. Thus, there is the problem of collision with objects in a dark room — stumbling over furniture in the bedroom or over toys on the living room floor. Both of these are statistically important sources of accidental injury. In the first case, either the plan of the bedroom does not make adequate provisions for the necessary furniture, or the furniture is not suitably arranged in the

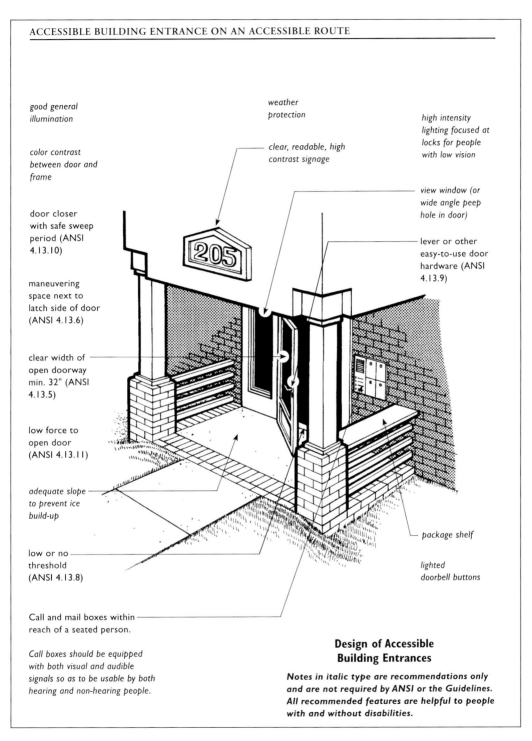

good general illumination

weather protection

high intensity lighting focused at locks for people with low vision

color contrast between door and frame

clear, readable, high contrast signage

door closer with safe sweep period (ANSI 4.13.10)

view window (or wide angle peep hole in door)

lever or other easy-to-use door hardware (ANSI 4.13.9)

maneuvering space next to latch side of door (ANSI 4.13.6)

clear width of open doorway min. 32" (ANSI 4.13.5)

low force to open door (ANSI 4.13.11)

adequate slope to prevent ice build-up

package shelf

low or no threshold (ANSI 4.13.8)

lighted doorbell buttons

Call and mail boxes within reach of a seated person.

Call boxes should be equipped with both visual and audible signals so as to be usable by both hearing and non-hearing people.

Design of Accessible Building Entrances

Notes in italic type are recommendations only and are not required by ANSI or the Guidelines. All recommended features are helpful to people with and without disabilities.

Figure 2–3 / Recommended features for improving the accessibility and safety of building entrances, as illustrated in HUD's Fair Housing Act Design Manual.

room, or the lighting is inadequate. In the second case, the children of the household should have either a room of their own or (at minimum) storage space for their toys.

Not all areas of the house are equally dangerous, nor are different types of accidents evenly distributed throughout the house. Bathrooms and kitchens are much more dangerous than living rooms and bedrooms. Outside stairs and porches pose their own unique hazards due to uneven, slick, or icy surfaces.

All too often, architects select interior flooring and exterior paving materials for their appearance with little regard to how slippery they may be when either wet or dry. The primary purpose of flooring and paving materials is to safely sustain foot traffic, not to look good.

Statistics provide impressive proof that accidents in the home are not due merely to human nature, but to very specific factors that can be isolated and eliminated by knowledgeable design. Where there's an accident there's a reason, and this reason may be partly due to what safety experts call "unsafe conditions" and partly to "unsafe practices."

Reference to industrial experience sheds new light on this situation. Here scientific research has yielded many control and preventive measures that have resulted in marked reductions in accident frequency and accident severity. In such industrial safety work, three factors are investigated: the condition of the building itself, the processes carried on in the building, and the practice of the workers. The same analysis must be applied to the home if we are to understand why it is so dangerous and how it may be made safer. Take the kitchen, for instance — the most dangerous area in the house. What characteristic processes are carried on here? To what extent can redesign of the room itself increase its safety (omission of live storage space above eye level, careful layout to facilitate movement within the kitchen, use of ground fault interrupters on outlets near the sink, etc.)? To what extent can the processes themselves be made safer (elimination of deep-fat frying or the washing of cutlery by hand)? And to what extent must people learn safer practices (i.e., to keep cleaning agents locked out of children's reach, to refrain from using ranges or ovens for space heating, and so on)?

The large-scale opportunity to apply safety analysis to house design occurred in public housing beginning in the early 1970s, resulting in standards that have achieved marked reductions in accident frequencies. Whether accidents result from poor building design or human frailty, it is thus amply clear that they are entirely susceptible to scientific analysis and prevention.

Since the first edition of this book, much progress has been made on issues of accessibility and safety. Federal laws now require accessible plumbing fixtures in housing built with public funds or that is operated by public programs. These are the Architectural Barriers Act, Section 504 of the Rehabilitation Act of 1977–78, and the Americans with Disabilities Act (ADA) of 1990. In addition, the Fair Housing Accessibility Guidelines require accessibility for all apartments in elevator buildings and all ground floor walkups. American buildings and workplaces are also becoming safer through loss prevention initiatives including substantial redesign of machinery to eliminate many of the hazards inherent in earlier models (e.g., increased use of guarding and interlocks).

American Buildings: Source of Illness and Disease

The foregoing applies only to one type of damage to the health of the building consumer — the accident. There is another (and perhaps even more important) type to consider: the contribution of buildings themselves to illness and disease. Current practice all too often makes a sharper distinction between accident and disease in relation to building use than the facts seem to warrant. Both constitute an impairment of health, and both may be wholly or partially traced to deficiencies in the building. Obviously, the sequence of cause and effect is more apparent in the case of a sudden fall down a flight of stairs (an accident) than an obscure and imperceptibly worsening of allergies from poor indoor air quality (disease). But the precise difference between the two is likely to be more important to the medical statistician than to the building consumer, who is merely interested in preserving good health against both forms of attack.

However, it is a difficult and risky business to try to plot the causal relations between deficient buildings and disease. The existence of excessive rates of sickness and mortality in the inner cities is an accepted fact, but the extent to which poor housing *per se* is responsible for these differences is very difficult to ascertain because of the interaction of many economic and sociological factors. For example, the Mayo Clinic reports that death rates due to asthma are almost 20 percent higher in metropolitan areas than in rural areas. Contributing to the difference may be the crowded living conditions that can spread respiratory infections; family stress; and dust, dust mites, cockroaches, and rat and mouse urine. In addition, residents of poor urban areas often lack health insurance and access to adequate medical care.[6] One must be careful not to attribute to deficient buildings those maladjustments, illnesses, and diseases that in fact are caused by deficiencies in the social order. Thus, the coincidence between tuberculosis and substandard housing at one time led many housing specialists to conclude that poor living conditions were the *sole cause* of this social evil. Subsequent experience has shown this to be incorrect. The resurgence of tuberculosis in the 1990s was spurred not by deficient buildings but by a combination of social factors: the AIDS epidemic, urban crowding, homelessness, immigration, drug abuse, prison overcrowding, the rapid disappearance of preventive medicine health clinics in major cities, and the short supply of isolation facilities. Tuberculosis returned to the United States in epidemic proportions, with drug-resistant strains so virulent that antibiotic treatment was largely ineffective. The message was clear: It is false economy to discontinue public health surveillance of infectious diseases that have not yet disappeared from society. While overcrowding of buildings may contribute to disease transmission, buildings should not be viewed in isolation. No clean, sunny interior can successfully immunize an individual from life-threatening risks they may choose to take, nor can ample space in which to relax prevent the destructive impacts of unemployment, drugs, and crime. These are the products of our social environment, against which no building yet devised can offer protection.

Efforts have been made to determine whether ethnic differences in disease and death rates may be traceable to environmental circumstances. Most of these connections are difficult to establish, with the exception of the adverse consequences (reductions in IQ and attention span, reading and learning disabilities, hyperactivity, and behavioral problems) associated with childhood lead poisoning, labeled by the Centers for Disease Control (CDC) as the primary environmental health hazard facing American children. Regulations and guidelines for abatement of lead-based paint hazards have been issued by the U.S. Department of Housing and Urban Development.[7] The older the dwelling, regardless of its location relative to social or economic class, the more prevalent lead-based paint is likely to be, with housing built before 1940 particularly suspect.

Within poor urban areas, many express the concern that, in addition to their burdens of substandard housing, poor health care, and inadequate opportunities for employment, they have also been burdened with more than their fair share of garbage dumps, landfills, and polluting industries. To address this larger issue of environmental justice, and recognizing the potentially large impact of federal construction projects on communities, President Clinton signed Executive Order 12898 in 1994. This requires that each federal agency identify and address disproportionately high and adverse human health or environmental effects of its programs and activities on minority and low-income populations.[8]

Nevertheless, many aspects of illness and disease have been demonstrably dependent upon bad building in the past, and have been demonstrably reduced by good building. In subsequent chapters we see in more detail what these aspects are and how buildings can reduce or eliminate them. Here it suffices to cite one historic example—and one which we as a society are now well beyond—even though it involves the leading cause of death in the world. It is the significant relationship between a group of digestive diseases (diarrhea, enteritis, colitis, typhoid, and paratyphoid fevers) and the presence or absence of private indoor flush toilets. Fortunately for Americans, on the eve of the twenty-first century, more than 99.8 percent of their homes are equipped with indoor flush toilets. Globally, infectious and parasitic diseases still account for nearly one third of all deaths annually (16.5 million in 1995).[9] More than 99 percent of these deaths occur in developing countries; in industrialized countries, infectious diseases now account for only about 1 percent of all deaths.[10]

The U.S. Public Health Service once found that the frequency of digestive diseases in households without sanitary facilities was 70 percent greater than in those with them! Any interpretation of such findings, the survey added, must bear in mind that

. . . in households not meeting this standard [of indoor toilets] there will probably be concomitant deficiencies [especially, lack of insect screening and poor facilities for refrigeration of food] which may have an effect on the illness rate from this group of digestive diseases . . . .We are confronted with an expression [or standard] which tends to measure poor housing as a whole.[11]

In other words, buildings that do not provide adequate protection against germs and insects are not likely to provide the special equipment necessary for food preservation. Deficiencies in one direction usually imply deficiencies in others; the task of exactly tracing out the relation of each to the maintenance of health only emphasizes the overall importance of good building.

The discovery of the relationship between buildings and health has served to expose a serious shortcoming of typical criteria used to analyze building performance. Most discussion of building has been in primarily visual terms. Consciously or unconsciously, explicitly or implicitly, judgments based on vision have dominated architectural opinion. Actually, of course, there is quite as much justification for measuring buildings on any other sensory basis: Have you *heard* the new Jones house? What does the kitchen *smell* like? How do the stairs *feel*? Do the windows *get on your nerves*? Does the home in winter *feel* dry? Though we are trained to think otherwise, we experience buildings through all our senses equally. Our entire sensory and muscular systems are involved in our use of buildings.

But the matter goes much deeper, for none of the senses is very reliable in estimating a building's day-to-day performance. How woefully inadequate they are is amply attested to by the number of persons who—despite the use of their senses—are annually killed or injured in buildings. The nose is sharp enough to smell only the smoke from the actual fire, not to detect the hidden defective wire that causes it. The eye can tell you if the column is perfectly proportioned, but it can't read the internal stresses or estimate how near it is to collapse. The ear accurately registers more noise than the nerves can stand, while the sense of touch comes into play too late to save you from breaking your neck on a slippery floor.

In addition, a host of situations arises in the day-to-day use of all sorts of buildings that cannot be sensed at all—these must be *understood*. Under such a heading fall accidents involving electric shock, spontaneous combustion, and explosions; health effects including allergies due to airborne contaminants; stress and fatigue due to bad lighting, ventilation, or acoustics. If unchecked, the harm inflicted by dust from lead-based paint in inner-city housing can permanently diminish the intellectual abilities of generations of children, who may already be at risk due to other social and economic circumstances. To accurately measure such factors, more than the rule-of-thumb techniques of the past are required. In the light of current knowledge and in the face of modern building requirements, it is no more possible to measure the performance of a building by the senses alone than it is to operate an airplane without instruments.

The corollary is obvious. It is no more possible for an individual architect (without the input of specialists) to design a complex building than it would be for a solitary engineer to design a space station. Thus, both from the standpoint of the user and that of the designer, health-protecting and health-extending building implies the fullest application of the scientific method and the widest use of technical resources. But urban society seems to create (at least) two new environmental problems for each one that it solves. The nineteenth century virtually completed the systems of utilities, services, and amenities that make possible the modern city. Many of the infectious and parasitic diseases that still wrack humanity as a whole were thus largely eliminated in this country by bringing under control the vermin and filth that are the vectors of those diseases. Many of them, such as malaria and plague, have all but disappeared from this country, and smallpox has been eradicated globally. Nevertheless malaria still claims two million lives annually in the world as a whole.[12]

Effective transportation guarantees the adequate supply, and sanitary measures the quality, of the food we eat and the water we drink. Collection systems effectively handle the removal of garbage, human waste, and materials to be recycled. These urban facilities make possible the comforts and amenities of modern urban architecture, constituting the environmental support system without which the individual building could not for a moment survive.

But cities, in the radical modifications of the natural landscape which they entail, produce their own ecologies, in which "natural" hazards to health and well-being are too often replaced with artificial ones. And there is mounting evidence in the area of indoor air quality and others that these hazards have disastrous implications. (See chapter 9.) The typical bathroom, served by municipal water and sewerage systems, permits the average city dweller to enjoy a higher level of personal hygiene than ever before. But these same systems, on a regional scale, are polluting the environment alarmingly. Particularly of concern are the combined sewer systems of most older American cities, which during heavy rainstorms combine the flow of wastewater with drainage runoff, bypassing sewage treatment facilities and discharging raw sewage into creeks, rivers, and the ocean. And the increasing volume of such wastes is astounding: our coastal waters receive 2.3 trillion gallons of municipal wastewater and 4.9 billion gallons of industrial discharges every year![13] The same mechanical systems that give us clean, conditioned air inside the building are simultaneously polluting the outside atmosphere with the waste ash and gases of faulty combustion. Mechanical engineers now more accurately use the term *outside air* rather than *fresh air* in locating intakes. About a third of the country's 2.55 million tons of particulate emissions in 1995 came from fuel combustion, used either for power production or heating.[14] The automobile, that paradigm of privatized luxury in transport, poses an even greater threat to our air quality, emitting its own weight in carbon in the form of carbon dioxide — the principal greenhouse gas — each year, in addition to hydrocarbons, fine particulates, sulfur, carbon monoxide, nitrogen oxides, aldehydes, and arsenic.[15] The manufacturing plants of the nation, despite complex, stringent, and often burdensome air pollution control regulations, also continue to emit a variety of hazardous air pollutants. The problematic smogs of Los Angeles, St. Louis, Tokyo, and London are the composite result of this atmospheric pollution. Meanwhile, in the agricultural hinterland, to facilitate the production of those foodstuffs required by the city, the wide use of insecticides, fungicides, and herbicides poisons the atmosphere, water bodies, and soils alike.

It has been suggested that this generalized pollution of the environment is the root cause of new epidemiological phenomena — the startling increase in the incidence rate of asthma, for example, by 30 percent from 1970 to 1982, and by a further 41 percent from 1982 to 1992. There are 12.4 million asthmatics in the country, as reported by the National Center for Health Statistics, and mortality rates rose 43 percent from 1994 to 1995.[16] Even though the exact mechanism has not been explicated, asthma is believed to be caused by environmental factors like exposure to allergens and air pollution; there may also be a genetic predisposition to the disease. (The direct results of smog are not open to controversy; following the London smog of December 13, 1952, death rates soared above normal: bronchitis 1,083 percent, influenza 720 percent, pneumonia 486 percent, tuberculosis 453 percent, high blood pressure 294 percent. While London may still have serious air pollution problems, nothing today compares with their notorious "killer smogs" of the 1950s.)

The scale and complexity of such ecological problems may outrun the comprehension, not to say the professional jurisdiction, of the average architect. And yet architects are an active party of the whole process, whether or not they will it or recognize it. Each time they provide parking space for another car, each time they cut down a tree, or replace a square yard of turf with one of blacktop, or install a heating plant burning fossil fuels—so, each time, they modify the microclimate in which the building stands. (In the United States, the equivalent land area of two New York Cities—some 415,000 acres—was paved over *each year* between 1982 and 1992, a result of land use planning decisions that should not be overlooked by architects.[17]) Sooner or later, they must face the consequences of their acts—if not as architects, then certainly as citizens.

The causal relation between building and accident, discomfort and disease is today a generally accepted concept; however complex the line of cause and effect may be and however much of it remains to be explored in detail. This in itself marks a great advance over the architectural theory of even a few years ago. Yet it remains merely the negative side of a much greater discovery, for techniques of environmental control promise not merely the eradication of age-old deficiencies in building; they also yield totally new concepts of human comfort, health, and safety.

Of course, given the present structure of the building field, the architect can argue that many of the factors contributing to the low performance levels of architecture and urbanism are beyond anyone's control. Few architects are offered the opportunity to design the fixtures and furnishings of a buildings. Not many have a voice in the way a building is maintained after it is finished. And almost none has had a hand in drafting the ordinances that regulate the atmospheric pollution that threatens the health of clients or the highways that despoil the cities. Legally, an architect's responsibility may be limited; morally, it is very great. In fact, the future of the profession rests in large part upon the degree to which it can formulate and then apply a comprehensive and unified theory of environmental design. Such is the evolving mission of practitioners of *green architecture*, where concerns for environmental stewardship, energy and resource efficiency, and healthy building conditions are paramount.

One of the leaders of the worldwide green architecture movement is William McDonough, an architect and the former dean of the School of Architecture at the University of Virginia in Charlottesville. In 1992 Mr. McDonough was commissioned by the city of Hannover, Germany, to formulate design guidelines for the World's Fair in the year 2000. Within the document, nine general principles were established, which articulate the philosophy for the sustainable design of buildings, cities, and products. These have become known as the Hannover Principles:

1. **Insist on the rights of humanity and nature to coexist** in a healthy, supportive, diverse and sustainable condition.

2. **Recognize interdependence.** The elements of human design interact with and depend upon the natural world, with broad and diverse implications at every scale. Expand design considerations to recognizing even distant effects.

3. **Respect relationships between spirit and matter.** Consider all aspects of human settlement, including community, dwelling, industry and trade, in terms of existing and evolving connections between spiritual and material consciousness.

4. **Accept responsibility for the consequences of design** decisions upon human well being, the viability of natural systems, and their right to coexist.

5. **Create safe objects of long-term value.** Do not burden future generations with requirements for maintenance or vigilant administration of potential danger due to the careless creation of products, processes or standards.

6. **Eliminate the concept of waste.** Evaluate and optimize the full life-cycle of products and processes, to approach the state of natural systems, in which there is no waste.

7. **Rely on natural energy flows.** Human designs should, like the living world, derive their creative forces from perpetual solar income. Incorporate this energy efficiently and safely for responsible use.

8. **Understand the limitations of design.** No human creation lasts forever and design does not solve all problems. Those who create and plan should practice humility in the face of nature. Treat nature as a model and mentor, not as an inconvenience to be evaded or controlled.

9. **Seek constant improvements by the sharing of knowledge.** Encourage direct and open communication between colleagues, patrons, manufacturers and users to link long term sustainable considerations with ethical responsibility, and re-establish the integral relationship between natural processes and human activity.

The Hannover Principles should be seen as a living document committed to the transformation and growth in the understanding of our interdependence with nature, so that they may be adapted as our knowledge of the world evolves.

It is heartening to see so many of today's architects begin to embrace the philosophy detailed in two earlier works that have led to the current volume of this book.[18] The dawning of the twenty-first century holds much promise over the unenlightened mid-twentieth century, as we emerge from a period of awakening which began with the energy crisis, as discussed in chapter 3.

Fair and Warmer

Control of the Thermal Environment

The thermal habitat of human metabolism is established by the play of solar radiation upon the surfaces that surround us and the oceans of air in which we are submerged. But this same solar radiation contains also those wavelengths of energy that we call *visible light*, and hence establishes simultaneously our luminous environment. The temperature, movement, and humidity of the atmosphere of course operate on our metabolic function and must consequently be reckoned as integral factors of our thermal environment. But the oxygen of the atmosphere is also a chemical prerequisite of metabolism. Hence human beings exist in coextensive environments — thermal, atmospheric, and radiational — and any manipulation of one causes repercussions in the others.

This confronts the architect with a bewildering range of problems. In order to manipulate them with precision, he or she must analyze them as though they were separate and distinct entities. Only by this analytical method have immense advances in heating, air conditioning, and illumination been possible. In order of magnitude, control of our thermal environment is first. The question as to why we should heat buildings in winter or cool them in summer seems too obvious to require an answer, but the obvious response — to heat or cool the people in them — is actually so crude as to be almost meaningless. Our very concepts of warmth and coolness are relative and highly subjective. Ultimately, they are inaccurate, as in thermodynamics there is no such thing as "cold" above absolute zero (minus 460°F), the point at which molecular activity theoretically ceases; above that point there are only varying degrees of heat. But buildings, in any case, neither warm nor cool us; our life processes do. Human metabolism, the whole life process, is one of slow combustion. Under all circumstances it produces more heat than it needs. Our body's basal metabolism produces about 250 British thermal units (Btus) per hour of sensible heat (about the same as a 75-watt incandescent lamp) and about 200 Btus per hour of latent heat (moisture). In its conversion of energy it is only about 20 percent efficient, hence the body must always dissipate to its environment approximately 400 out of every 500 Btus it produces.*

What is decisive in the body's thermal equilibrium is the *rate* at which this heat is dissipated. If the rate of heat loss is too slow, we say we feel hot; if it is too rapid, we say we are cold. Of course, the amount of heat produced by the body varies widely with activity, age, sex, and health. A man walking rapidly up a stairway produces about five times as much heat as he does when sleeping. A ten-year-old boy produces more heat than his grandfather at the same task (chapter 7).

Body heat must be dissipated at a rate exactly balanced with the rate of production. Otherwise, it begins to accumulate—a condition to which the body is extremely sensitive. Indeed, maintenance of this thermal balance is the fundamental condition of existence, not merely the fundamental requirement of comfort and well-being. Studies show that as heat accumulates, thermal stress increases, the body passing through a characteristic spectrum of response from comfort to discomfort, distress, and failure (Fig. 2–1, p. 25). A strong motivation may make possible the temporary extension of these limits (e.g., a group of roofers enclosing a house at the end of a very hot day may push their level of endurance when rain is expected). Continued exposure to moderate stress can also lead to a certain degree of acclimatization, with people in tropical climates more accustomed to heat. But the upper and lower limits of thermal existence are fixed and obdurate.[1]

Regardless of climate, whether we live in the Arctic or the tropics, our normal internal temperature range differs by no more than a fraction of a degree. Our extremities are generally cooler than the rest of the body, and our daily body temperature profile exhibits its lowest value during sleep. Within these limits, however, the human body has an extraordinarily effective system for balancing heat loss against heat production to maintain a constant interior temperature close to 98.6°F. Only when its core temperature rises toward 105° or falls below 95° is the body brought into imminent collapse and death.

To maintain this steady state, called *homeostasis* by physiologists, the body employs a complex system of feedback and control. As the exterior environment grows colder the pores of the skin contract, the rate of perspiration drops, the capillary veins contract, and the heart—initially pumping at an increased rate to compensate for the loss of body heat—slows, pumping at a slower rate to husband the blood in the deep body cavities. (This withdrawal of blood from the body's surface explains the phrase *blue with cold*.) Cold also may cause a semiconscious increase in activity, such as foot stamping and dancing about. In animals, fluffing of the feathers or fur creates an insulating layer against the

---

* In contrast, conventional noncondensing heating appliances (e.g., boilers and furnaces) are approximately 80 percent efficient.

cold; in humans, goose bumps cause the hair on the body to rise. Humans usually supplement this level of insulation with extra clothing. If these measures are inadequate, shivering takes place to create muscular heat. As a last resort, the body assumes the so-called fetal position to reduce the exposed body areas to a minimum. If these measures are inadequate, collapse and death ensue, as the core temperature continues to drop and as the cardiac rate, blood pressure, and cerebral, respiratory, and metabolic functions are depressed until they literally cease.

Under opposite conditions of high external temperatures, the body reverses this procedure. Now the heart rate accelerates, the arteries and veins dilate, and the blood is moved from inside the body to the surface for more rapid cooling. If this proves insufficient, the pores expand and the sweat glands increase their production. (Hence the expression *damp and flushed with fever*.) But beyond this, the body has no further resources. Either the rate of heat loss must be externally increased by lower radiant and ambient temperatures, lower humidity or higher air movement around the body, or some combination of these, or the body will slip into irreversible coma and death.

The responsibility for maintaining a stable internal temperature rests with a complex feedback system, ultimately monitored by the hypothalamus. In periods of overheating, it is the sole mediator of the temperature control mechanisms described above. In periods of heat deficit, it teams up with the thermodetectors in the skin to accelerate all forms of muscular activity.

The body has four channels for disposing of its excess heat: under normal room conditions, about 60 percent by radiation to surfaces colder than itself, about 15 percent by a combination of convection from skin and mucous membrane, and conduction, and about 25 percent by evaporation from skin and mucous membrane.[2] All these means of heat exchange are employed by the body at all times, as nowhere in nature could conditions be otherwise. All four seem to be equally effective physiologically. The body does not prefer one means over another, though it does react unfavorably to uneven rates of loss from different parts of the body at any given moment (e.g., a draft on the back of the neck, chilled hands, wet feet). But the degree to which these channels of heat dissipation are individually effective depends upon the balance of external thermal factors. This is the algebraic sum of (1) the radiant temperature of the immediate environment, (2) the ambient air temperature, (3) the moisture content of the air, and (4) the rate of air movement across the body. These establish the thermal habitat (Fig. 3−1). Under natural conditions, all four factors are in continual flux and very infrequently achieve the exact balance that we describe as *comfortable*.

The body is always losing heat by direct radiation to surfaces cooler than itself (e.g., a cold, uncurtained single-glazed window on a winter's night) or gaining heat by radiation from bodies warmer than itself (e.g., the unshaded asphalt of a parking lot). Because all objects radiate some heat above absolute zero, this radiant heat exchange is always operative and can either favorably or adversely affect human comfort. On a sunny winter day, for example, the heat of the sun reflected off the snow makes it possible to ski in summer clothing, even though the air temperature may be well below freezing.

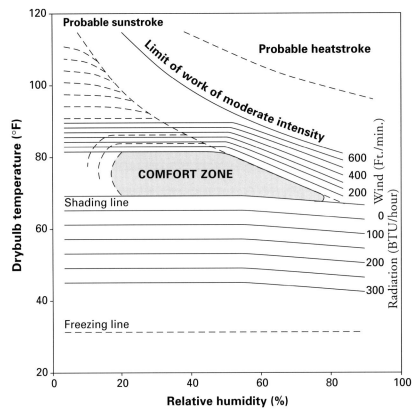

Figure 3–1 / Bioclimatic chart. Our thermal habitat is defined by four interacting environmental forces: radiant and ambient temperatures, relative humidity, and air movement. "Comfort zone" is for an adult, young, healthy, lightly clothed, doing light work at sea level.

When the air temperature is below that of the skin, air movement across the skin removes heat by convection; the more rapid the movement, the greater the cooling effect. Even when the air is warmer than the skin, its movement can still remove body heat by evaporation of sweat. However, the evaporative process is always limited by the relative humidity of the air; the higher the humidity, the lower its cooling capacity. In any case, increased velocity is effective only up to a given temperature, beyond which the air adds more heat to the skin than it can remove by vaporization. (Thus, in desert climates, cross ventilation is not always desirable.)

Conduction—due to walking barefoot on cool floors or sitting on cold stone, for example—is experientially the least important form of heat transfer, the rate of which is dependent upon the thermal gradient, or temperature difference. For persons swimming in cold water, conduction is a rapid method of heat exchange and can have disastrous results: when persons saved from drowning in cold seas subsequently die from "exposure," they are victims of conductive heat loss carried beyond the point of no return.

Figure 3 – 2 / Diners at the Harvard Business School's Kresge Dining Hall complained of inadequate heating system performance and a lack of comfort. Several engineering studies were conducted and the heat loss calculations showed that sufficient heat was being provided. The overlooked issue, however, was the cold, single glazing of the windows and its chilling radiant effects during the winter. Only an improvement in glass type to double-glazing (the only option available at that time) could have improved the situation.

Heat, Cold, and Human Well-Being

The actual metabolic relation of the human body to its thermal environment can thus be described in largely objective terms. But human consciousness complicates this relationship for, in addition to mechanisms for responding to changes in the thermal environment, the body has very flexible sensory means for perceiving them. The thermosensors in the skin register the effect of heat as radiation (an open fire), as conduction (a hot bath), and as convection (a blast of hot air from an oven). This perception undoubtedly acts to reinforce our state of thermal comfort or distress at any given moment. Finally, there are purely subjective factors, unconnected to our thermal condition, that can further complicate a given situation (e.g., anxiety about the task at hand, worry about health or finances). Clearly, architecture can only hope, at best, to alleviate the objective aspects of this complicated problem of thermal stress.

It is easy to dramatize extremes of thermal stress — heat so intense or cold so severe as to lead directly and spectacularly to disablement or death. Surprisingly, these events are not as unusual as we are likely to think. Somehow we find it easy to forget the extremes of weather-related heat and cold that we do experience. These events play a critical, yet often unrecognized, role in the habitability of our cities. In the United States, exposure to excessive cold in winter typically claims the lives of about 600 people, and excessive heat in summer claims up to 1,500 lives. Recent history includes a number of thermal weather-related events that qualify as disasters:[3]

Year	Date	Type and Location	Number of Deaths
1995	July 11–27	Heat wave in Chicago	465
1995	July	Heat wave in Milwaukee	85
1993	July	Heat wave in Philadelphia	118
1993	June–July	Heat wave in Southeast	100
1980	July	Heat wave in St. Louis	100
1978	January 25–27	Blizzard in Midwest	80
1978	February 5–7	Severe snowstorm in Northeast	50

For each of these heat- or cold-related deaths, there are millions of people who, in a long life, will never be subjected to stress approaching this intensity. Nevertheless, they will suffer from much less apparent deficiencies in their thermal environment, and the long-range consequences for them may be quite as disabling as heatstroke or exposure. Unfortunately, even for specialists in the field of environmental health, this sequence of cause and effect is not easy to trace. Few cases of disablement or death can be attributed to any single environmental cause. Life is seldom that simple. A nexus of interacting factors centered on the individual are usually involved, each of which may contribute to the end result. This necessarily ambiguous situation often serves to discourage any serious architectural diagnosis. Too often, instead, a sort of shell game is played in which cause (bad building, bad diet, bad lifestyle) can never be directly related to effect (discomfort, distress, disability, disease, death).

In today's America the typical urban experience with heat stress and dehydration occurs on hot, dry summer days when heat radiates from the sidewalks, streets, and the surrounding buildings, and there is no relief in the form of canopies or shading from trees. From the streets the urban dweller descends to crowded, oppressively hot subways whose windows are often sealed. On the top floors of unshaded apartment buildings without air conditioning, conductive heat gain from hot asphalt roofing can become unbearable. These conditions can become life-threatening to susceptible members of the population, including the elderly and those with heart conditions or respiratory problems (for example, asthmatics).

We are just now beginning to understand and prepare for heat-related emergencies, after recently suffering unexpectedly heavy death tolls in our cities. Heat, rather than lightning, hurricanes, or tornadoes, is the leading cause of climate-related death in the United States.[4] Particularly vulnerable are midwestern and northeastern cities that experience sporadic heat waves to which people are unaccustomed. Often they live in row-houses or apartments with uninsulated black asphalt roofing, as compared to housing in the South, which may be light-colored and cross ventilated. Most of the 465 heat-related deaths in Chicago during July 1995 took place in the poorer neighborhoods on the South Side. Tragically, most of these housing units did not have air conditioners, and many residents were found with their windows locked or sealed shut, apparently preferring to endure the heat rather than to allow ready access to intruders. At that time, city officials did not appreciate the dangerous conditions nor did they institute ameliorating actions until it was too late. Several public air-conditioned shelters were available in office buildings, but with no means or mechanism of transporting people to them.

Nowhere are the unfortunate consequences of thermal stress more clear than in the race riots that were a prominent feature of American cities during the 1960s. Although the basic causes of those disturbances were profound social and economic injustices, it is not at all accidental that the riots occurred in the hottest months of the year. The micro-climates created by our masonry deserts exacerbate the already difficult summers of major cities. Substandard conditions inside urban apartment buildings (absence of cross ventilation, lack of fans, insulation, air conditioning) drive the people out into the streets.

But the neighborhoods are as unbearable as the individual buildings that comprise them. Urban amenities that might compensate for lack of private comforts are missing despite numerous government programs over the last several decades. Shadeless pavements, the paucity of parks and green spaces, the scarcity of swimming pools—in short, the lack of any possibility of escape from high radiant and ambient temperatures and high humidities—combine to make life literally intolerable. Explosions are inevitable and easily set off by any number of provocations, such as the Rodney King incident in Los Angeles. It would be nonsense to argue that reconstructing the poorer neighborhoods would, by itself, suffice; the grave inequities that underlie them must also be wiped out.

It is perfectly obvious that most American experience today has its actual locus in real buildings and real cities; it is therefore inconceivable that architecture and urbanism do not play a vital role in their health. As the physiologist C. E. A. Winslow put it in his study of human thermal requirements:

[W]e can predicate with certainty that extremes of heat and cold are harmful; and that even moderately hot conditions increase susceptibility to intestinal diseases, and moderately cold conditions increase susceptibility to respiratory disease. These are simple conclusions but they are of far-reaching significance both from an epidemiological and from a physical standpoint.[5]

Environmental health specialists and human ecologists recognize that thermal stress and atmospheric pollution play roles of prime importance in respiratory ailments like childhood asthma, acute infectious bronchitis, and influenza. Debilitation and breakdown in human resistance to cold in ill-heated and ill-ventilated buildings are conducive to such ailments, and dampness and cold are predisposing factors to rheumatism.

Excessive heat has always been a serious environmental hazard in heavy manufacturing and extractive industries, but only in recent times have we developed the rational means for evaluating the stresses imposed by hot environments, identifying contributing factors, and thus predicting and preventing the resulting physiologic stress. Architects involved in the design of industrial buildings now have access to skilled assistance that makes error unnecessary, indeed impermissible. As a matter of fact, however, with the rise of automation in heavy industry, the problem of extremely hard or hazardous labor begins to recede into the background. The day may not be far off when such noisome and destructive jobs are entirely eliminated by mechanized, automated, and computerized production methods. As the economy has shifted away from heavy manufacturing toward services, offices have become the workplace of more and more Americans. With the increased use of office equipment (e.g., computers, printers, copiers), the heat load generated in these buildings has grown significantly, to the point where interior portions of most office buildings need to be cooled whenever occupied, even in the depth of winter.

But if architects are seldom involved in designing for processes that demand heavy or laborious work, they are increasingly charged with creating satisfactory thermal environments for a wide range of less strenuous but more exacting tasks. Modern industrial processes have their own precise environmental requirements. Many of them demand an absolutely constant thermal environment; some manufacturing and production processes, for example, are intolerant of even small variations of ambient temperature and humidity. Such process requirements do not always coincide with human requirements. Typically, they deviate; sometimes, they are irreconcilable. Hence modern human beings at work-a-day tasks are often submerged in thermal environments not tailored to their own psychic and somatic requirements.

Even where process requirements are not stressful from thermal overload, the opposite may often be the case—that is, under- rather than overstimulation. The monotony and boredom of modern work is almost without precedent in human history. Only the galley slave of classic antiquity experienced the monochromatic, atomized, and repetitive experience characteristic of many jobs today. This new situation raises many vital but extremely subtle problems of comfort, efficiency, and productivity. If modern work, by its necessarily fragmented and repetitive character, suggests the need for variety in the environment in which it occurs, it is the task of the architect to supply it.

Each level of activity has its own metabolic rate and thus its own internally established rate of heat loss. But, as seen in chapter 1, even this is not indefinitely extensible in time. A person using a computer at 9 A.M. may very well require a different thermal environment at 3 P.M. even though the difference may be below the level of conscious perception. (The same proposition holds true for other areas of sensory perception—light, sound, odor, posture, etc.) In any case, contemporary misgivings about the anesthetizing effects of "controlled environments" probably have a sound basis in day-to-day experience. The word processor, like the schoolchild or assembly-line worker, requires the sensory stimulation of change and variety. But change and variety must lie within a golden zone of thermal balance and — if the work is not to suffer — the changes must be structured and not indeterminate. (If change alone were all that was required, the typist could work unprotected in an open field.)

Personal control of one's work environment (e.g., control of the thermostat setting, selection of lighting level and type, choice of chair and adjustable desk height, use of accessories such as antifatigue mats, radios) can go a long way toward making the workplace an acceptable, enjoyable, and productive place to be. The architect's primary task, therefore, may be to create an environment that enables or empowers the occupants of a building; the building must also continue to function efficiently as a system, even with variability on a workstation by workstation level.

In many activities, of course, questions of boredom or monotony do not arise. Buildings designed for entertainment and play — theaters, stadiums, swimming pools, ball courts — shelter experiences that have their own built-in patterns of variety, suspense, satisfaction. Each is complete and intelligible in itself. Thus each can have a thermal environment designed for its particular level of metabolic activity.

How Buildings Are Heated and Cooled

The task of architecture, then, is not merely to abolish gross thermal extremes (freezing to death, dying of heat prostration) but to provide the optimal thermal environments for the whole spectrum of modern life. The technology of heating and cooling aims not merely at introducing the proper amount of heat into, or extracting the proper amount of heat out of, the building but doing it in such a manner as to achieve a thermal steady state across time — and a thermal equilibrium across space. Neither of these criteria is easy to achieve, as radiant and ambient heat are variable forms of energy. As long as we had to depend upon simple combustion in fireplaces and stoves, the fire itself was a point source of heat, so that its effectiveness diminished rapidly with distance (Fig. 3−3). Moreover, the enclosing surfaces of the heated space were always subjected to the shifting stress of sun and wind. Because the insulation properties of walling materials were incompletely understood (see chapter 8), a thermal environment constant across time and symmetrical across space was an impossibility in preindustrial architecture (Fig. 3−4).

Today's building designers, however, have at their disposal two increasingly refined instruments: mathematical methods and computer software for accurately calculating building energy flows, and a sophisticated range of building materials (e.g., low emissivity ["low-e"] glass) and heating/cooling equipment for producing the desired thermal regimes. In real life, one builds the thermal vessel and then installs the heating and cooling equipment. Conceptually, it is the other way around: one cannot design the enclosing vessel until one has a clear concept of the internal environments to be created and maintained. The criteria for these environments must, in turn, be derived from the needs of the people and the processes that will inhabit the building.

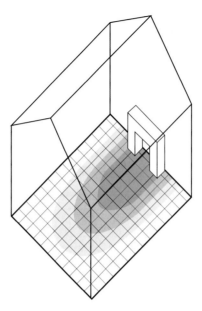

Figure 3 – 3 / Early heating methods could not achieve a thermal steady state across time or space. Simple combustion of wood or coal in the fireplace was inefficient and uncomfortable. Introduction of the freestanding metal stove increased control of radiant temperatures, but air temperature and movement remained uncontrollable.

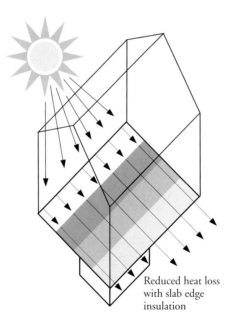

Reduced heat loss with slab edge insulation

Figure 3 – 4 / Traditional structural methods and building materials offered limited means of thermal insulation. The efficiency of the building as a thermal container was low; this was exacerbated by the fundamental asymmetry, across time and space, of the natural thermal environment around it. Newer construction details such as slab-edge insulation can now limit heat loss from concrete floors and other potential thermal bridges.

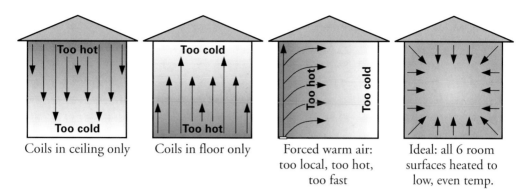

Coils in ceiling only   Coils in floor only   Forced warm air: Ideal: all 6 room
                                                 too local, too hot,   surfaces heated to
                                                       too fast   low, even temp.

Figure 3–5 / Basic types of heating installations. Even with modern equipment, heating systems often fail to meet normal criteria of comfort and health. Optimal application is one in which the transfer method is exclusively radiant (right above), with heat source distributed across all enclosed surfaces, but this is seldom practicable.

All conventional thermal control systems have common functional characteristics, whatever their special features (Fig. 3–5). They all require a primary source of energy — usually oil, gas, electricity, or wood. They must convert this energy into heat or cold by the processes of combustion, compression, evaporation, or electrical resistance. They require a medium of distribution for this manufactured heat or cold — air, steam, water, or other fluid having special properties. Finally, they must employ one of two methods of heat transfer — convection or radiation.

It is within these limits that heating and ventilating engineers have been working for approximately two centuries as evidenced by Thomas Tredgold's treatise, which marked the first theoretical attempt to explore the field.[6] (Table 3–1). The direction of these efforts, however, has been largely conditioned by historical chance. Because wood, coal, gas, and petroleum became available as fuels in approximately that order, eighteenth- and nineteenth-century heating systems were premised upon simple combustion. But the forms in which these fuels were available made possible increasingly sophisticated equipment, notably in automatic fueling and controls, as is obvious in the sequence: fireplace, stove, furnace, stoker, oil burner.

The fireplace had many disadvantages: it was wasteful, dangerous, messy, and limited in its effect. In the eighteenth century, Benjamin Franklin took an early step away from this with his lightweight, prefabricated, and demountable cast-iron stove. (Even the stove had the disadvantage of being a point source of heat.) This led naturally to the idea of the furnace, lost since Roman times, of heating air in a central plenum and carrying it by ducts to the various rooms. Such early furnaces relied entirely upon gravity-flow — that is, the natural tendency of heated air to rise — and this placed obvious limitations upon the size and efficiency of such systems. The use of fans to push the air through the ducts awaited the perfection of the electric motor as a prime mover; this appeared in the last quarter of the nineteenth century. From this point it was but a step to the modern

Table 3 – 1 / *Components of Modern Thermal Control Systems*

Energy Source	Conversion Method	Conversion Unit	Delivery Medium	Delivery Means	Transfer Method
gas, oil, coal	combustion	furnace	warm air	fans, ducts, registers	convection
		boiler	hot water	pumps, pipes, radiators	convection
				pumps, pipes, panels	radiation
			steam	pipes, radiators	convection
electricity or gas	compression	compressor	warm or cool air	fans, ducts, registers	convection
			hot or cold water	pumps, pipes, panels	radiation
gas	evaporation	evaporative condenser	warm or cool air	fans, ducts, registers	convection
electricity	resistance			wires, resistance coils	radiation

air-conditioning system in which air is heated or cooled, moistened or dried, filtered, and then forced through ducts at any rate or volume desired.

But early experience with the steam boiler led to another set of developments in heating. Unlike the furnace, the boiler used either steam or hot water as a heat delivery medium, steam having the obvious advantage of being under pressure and therefore requiring no auxiliary pump or fan. (Gravity-flow in hot water systems was also moderately effective in small systems.) Hence the early perfection of central steam and hot-water systems, with a central boiler supplying radiators in each room. The radiator, incidentally, is misnamed; less than one half of its heat is emitted radiantly, the balance being discharged by convection. When a fan was placed behind the radiator and air forced across the surface of its heated fins, the element was converted into an almost pure convector.

The efficiency of combustion heating appliances has advanced markedly in the recent past. By federal law, conventional appliances now offered for sale in the United States must have a minimum annual fuel utilization efficiency (AFUE) of at least 80 percent. Improvements in technology make it possible to harness much of the remaining 20 percent. The pulse furnace first introduced in the mid-1970s uses a spark plug to begin a self-sustaining combustion process that is over 90 percent efficient. Such an efficiency is achieved in large part by passing the high-temperature combustion gases over a large heat exchange area to reduce the gas temperature to below 212°F, at which point water vapor condenses and gives back the heat that was needed to produce it during the combustion process. In conventional heating appliances, this water vapor is simply vented up the chimney at a temperature of 300°F or greater, taking with it 10 percent or more of the fuel's heating potential.

Techniques and equipment for the cooling of buildings are of much more recent origin. Most early developments in refrigeration occurred in the food processing industries and were only subsequently applied to the cooling of buildings. All the necessary components for cooling and drying air, including appropriate electronic controls, were available in the United States in the 1930s. But, except for industrial applications and in some building types like theaters, they were not widely applied to architecture in general until the end of World War II. Since that time, however, development has been so rapid that a new building without summer cooling is almost as obsolete as one without heating would have been in 1920. In 1995, 80 percent of all new one-family housing built in the United States had central air-conditioning; in the South, the figure was 98 percent! In new privately owned multifamily buildings, an average of 86 percent were air-conditioned in all parts of the country. This number rose to 99 percent in the South.[7]

Endless permutations and combinations of air-conditioning systems are in common use (Table 3–1). Together with parallel improvements in combustion, propulsion and refrigeration (burners, pumps, fans, compressors), and in automatic control devices (thermostats, aquastats, time and pressure controls), control of the thermal environment has become a reality. The mechanical efficiency of such equipment is now so high that it has, for all practical purposes, removed all limitations of size and location from our building activity. A small house or an entire city can be automatically conditioned by a single plant. Any kind of thermal environment can be created and maintained anywhere—at the equator, at the poles, even in outer space. This is a historic accomplishment in the evolution of architecture, permitting thermostable states comparable to homeostasis in humans.

The Convective Systems

The majority of thermal control systems are largely convective in their method of heat transfer; those involving summer air-conditioning are almost wholly so, as radiant cooling raises such serious condensation problems as to be impractical in most cases. Convective systems have certain advantages over other methods, including economy and simplicity. But they all have real shortcomings. The first is their general sluggishness in responding to changing external conditions. Because they depend for effect upon manipulation of the entire air mass inside the building, a time lag in completing the change is inevitable. In old-fashioned masonry buildings with high-heat-capacity walls this lethargy was not too serious, as the building itself was slow to respond to external changes. But modern architecture, with its wide use of glass and lightweight wall materials, results in a thermal container of quite different properties. Its transparency implies rapid heating up and cooling off and hence demands instantaneous response on the part of the thermal control system. This the air system cannot do, as it depends for its effect upon the temperature of the whole air mass in the vessel in question. Moreover, a large part of the heat gain through glass is radiant and not directly modified by air temperatures.

Of course, the convective system *ultimately* catches up, but it is small consolation to the occupants overheated by the radiation to know that in thirty minutes or an hour they will be cool again. Thermal stress is metabolic and immediate, not a matter of statistical averages. For this reason, serious discomfort is all too common in many glass-walled buildings, despite their advanced air-conditioning.

Convective systems have another related disadvantage. Because warm air rises and cold air falls, the tendency toward vertical temperature stratification inside the building is always operative. Most rooms show higher temperatures at the ceiling than at the floor. From a physiological point of view this is almost the exact reverse of the desirable: ambient temperatures at the feet should be equal to or higher than those at breathing level. Modern air systems can overcome this tendency toward stratification, but to do so without drafts and noise requires a more sophisticated duct and damper system and redundant capacity in the system as a whole.

The Radiant Systems

Well known to the Romans and the Chinese, and widely used in their more important buildings, radiant heating had been all but forgotten in Europe and America. Increased experience with it in recent years has led to important advances in both theory and technique. Mechanically, the radiant system differs in only one important respect from convective systems — the actual method of heat transfer — but it is an important difference.

Using a plane surface (ceiling, walls, or floor) as the actual heating element, radiant panels offer an almost ideal method of manipulating the thermal environment. If installed in all six surfaces of the room, as the Romans often managed to do, they surround the body of the occupant with a balanced thermal perimeter — that is to say, the rate of heat exchange between the body and its surrounding surfaces is equal in all directions (excepting, of course, the soles of the feet, where the heat exchange is conductive) and constant in time. This exchange is independent of the temperature, humidity, and movement of the surrounding air. For example, a convective system surrounds a normally clothed person at rest with 70°F air in order to maintain comfort. But with radiant surfaces at 80°F, the air temperature could drop to 55°F and the same person would be comfortable. Contrariwise, air temperatures could rise to 85°F and, with walls held at 60°F, the person would be quite at ease. It is this relative freedom from having to manipulate ambient temperatures that makes radiant heating so attractive.

From an experiential point of view, radiant systems have the obvious advantage of acting directly and immediately upon the occupants of the building and only indirectly and secondarily upon its air mass. Obviously, in any closed and unventilated room the atmosphere ultimately reaches the same temperature as the enclosing surfaces. In actuality this seldom, if ever, occurs. In any case, if these systems use hot water or electricity as a medium, they eliminate space-consuming fans, plenums, and ductwork. For the same reason, they are simpler to install and operate. The elements themselves are invisible and, because of the low temperatures at which they operate, permit any type of decoration.

In practice, however, there are limitations to radiant systems, too. The optimal installation, from a physiological point of view, uses all six room surfaces as radiant sources. But construction methods and budgetary limitations often make this ideal distribution impractical. Then the coils are concentrated in one or two planes only — for example, floor and/or ceiling. But because the area is so restricted, surface temperatures may have to be raised beyond comfort level; hot feet or headaches can be the result. Also, if heating coils are confined to one plane, such as the ceiling, desks and tabletops block the rays, producing cold spots under them. A hazard in systems using water as a delivery medium is the danger of leaks developing in coils embedded in plaster ceilings or concrete slabs. Thus, the electric resistance coil must be judged as the safest installation.

The Roman system employed heated air, circulating it through continuous ducts in floors, walls, and ceilings. It was wood-fueled and gravity-flow, a simple and comfortable method of heating. Its limitation was that it presupposed heavy load-bearing masonry structures of the sort one would rarely find practical today. A combination of such labyrinths in a masonry floor with conventional convective air systems, however, makes a highly satisfactory setup for single-story buildings. Today, some contemporary houses utilize warm air radiant design by employing a system of vaulted metal formwork that first serves as the formwork for a poured concrete subfloor and then is used to distribute warm air through the openings.

Though the high cost of electricity in many parts of the country limits the use of the electric resistance coil in radiant heating, it is the most attractive of all methods. It requires almost no space, has no moving elements, is relatively simple to install, is all but foolproof in operation, and is low in first cost. The coils themselves can be embedded in plaster walls and ceilings, somewhat less frequently in masonry floors, but a wide variety of supplementary applications suggest themselves. For example, the elements used in electric blankets have been incorporated into curtains for large glass areas. Fabricated panels providing electric radiant heat can be inserted into a framing system such as a hung ceiling grid. They can also be built into folding or sliding screens and shutters. In the future the use of electric radiant heat is likely to increase dramatically as technological advances in photovoltaics increase and production costs are reduced.

In cold climates, where the low surface temperatures of even insulating glass raise serious comfort problems, such applications would make significant contributions to the overall thermal balance of the room. The coils would be employed to slow radiant heat loss from the room's occupants to chilled glass surfaces, not to raise the air temperature of the room as a whole.

The above considerations apply to the use of radiant panel systems for heating, but air and water systems also offer interesting potentials for summer cooling. In hot weather, as we have seen, comfort can be maintained quite as well by losing heat to cool surfaces as to cool air. Thus, by circulating chilled water or cool air through the coils, we would have "radiant cooling" independent of the temperature, humidity, or movement of the surrounding air. The drawback here is condensation; except in the Southwest, summertime humidities in the United States are high and chilled surfaces would produce heavy sweating. Thus radiant cooling could be used only in conjunction with dehumidification equipment that could hold room air at low humidities. From a physiological standpoint, however, radiant cooling, like radiant heating, can offer an exhilarating thermal environment.

Because it operates independently of air temperatures, radiant panel heating can be productively employed in a wide range of outdoor installations — for example, in theater and hotel marquees, in sidewalk cafés, and for removal of ice and snow on sidewalks, streets and plazas. Moreover, because infrared radiation can be focused, like the visible wave band, all sorts of special problems can be solved by means of radiant heating and cooling that could not readily be met with convective systems. Thus, for example, a surgical team in an operating theater might be cooled by radiant cooling panels focused on them from the walls while the patient is submerged in the warm, moist air supplied by the central air-conditioning system.

Animal Analogues for Thermal Control Systems

The objective of all these heating and cooling systems is, of course, to produce a stable, balanced, and symmetrical thermal environment — that is, to achieve in architecture that homeostatic state that Harvard physiologist Cannon called the highest stage of evolutionary development in animals. The analogy is apt, for the building confronts the same paradox as the animal body. It seeks to establish and maintain its internal thermal equilibrium while being submerged in a continually fluctuating set of external forces. The analogue is that the building, as a thermal vessel, requires a skin or enclosing membrane that, like the animal epidermis, is capable of variable response to shifting environmental stresses. This is why the wall cannot be thought of as a simple barrier but must rather be visualized as a permeable filter, capable of admitting, modifying, or rejecting the various forces that play upon it (Fig. 8–5).

Hence, in thermal control, the design of the building wall is quite as important a matter as design of the systems. The malfunction of much modern architecture can be traced to neglect of this principle, where stereotyped curtain walls are used in highly formalistic designs that seldom pay serious attention to climate, latitude, and orientation. The entire task of maintaining required internal conditions is thrown upon the heating and cooling systems, with inevitable waste, inefficiency, and malfunction. The advantages of standardization of industrially produced parts and components are obvious. But a comparable standardization of entire buildings makes no sense at all, considering the wide climatic variations discussed in chapter 9. A building in Bangor and a building in Tucson may well use identical materials — metals, insulation materials, glass, and plastics — but the way in which they are assembled into a wall must be quite dissimilar if the walls are to function equally well.

It is possible to visualize in broad terms the characteristic features of several different types of building skins to meet these requirements.

1. The most direct analogue of the animal epidermis is a solid opaque membrane (with few windows of limited size) with an overall capillary system of coils embedded near the outer surface (Fig. 3–6). The coils circulate either chilled or heated water as called for by individual thermostats for each exposure of walls and roof. In cold weather, such a capillary system circulates heated water in those walls chilled by wind or shade, transferring heated water from sunny exposures and supplementing it as required. In summer, when heat gain is excessive on all walls, the capillaries circulate chilled water on all outer surfaces, transferring heat thus accumulated into a central storage system. Such a capillary system is supplementary to conventional conditioning of enclosed volumes, serving largely to hold the perimeters in a thermally symmetrical state. It is most valuable in building types where precise environmental controls are required. It has the obvious disadvantage of opacity for any building type that requires natural light or view.

2. Other dynamic solutions to the problem of equalizing the unequal and continually shifting thermal stresses upon the building have stirred the imagination of architects who have experimented with it over the years. One response is to design the building so that two adjacent walls are opaque to thermal transmission and the opposite pair transparent. The building could then be rotated so as

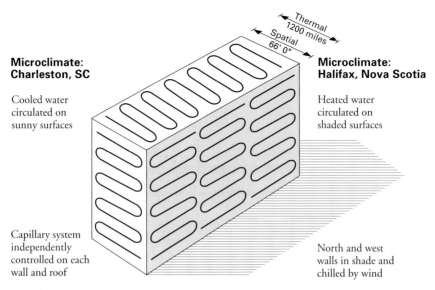

Thermal
1200 miles

Spatial
66' 0"

**Microclimate:
Charleston, SC**

Cooled water
circulated on
sunny surfaces

Capillary system
independently
controlled on each
wall and roof

**Microclimate:
Halifax, Nova Scotia**

Heated water
circulated on
shaded surfaces

North and west
walls in shade and
chilled by wind

Figure 3 – 6 / The asymmetry of the thermal environment in which a freestanding building is submerged is marked. During daylight hours, it becomes acute. Then the spread between thermal environments along sunlit and shaded walls is the equivalent of hundreds of miles rather than tens of feet. A capillary system in the building's epidermis, operating independently of internal heating and air-conditioning system, facilitates the maintenance of an internal thermal steady state. It also reduces redundant capacity and yield economies in energy consumption.

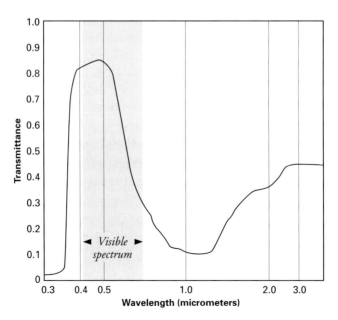

Figure 3 – 7 / A spectrally selective glass with the performance characteristics shown allows much of the daylight in the solar spectrum to pass through while longer-wave infrared heat energy is blocked out. Such glass is ideal for many types of commercial buildings that can benefit from the entry of natural light but have little need for heat.

to keep the opaque walls normal to the sun in periods of overheating. In cold weather, the cycling would be reversed—that is, the transparent walls would be held normal to the sun.

A less complicated version of the same principle is to rotate a freestanding screen, large enough to shield the building, around it, cycling it to correspond to periods of over- or underheating as above. Such methods are especially adapted to dry climates of extreme insolation (Yuma, Phoenix, Las Vegas) or to regions with high winter winds (Duluth, Buffalo). Because either building or screen is floated on tracked pontoons, the mechanical energy for such rotation is moderate—probably less, in fact, than the redundant cooling capacity saved.

It is now clear that thermal control of buildings can be achieved without such applications of technology as rotation of buildings or moving and sun-blocking screens. Spectrally selective glazing can be chosen that admits a large portion of the visible light spectrum while keeping out a large portion of the infrared heat (Fig. 3–7). Today's glazing choices are like ice cream, with a multitude of flavors available.

3. The most familiar architectural response is that of shading the wall by manipulating the forms and materials of the wall itself. This response takes two forms: (a) planar extensions of the wall, in the form of vertical and horizontal *brise-soleils*, louvers, screens, etc., and (b) use of materials with special photothermal properties—heat- or light-rejecting glasses, plastics, etc., or some combination of the two. Because of the constantly shifting path of the sun, the geometry of the first method is complex. Consequently, many sun-shading devices are often the result of an esthetic decision rather than a concern for functionality (Fig. 3–8). Automatically

Figure 3–8 / Apartment Building, Vancouver, British Columbia, Canada. Projecting overhangs above glazing are more photogenic than functional.

Figure 3–9 / Occidental Petroleum Building (built originally by Hooker Chemical Company), Niagara Falls, New York, 1979. Cannon Design, architect. Left: Exterior view of the building designed as a glass box within a glass box for improved energy efficiency. Right: Within the wide space between the glazing layers are operable louvers that open and close to reduce thermal loads and allow heat to be delivered where needed around the building.

powered louvers can be used in various ways to overcome the limitations of fixed shading devices. One approach to load reduction is the construction of an all-glass box surrounded by another all-glass box several feet away (Fig. 3–9). Operable louvers located in the air space on all sides of the building then open and close so as to advantageously direct energy flows. From a Btu standpoint the building is energy efficient and the size of the heating and cooling plants is reduced. This is at the cost, however, of expensive glass skins.

Operable louvers can also be used more selectively, outside windows high on a wall (above vision glass) to deflect direct daylight onto the ceiling and further into a building (Fig. 3–10). During the heating season such louvers close at night to reduce heat loss. When using operable louvers, care should be taken to install products that can withstand icing, corrosion, and mechanical failure.

The most sophisticated solution to this particular problem is the type of wall analysis and design suggested by the work of Ralph Knowles (Fig. 3–11). Here a cellular geometry is developed by computer analysis to optimize building form, inviting solar heat in when needed during the colder months and blocking it out

Figure 3–10 / Mart Library and Computer Center, Bethlehem, Pennsylvania. Warner, Burns, Toan & Lunde, architects, completed 1984. Top: Operable louvers outside the high glass area act as horizontal light shelves to reflect daylight deep into the building. During the winter the louvers close at night to reduce heat loss from the building. Bottom: Interior view. The design achieves much of the energy advantage of the Occidental Petroleum Building (Fig. 3-9), but without as much of an initial cost premium.

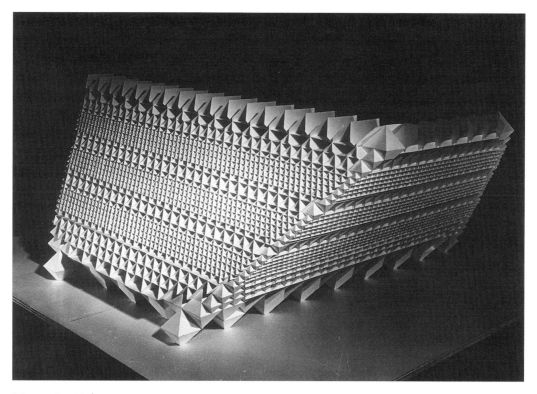

Figure 3–11 / Hypothetical study for an office building at 30 degrees N. Ralph Knowles, architect. For more than twenty years Knowles studied orientation to derive geometric shapes for buildings that optimize sun control. Result is a kind of bearing wall in which structural material is organized normal to wall plane. This assures complete diurnal and seasonal control of sunlight, maximum transparency from inside, and wide spans.

during warmer periods. In addition to being highly effective, the resulting patterns are extremely handsome and suggest once again that the origin of rich and satisfying esthetics is always to be found in functional effectiveness.

Response to Crisis: Thermal Design Evolution

As the 1970s began (when the previous edition of this volume was published), most American architects were confident that they were in complete control of the thermal environment of the buildings they designed. This was principally accomplished by employing mechanical engineers who selected equipment that could overcome any architectural design shortcoming. No matter how much unshaded west-facing glass a building had, there was a chiller big enough to keep the inside of the building comfortable. However, not all American architects thought that way at the time. In the summer of 1973, Richard Stein wrote in *Architectural Forum* magazine:

There is an anomaly amongst us, and it has to do with the fact that we are designing and building structures that are the very opposite of what they purport to be. The underlying idea—found in all architectural design and criticism—is that design decisions derive from programmatic needs, and that resulting building forms derive from solving those needs rationally, using materials and techniques at hand and considering their placement in a setting.

The tremendous increase in energy use by these buildings has forced a re-examination of whether we do, in fact, do what we say we do. Has our fourfold increase in electric energy use, in the past two decades, produced a comparable increase in the quality of life? If not, how do we explain the path we have chosen? [8]

Stein's article, "Architecture and Energy," which was later expanded into a book of the same title,[9] was prophetic and timely. By the fall of 1973, the ability to control the thermal environment inside our buildings was threatened by an energy crisis. The cost of fossil fuel products skyrocketed and their very availability became uncertain. No longer could we take energy for granted.

Some began looking upward for answers—and saw the sun. A resurgence of solar design began with the use of active solar collectors to produce domestic hot water and, to a much smaller extent, hot water or hot air to assist in the heating of entire homes. The typical configuration at the time was a flat metal plate painted or coated so that it would absorb the maximum amount of heat when installed in a glass-covered box insulated on the back and sides. To facilitate their handling and installation, flat plate collectors are typically manufactured in modules 3 to 4 feet wide and 6 to 8 feet high.

Flat plate collectors are often made of metal for a fundamental reason: it absorbs heat well. Metals are, however, heavy and expensive. As an alternative, some flat plate collectors are made of rubbers and plastics that admittedly do not absorb heat as well, but are less expensive to manufacture and install. Flat plate collectors enjoyed about a decade of

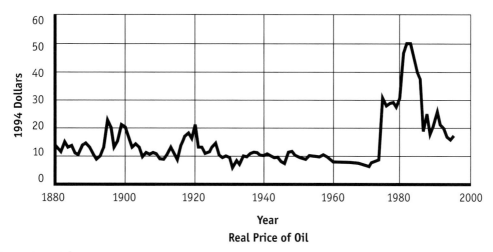

Figure 3–12 / The real price of oil from 1880 through 1994 (in 1994 dollars per barrel. Note that there are forty two gallons in a barrel of oil.) Reprinted with permission from The Worldwatch Institute.

widespread interest (until the early 1980s) aided by federal and, in some cases, state tax credits. When conditions are ripe for another boom in solar water heater use, collectors are likely to display a new esthetic, perhaps similar to the high-strength plastic bag collector design developed at the Brookhaven National Laboratory in the 1980s. These lightweight collectors are manufactured by fusing various layers of high-strength, very-low-weight plastic to provide spaces for water to pass through and be heated. Reduced fabrication and installation costs should improve cost-effectiveness.

Another immediate response to the energy crisis was the development by the American Society of Heating Refrigerating and Air-Conditioning Engineers (ASHRAE) of a standard, first adopted in 1975, that provided prescriptive guidelines for the energy efficient design of buildings (i.e., insulation levels, types of glazing, lighting systems, efficiency of HVAC equipment, etc.). Known as ASHRAE 90–1975, this standard soon became codified and states were required to adopt it or to develop provisions that were at least as stringent (the choice of New York and California) if they were to be eligible for certain federal funding. The American Institute of Architects (AIA) did not join ASHRAE in the sponsorship of ASHRAE 90 although given the opportunity. AIA's position was that such a prescriptive approach was too limiting on design. AIA preferred development of Building Energy Performance Standards (BEPS) based on meeting or exceeding performance targets of Btus per square foot per year that varied by building type and climate zone. But ASHRAE 90 endured as the relevant energy standard for commercial buildings, having weathered several revisions and eventual reformatting as ASHRAE 90.1 (for commercial buildings) and ASHRAE 90.2 (for residential buildings). Through its revisions it has become more flexible and less prescriptive.

As the 1970s continued, much of the attention of energy-concerned architects switched from solar collectors on roofs to the houses and buildings themselves. The modern era of passive solar heating gained momentum during this period; for a small but thoroughly convinced segment of architects it continues, albeit without a great deal of fanfare. Various techniques and design forms began to evolve and be refined, making part of the house a heat collector that could be comfortably, even delightfully, inhabited. These include direct gain, thermal storage walls, and sunspaces (Fig. 3–13).

An architecture that encourages well-conceived use of the sun provides more than thermal benefits: it provides luminous and emotional benefits as well. Comfort, satisfaction, and improved productivity all result from energy-conserving design, as demonstrated by numerous architectural examples. As might be expected, in a period of invention and experimentation, not all design approaches that received attention and praise lasted. One such example is the double envelope design, which provided for the collection of solar heat in a south-facing sunspace. The heat rose into a cavity of double construction over the ceiling at the roof and then down through double-wall construction on the north side of the house. Finally, the heat arrived in a shallow area below the first floor, where it was held in rock storage until needed. This design type was considered magical for a time, as if the journey of heated air over and around the building were somehow adding to the bounty of Btus that the heated air had collected.

Figure 3–13 / The Brookhaven (Laboratory) House, Brookhaven, New York. This demonstration house designed by Lisa Heschong of Total Environment Action (TEA), and completed in 1979, utilizes direct gain (through south-facing windows), a thermal storage wall (surrounding the windows in the living room below an operable awning), and a sunspace (similar to a greenhouse, but a space that transfers heat to the house).

In the 1980s, the search for energy-conserving design lost momentum. The energy crisis was perceived to be over. By and large, people were once again interested in energy conservation only if it also meant assured and significant dollar savings as well. Luckily, at that time Dr. J. Douglas Balcomb and his associates at Los Alamos National Laboratory developed a simple yet elegant method of measuring passive solar performance. Simply defined, the method compares the need for heat in a building (a measure of heat loss) to the area of south-facing windows incorporated in the design (Fig. 3–14). This value is known as the load collector ratio (LCR). Based on the ratio obtained, performance in different climates can be predicted for designs that vary by south-facing window glass type, whether the glass is covered by night insulation or not, and the amount of thermal mass available. Table 3–2 provides the solar savings fractions (amount of annual heating provided by the sun) that would be achieved by houses of identical design, including low-emissivity south window glazing and a low amount of thermal mass, when placed in various American climates. As can be seen, the house design that yields a 44 percent savings in heating fuel if located in Albuquerque yields only 10 percent if located in Buffalo.

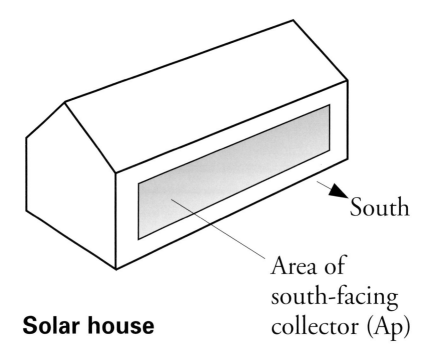

South

Solar house

Area of
south-facing
collector (Ap)

Figure 3–14 / The heating benefits of passive solar heating can be estimated through use of the load collector ratio LCR method. Rather elegantly, the method compares the need for heat (the *load* in units of Btus per degree day not including the heat loss through the south-facing window area) with the square foot area of south-facing window area (the *collector*). This ratio is used to determine the solar heat contribution or solar savings fraction (SSF), as illustrated in Table 3–2.

Clearly, architects must fully understand local climatic conditions if energy-conserving, climate-responsive design is to result.

Portions of many nonresidential buildings are not well suited to passive solar heating. In modern commercial buildings, much of the warmth needed for comfort is provided by the people themselves, along with the heat from artificial lights and office equipment such as computers and copiers. Moreover, in many building types it is hard to incorporate well-placed thermal mass, and uncontrolled sunlight can produce glare for workers who are unable to change their position and location. However, many other building types and portions of buildings (e.g., lobbies, atriums, circulation spaces, warehouses) can benefit from passive space heating design (Figs. 3–15 and 3–16).

For most nonresidential building types, passive solar suggests one primary design approach: use of daylight, as discussed in detail in chapter 5. Fortunately, today's architects can investigate design strategies such as passive solar heating and daylighting even during the predesign phase of a project using software such as *ENERGY-10*. Developed by the National Renewable Energy Laboratory under the guiding vision of J. Douglas Balcomb, the *ENERGY-10* program is intended primarily to aid in the identification of

Table 3 – 2 / *Comparative Passive Solar Performance*

East	%	Central	%	West	%
Albany	14	Chicago	18	Albuquerque	44
Asheville	31	Cincinnati	19	Billings	23
Baltimore	24	Cleveland	14	Bismarck	17
Binghamton	9	Detroit	16	Boise	29
Boston	19	Des Moines	18	Casper	29
Buffalo	10	Indianapolis	18	Denver	36
Caribou	13	International Falls	10	Dodge City	34
Concord	15	Kansas City (Kans.)	25	Fargo	14
Hartford	16	Louisville	22	Portland (Oreg.)	25
Newark	22	Madison	17	Prescott (Ariz.)	45
New York	19	Minneapolis	15	Reno	39
Philadelphia	22	Rapid City	23	Salt Lake City	30
Pittsburgh	15	North Omaha	21	Mt. Shasta (Calif.)	30
Providence	19	Springfield (Ill.)	21	Seattle	24
Roanoke	29	St. Louis	26		
Syracuse	11				
Washington, DC	22				
Wilmington (Del.)	23				

Comparative Passive Solar Performance of solar houses that meet the description of the DG-A2 reference design (low mass, low-e glazing with an LCR of 40), as put forth in the *Passive Solar Design Handbook, Vol. III*, published by the U.S. Department of Energy. Values shown are the solar savings fraction (SSF), which is the reduction in annual heating energy requirements compared to a similar house design without any south-facing windows.

A

B

C

Figure 3–15 / Environmental Education Center, Milford, Pennsylvania. Kelbaugh & Lee, architects, completed 1982. (A) Exterior view showing design that combines direct gain and thermal storage wall. (B) On sunny winter days insulated reflectors are lowered from in front of the thermal storage wall. (C) The interior view shows sunlight entering the massive structure, with much of the heat being stored in the floor and walls for release later in the evening, for overnight guests.

Figure 3-16 / Girl Scout Building, suburban Philadelphia, Pennsylvania. Bohlin, Cywinski & Jackson, architects, completed 1983. (A) South-facing elevation featuring high (sun-shaded) windows at top with single-wythe thermal storage wall below. (B) Interior view with infill thermal storage wall at left. Thermal storage wall is only 4 inches thick because the building is used primarily during the afternoons—not overnight, like a residence, where thicker walls would improve performance.

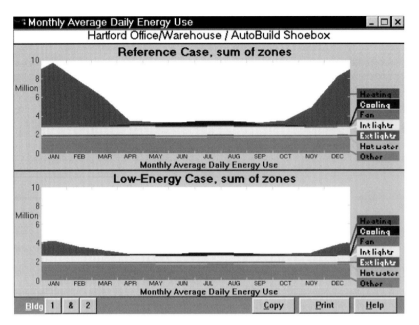

Figure 3–17 / The *ENERGY-10* program provides many graphic results for the energy performance of two buildings: (1) a reference case that initially represents typical commercial construction; and (2) a low-energy case that has a wide range of energy efficiency strategies applied. An outstanding feature of the program is the myriad of default values (all editable) that come preloaded with the program for nine building types. Results are presented in many colorful output graphics such as the one shown.

Figure 3–18 / A variety of photovoltaic design types undergoing long-term exposure testing at the National Renewable Energy Laboratory, Golden, Colorado.

appropriate energy efficiency strategies for small buildings of a specific building type in a specific climatic location. The program is meant to be first used before the building has even been designed, with refinements made as the design is developed. (Fig. 3–17).

Architectural concern for energy conservation in buildings has broadened in scope and vision over the years. As we approach the twenty-first century, the desire for cost-effective energy-conserving design is increasing, in large part due to environmental linkages. As discussed in chapter 4, the generation of electricity produces significant atmospheric pollution. Architects are now exploring emerging technologies such as photovoltaics (solar cells that produce electricity) for roof mounting and possibly for use as the very skin of the building (see chapter 11). Through the use of such technologies and design strategies, architects can serve as more responsible stewards of our resources.

Pure as the Air You Breathe

Control of the Atmospheric Environment

In popular opinion, the ideas persist that somewhere—in Cape May, in the Smoky Mountains, at Yellowstone—there is such a thing as pure air, that such atmospheres are good for you, and that they constitute the ideal habitat for all of our activities. The first opinion is wrong and the latter two are only relatively right. There is no such thing in nature as "pure"—that is, completely clean and sterile—air and there never has been. The nearest approach to such an unnatural state is found either at the poles or in the upper levels of the atmosphere. But scientists have found dusts and pollens deep in the ancient ice of Antarctica, and some terrestrial impurities are carried to the outer limits of the earth's atmospheric envelope. The great air currents of the globe are nature's most important transportation network, and they are used to the maximum. Natural atmospheres are by definition impure, freighted with a vast cargo of bacteria, molds, viruses, pollens, spores, and dusts—not to mention flying insects (which are the vectors of some of humanity's worst diseases) and birds.

What we usually mean when we speak of pure air is air that is free of manmade pollution—and here, of course, conventional wisdom is correct. There are few manmade pollutants that are not actively inimical to us, and the amount of them now being discharged into the atmosphere is verging on the catastrophic. In the undisturbed natural atmospheres of the Siberian taiga or the Canadian far north, however, only people with allergies or asthma have cause for alarm. The botanist Fritz Wendt has pointed out that Longfellow's

Earl Dotter, photojournalist

Figure 4–1 / The all-too-familiar scene of atmospheric pollutants being discharged into the atmosphere—often near our poorer residential neighborhoods, too often also near playgrounds, as in this location in Hopewell, Virginia.

"whispering pines and hemlocks" are among the world's greatest sources of pollution, discharging molecular substances known as *terpenes*. Some plant species have such noxious discharges that other plants cannot grow near them![1] But in common experience, such discharges are the source of some of our most pleasant olfactory sensations: the scent of the lily, the rose, the pineapple.

We are completely submerged in this ocean of air and we are as completely dependent upon it as any fish upon the sea. Our relationship with it is very complex. As we saw in the preceding chapter, the thermal balance of the human body is largely dependent upon the temperature, humidity, and movement of the air around it. These become, in fact, functions of the thermal environment (and this is confirmed by thermal engineering practice, where the handling of air masses within the building is regarded as an integral part of heating and cooling). But this relationship can only partially be described in thermal terms, for the air is also the habitat of our respiratory system, including the sense of olfaction, for which the free oxygen of the atmosphere is a prerequisite. Animal life is fundamentally a process of slow combustion—thus the air plays a critical internal role in the metabolic process, this time on the heat-producing side of the metabolic cycle. Of the body's three requirements for combustion—air, water, and food—air is most urgently needed. The average adult consumes five pounds of air for every one of food or water, and a few seconds of lack exhausts all reserves; collapse, coma, and death follow within moments of a cutoff in the supply.

Thus, while the respiratory system is only indirectly involved with the temperature, humidity, or motion of the air, it is vitally linked to its pressure and composition. It is to this latter relationship that we must now turn, as it plays an increasingly important role in design at both the architectural and the urbanistic level.

The Habitat of the Respiratory System

The natural habitat of the human respiratory and olfactory systems can be described in terms of *pressure*, *gaseous composition*, and *nongaseous aerosols*. The normal pressure—that is, the level to which our lungs, heart, and blood circulation are adjusted—is that of sea level, about 14.7 pounds per square inch. In undisturbed conditions the air is a gaseous mix of nitrogen, oxygen, argon, carbon dioxide, and water vapor with minute traces of neon, helium, krypton, and xenon, together with varying small amounts of ammonia and nitrous and nitric acids. Until comparatively recent times, this mix supported a physical burden of aerosols of predominantly natural origin: bacteria, viruses, pollens, etc.; water particles; dusts from storms; and smokes and ashes from forest fires and volcanic eruptions.

Normal preindustrial human beings, going about their daily tasks, never experienced violent shifts in the pressure or composition of the atmosphere comparable to those diurnal and seasonal fluctuations characteristic of the thermal and luminous environments. They encountered stressful changes in pressure only in the case of such activities as diving or mountain climbing. The chemical composition of the air was only rarely disturbed by natural phenomena (marsh gas, volcanic eruptions), and, aside from allergens, the only noxious particles were dusts or insects. The design of their respiratory systems reflected these relatively stable conditions. Their lungs had the built-in capacity to accommodate the low pressure and thin oxygen of high mountains and even the capacity to acclimatize them to life on the *altiplanos* of Tibet and Peru. But against poisonous gases they had only the warning system provided by their sense of smell.

Impurities in Suspension

All atmospheres carry a suspended burden of foreign matter—spores, pollens, dust, and particulates of all sorts. But if nature produces all these pollutants, nature has also evolved a series of mechanisms for holding them in check. Washing them out with rain is, of course, the most general, but a natural landscape of forest or meadowland acts as a vast impingement filter, trapping many aerosols as air moves across it. This natural filtration effect produces atmospheres at the center of the forest that may be 25 percent cleaner than at its fringes, while a mown lawn is also an extremely effective filter of larger airborne particles (see chapter 9).

It is only within the last several decades that we have been able to define—much less to construct—a perfectly pure and sterile atmosphere. Yet people have for centuries understood that apparently clean air could, on occasion, carry a lethal burden. Thus, during medieval periods of plague, people wore masks against contagious diseases, some of which are, in fact, airborne. (Others were carried by water, food, or personal contact, of course.) A fear of "night airs" was widespread in the Western world. And not without reason: in antebellum New Orleans there was a great fear of the "miasma" that rose at night from the swamps, carrying the danger of malaria (literally *bad air*) to all who inhaled it. Buildings were supposed to offer some protection against this menace, though in both Rome and New Orleans a flight to the hills was considered advisable in hot weather. Even so great a scientist as Darwin, lacking the assistance of bacteriology, was forced to fall back upon the miasma theory to explain the propagation of certain tropical diseases. It remained for Walter Reed, the great American doctor and epidemiologist, to convict the swamp mosquito (and not the swamp air) as the vector of malaria and yellow fever. Without this discovery, construction of the Panama Canal would have been impossible.

The natural atmospheric environment has always been immensely important to nature as an avenue of propagation, and nature has loaded it with spores and pollens. Not all of these are good for the human respiratory system and it is probably erroneous to think that our predecessors were any more comfortable, submerged in them, than we are today. There is no reason to suppose that asthma and allergies are modern inventions, though there is every reason to suspect that manmade pollutants have enormously complicated the picture in recent times. The prevalence of asthma in Westernized societies has doubled in the last twenty years, accounting for one third of pediatric emergency room visits in the United States.[2] Rates are highest in poor urban neighborhoods, where children are hospitalized at nearly twice the national rate.[3] Asthma is not believed to result from just one cause but from a host of factors including allergens, air pollutants and irritants, smoking, respiratory infections, exertion in cold weather, medications, sulfites, and, finally, emotional stress.[4] While air pollution is known to aggravate existing asthma, it is not clear that it causes it; comparisons of populations in highly polluted areas in Europe and those in cleaner areas have actually shown higher prevalence of asthma in less polluted areas.[5]

The dust mite—and millions inhabit a typical house—has been implicated as an important source of allergens (i.e., proteins in their excrement). These, along with cat saliva, cockroach feces, mold, animal dander and excreta, insect fragments, and pollen, lead to allergies and asthma attacks.[6] Dust mites thrive in warm, moist conditions (relative humidities of 70 to 90 percent are best, but they can survive when the relative humidity drops to 45 percent), in carpeting, bedding, draperies, and upholstered chairs.

To trigger-proof one's home, the Mayo Institute recommends "minimalist" interiors: replacing upholstered furniture with leather or vinyl; replacing carpeting with hardwood, vinyl, or tile; replacing heavy drapes with blinds, shades, or washable curtains; and using two-ply microfiltration bags or an electrostatic filter that fits over the exhaust outlet on a vacuum cleaner, or a special vacuum cleaner with high-efficiency particulate air (HEPA) filters.[7] Interestingly, in Japan asthma rates increased just when the population moved away from the traditional bare and well-ventilated house to Western-style architecture.[8]

We are constantly learning more about most of the diseases that afflict us. Our diagnoses grow more accurate all the time, so last year's statistics are not comparable with those of fifty or even ten years ago. Fresh insights into the complex process that produces allergies have come from molecular biology and genetic engineering. We have no precise information on how many persons suffer from pollen- and spore-induced disturbances. But at least we now understand something of the pathology of allergy, and we have perfected equipment that can filter out a large proportion of allergens.

The ocean of air also supports another complicated hierarchy of microorganisms: bacteria, molds, protozoans, and viruses. Many of these are beneficial. Some of them (the antibiotics, yeasts, and bacilli like those that sour milk or fix nitrogen in the soil) are indispensable. Collectively, however, these organisms cause most contagious diseases, and some, while not spreading disease, cause allergic reactions in susceptible people. Some of them are free agents, riding around on drops of moisture from human throats or nostrils; many of them hitch rides on insect hosts. For many others the exact method of transmission is not fully understood. Most bacteria are harmless, but the notorious disease-causing ones capture the headlines. For example, the term *Legionnaires' disease* was coined following an outbreak at the American Legion conference in Philadelphia in 1976; 221 attendees fell ill with acute pneumonia and other symptoms, and 34 died.[9] It was subsequently reported that aerosol (containing bacteria now called *Legionella pneumophila*) wafted from a cooling tower into the fresh air vent of the Bellevue-Stratford Hotel, where the conference was being held, and was dispersed throughout the building. Currently, about 25,000 cases of Legionnaires' disease are reported each year in the United States. It can be treated with antibiotics, but the fatality rate in an outbreak can be as high as 15 percent. The organism has been cultured from showerheads in hotels and hospitals where Legionnaires' disease has been reported. A less severe, flu-like illness without pneumonia, called Pontiac fever, was reported earlier, in 1968, as a result of a building-related epidemic in Pontiac, Michigan, attributed to a contaminated air conditioning system.

We now know that *Legionella pneumophila* thrives in warm water, not above 125°F, at a pH of 6.9 to 7.0. It (and related organisms) may proliferate in wet systems such as cooling towers, evaporative condensers, whirlpool spas, and showerheads. Many hospitals follow strict maintenance and disinfection procedures to protect their patients and staff from *Legionella* and monitor hospital patient specimens as an immediate warning of its presence. In such a dynamic and sensitive environment, routine changes in space requirements may involve seemingly insignificant measures such as capping off hot water lines

Figure 4–2 / Visible plume of moisture rising from cooling tower operation. ASHRAE has proposed a minimum distance of 15 feet between cooling towers and outdoor air intakes on buildings in order to minimize introduction of contaminants. Prevailing winds and air flow patterns around the building and building elements should also be considered in locating intakes. Highly efficient drift eliminators can be used to contain spray.

to certain areas. This measure alone may create stagnating conditions where *Legionella* can proliferate. From the architect's perspective, there are a number of design factors to consider—for example, the prudent location of the air intake for a building's HVAC system is upwind and away from cooling towers and evaporative condensers (Fig. 4–2).

Also a source of infections and allergies are the fungi—molds, mildew, yeasts—and the spores they produce. New buildings are not immune, as illustrated by the abandonment of the three-year-old Martin County, Florida, courthouse in 1993 by the building occupants, who deemed it uninhabitable. Excessive moisture had permeated the walls of the building, and it was severely contaminated with fungi, including *Stachybotrys chartarum (atra)* and *Aspergillus versicolor.* The building was subsequently remediated using asbestos abatement techniques, including removal and disposal of the interior finishes as hazardous waste. The structure was gutted and rebuilt, with an entirely new HVAC system. The mold growth was thought to result from a violation of the rule that vapor retarders (formerly called vapor "barriers") are to be installed on the winter warm side, which in warm, humid climates like Florida is on the outside, with the insulation inside (in the cold Northeast, vapor retarders are installed on the inside with the insulation toward the exterior). In this case, vinyl wallpaper (functioning as a vapor retarder) was installed on the inside of the exterior wall; vapor condensed in the wall behind the wallpaper creating, in combination with nutrients in the gypsum board, ideal conditions for fungal growth.

Mold growth in water-damaged buildings has become a major building-related issue.[10] Most buildings contain the two essentials for mold growth: a source of carbon and moisture. Fungi will not grow if building materials are dry, but *dry* is a relative term, with some molds capable of growing on hygroscopic materials such as cotton, which simply draw water from the air. Others proliferate after leaks or floods, or following condensation in construction assemblies.

Some types of mold produce toxins—for example, trichothecene toxins produced by *Stachbotrys atra* have been the focus of controversy, following reports of a case of poisoning in Chicago as well as outbreaks in the early 1990s of bleeding in the lungs of infants in Cleveland (33 in Cleveland's poor east side, 9 of whom died) and Chicago (10 in all, with no fatalities). *Stachybotrys* and its toxic byproducts were found in building materials, including air ducts and damp fiberboard.[11,12] Some water-damaged houses in Cleveland that were not involved in the outbreak also had evidence of the mold. To date there have been no epidemiological studies to establish an association between the presence of this mold on building surfaces and respiratory disease. In the absence of such studies, it is unclear what the relationship is, or even if there is one. Only one case of human exposure to *airborne spores* of this mold apparently resulting in medical symptoms has been reported.[13]

While the link between *Stachybotrys* and its toxic byproducts and the health effects experienced by the infants was not conclusively demonstrated, much panic has ensued, and the effects have been felt within the field of building technology. Unfortunately, much of the information on health-related effects of mold and other biological contaminants appears anecdotally in the popular press rather than in standard peer-reviewed journals, which require a more thorough, objective analysis of the available data. Thus there remain many unanswered questions.[14, 15]

Ironically, a cure for one problem may be the cause of another. When building managers or homeowners install humidifiers to relieve respiratory discomfort, they may actually be worsening air quality; if the relative humidity reaches 50 percent or more, or if moisture condenses, mold flourishes. Ultrasonic humidifiers disperse water vapor (and mold) into the air. Dehumidifiers can also become moldy unless they are emptied and cleaned frequently.

Protozoans feed on bacteria and are able to colonize standing water in humidifier reservoirs and condensate trays. When their cells become entrained in the airstream, potent allergens are formed, which may cause ill effects in building occupants, ranging from pneumonitis, humidifier fever, and asthma to allergic rhinitis.[16]

The viruses—those strange substances that bridge the gap between the living and the nonliving and thus obscure what was once considered to be a sharply defined line between living cell and chemical molecule—can apparently move on the tsetse fly to cause encephalitis, on the housefly through direct contact to spread infantile paralysis, and on droplets from the nostrils to scatter influenza and the common cold.

There is now no doubt that airborne pollens cause hay fever, that airborne mineral dusts and fibers (e.g., crystalline quartz, tridymite, cristobalite, and asbestos) lead to respiratory diseases such as silicosis, asbestosis, and lung cancer, and that tobacco smoke causes lung cancer and emphysema; together, these constitute a large percentage of American disabilities and deaths. But, oddly enough, the theory of infection by airborne microbes is still the subject of cautious speculation, though there is growing evidence to support it. Average citizens who think they catch colds from exposure in crowded buses or elevators have common sense on their side but not yet completely proven fact; some medical references indicate that person-to-person contact (i.e., via the unwashed hands of someone who blew his nose) may be more often the cause of the spread of viral infection.[17]

For scientific investigators, the problem is complicated by the fact that viruses appear to be the cause of many ailments. While viral behavior is not completely understood, viral research accelerated by the AIDS epidemic is yielding much insight. Even though several hundred different viruses infect us, many produce subclinical disease, and diagnosis and treatment remain difficult. The common cold itself is associated with several different types of viruses.[18] We know that influenza and measles spread through instantaneous transmission of droplets in the air (e.g., from sneezing). Therefore, it is more likely that viruses are spread by close contact among building occupants themselves rather than by the building or by distribution through the building's HVAC system.[19]

If architects must, with the experts, withhold final judgment on the airborne transmission of disease, they might at least observe that the air inside any building supports billions of organisms of all sorts, that the population of such organisms per cubic foot rises in direct proportion to human occupancy, and that many of these organisms closely resemble those known to cause respiratory disturbances. To this can be added the notorious coincidence of overcrowding and contagious disease—and the moral responsibilities of the architect as well as the social urbanist in this area become clear.

Finally, the atmosphere is the habitat for many insects, most of which are a nuisance to human beings. A few, of course, are essential: aside from the no longer significant task of producing honey, the honeybee carries on the immensely more important task of pollination. But relative to most modern human activities, especially those that occur in cities and buildings, insects are uniformly *personae non gratae*. For the average middle-class American city dweller, municipal sanitary measures have largely eliminated the problem of airborne insects. (The problem of eradicating land-based vermin—roaches, rats, mice, ticks, bedbugs, lice, fleas, and termites—is altogether another matter, as most low-income apartment dwellers can readily testify. But the elimination of these vermin is also a matter of social responsibility, not technical competence.) Nevertheless, in rural areas and especially in tropical and semitropical climates, insect control is a prime architectural problem, from not only a sanitary but also an esthetic point of view. The necessity for insect screening works directly against the open plan, with its integration of indoor and outdoor space that a tropical climate makes desirable. Before air-conditioning, the tendency, especially in

Figure 4–3 / Aerial pesticide applicator spraying methyl parathion on cotton crop in Bolivar County, Mississippi. Cotton accounts for 10 percent of the world's annual pesticide consumption,[24] causing "green" architects to debate whether cotton, a renewable resource, is indeed an environmentally friendly material. Cotton has been proposed as a substitute for fiberglass as wall insulation.

residential buildings, was to place the entire house and garden in a single screened cage, thus placing this environmental filter at the outer perimeter of family life.

Insect control at an urban or even regional level has been immensely advanced by the use of chemical pesticides sprayed from the air (Fig. 4–3). Thus whole sections of the Florida Everglades have been ridded of the mosquito, the Mississippi Delta of the boll weevil, Adirondack resort areas of the deer fly — if only on a local and/or temporary basis. But, unexpectedly, such aerial use of pesticides has had disastrous ecological side effects, not only in the insect world itself (e.g., the destruction of the Florida honeybees upon which fertilization of the orange groves depends) but also upon bird life and aquatic life. More than half of the honeybee colonies in the United States have been lost in the last fifty years, with one quarter of this loss occurring from 1990 to 1995. Among the threats to nature's pollinators — bees, other insects, birds, worms, and microorganisms — are such factors as intense exposures to pesticides, habitat fragmentation and disturbance, loss of nesting and overwintering sites, exposure of nectar plants to herbicides, and breakdown of nectar corridors, which provide food sources to pollinators during migration. Agricultural losses from reduced pollination may reach $4 billion annually.[20,21]

Pesticide use in the United States is substantial, with 21,000 commercial products containing 860 active-ingredient pesticide chemicals currently on the market.[22] The intricate and far-reaching consequences of this kind of chemical warfare are leading to legal limitations on a global scale. In 1995, 110 countries agreed to begin working on an international ban on persistent organic pollutants (POPs) including nine pesticides and three industrial chemicals suspected as having endocrine-disrupting effects.[23] It seems entirely possible that, as a result of our growing knowledge, many more pesticides will ultimately be outlawed altogether, as called for by Rachel Carson in her epochal book, *Silent Spring*. And yet, even with the growing list of pesticides banned from use in this country and others, international trade in banned or severely restricted pesticides persists. Carson's book gave us early and specific warning on pesticides; unfortunately, over thirty-five years have passed and resolution of this issue is still incomplete.

Modern life confronts us with new atmospheric situations, as when it takes human beings deep under the sea or far out into space. Here people are exposed to barometric pressures that would either collapse or explode their respiratory systems were they not encapsulated in a submarine, or a spacecraft, or tethered to the mother ship in a self-contained spacesuit. These remarkable inventions have required the development of a paramilitary technology that is very advanced. This investment in research, particularly in the aerospace arena, has had dramatic payoffs in more terrestrial spheres. For example, there have been significant spinoffs in materials science, in remote sensing technologies, in communications, in our ability to identify the elements of our environment that are essential to our survival, and the limits of human tolerance. In addition, the totally encapsulated suits worn at hazardous waste sites bear a striking resemblance to moongear!

Research needs its vacuum chambers, aviation its wind tunnels; there are specialized medical procedures in which atmospheric pressure is manipulated for therapeutic purposes—for example, hyperbaric chambers (enclosing the patient in an atmosphere of 100 percent oxygen at greater than 1 atm pressure) for the treatment of caisson disease (the bends), carbon monoxide poisoning, smoke inhalation, or gas gangrene. However, the architect is seldom called upon to design buildings for anything other than normal ambient pressures. The one important exception to this generalization is in the exciting field of inflated structures, in which internal air pressures are slightly higher than outside in order to support the nonrigid envelope. The differentials are too small to be physiologically significant and the structural possibilities are spectacular (see chapter 8).

The Poisoned Air

It is above all the chemical composition of the atmosphere that is being radically altered by modern industrial society. Every human activity has always produced waste products, and much of this waste has always been dumped into the open air. But in preindustrial times, neither the nature nor the concentration of these wastes was ever a matter of much consequence. It is urban life and modern technology that have brought about a qualitative change in this atmospheric sewage, as it has been quite aptly called. There is incomparably more of it, and it is composed of thousands of new substances, gaseous and particulate, whose actions upon one another and upon human life are scarcely guessed at. It is true that many activities require atmospheres whose composition, purity, or cleanliness are without precedent in the natural world (e.g., pharmaceuticals, surgery, baking, brewing, and food processing). But it is simultaneously true that these same industries, along with all our activities (heavy industry, transportation, space heating) are annually dumping billions of tons of pollutants into the American atmospheric environment. We are destroying the "old-fashioned" natural atmospheres on which all biological existence is premised.

It was not until we were able to see the early photographs of the earth taken by astronauts and cosmonauts that we really began to recognize that our sky is not infinite but instead is actually quite limited. In Vice President (then Senator) Al Gore's 1992 book, *Earth in the Balance*, the atmosphere is described as a very thin blue translucent blanket.[25] The distance from the ground to the top of the sky, he stated, is no farther than an hour's cross-country run, and we are filling up this volume, profoundly changing its makeup, every hour every day, everywhere on earth. Things have already reached critical proportions. In fact, beginning with visionaries such as Rene Dubos in the 1960s, a growing number of ecologists fear that this pollution—the result of over two hundred years of fossil fuel combustion—may have already irreversibly altered the structure of the upper atmosphere and hence the future climates of the earth![26]

In the light of current research in environmental health, it seems incredible that the smoke and fumes of industry once were considered beautiful—at least by those upper-

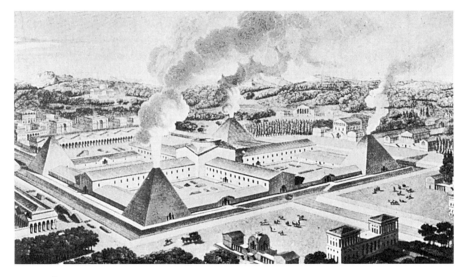

Figure 4–4 / *Forge à Canons*, project for a metallurgical plant for the French military establishment, 1804. Charles Nicholas Ledoux, architect. In this early scheme for a model factory town, the utopian designer celebrates the smoke, flame, and noise of a coal-powered industrialism. It was too early to visualize the disastrous consequences for the atmospheric environment of inefficient combustion of fossil fuels.

class people who were not compelled to toil in the factories and mills. The smoke and flame of the iron foundry were even raised to the level of architectural ornament in Ledoux's design for the royal French munitions monopoly (Fig. 4–4). It is now apparent that, from the very beginning, these industrial wastes of gases, smokes, and ashes had profoundly serious implications for the health of working people. The striking thing is how long it took to establish the causal links between air pollution and disease. Even when the first movements against air pollution appeared, in the early part of the twentieth century, they took the form of smoke abatement or smoke prevention campaigns. Although the potential health hazards of pollution were suspected, there was little concrete medical data to support these concerns. Hence these campaigns used arguments of a largely visual nature — that is, smoke should be eliminated because of the way it cut out sunlight, damaged plants, soiled buildings and clothes, etc.[27] Obviously, these are perfectly valid arguments against atmospheric pollution; they merely turn out to be, in the light of current knowledge, much less serious than those involving health and well-being.

Atmospheric pollution had to reach the level of major natural disasters in order to attract adequate scientific attention to the pathological consequences of even low concentrations of pollutants. A review of the historic chronology of such disasters is informative and noteworthy. All these incidents occurred within a fixed environmental reference frame. The underlying cause (retention of large amounts of industrial waste in the air) had to be triggered by a meteorological phenomenon. This occurs when, because of both topographical and meteorological reasons, a metropolitan region finds itself submerged in a cold, moist air mass that is trapped under an overlying mass of still, warm air. As the condition is the reverse of normal, it is called an *inversion*. Typically, these cause fogs, and because the inversion prevents dispersion of pollution to the upper atmosphere, the concentration of pollutants increases and we have a poisonous mixture now called a *smog* (a term used for a mixture of smoke and fog, first introduced by Dr. Harold Antoine Des Voeux in describing the great London air pollution disaster from coal burning in 1911).

Industrial or gray smog, experienced in older cities like New York, Baltimore, Chicago, London, Philadelphia, and Pittsburgh, is most often associated with extensive use of coal or oil for heating, manufacturing, and electric power generation (Fig. 4–5). This type of combustion produces particulates and sulfur dioxide. Industrial smogs occur most frequently in winter, when the heating season is at a peak and effluents from thousands of boilers and furnaces are dumped, so to speak, on top of the normal industrial wastes. Wintertime smogs are more significant physiologically because cold weather produces the peak of respiratory diseases — bronchitis, influenza, common colds. Even with clean air, the largest number of persons have respiratory problems in winter. Thus, all factors combine to make the smog most severe just when the population is most vulnerable to added environmental stress.

One of the first serious air pollution disasters to be recognized and studied as such was that which occurred in the heavily industrialized Meuse Valley in Belgium.[28] Submerged in a heavy fog for four days in December 1930, with the atmosphere more poisonous hour by hour, the population witnessed 63 deaths and 6,000 illnesses serious enough to require medical attention. This represented a death rate 10.5 times the normal; most of the victims,

Earl Dotter, photojournalist

Figure 4–5 / Industrial or gray smog results from fossil fuel combustion in our older industrialized cities, as shown here in the Lower East Side in New York City in 1968. Thirty years later, approximately three hundred of New York City's schools are still being heated by coal-fired boilers, which typically emit more soot, sulfur oxides, nitrogen oxides, and heavy metals like lead than boilers fueled with cleaner-burning alternatives such as natural gas.

in what has since come to be recognized as a typical pattern, turned out to have had previous histories of respiratory or cardiac disturbances. The effects of the smog can thus be seen as most severe on those with serious ailments. Now there is established evidence that many of those ailments were themselves the pathological results of longtime exposure to lower concentrations of exactly the same pollutants that finally killed those individuals.

Almost identical environmental circumstances produced the first well-documented American disaster at Donora, Pennsylvania. A manufacturing town of 13,000, Donora extends along the banks of the Monongahela River, which forms a crescent-shaped valley sunk between 400-foot-high hills. In the town at the time of the disaster were three big plants fabricating steel and zinc products twenty-four hours a day. In a classic topography for inversions, this one began with a fog on Tuesday, October 26, 1948, and did not lift until the following Sunday. The deadly concentration of pollutants from trains, tugboats, and factories rose steadily—and with it, the roster of dead and disabled. At week's end there were twenty dead (as against a usual rate of one or two) and almost

6,000 cases of respiratory distress of varying degrees of severity (many of these sufferers were saved by oxygen inhalators belonging to the fire department). Scientists of the U.S. Public Health Service found that "pre-existing diseases of the respiratory system appeared to be a single common factor among the fatally ill." They also found that of Donora citizens who were 65 or over, more than 60 percent had reported some discomfort from the smog, almost half of them having been severely affected. In trying to isolate the exact mechanism of the attack, the investigators were forced to conclude that it was "probably a combination of [such] substances, rather than one, which was responsible for the trouble."[29]

London was famous for fog long before Dickens, but the city only began seriously to analyze it from an epidemiological point of view after the disastrous smogs of December 1952 and January–February 1953. Here again a durable inversion was responsible, accompanied by unseasonably cold weather. Deaths during the first smog ran to 4,000 above average for the period, while those during the second soared to 8,000 above normal. Again, the hardest hit by these two atmospheric disasters were persons with histories of cardiac and respiratory diseases.[30] Analyses of historic New York City smogs reveal comparable situations. In one that ran from January 29 to February 12, 1963, mortalities ran 647 above normal for the period. Even allowing for the fact that it was the coldest such fortnight in ten years, and for the concurrent epidemic of influenza, investigators figured that at least 400 deaths could be directly attributed to the smog.[31] Another classic Public Health Service study of that time in Nashville, Tennessee, a city then known as Smoky Joe, revealed a significant correlation between income, place of residence, and death rates from respiratory ailments. The study showed that the lowest-income groups in the city (African American, in this instance), living in those wards where air sampling stations showed air pollution to be highest, had a mortality rate almost two and a half times as high as that of higher-income groups living in the much cleaner suburbs.[32]

While winter inversions are often associated with industrial (or gray) smog from the industrial and residential burning of oil and coal (generating sulfur oxides and soot), photochemical (or brown) smog from motor vehicle use has become a greater hazard in many cities, and particularly those in warmer, drier climates with populations exceeding 100,000 people — cities like Los Angeles, Tokyo, Mexico City, Buenos Aires, and Sydney. Nitric oxide from car exhaust reacts with the oxygen in the air to produce nitrogen dioxide, a reddish-brown gas that forms a brownish haze. When exposed to sunlight, the nitrogen dioxide and the hydrocarbons from unburned gasoline react to form ozone and peroxyacetyl nitrate (PAN), or photochemical smog.

The smogs of Los Angeles are perhaps the most notorious of all, because of three special conditions: the Los Angeles basin is ringed for the most part by mountains, it has a semitropical climate, and its residents rely heavily on the automobile.[33] Because of the climate, there is comparatively little need for winter heating, and because the winters are mild and dry, there has been (until recent years, at least) a low incidence of bronchitis, influenza, and colds. But this same preponderance of clear, sunny days exerts an exaggerated photochemical effect upon the effluents of millions of automobiles, many oil refineries, and thousands of trash burners, to produce complex gases in the atmosphere. The most widely publicized result of such smogs is their tear-gas effect on the eyes, but because several of the pollutants are known to be carcinogenic, the long-range impact upon the health of Los Angeles residents may be more serious. More rigorous regulations than the federal standards were adopted in California and have proven successful over the past twenty-five years; conditions in the Los Angeles area have improved. The statistics show that in the South Coast basin of California (home to millions of Californians, including those in Los Angeles, Orange, and portions of San Bernardino and Riverside counties), there was a health advisory due to high levels of ozone (0.15 ppm) for 59 days in 1995. By contrast, from 1976 until 1981, there were health advisories for at least 152 days each year. Moreover, very serious Stage 2 episodes (occurring when ozone levels exceed 0.35 ppm) were reached an average of 15 times per year from 1976 through 1980. Since 1986, however, Stage 2 has only been reached twice.*

By dint of heroic control measures adopted in the past several decades, Los Angeles has succeeded in greatly reducing air pollution from stationary sources — that is, oil refineries, power and heating plants, trash burners, and incinerators.[34] Photochemical smog in Los Angeles is also surely responsible for the national emission control standards for automobiles and the stringent air pollution standards adopted by California. Moreover, the California Air Resources Board requires that 10 percent of the new automobiles put into service (i.e., approximately 200,000 cars) by the year 2003 be zero-emission electric cars and 17 percent by the year 2010.

Skeptics have labeled zero-emission cars "elsewhere-emission cars," as they charge their batteries with electricity from power plants, which are often coal-fired. As an alternative to electric cars, an ultralight hybrid, or hypercar, has been proposed, weighing in at only a few hundred pounds, and fabricated of moldable composites. This car would burn compressed natural gas or hydrogen fuel (or liquid fuels from farm or forestry wastes) as needed in a tiny onboard engine to make electricity to run the wheel motors; alternatively, it could be powered by solar cells. A few batteries (or a carbon-fiber superflywheel) would temporarily store the braking energy recovered from the wheel motors and reuse most of it for hill climbing and acceleration.[35]

Ironically, just as technology is advancing in a direction that allows us to design more compact, more efficient vehicles, American carmakers are headed in the opposite direction. There has been a sudden surge in demand for big sport utility vehicles (SUVs), pickup trucks, and minivans to replace the family car. They have fuel economy ratings of

---

* A 1989 study funded by the South Coast Air Quality Management District (SCAQMD) and conducted by Dr. Jane Hall of California State University at Fullerton found that meeting federal clean air standards for ozone and fine particulates in the South Coast region would yield $9.4 billion in health-related savings each year. The study found that 98 percent of the four-county basin's population of 13 million was exposed to unhealthy air, with children especially vulnerable. In addition, it was estimated that, each year, 1,600 people died prematurely as a result of exposure to air pollution. In 1991 a follow-up study reported that minorities as a whole were exposed more often to poor air quality because they tend to live in areas of affordable housing where the air is more polluted.

14 miles a gallon or less and their emissions are generally dirtier. Although these heavy vehicles are safer for their passengers, the U.S. Department of Transportation has concluded that they represent a growing danger to the occupants of the smaller, lighter, more efficient cars currently on the road. Because they come with four-wheel drive and high bumpers, they tend to override the strongest sections of a car body and drive into the passenger compartment during collisions. Ford Motor Company has recently unveiled its design for an 18-foot giant SUV that accommodates eight adults in three rows. Like the heaviest Suburban models and the AM General's Hummer, an SUV adapted from a military transport, the giant Ford exceeds the government's limits for classification as a light vehicle at a weight of over 3,000 pounds. As such, it would not be covered by federal fuel economy regulations.[36]

Lest we think that gas-guzzling automobiles and unhealthy smog conditions are uniquely American, let us consider Brazil, which has doubled its production of automobiles since 1990. Accompanying this car boom is the pollution (an estimated 5,000 tons of carbon monoxide released daily in São Paulo) and associated respiratory afflictions. Worldwide, emissions from automobiles have escalated. In 1950 there were 50 million cars for the earth's 2.6 billion people. Today, the world's population has doubled to 5.5 billion, while the number of automobiles has increased tenfold to 500 million. Consider conditions in Southeast Asia, where air quality is getting increasingly poor as the region modernizes. Adding to already poor conditions, the deliberate burning of rain forest created incredibly unhealthy and dangerous conditions in September 1997. According to the Malaysian Department of Environment, the air pollution index in Kuching on September 24, 1997, was 638, and hovered near 200 for weeks. A rating of 100 (measuring carbon dioxide, carbon monoxide, dust, ash, sulfur dioxide, and nitrogen dioxide as set by the U.S. Environmental Protection Agency [EPA]) is considered unhealthy.

With smog events, the historically chilling statistics are of human deaths and serious health impairment. In the case of acid rain, the statistics are more often expressed as the ecological death of thousands of lakes and streams in the northeastern United States, Canada, and Scandinavia. Acid rain also damages forests and erodes building façades and monuments. Ironically, acid rain first became an issue when tall smokestacks were built on coal- and oil-burning plants and smelters to reduce local levels of airborne sulfur dioxide and nitrogen oxides. This strategy simply transported the pollutants elsewhere — carried them from power plants in the Midwest to the forests of the northeastern United States and eastern Canada, and from Great Britain and Scotland by predominantly westerly winds across the North Sea to Denmark and Norway. Tall stacks send sulfur dioxide and nitrogen oxide high into the clouds, where mild solutions of sulfuric and nitric acids are formed. The strength of the acid is measured on the pH scale, with progressively lower values associated with stronger and stronger acids. Natural rainwater is slightly acidic; its pH of about 5.6 is due to the interaction of water droplets and atmospheric carbon dioxide. Rainfall data from the National Center of Atmospheric Research has included pHs of 3.0 and below — approaching the acidity of vinegar. In some areas, lakes and streams have the ability to buffer the effect of acid rain, but when the buffering capacity is exceeded, algae, plankton, and other aquatic life that supports fish, including commercially valuable trout, salmon, and bass, cannot be sustained. Acid rain has also slowed growth in and damaged extensive tracts of forest.

Since the first reports of acid rain in the mid-1970s, the primary cause was generally understood to be the burning of fossil fuels. From 1940 to 1970, nitrogen oxide emissions in the United States more than doubled to 19.9 million tons (Mtons) and sulfur dioxide emissions increased by half to 27.9 Mtons. In recent years nitrogen oxide emissions have held relatively steady (21.0 Mtons in 1992), with sulfur dioxide emissions somewhat reduced (20.7 Mtons in 1992).[36] The Clean Air Act Amendments of 1990 require a 50 percent reduction in sulfur dioxide emissions from 1980 levels by the end of the year 2000 along with major reductions in nitrogen oxides. The EPA set more stringent emission targets for older coal-burning plants—about half of the existing 850 plants—to have been met by 1995, with the remainder having to attain their goals by the year 2000.

To accomplish these reductions, power plants use scrubbers to remove pollutants from the airstream by one of several dry or wet chemical processes. One landmark wet scrubber project is the 2,250 megawatt Salt River Project, a retooled coal-fired plant (that burns 25,000 tons of coal per day at full capacity) on Navajo Nation land near the Grand Canyon. In addition to pollution reduction, concern for clarity and visibility at the Grand Canyon were important considerations that resulted in a design exceeding EPA goals. As a result of negotiations with the EPA, the scrubbing equipment was designed for a 90 percent reduction in sulfur dioxide emissions—from 70,000 tons/year (on a 365-day basis) from stacks 775 feet high! The wet scrubber desulfurization technology converts, on an annual basis, 210,000 tons of limestone, 63,000 tons of particulate, and water into 350,000 tons of gypsum that is currently planned to be landfilled on site, but perhaps will be used as construction material elsewhere (e.g., gypsum board), in the future.[38] The Clean Air Act Amendments of 1990 also include provisions for the transfer of pollution rights. Leave it to American lawmakers to legitimize one's inherent right to pollute. The law allows a company or utility (such as the Navajo Generating Station at Salt River) that reduces its sulfur dioxide emissions by more than the law requires to sell the unused allowance.

The formation of acid rain and the magnitude of its effects are now believed to be controlled by more variables than simply the emission of sulfur dioxide and nitrogen oxides into the atmosphere. Recent studies reveal the critical role of alkaline minerals (e.g., calcium and magnesium carbonate) in atmospheric dusts, which neutralize the acidity in rain and increase the buffering capacity of soil and water. Sources of such dusts include cement manufacturing, mining operations, metal processing, forest fires, and natural erosion. Although sulfur dioxide and nitrogen oxides are regulated by governments in North America and the European Union, these reductions have not yet rejuvenated the lakes, streams, and forests to the extent anticipated. These governments also established air quality standards to limit dust emissions, which are associated with a range of health and environmental problems, and by so doing unwittingly removed a large airborne reservoir of alkaline dusts that were interacting with and neutralizing the effects of acid

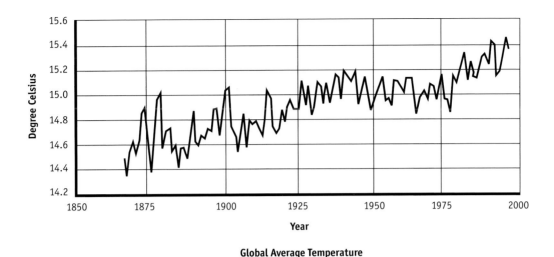

Global Average Temperature

Figure 4-6 / Global average temperature. Proponents of the global warming theory present as evidence the increase in the global average temperature by approximately 1°C over the last century. Reprinted with permission from The Worldwatch Institute.

rain. It is clear that the solutions to the environmental issues that confront us are not always obvious, nor can linear thinking always promise us the results we expect.[39]

It is undeniable that industrialized society depends on the combustion of fossil fuels. From these are liberated vast amounts of carbon dioxide in quantities that outpace the earth's absorptive capacity. Therein lies the greatest dilemma for the earth's industrialized and developing countries: either drastically curtail the use of fossil fuels or face potentially catastrophic global warming. The global warming theory holds that a layer of greenhouse gases, particularly carbon dioxide, traps heat (long-wave or infrared radiation) in the lower atmosphere, functioning like glazing on a greenhouse. As the atmosphere, land masses, and oceans are warmed (if only by a few degrees centigrade), the relatively constant range of global temperature will be disrupted and climates will change (Fig. 4-6). The polar ice may melt and in the process cause the level of the oceans to rise, flooding of many of the world's major seaports.[40]

Many experts are actively studying this issue — often with dramatically different findings and conclusions. For example, a team from Victoria University in New Zealand concluded from fossil evidence that the Antarctic ice melted completely three million years ago, when global temperatures were only a few degrees warmer than in 1994. It is estimated that if that were to happen today, the world's oceans would rise 215 feet.[41] Nor is this issue purely academic. In March 1997 it was reported that the Marshall Islands, near the equator in the central Pacific Ocean, experienced strangely rising water levels that flooded the homes of some of the inhabitants and much of their islands during calm weather conditions. The sea is viewed by the inhabitants as their main provider; they now are beginning to wonder if the rising sea will in the not too distant future take everything away.[42]

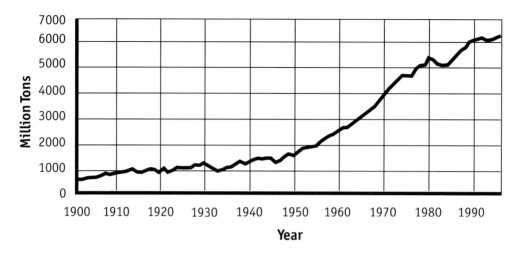

Figure 4–7 / Worldwide emissions of carbon, which includes carbon dioxide, reached 6.06 billion tons in 1995. Reprinted with permission from The Worldwatch Institute.

And so, how are we as a global community controlling the production of potentially damaging carbon dioxide? In 1995 worldwide global emissions of carbon from fossil fuel burning broke a new record at 6.06 billion tons (Fig. 4–7). The United States remained the largest contributor at 1.4 billion tons (other leading emitters were China, Russia, Japan, and Germany). About one third of U.S. carbon emissions are the result of electricity production, a fact that motivated the EPA to develop programs and initiatives to reduce electricity use for lighting, HVAC office equipment, and motors. The concern is that developing countries (e.g., China, India, and Brazil) may soon outpace industrialized countries in their rate of increase in carbon emissions.[43]

Ozone, a substance that so irritates our respiratory system here on earth, has a far more useful purpose in the stratosphere (approximately 5 to 30 miles above the earth's surface). There it serves the vital function of protecting the earth from harmful quantities of ultraviolet radiation from the sun. Without such protection we would experience a sharply increased incidence of skin cancers and cataracts, greatly reduced crop yields (leading to an increase in carbon dioxide), and extensive damage to aquatic life. Fortunately, the greatest threat to earth's ozone layer appears to have been identified. And perhaps even more fortunately, an international protocol to reverse a disturbing trend appears to be in place.

Concern for the condition of the ozone layer and the circumstances under which it may be damaged is relatively recent. It was only in 1974 that Mario Molina and Sherwood Rowland (chemists at the University of California at Irvine) published an article in *Nature* that explored the properties of chlorofluorocarbons (CFCs). CFCs (freon) have been used widely in industry since their invention in the late 1920s, and in particular as refrigerants for air-conditioning equipment. Molina and Rowland noted that the chemical stability of CFCs, an asset in commercial applications, could allow them to drift from earth to the stratosphere intact. The more intense solar radiation at that height would free reactive chlorine atoms in the CFCs and initiate a series of chain reactions that would destroy portions of the thin, vital ozone layer. This theory was received with skepticism. However, as corroborators validated the basic theory, the research team received the 1995 Nobel Prize in chemistry for their work (along with Paul Crutzen of Germany's Max Planck Institute).[44]

Recognition of the link between CFCs and ozone damage was remarkably swift. When CFCs were developed and became available for commercial use, they were viewed as miracle compounds, being nonflammable, nontoxic, noncorrosive, and stable. World production (albeit by a limited number of producers) grew rapidly from less than 50 thousand tons in 1950 to over 1,200 thousand tons in 1988, primarily for use as coolants but also as cleaning solvents for circuit boards and computer chips. The significant reduction in CFC production in recent years is due to an agreement, reached in 1987, known as the Montreal Protocol on Substances That Deplete the Ozone Layer. It was originally signed by 24 countries (including the United States) and the European Community and then ratified by more than 150 countries.

The schedule includes phasing out CFCs in developing countries by 2010 (they have already been phased out in developed countries as of January 1, 1996). By January 1, 2010, there is to be no manufacturing of new equipment that uses HCFC-22. HCFC-22 and HCFC-141b will be phased out by January 1, 2020. This is also the deadline for new equipment using HCFC-123 and HCFC-124. Both of these refrigerants will be phased out by January 1, 2030. A replacement for refrigerant CFC-11, used in large chillers, is still being researched.

The Montreal Protocol led to an almost total suspension of CFC production by the signatory nations (Fig. 4−8). However, loopholes and problems exist, including illegal pro-

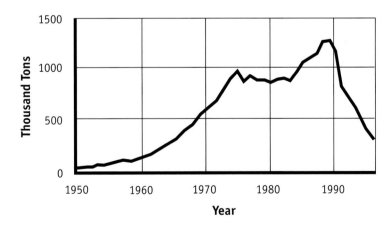

Figure 4−8 / World production of chlorofluorocarbons. Production doubled roughly every five years from the 1950s to the early 1970s. A production peak one year after the signing of the Montreal Protocol was followed by a precipitous decline. Reprinted with permission from The Worldwatch Institute.

duction in Russia, and a black market for CFCs of approximately 30,000 tons per year (1997 estimate). Moreover, the populous and rapidly industrializing countries of China and India have not yet signed the protocol.

Still, the prognosis is promising. With general adherence to the Montreal Protocol, it is estimated that the damage caused to the ozone layer by CFC use (over a period of fewer than sixty years) will begin to reverse by the year 2000, with a full recovery by about 2045.[46] Meanwhile, industry and the HVAC field have begun to adjust to life with substitute refrigerants and propellants which are, presumably, more environmentally-friendly. But, in addition to their potential to deplete the ozone layer, refrigerants can also contribute to global warming if released to the atmosphere. On a per-pound basis, like the older CFCs, some of the new replacement refrigerants are hundreds or thousands of times more powerful greenhouse gases than carbon dioxide.[45]

Over the past half-century, the growth of American industry has been astonishing. Unfortunately, many of the industrial processes involved result in toxic releases into our atmosphere. Of particular and growing concern is the effect of small particles that remain suspended in the air as a result of the combustion of fossil fuels (some of which may be helpful in curbing acid rain, as described above). Studies by the EPA and the Harvard School of Public Health suggest that as many as 60,000 Americans die each year as a result of particulate pollution—a far larger number than for any other type of atmospheric pollution.[47]

Some solace can be taken from the measurable strides being made to control or eliminate emissions into our atmosphere by the major chemical producers. Perhaps the most positive sign of this trend is that pollution prevention has become the watchword of the chemical industry, replacing older attitudes toward pollution that focused on the end of the pipeline, or the end of the smokestack, with dilution being the solution to pollution. Pollution prevention, when carried out with true finesse, makes adjustments to the entire production process, from raw material selection through manufacturing and through salvage and reuse of the byproducts of manufacturing as well as through product stewardship. Not only are emissions reduced and wastes minimized but byproducts are consumed through materials exchange or reuse. This is the adoption of an entirely different philosophy, with historical roots that can be traced back over seventy years to Henry Ford in his 1926 book, *Today and Tomorrow:* "We will not so lightly waste material simply because we can reclaim it. . . . The idea is to have nothing to salvage." [48]

Much of the impetus behind this new attitude is the spate of environmental laws and regulations that have raised financial and legal barriers to business as usual. Not to be overlooked are the regulations requiring public disclosure of chemical use, permitted discharges, and accidental releases. Perhaps as a result of the need for and the reaction to such public disclosures, the emissions of selected industries were reduced by 31 percent from 1987 to 1992. We still have a way to go, however; companies were still emitting 3.8 billion pounds of toxic chemicals in 1992.[49]

Not all releases of toxic pollutants are predictable or, for that matter, fully disclosed in time to prevent serious injury. Consider the 1984 chemical release at the Union Carbide plant in Bhopal, India, which killed over 2,000 and led to the EPA's accidental release prevention rule (in effect in 1999). Or the 1986 explosion and fire at the Chernobyl nuclear power plant in northern Ukraine near the Belarus border, when the cooling system of the plant's 1,000-megawatt No. 4 reactor failed during a test and overheated. This was the world's worst nuclear reactor accident, estimated to result in the deaths of as many as 8,000 during the accident and its cleanup, and whose fallout contaminated a large part of Eastern Europe and Scandinavia. Or the massive ecological damage sustained in 1991 as a spiteful postscript of the Persian Gulf War, when hundreds of deliberately set oil fires continued burning, generating unprecedented amounts of pollution in the air, on the ground, in the Gulf, in underground aquifers, and damaging marine environments.

Putting modern atmospheric disasters aside, serious concern also needs to be directed to the proposition of using the atmosphere (through incineration) to alleviate our solid waste dilemma. Consider New York City, for example, whose primary landfill (Fresh Kills on Staten Island) is almost at capacity, even though it covers more than 1,000 acres, with closed sections now having mounds of buried trash more than 150 feet high.[50] The two principal alternatives are recycling, which requires cooperation and ready markets (see chapter 11), yet often garners apathy, and incineration, which engenders fear (of pollution and cancer) and community opposition. (In 1992, the New York City Council voted to approve construction of an incinerator on the site of the old Brooklyn Navy Yard in the borough of Brooklyn. The project was vehemently opposed by the residents of the adjacent and heavily populated neighborhoods of Williamsburg and Fort Greene. To the relief of the community, the project was not built after failing to receive the required air and solid waste permits.[51])

Our proclivity to discard much more material than we are willing or able to recycle continues to be a national burden warranting vigilance. Such waste is endemic to the building industry, with construction debris but one example. Consider the proposed 2,000-acre Eagle Mountain Landfill to be constructed adjacent to Joshua Tree National Park in California's southern Mojave Desert. The merits of the project, which would receive 20,000 tons of solid waste from the Los Angeles area, have been debated for more than ten years and are expected to be decided on soon. Ecologist Jerry Freilich, who worked at Joshua Tree for ten years, says the dump will inevitably do harm. He says the availability of trash to scavenging wildlife, the disturbance of the earth, and the withdrawal of groundwater will have a rippling effect across the park ecosystem. For example, ravens drawn to the dump will also prey on young desert tortoises, a threatened species. Voicing indignation, Brian Huse of the National Parks and Conservation remarked, "You couldn't pick a worse place to put a mega-scale garbage dump. If you permit this dump to go in here, what does that suggest for other parks?"[52]

For architects, the situation is full of paradox. From a social point of view, they are parties to the act of pollution, as most of the wastes involved are generated in buildings designed by members of their profession. Yet the architect *qua* architect is usually powerless to intervene at any scale larger than the individual project. Architectural clients have neither the power nor the inclination to control more than the air in their own buildings, nor the desire to meet more than the minimum legal standards imposed on the disposal of their own building wastes. From a purely technical point of view, the paradox is that architects are called upon to correct atmospheric conditions that are largely or wholly of their own collective making. Unlike the thermal or luminous environments, which architects must manipulate to correct all sorts of natural deficiencies by means of heating and cooling, illumination, and the like, the natural atmospheric environment has little wrong with it, as we have seen. Theoretically, architects need only let it fill their buildings as water fills a bowl. Instead, however, they are compelled to spend more and more of the building dollar on elaborate equipment designed merely to return the air to its normal state. The result is another of those misapplications of technical virtuosity with which America is filled. In the last analysis, no isolated architectural solution to the problem is possible—there can only be an urbanistic or regional one. Architects would be well advised to consider Henry David Thoreau's query: "What is the use of a house if you don't have a decent planet to put it on?" [53]

Uses of Filtration

All the foregoing is recent history. It is only within the past few decades that we have begun to realize the degree to which the atmosphere is loaded with impurities, gaseous and particulate, natural and man-made. Indeed, it was only in the 1980s that the term *multiple chemical sensitivity* (MCS) was coined, although the same symptoms may have been experienced since 1880 (as organic solvent intolerance, intolerance to smells, odor-triggered headaches, etc.).[54] Other terms that have recently become popular include *sick building syndrome* (SBS), *chemical* or *environmental hypersensitivity*, *chemical-induced immune dysfunction*, and *twentieth-century disease*. In 1991 the National Academy of Sciences defined MCS by the following:

Patients must have symptoms or signs related to chemical exposures at levels tolerated by the population at large. (Reactions to such well-recognized allergens as molds, dusts, and pollens are not included.) The symptoms must wax and wane with exposures and may be expressed in one or more organ systems. A chemical exposure associated with the onset of the condition doesn't have to be identified, and preexistent or concurrent conditions—such as asthma, arthritis, or depression—should not exclude patients.[55]

In extreme cases, those with MCS are housebound, living in a "space bubble" with high-efficiency air filters and fans, unable to interact with the rest of the world because of fear of contact with common chemicals—pesticides, insecticides, herbicides, chemicals in building materials and furnishings, perfumes, deodorants, hairspray, cigarette smoke, emissions from carbonless copy paper, laser printers—that might trigger violent illness. Controversy continues in the medical community as to whether all of these cases are chemically induced illnesses or whether the cause is sometimes psychological.

Nonetheless, the U.S. Department of Housing and Urban Development (HUD) recognized MCS in 1992 as a handicap under the Fair Housing Amendments Act (FHA), protecting those with MCS from discrimination when buying or renting housing. This has significance in multifamily housing (apartments, attached townhouses, cooperatives, and condominiums), where activities involving chemicals (building maintenance, pest control, housekeeping, carpet cleaning, renovation and remodeling work, roof repairs, etc.) are routinely conducted without the foreknowledge or approval of residents. Because those suffering from MCS now have legal recourse under the FHA, more control over chemical use may be available to occupants of multifamily housing. As a result, no- or low-chemical alternatives such as integrated pest management (IPM) may find more widespread use. While this type of initiative holds promise, building occupants still have to rely on other means, such as filtration technology, to protect themselves from pollutants released within the community at large.

In the past few decades, sophisticated filtration equipment has been developed. Characteristically, the first steps were taken by industry, more to promote efficiency than employee health per se. It was in those industries where pollution interfered with the process itself that the first effective measures were taken and the most efficient filters evolved. Industrial dusts in the paint shops of Detroit's auto plants and the film laboratories of Hollywood made first-rate paint jobs and films impossible. In mining or quarrying, on the other hand, dust did not affect the process itself, though it had most destructive effects on the lungs of the miners and quarry workers. In the first instance, industry eagerly fostered the development of advanced filtration equipment; in the latter case, Congress itself was reluctant to pass legislation protecting the most elementary health demands of the workers.

Several methods of ridding the air of its unwelcome burden of particulates have been developed. Others, such as adsorption, have been perfected to remove gaseous substances. Air can be *washed* by passing it through a fine water spray; this removes most of the larger particles—ashes, dusts, pollens. However, smaller particles are not caught, and the air comes out of the spray much wetter than it went in, which is often undesirable. A second method is *mechanical filtration*. Here the stream of air is forced through fabric or fiber filters; sometimes these filters are covered with oil to hold particles by impingement. Viscous impingement filters have a high efficiency on lint but a low efficiency on dust. When very small particles must be filtered from the airstream, high-efficiency particulate air (HEPA) and ultra-low particulate/penetration air (ULPA) filters are used, often in conjunction with a prefilter that eliminates larger particles from the airstream. HEPA filters have efficiencies ranging from 99.99 to 99.9999 percent for 0.3 micron particles—for example, smaller particles found in tobacco smoke and auto exhaust having diameters of about 1/100,000 of an inch. For clean-room applications (environmentally controlled with respect to airborne particulates and other conditions) or when radioactive particles are present, ULPA filters can be used with even higher efficiencies. They have the disadvantage of offering high resistance to air passing through them.

In a third method, *electrostatic precipitation*, air passes through a charged grid or ionizer that bombards the particles and thus gives them an electrical charge. The air then passes through another grid whose plates are alternately positive and negative. Here the charged particles are caught and held; they are periodically removed by slipping out the grids and washing them. Two other types of electronic air cleaners are now commercially available: charged media nonionizing and charged media ionizing. The charged media nonionizing type combines characteristics of dry filters and electronic air cleaners. It is constructed of a dielectric filter (e.g., glass fiber mat), often arranged in pleats, in contact with a gridwork of alternately grounded and charged members that generate an intense and nonuniform electrostatic field in the filter. Charged media ionizing electronic air cleaners combine the features of the other two, charging dust in a corona-discharge ionizer, then collecting on a charged media filter mat. However, these ionizers can also generate ozone, which can interact with unsaturated hydrocarbons indoors to form irritating aldehydes and other indoor air contaminants. Electronic air cleaners offer a low pressure-drop alternative to high-performance dry filters for removing dusts, pollens, and bacteria. Their applications have been many; however, high-efficiency dry filters currently dominate specialty applications such as those for laboratories, clean rooms, and biological safety cabinets.

Despite their high efficiency, however, HEPA filters are not wholly effective against bacteria and viruses. They can remove over 90 percent of all particulate matter, but the smallest of these organic substances may still slip through. Besides, the only safe germ is a dead one; it is not enough to catch it—it must also be killed. For this purpose, the germicidal lamp (a low-pressure mercury vapor lamp emitting ultraviolet [UV] radiation) can be used to irradiate the air after filtration. Emitting radiation in the invisible portion of the spectrum, the UV lamp has been found highly effective against both microbial and viral populations and can be employed in several ways besides being tied into the filter. It has been tested most recently for use in reducing tuberculosis (TB) transmission in high risk environments in shielded ceiling fixtures or within air ducts of recirculating systems.[56] It can be used to irradiate the air in any room or portion of a room through use of shielded fixtures that direct the radiation toward the ceiling and out to the sides. The lamps are shielded so that room occupants are protected from prolonged exposure to UV radiation, which can damage skin and eyes (one should never look directly at UV lamps for more than a few seconds). UV light has been proved effective against infectious microorganisms on any surface on which the rays fall. It does not penetrate and therefore destroys only surface microorganisms and those not shielded by dust. Finally, the germicidal lamp can be used to form an invisible germ lock between different areas of the same building through use in corridors, stairwells, and elevator shafts.

Obviously, this type of irradiation could be applied to many building types. Certain areas of hospitals, such as surgical suites, emergency rooms, intensive care units, laboratories, and neonatal wards, TB clinics, AIDS clinics, shelters for the homeless, correctional institutions, and nursing homes, where contagious disease transmission is a critical issue, can be effectively isolated to prevent cross-infection—a particular hazard with central air-conditioning systems. Understanding the benefits of UV irradiation under properly controlled conditions is not new. In controlled experiments in three Pennsylvania schools over twenty-five years ago, UV irradiation of primary-grade classrooms reversed the trend of a measles epidemic; only a third as many cases were reported there as in the upper classes, whose rooms were not irradiated. (There are usually three times as many such cases in lower grades than in the upper ones.) Studies by the U.S. Navy during the same period found that similar equipment installed in selected barracks reduced cases of common colds, German measles, and scarlet fever by 25 percent; samples of air from these barracks showed only half as many microorganisms as that from nonirradiated buildings.[57] Application of this type of light has also proved valuable in theaters and in public transport.

In some specialized processes, on the other hand, the presence of certain microorganisms is essential; thus, in brewing and baking, a particular strain of cultivated yeast is introduced into the atmosphere. Thereafter, contamination by wild airborne yeasts and other fermentative agents must be avoided. Cheesemaking requires both bacteria and molds, but certain cheeses require special cultures and close control of atmospheric and thermal conditions. Prior to the development of carefully controlled air-conditioning equipment, such cheeses could only be produced in some special cavern in Greece or Italy. Now, of course, it is possible to recreate and maintain these exact atmospheres—complete with their special microbical population—in any building anywhere. Other fields require clean rooms, including the manufacture of pharmaceuticals, semiconductors, and cosmetics, food processing, aerospace, bioscience, and computing.

Advanced equipment of this sort should, in theory, be employed to create the new and special environments required by modern life, for which there are no precedents in nature. Yet all too often it is employed merely to reestablish conditions that under ordinary circumstances would be free for the asking. Thus, many a modern building employing electronic filtration and irradiation internally is simultaneously dumping the wastes from its own heating, cooling, and power plants into the outside air around it! The insanity of this proposition does not make it any less common. On the contrary, it is a characteristic contradiction of architecture and urbanism today. Yet it becomes ever clearer that either the whole environment must be cherished and maintained intact or ultimately even the finest building is doomed to fail.

The Aerodynamic Behavior of Buildings

The need for structural stability long ago compelled architects and engineers to come to terms with the force of moving air. Relatively wind-resistant structures were designed empirically—that is, on the basis of trial and error—for millennia before the development of mathematical means for calculating wind loads and converting them into stress formulas that yield structural members of appropriate size and shape. Such computations are today routine, and now, with the computer, mathematical models of any conceivable aerodynamic condition can be easily simulated.

Of course, the impact of moving air on buildings has consequences other than purely mechanical ones. Air currents moving through and around the building have important effects upon the thermal state of that building as a whole. The factor of wind chill is especially critical in cold climates, as it greatly exacerbates the thermal stress of submersion of the human body in cold air.

But there is still another side to this question, for, if the problem of what moving air does to buildings has been rather thoroughly explored, the reverse — that is, what the building does to this moving air — has been almost completely ignored by architects and landscape architects alike. True, the consequence of this aerodynamic interaction is microenvironmental in scale, but this is precisely the scale at which human experience takes place. It is obvious that any building, no matter how small, modifies preexistent wind patterns by its sheer presence in the airstream. It is equally apparent that when the exterior surfaces of the building are heated, whether externally by the sun or internally by the heating plant, convective air currents are set up. These interact with local winds, still further complicating the aerodynamic situation in the immediate environs of the building.

Such factors have always been fairly well understood by preindustrial societies and compensated for in their architecture and town planning. But the small scale and low height of preindustrial buildings held them within manageable (or at least tolerable) limits. The great height of modern buildings and their unprecedented density in modern cities has raised the problem to new levels of acuteness. Any modern complex, with its masonry masses and paved streets and parking lots, absorbs and then reradiates immense amounts of solar energy. This effect alone is enough to set up strong convective currents, but superimposed upon this is the effect of large vertical surfaces that create powerful rising and falling currents. If these surfaces are in close juxtaposition, as they usually are in downtown districts, these currents are often accelerated into gale-force winds.

As a result of these accumulated factors, the microenvironment of most urban areas is radically altered from its natural state. Because this is seldom taken into account in either the design of the individual building or the complex of which it is a part, the alteration is usually for the worse. There is an unanticipated drop in the levels of amenity, comfort, and safety that the designs were supposed to have raised and reinforced. The wind-chill factor reduces the time span in which plazas in northern climates are actually pleasant to be in or possible to use. Blowing dust and trash is an offense to eye and nostril alike. Snow is drifted into unsafe and unpretty patterns. Entrance doors become difficult to operate and lobbies drafty. Falling icicles and window glass sucked out of curtain walls by pressure differentials become a serious hazard to pedestrians. Such aerodynamic dysfunction is familiar to all city dwellers — except, ironically, the building designers themselves!

It is, of course, impossible to prevent the generation of local wind systems in built-up areas. (In hot climates it might even be desirable!) The real point at issue here is their control. Though such control involves many variables, aerospace technology has raised to very high levels the possibility of analyzing the interaction between the built form and the moving air around it. The principal research tool is the wind tunnel; these are widely distributed across the country and could readily be used to test scale models of individual buildings, building complexes, and, indeed, entire towns. Such analyses should become an integral part of all major architectural and landscape designs.

Wind tunnels have been in use since the 1890s, when scientists W. C. Kernot in Australia and J.O.V. Irminger in Denmark placed models of small buildings in wind tunnels to measure pressures against them. Over the last thirty years or so, the need for increasingly sophisticated wind tunnels has become better understood. This is because the atmospheric boundary layer that is close to the earth (perhaps as low as 500 feet over water, up to 1,500 feet above large cities) is generally turbulent, with the wind changing speed and direction rapidly. Such factors are hard to model mathematically and require simulation in special wind tunnels that include a turbulent boundary layer over the floor to simulate these effects as compared to the free air conditions most often modeled for planes in flight. In response to such needs, just such a wind tunnel has been constructed at the University of California at Davis (UCD) with funding from Lawrence Livermore National Laboratory. Where wind engineers previously focused on how winds affect structures, they now increasingly concern themselves with environmental problem solving, including studying how gases like chlorine, ammonia, and liquified natural gas dis-

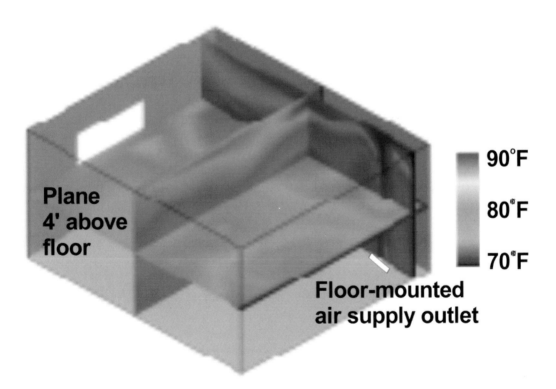

Figure 4-9 / Natural and mechanical air movement within buildings can now be studied and improved through the use of computational fluid dynamics (CFD) modeling. Distribution of conditioned air can be evaluated as shown here, with temperature contours depicted on a horizontal plane four feet above the floor.

perse when released into the atmosphere. It is also interesting to note that NASA's Langley Research Center Transonic Dynamics wind tunnel is converting its testing medium from the ozone-depleting refrigerant gas R-12 to the replacement refrigerant R-134a. The one-million-cubic-foot wind tunnel uses this refrigerant gas as the test medium because it is heavier than air and thus is ideal for aeroelastic testing within the tunnel.

The Habitat of Olfaction

To *be* in the atmospheric environment is the basic fact of animal existence. To be able to *perceive* some of its qualities is an altogether different aspect of the same experience. A room could simultaneously be filled with attar of roses and carbon monoxide: the olfactory sense would register pleasure with the one without detecting the mortal danger of the other. Contrariwise, the atmospheric environment might meet all objective criteria for health and still be rendered esthetically unsatisfactory by harmless concentrations of a noisome odor (rotten eggs, putrefaction). It is an odd fact that the critical literature of architecture pays so little attention to its olfactory behavior, as odor plays an important experiential role in all buildings. Anyone who enters the old churches of Italy and Greece realizes that the experience is conditioned, in about equal parts, by four factors: illumination, acoustical response, ambient temperatures, and the *odors* in those great masonry vessels. Stepping into them, one is immediately submerged in coexistent pools of light, sound, temperature, and odor that differ sharply from the work-a-day world outside. The sensuous impact is powerful, even on the nonbeliever, and the scent of candles, flowers, and especially incense is an important constituent of the total experience. (As a matter of fact, the extensive use of incense in Orthodox and Catholic churches has important visual consequences as well, because without the incense in the cool, still air, the rays of sunlight coming in through the windows would be invisible. This "finger of God" effect is especially important in baroque churches, where the size, shape, and location of windows are often calculated to focus such rays on a given spot at a given time of day.) All buildings generate their own olfactory environment, whether or not architects anticipated this fact. Too often, in the modern world, they did not. Here, as in other aspects of the design process, purely visual criteria often dominate design decisions, to the detriment of other avenues of sensory perception. For example, the open plan of upper-class suburban houses often yields visual sequences more dramatic than would be possible with conventional rooms. But the plan through which space flows without interruption is one in which odors (and sounds) behave the same way. This condition does not show up in the photograph and is not apt to be mentioned in the caption, but many open plans are, in experiential reality, disastrous.

Every act of the architect has olfactory consequences, which at the very least should be anticipated. This becomes especially important in buildings like schools or hospitals, where the ducts of centralized air-conditioning systems introduce the hazard of accidentally distributing obnoxious odors across the whole building. (This is the olfactory

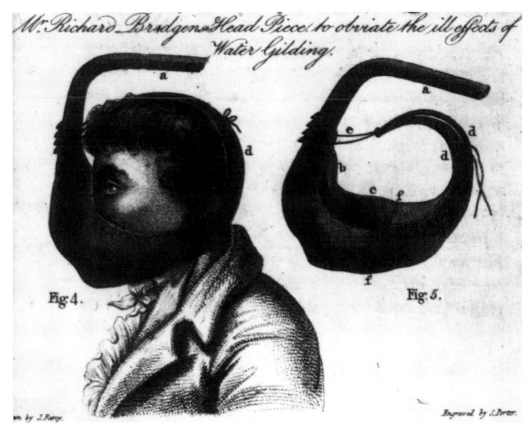

Figure 4–10 / Patent drawing for nineteenth-century masking device designed in England by Richard Bridgens. The purpose of the device was to provide a worker in a gilding factory with uncontaminated breathing air from behind the head.

dimension of the danger of cross-pollution discussed earlier in this chapter, though it might not involve identical gases or aerosols.) Such considerations raise basic questions: What is odor? How is it perceived? How can odors be manipulated architecturally?

For a substance to be olfactorily perceptible, it must have two physical properties. It must be at least partially volatile (otherwise the atmosphere would not support it), and it must be soluble in water (otherwise it could not penetrate the watery film that covers the mucous membrane of the nose). Beyond this, surprisingly little is known about odors; this is expressed in the absence of an objective, quantitative unit of measurement for odor in common everyday use, unlike for light and sound. Attempts have been made to develop units of measurement for odor, though such measurements tend to be subjective. For example, there is the *decipol*, where mountain or sea air is assigned a value of 0.01 decipol; cities with moderate air pollution typically span a range of 0.05 to 0.3 decipols, and a rating of 7.4 decipols is deemed to characterize acceptable indoor air quality. The *olf* is a perceived air quality term, with each person creating about one olf of bioeffluents. It is believed that a minimum of 5 cubic feet per minute (5 cfm) per person of outdoor air is required to dilute bioeffluents to acceptable limits. Emissions from building materials, furnishings, and office equipment may require additional dilution to maintain an acceptable indoor environment.

We do not yet have a means of describing or identifying various odors except by analogy. The average person can name only a few common odors, but this is thought to result not from our inability to detect differences between the odors but our inability to name them.[58] We are only now beginning to understand the process of olfaction. Remarkably, 1 percent of all our genes are devoted to odor detection! This demonstrates how critical the sense of smell is to our survival. How we detect odors is analogous to how we see. In vision, the brain analyzes an image by interpreting the individual components: form, location, movement, color. The unity of an image is accomplished by reconstructing the signals in the visual centers of the higher cortex. In comparison, the brain analyzes an odor by dissecting the structural features of the scent. The odor is then reconstructed by the olfactory cortex.[59] It is a chemical sense and, to the chemist, its sensitivity is astounding:

The mechanism through which a tiny area within the nasal fossae is able to receive an unlimited number of dissimilar odor stimuli, sometimes from a remote distance and sometimes in dilutions as weak as one part in billions of air, constitutes a prime biologic mystery. In the case of the eye and the ear, the perceptive apparatus is confronted with a limited and precise range of vibration. Exactness attends the two sensations. [Even] for taste, only four primary stimuli are involved. Not so for odors. The varieties of odor stimuli requiring appraisal and identification are to be reckoned in tens of thousands.[60]

Moreover, the capacity of the human nose (let alone that of animals in the wild) to sort out and characterize various substances is almost beyond belief. It deals with complex compounds in amounts so small that, for some compounds (e.g., 4-PC or 4-phenylcyclohexene, found in the latex backing of carpets, has an odor threshold in parts per trillion) it rivals the best analytical techniques of the modern laboratory, and it identifies them instantly.

And yet we cannot yet accurately measure the habitat of olfaction nor describe in precise terms the mechanism whereby we perceive it.

But how does the olfactory cortex, which receives signals from the olfactory bulb, decode the map provided by the olfactory bulb? This question is one of the central and most elusive problems in neurobiology. . . . How does the cortex prompt the range of emotional or behavioral responses that smells often provoke? To what extent is the recognition of odors in humans conscious or nonconscious, and how much of behavior or mood is governed by the perception of odors in our environment? We have only begun to explore the logic of smell and how it can evoke the "vast structure of recollection."[61]

Nevertheless, this habitat must be conceived of being as concrete as those of vision and hearing.

Like vision and hearing, olfaction is a scanning sense that permits us to analyze the middle reaches of our environment. (The sense of taste, with which smell is closely allied physiologically, depends, of course, upon actual contiguity.) The horizontal dimension of its habitat is a spectrum of thousands of mixes of the seven primary odors, though these odors cannot be arranged into an orderly progression, like those of light or sound, because different substances can have the same smell. Along this scale lie all those pleasant olfactory experiences that we associate with roses, incense, or *boeuf Bourguinon*, and the unattractive or repellent ones connected with sweat, feces, or putrefaction. The vertical dimension of the olfactory habitat is one of intensity, ranging from a lowest threshold of perception to an upper one of concentrations so intense as to be stressful, nauseous, or asphyxiating. The third dimension of the habitat is that of time. Continued exposure to a steady concentration of a given substance leads to a steadily declining capacity to perceive its odor. As with the other senses, steady stimulation tends to anesthetize perception itself.

Not only are odors hard to quantify, they are even more difficult to arrange according to any valid esthetic scale. The qualitative judgments we pass on any given set of olfactory conditions are highly subjective, deriving in about equal parts from personal experience (e.g., the scent of lilies at the funeral of a parent) and culturally derived criteria (e.g., the Elizabethan attitude toward body odors). Sometimes even the same odor provokes different value judgments, depending upon our knowledge of its origin (e.g., the scent of putrefaction in meat as against certain cheeses). This cultural component of what "smells nice" and what "smells bad" varies widely from one society to another, as both Hall and Bedichek have demonstrated.[62]

Olfaction clearly plays a larger role in the life of animals than it does in the life of contemporary human beings. Part of this loss of acuity may indeed be evolutionary, but it is probably more due to a kind of acclimatization to the conditions of modern life, which do not compel us to exercise our ability in the same ways or to the same ends as earlier cultures did. This becomes apparent with people who are blind and therefore compelled to develop their other perceptual senses to compensate for the loss of vision.[63]

Interestingly, those who lack a functional sense of smell (*anosmics*) nevertheless respond to airborne chemicals by registering their nasal pungency. This sensory channel is known as common chemical sense. Pungent sensations include stinging, prickliness, tingling, irritation, burning, piquancy, and freshness, among others. Anosmics have reported that the pungency evoked by chemicals ranges from "sharp" or "biting" to "dull" or "pastel." Unlike smell, this response relies on free nerve endings, particularly from the trigeminal nerve. In addition to nasal response, nerve endings in the conjunctiva are also affected, resulting in eye irritation, or ocular potency. In general, at very low concentrations in the environment, only odor is perceptible, but as concentrations increase, we are attuned to a chemical's pungency as well. Whereas odor sensations tend to diminish with time (olfactory fatigue), nasal pungency can build up for thirty or more minutes (temporal integration or summation) before adaptation. These two sensory channels (and their temporal properties) must be considered together in any comprehensive analysis of this subject.[64]

It may well be that the polluted urban atmospheres discussed earlier in this chapter are not only deleterious to the respiratory tract as a whole but also exercise an anesthetic effect on the olfactory mechanism. In any case, olfactory monotony is only another sensual expression of the monotony of the urban landscape as a whole. Part of it is due to personal and municipal hygiene, whereby body cleanliness is extended to the social aspects of eliminating wastes of all kinds, including the noisome odors which were an integral part of any pre-twentieth-century city.

The other side of the same coin — the disposal of obnoxious odors (your own or your neighbor's) — is not a pressing problem in rural America today; before the Civil War it would not have been too serious even in the American city. Densities were low enough to permit one to open up the windows and air the place out. By the same token, few operations were large enough to pollute large areas around them. Some of the earliest sources of industrial stench on a neighborhood scale were the tanneries, meat-packing houses, and soap and tallow factories of Cincinnati and Chicago. Today, on the other hand, noisome industrial wastes have become regional in scale (e.g., along the middle Northeast Corridor from Baltimore to Staten Island). Even a single large plant can pollute an entire city, as the citizens of Charleston, Savannah, and Mobile who have lived downwind of the sulfurous odors of big paper mills can attest.

Diametrically opposed reactions to our olfactory landscape have emerged in recent times. Aromatherapy has regained popularity; it is based on the belief that essential oils have healing powers, eliciting various physiological or emotional effects when inhaled or rubbed into the skin. Taken one step further, some architects in Japan have employed air-conditioning systems that deliver a variety of odors to the building throughout the day on the premise that work performance is improved or a sense of well-being instilled among the occupants.[65] Many people in this country would consider such a practice manipulative and beyond the realm of acceptability, even though American architects and interior designers already have modified many parameters to maximize productivity — lighting, wall color, acoustics, spatial layout. There is instead a growing constituency for fragrance-free zones — areas in buildings where people are not allowed to wear perfume or cologne. A host of unscented consumer products (e.g., tissues, detergents, cleaners) have emerged in response to their demands and to a growing intolerance of odors generally.

Architectural Control of Odors

Under circumstances such as these, it is literally true that the only effective way to control obnoxious odors is to prevent them — often a complex and expensive process. Inside a given building, odor control usually falls to the air-conditioning engineer, who has three stock responses: dilution, masking, or removal.

1. *Dilution*: This is the commonest method of odor control when the odor is of internal origin. This involves simply recirculating less of the used air and adding more outside air to the mix. (But this is merely a technical way of saying that more of

your odors are being dumped on your neighbor. Very tall chimneys serve at least to distribute them more widely, as in the case of the paper mills.) This method involves the moving and conditioning of greater volumes of air per cycle, with corresponding increases in fan, duct, and conditioner capacities. Besides controlling odors, dilution is also employed to reduce airborne levels of viable and infectious microorganisms — particularly to control transmission of tuberculosis (via *Mycobacterium tuberculosis*) and colds (rhinoviruses).

2. *Masking:* Some objectionable odors can be masked by superimposing a stronger concentration of a putatively more pleasant air-freshener scent on top of them. This is the technique commonly applied in public washrooms in lieu of better ventilation. Lemon- or pine-scented fragrances are often used, as people associate these with clean environments beneficial to their health. As long as the original stench is not toxic, this technique is permissible, although it is not apt to be successful esthetically.*

3. *Removal:* Some of the techniques already described for cleansing the air of particulates may also have the side effect of reducing odors associated with those offending substances. The most direct method of odor removal, however, is by chemical adsorption. Here the air to be deodorized is passed across a thin bed of activated charcoal that adsorbs (i.e., physically catches and holds) the offending gas molecules. This method requires that the beds be periodically removed for cleaning and reactivation. Adsorption (or some of the more complex methods, like vapor neutralization and catalytic combustion) nevertheless should be mandatory for any industrial process yielding noisome or noxious airborne wastes.[66]

The control of the olfactory habitat is not an easy task for the architect, involving, as we have seen, a number of incompletely explored areas of experience. But that should constitute no reason for abdicating responsibility for it, as is too often the case. Olfaction constitutes an important dimension of the sensory perception of architecture and hence of the total esthetic experience of it.

---

* It is paradoxical, to put it mildly, that this masking technique is widely used in insect sprays for household use when the toxicity of the basic chemical is prominently announced on the container itself. One might expect the printed warning to be reinforced with an *unpleasant* odor rather than a pleasant one!

"Oh, Say, Can You See . . ."

Control of the Luminous Environment

A sunset is a pretty thing to look at and a leaping deer a lovely thing to see. But it is scarcely in such terms that the evolution of human vision, or its uses today, can be productively analyzed. Vision is indeed the material basis for many of our richest esthetic experiences, but we did not, as Hans Blumenfeld once succinctly put it,

. . .develop the ability to see just for the fun of it, but in order to grab and avoid being grabbed. The good, the true and the beautiful light is the light which enables us to perceive real bodies. We want to perceive their exact size, shape and distance; and to perceive them safely, easily and quickly.[1]

Of all the sensory means of perceiving the qualities and dimensions of the real world, the visual is by far the most comprehensive. Psychologists estimate that, for adults, as much as 90 percent of all information about the external world comes in the form of visually perceived data. Because, as Edward Hall says, "the optic nerve contains roughly eighteen times as many neurons as the cochlear nerve, we may assume that it transmits at least that much more information . . . the eyes may be as much as a thousand times as effective as the ears in sweeping up information."[2]

For the literate person, the relative weight given to visually received information is enormous and unbalanced, outrunning by far the importance we attach to data perceived by other sensory means — hearing, touch, olfaction, and taste. The implications of this visual bias are serious and by no means fully comprehended.

Visually acquired data is the bedrock of all specialized education. But by this same token of ubiquity, we consistently overlook the dangers implicit in this visual bias, which leads us to act as though the entire esthetic process were exclusively a matter of vision. Common sense should tell us that much of the data we think of as visually acquired has actually been perceived by other sensory means and only subsequently abstracted and synthesized into visual constructs. Thus vision-based estimates of the shape, size, and relation of objects would be impossible without previous tactile and kinesthetic explorations of them. When we say, "It looks far away," or "It looks like velvet," or "It looks like a pineapple," we are actually recasting in visual terms a whole body of information that we originally acquired, in whole or in part, by other sensory means—that is, by walking, reaching, feeling, smelling, tasting. The architect conventionally expresses concepts of spatial phenomena in visual terms. We see distances and dimensions, but our original understanding of distance, and of the friction and gravity to be overcome in exploring it, comes originally from kinesthetic experience. Architects talk of balance, rhythm, symmetry as though they were purely visual qualities, but our perception of them rests on complex factors of heartbeat, vestibular apparatus, and sensors in skin and muscle. (See chapter 7 for a more extensive treatment of the role of touch in architectural experience.) Finally, of course, there is the fact that many important aspects of human experience cannot be visually perceived at all—for example, electric shock, the smell of roses, the taste of wine, symphonic music, sexual orgasm.

Nevertheless, the visual experience of architecture remains the dominant one, above all for architects themselves. The failure to recognize the enormous significance of the nonvisual impact of architecture leads to the impoverishment of all perceptual experience—including even, ironically, that of vision itself! For if the satisfaction of our complex sensory requirements is vulgarly simplified in such a fashion, then whole areas of environmental manipulation, with all their important visual consequences, are excluded from the design process. Having thus abandoned the one real source of originality, the architect is reduced to the mere *invention* of novel forms, and these, as in modern painting and sculpture, tend to become increasingly idiosyncratic, subjective, frivolous.

Actually, as the whole history and prehistory of architecture demonstrates, visual richness is the almost automatic byproduct of the correct solution of most environmental problems. Their very complexity assures this. As both primitive practice and the most advanced research demonstrate, the proper control of sunlight, with its inordinate number of luminous and thermal variables, yields far more photogenic surfaces than any amount of formalistic invention. And precisely because the forms are derived in response to environmental necessity, they are bound to be more durable, structurally and stylistically.

The paradox is that, despite contemporary architects' obsession with the visible aspects of their work, they often have little knowledge or understanding of the visual performance field. This is expressed in many ways. For all the new means at their disposal, their use of color—either as pigment or as light—is both more timid and less expert than in many previous periods. For all their extravagant use of glass, they seldom recognize the basic optical fact that glass is only transparent under certain objective con-

Figure 5 – 1 / Mud-walled huts in Ethiopia. For primitive societies living in hot climates, most work takes place out of doors. Hence, control of the luminous environment indoors is less critical than protection against thermal extremes. Mud masonry is topped by thatched parasol roofs as protection against the short wet season. Note the stabilizing horizontal members in the structure to the right similar to that used in modern cavity wall construction.

ditions. For all their wide use of artificial, non-daylit illumination, all too many buildings are poorly lit with improper fixtures for the task.

The field of lighting design has changed tremendously since the first energy crisis of 1973. All facets of technology have improved, including more efficient lamps, improved fixtures, and various controls to reduce waste. Laws, codes, standards, and basic operational economics have reduced the luminous power density of most buildings substantially. However, notwithstanding these changes and increased knowledge of insolation and orientation, many new buildings still display serious malfunction, expressed in glare, overheating, and faulty integration of natural and artificial light sources. In short, the architect pays at once too much and too little attention to the visual world — too much to its formal superstructures, far too little to its experiential foundations.

Historic Changes in the Visual Task

The natural luminous environment shares with the thermal and the atmospheric the quality of discontinuity. There is not only the regular alternation between night and day

A

B

Figure 5 – 2 / Millowners' Association Building, Ahmedabad, India. Le Corbusier, architect. The great French pioneer was among the first of modern architects to recognize the sheer esthetic possibilities of the geometry of sun control. Views: (A) exterior of building, (B) from interior showing how effective building geometry is in blocking entry of sunlight.

but the constant fluctuation in both intensity and color composition of daylight itself. Unlike variations in the other environments, however, such fluctuations were not of themselves either stressful or the cause of much inconvenience to preindustrial humans. Nightfall, naturally, brought terror as well as rest to primitive peoples, but it did not seriously interfere with their activities. Or rather, their activities were geared to the diurnal luminous rhythm. There was ample daylight for hunting and fishing, agriculture, and shepherding, and long, unilluminated nights provided for the necessary recovery of energy from the day's activities. This remained true for even so relatively advanced a society as that of pre-Revolutionary America. An occasional cobbler or engraver might have felt that "God had made the night too long"; certainly, the means of artificial illumination at the time were primitive and expensive. But by and large, the day was long enough and bright enough; all society remained geared to a dawn-to-dusk rhythm.

It remained for the industrial revolution first to raise the question of, and then to produce the means for, continuous illumination around the clock. George Washington's America had relatively little need of artificial lighting. In his day, nineteen out of every twenty workers spent their days producing food for themselves and the twentieth person. In Lincoln's day, eight people out of ten worked the soil to feed the whole ten. Today, agribusiness needs less than one person to feed hundreds. It is thus apparent that 95 percent of early Americans had relatively little need for artificial illumination, as agriculture then (as now) was a daytime operation. Our ancestors rose with the dawn, worked by the light of the sun, and stopped at dark. They went to bed early both from choice (manual labor made them sleepy) and from necessity (they had few sources of artificial light to read by, few books, and most of them were illiterate anyway).

But today this situation is almost precisely reversed. The great majority of Americans work (often on a computer) in a largely synthetic luminous environment because neither the quality nor quantity of daylight is adequate for the tasks at hand. Today almost all Americans are literate; newspapers, magazines, and books are published in the billions; artificial light sources are cheap and plentiful.

A parallel changeover must be observed. The great majority of pre-Revolutionary Americans used their eyes naturally. Their seeing tasks nearly all lay in the fields of middle and far vision—stalking game, guiding a plow, or sailing a ship. Only the bookkeepers, printers, jewelers, and tailors had tasks that lay primarily in the field of near vision. As noted, books were few, literacy low. Few children went regularly to school, so most of them used their eyes in a completely natural mix of near, middle, and far vision during their formative years.

Today this situation is reversed. The vast majority of us move in the world of near vision, of prolonged and critical seeing tasks, of concentration on a visual field rarely farther from the eye than the arm's reach. With universal education, American children are pushed into the world of near vision in nursery school and can easily remain there for twelve, fourteen, or twenty years.

It is hard, even today, to visualize the consequences of this shift from a largely natural to a largely synthetic luminous environment; the conceptual lag is apparent in the scanty and uneven research on the subject. Certainly the consequences were not anticipated at the beginning. Nineteenth-century enthusiasm for artificial illumination found its initial outlets in such applications as street lighting — understandably, for natural laws seemed to have been repealed. With the appearance of illuminated streets and plazas, the temporal limits of social intercourse were measurably extended across areas that night had closed to all but the hardy or the suspect. This is the new potential that Edward Bellamy celebrated in his utopian Boston in *Looking Backward,* and that the outdoor electric illumination of the Columbian Exposition demonstrated to a dazzled public in 1893. These were spiritual as well as physical proofs to the Victorians of their conquest of darkness.

However, it was scarcely to make streets safe or fairs beautiful that American society spent so much on the development of artificial light sources. These were byproducts of the central understanding that *industrial technology could not develop in the natural luminous environment*. The need of industrialism for a luminous environment that could be extended in time and space and manipulated in any desired direction sprang from two distinct but closely related facts. The first was the discovery that a machine, unlike a horse, is most economically operated when it runs all the time. The second was that, even in its primitive stages, a machine is a precision instrument — that is, it works to close tolerances and hence demands visual acuity on the part of its operators. Both of these facts imply artificial illumination: the first, *more* light in time and space, the second, *better* light than nature gives us.

Thus the economy and culture of industrialism changed not only the luminous environment of our workplaces but also the physical setting of our entire lives. It even changed the way we use our eyes, in ways that are both historically and physiologically unprecedented. In general terms, we developed artificial light sources to the point where, in many building types, they long ago supplanted natural illumination. There is no question that our vaunted technological accomplishments would have been impossible without this mastery of the luminous environment.

Yet it is a debated point as to whether today's average American eye is any better off in this new habitat than was its colonial predecessor. (Comparable studies on hearing acuity suggest strongly that environmental attrition is much lower among aboriginal peoples than in civilized urban societies; see chapter 6.) Certainly, for one American building that offers its inhabitants optimal luminous conditions there must be ten where conditions range from inadequate down to dangerous. Historically, illuminating engineering was developed primarily to improve process and only indirectly eye health or well-being; today it bears the characteristic imprint of this history. Its development has been uneven, with enormous qualitative discrepancies between its highest and lowest examples and instances of gross deficiency side by side with extravagant waste. This paradox is clear in our mechanical separation of problems of artificial illumination and daylighting when, in most building types, they could be thoroughly integrated to the benefit of both.

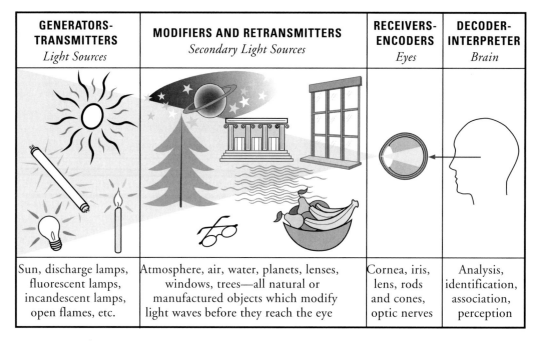

GENERATORS-TRANSMITTERS *Light Sources*	MODIFIERS AND RETRANSMITTERS *Secondary Light Sources*	RECEIVERS-ENCODERS *Eyes*	DECODER-INTERPRETER *Brain*
Sun, discharge lamps, fluorescent lamps, incandescent lamps, open flames, etc.	Atmosphere, air, water, planets, lenses, windows, trees—all natural or manufactured objects which modify light waves before they reach the eye	Cornea, iris, lens, rods and cones, optic nerves	Analysis, identification, association, perception

Figure 5–3 / The process of vision is enormously complex, involving physical, physiological, and psychological phenomena. It is our most important source of information on the shape, size, location, and physical characteristics of the world of objects.

The Human Eye and Its Habitat

Human vision is today the subject of close study on the part of a wide range of specialists in the fields of psychology, ophthalmology, optics, and engineering. An enormously complex psychophysical process, it defies any simple description. Yet, just because vision plays so large a role in the experiencing of architecture, a holistic approach to the subject is of great value to architects and designers.

One psychophysical theory of how the visual system works suggests that:

. . . it scans across space, over time, so that first one and then another point in space is "interrogated" by a neural mechanism in the brain. This scan is repeated perhaps as many times as ten times per second. Thus, during a fixational pause, the entire field may be scanned at least twice, with items of information being assimilated from various points in visual space during each neural scan.[3]

The visual system may thus be compared to an iconoscope, though an incomparably superior one. Its capacity to perceive the limits and qualities of its environmental habitat may be defined in both spatial and luminous terms. Spatially, it is capable of scanning a wide range of distances with marvelous precision and flexibility. Basically, however, it is

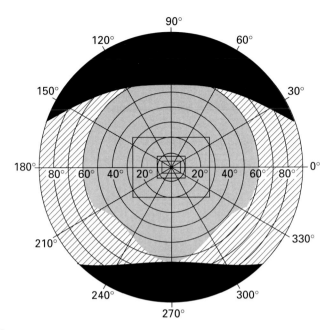

Figure 5–4 / The spatial parameters of binocular vision are partially represented in this diagram of the visual field. Shaded portions (right and left) are seen only by the right and left eyes, respectively. The rectangles represent the sizes of various typical visual tasks.

an instrument of far and middle vision.* The angular limits of the binocular visual field extend horizontally across more than 180 degrees and vertically for almost 130 degrees (Fig. 5–4). However, the central cone of the visual field, which provides our most accurate vision, is smaller.

The eye resembles the ear in that it perceives only a small portion of the sea of electromagnetic energy in which it is submerged—that is, the visible portion of the spectrum (Fig. 5–5). Within these wavelengths, neural stimulation is highest in the yellow-green (around 550 nanometers [nm]), while down below the violet band (400 nm) or above the red (720 nm), stimulus and, hence, perception fall away rapidly to zero. Like the ear again, the range of energies to which the naked eye responds is enormous—from that of a lighted candle viewed in the dark from a distance of 14 miles (as revealed by studies conducted under ideal conditions, our vision has a sensitivity that closely approaches theoretical limits) to a landscape flooded by more than 10,000 foot-candles (fc) of sunshine. Illuminance—light falling *on* a surface—is measured in foot-candles. Lumi-

---

* The normal eye focuses from a point approximately 15 feet in front of the cornea on out to infinity. However, 3 percent of first-grade schoolchildren are myopic (nearsighted), and this percentage rises to 9 percent in the sixth grade; about 19 percent of the first grade is hyperopic (farsighted), and this declines to 9 percent in the sixth. The U.S. Naval Academy found a consistent 25 percent rate of attrition in visual acuity in each four-year class; this rate appeared to be independent of any environmental or vocational factors.

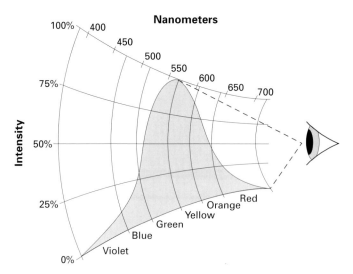

Figure 5–5 / The human eye perceives only a small portion of the ocean of electromagnetic energy in which it is submerged—the visible spectrum. Perception is highest in yellow-green bands, lowest in violet and red. It can adjust to large variations in intensity.

nance—light flowing *from* a surface—is measured in foot-lamberts. To accommodate itself to such a range of stimuli, the eye has a series of modulating devices: the pupil, which by expanding and contracting controls the amount of light admitted, and the eyelid, eyelash, and eyebrow, which shade it from stressful intensities.

The quantitative boundaries of the visual habitat are thus established by physics and physiology, but how well the visual system performs within this habitat is a function of several variable factors: the condition of the eye itself, age, the nature of the seeing task assigned to it, and the specific luminous environment under which the act of seeing takes place. Like all physical activity, the performance of any visual task involves stress, whether at work (word processing, assembling parts, chauffeuring) or at play (tennis, skiing, card playing). The visual component of any task requires definite inputs of energy and ultimately becomes tiring, no matter under what subjective motivation or objective conditions it transpires. Here, as elsewhere in the world of sensory experience, an optimal environment, one designed to facilitate the specific task in question, lightens the load and delays the onset of fatigue. A deficient or hostile set of luminous conditions, on the other hand, tends to exaggerate stress and accelerate fatigue.

But the need to define the mechanism of fatigue is not made any easier by the historical inability of the experts to trace its causal relationships or agree upon meaningful ways of measuring it. John L. Brown once postulated that the concept of fatigue implies a reduction in the ability of the sensory receptors to respond to visual stimuli and a resulting depressed neural activity for a given level of stimulation.[4] But many investigators have found no evidence of sensory fatigue *per se*. To resolve this apparent paradox, H. C.

Weston distinguished between visual and retinal fatigue, because vision involves motor functions as well as sensory process. Though he found little evidence to support the idea of fatigue of the neural sensors, he found a great deal of evidence to suggest that visual fatigue is principally due to movements of muscles within the eye, such as those that control convergence and accommodation.[5]

In any case, the eye — like any other organ of the animal body — can accomplish its tasks only by the expenditure of energy. This cannot occur without cost to the body as a whole, however complex or obscure the cost-accounting of the process may be. Some observers, therefore, take a holistic view of the process.

Vision, though primarily a function of a specific visual pathway, involves the participation of the whole organism. Since vision depends upon so many diverse components, visual fatigue is so complex a phenomenon as to be variously understood and diversely defined.[6]

With computer usage increasing from preschool age on, vision problems have proliferated, termed *computer vision syndrome* by the American Optometric Association. Symptoms may include temporary myopia (the inability to focus on distant objects minutes or hours after using the computer), eyestrain or eye fatigue, blurred vision for near or far objects, double vision and afterimages, dry, irritated eyes, and increased sensitivity to light. There is no evidence that computer usage causes permanent myopia any more than reading does. Design decisions that may contribute to these effects include inadequate lighting, overhead lights or desk lamps that create glare or reflection, and poor placement of workstations relative to windows (these should be at right angles to the computer rather than in front or behind).

The causal relation between the eye and its task can be expressed in either of two ways, each of which is an obverse of the other: (1) how well the visual system performs its task in terms of speed and accuracy of work accomplished, and (2) at what cost it does so in terms of tension, blink rate, etc. The luminous conditions under which the task transpires — that is, the visual "fit" — are an important factor in either case. It is the duty of the architect to provide conditions of luminous quality without excess. Generally speaking, performance improves and fatigue rates drop in direct proportion to increasing levels of illumination in the visual field (Fig. 5–6), though this is modified by other factors such as the distribution, direction, and color of light. However, too much light can cause glare, which increases fatigue and causes eyestrain.

A satisfactory adaptation of the eye to its task clearly implies a dynamic balance between three factors: the eye, the task, and the environment. It hardly needs saying that, in experiential reality, such a balance is rarely automatic. Usually, some adjustments are called for, and they can be made at any or all of several junctures. By being fitted with eyeglasses, the eye can be modified optically so that its seeing task can be performed with less strain (e.g., corrective lenses adjusted for a distance of 20 to 24 inches and an angle of 10 to 15 degrees are more suitable for computer use than are reading lenses, which are adjusted for an eye-to-page distance of 16 inches at an angle of 25 degrees). A particular task can be assigned to another person whose eyes are better suited to it (hyperopic for

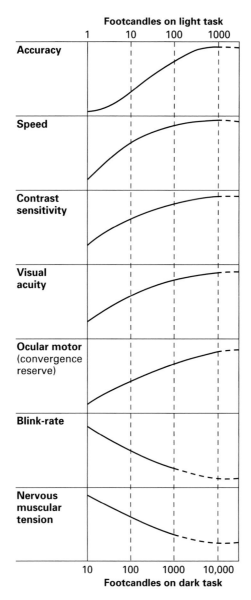

Figure 5–6 / Visual strain is a function of many factors, one of which is the luminous environment in which the seeing task occurs. Experimental data show that raised illumination levels lead to increased visual efficiency; physiologically, this lowered stress is expressed in lower blink rate and lower muscular tension.

distant view, myopic for close work). The entire task can be automated, with the load of visual discrimination transferred to electronic devices—which can often do it better anyway. In almost all cases, the luminous environment in which the visual task takes place is restructured in favor of the task itself. Only this last accommodation lies within the province of the architect's responsibility.

Manmade Luminous Environments

The provision of the proper luminous environment for a given visual task or activity is clearly a prosthetic measure, not merely for the eye but for the body as a whole. It extends the body's capacity to accomplish its task by making vision easier, more precise, less stressful. It must be reckoned as a therapeutic measure as well, for in lessening strain, it reduces the cost of seeing. This relationship is enormously complex and has been inadequately investigated in holistic terms, but if vision plays as decisive a role in total sensory perception as psychologists and neurologists claim for it, then it is of fundamental importance to behavior. Posture, gesture, movement are all conditioned by the luminous environment. Such effects can be observed and quantified. However, it is much more difficult to determine the long-range cumulative effects of good or bad illumination upon our health and well-being. Here, as in other areas of organism-environment interaction, we can only assume that the connection is real and important.

Generally speaking, the eye is most comfortable in a habitat that confronts it with no great contrasts in the field of vision. But this does not imply that the eye "wants" evenly distributed, directionless illumination. On the contrary, objects seen under diffused light exclusively are difficult to appraise correctly. Here we meet the same paradox that is to be observed in regard to other areas of sensory stimulation: optimal conditions seem to imply variations in stimuli strong enough to be perceived but not strong enough to be stressful, and for these variations to occur in time as well as space. The amount of light in the visual field is called *brightness*. As noted, the visual system has the capacity to adjust to a wide range of brightness levels. Until the energy crisis in 1973, there had been a steady escalation of minimum standards for various types of visual activity. Since then much research and product development has placed a greater emphasis on acceptable lighting conditions without excessive brightness. The Illuminating Engineering Society of North America (IESNA) Lighting Handbook recommends illuminance levels (foot-candles on the work surface) for a variety of seeing tasks (types of activities). Ranges are provided to give designers the freedom to consider site-specific conditions such as the importance of speed and accuracy and worker age. The IESNA also publishes recommended practices (RP): e.g., RP1 on office lighting and RP24 on office video display terminal (VDT) lighting.

For tasks involving critical seeing (proofreading, sewing, watch repair), two qualities are important: the illumination of the task itself should be high and the brightness levels of surrounding surfaces should not be less than one third this value. No surface anywhere in the field of vision should be much brighter than those of the materials and tools of the task itself. Of course, many tasks in the modern world require far higher levels of illumination: a machine toolmaker at a bench or a surgeon at the operating table may need hundreds of foot-candles on the task. (All such brightnesses are relatively low for the animal eye, which developed in a natural environment in which levels of 8,000 or 9,000 fc are not unusual, and stressful only in desert or snow-covered landscapes.)

When we illuminate the interior volumes of a building by either natural or artificial means, we are actually creating a new luminous mesoenvironment, designed and maintained for some specific set of visual needs. The luminous criteria derive from the task itself (sewing, card playing, word processing, study, etc.). Ordinarily, they are symmetrical in space (i.e., every child in a classroom will enjoy similar brightness levels) and constant in time, at least for the duration of the task itself. For many years it was unclear whether — to maintain a given level of visual acuity throughout a working day — the prescribed light level should remain objectively constant (e.g., 200 fc for color grading) or whether it might be advisable to raise it as the day progresses and the worker becomes more tired and consequently less speedy and less precise. Yet such parameters of work and fatigue should be established if the building is to perform at optimal levels of therapeutic intervention. New research, published by George C. Brainard and Craig A. Bernecker in 1996, reveals that increasing fc levels during the course of a work shift leads to an increase in productivity and a decrease in errors.[7] Often the architect is guided by IESNA recommendations, such as a range of illuminance from 20 to 50 foot-candles for visual tasks of high contrast or large size in offices. A computerized lighting program can then be used to evaluate the light levels that would arrive on the task using alternative lamps, fixtures, and arrangements. But our attempt to establish such stable mesoenvironments occurs in the larger context of the natural world, where the light of the macroenvironment is constantly shifting in amount, direction, color, and quantity. To resolve this paradox of establishing a stable state in a condition of flux, architects have at their disposal the structural devices of architecture (walls, roofs, windows, overhangs, etc.) and artificial lighting systems (lamps, fixtures, controls, etc.).

By its very presence, any building modulates the sunlight that falls directly on it and the daylight and darkness in which it is diurnally submerged. If it is properly shaped, sited, and oriented, with its fenestration properly designed for the visual tasks inside, the building extracts the maximum assist from the natural luminous environment. But, except for very simple building types located in the open country (with unobstructed access to all quadrants of the sky), satisfactory illumination by daylight alone is not probable. It must be supplemented by artificial sources, and for a vast range of contemporary social and technical processes, each with its own specialized luminous requirements, reliance upon natural light is out of the question. Artificial lighting systems of great complexity are required.

The integration of natural and artificial illumination is thus an extremely complex problem. From the point of view of the architect and illuminating engineer, it would be simplified if all visual tasks took place in opaque, sealed containers from which all natural illumination was excluded. With the perfection of a wide range of electrical light sources over the past century, this has become entirely possible. The windowless building has become commonplace. For those processes requiring absolute and unvarying control of luminous conditions, such sealed containers are obviously appropriate. However, it would be all too easy to extend such special cases into a general rule. As we have seen before and shall see again, the preponderance of experiential circumstances, even for modern urban people, has no such fixed or unilinear characteristics. Many activities and processes have no inherent requirement for opaque enclosure and many more actually

Figure 5 – 7 / Daylight can be used in many architectural applications. Here the canopy of the on-grade railway (subway) station near O'Hare International Airport has openings to allow the entry of daylight. As a result, lighting quality is improved, contrast is reduced, and passenger safety enhanced.

require transparency for easy visual access (e.g., lobbies, stores, and banks, airport control towers, view windows). Moreover, in many situations the eye is, so to say, at liberty, not engaged in any specific visual task. When we wait for a friend, walk in the park, or listen to a symphony, the visual system is stimulated by a wide range of optical conditions. This idle scanning of the visual field is not only pleasant—the chances are very high that it is a psychophysiological necessity.

Instead of the deep views of nature, urban people move in the shallow frame of man-made perspectives. Aside from the fact that most modern work lies in the field of near vision, there is the added problem that most of our leisure time is spent in the same kind of unnatural habitat. Our horizon is usually limited by the surfaces of a room (bedroom, classroom, workshop, office) or a very limited perisphere (out the window, down the block, through the windshield of a moving car). This raises problems for building design that are only obscurely understood and little investigated. Ever since the twin developments of year-round air-conditioning and artificial illumination made possible the windowless building, observers have been conscious of hidden factors that were not fully accounted for. There is accumulating evidence of employee dissatisfaction, not to say actual discomfort, in many windowless workplaces. Workers complain of feeling all cooped up, of not being able to tell what the weather's like outside. Indeed, research has shown that to satisfy most workers, windows must account for at least 20 percent of the perimeter walls of the building. Windows are thus openings to the outside world in more ways than one. When desk workers or students look out the window instead of down at their work, they are not wasting time: they are seeking psychic as well as optical relief from a highly structured and unnaturally monochromatic experience. In fact, computer operators are counseled to take frequent rest breaks for the eyes by glancing at objects in the middle or far field of vision. From this broader point of view, many of the arguments for the windowless building may turn out to be illusory, if not worse.

In designing the required visual habitat inside a building, the architect exercises control at two phases in the overall design process (1) by manipulation of natural light across the interface between the macroenvironment and the building's synthetic mesoenvironment, and (2) by manipulation of artificial light sources and surface response within this mesoenvironment.

The two aspects are, of course, inextricably linked. The architect must analyze them separately for purposes of precision, but to guarantee their successful reintegration in the final design, the architect must make sure that solutions to each are developed simultaneously — in tandem, so to say. To do this in buildings of any complexity, the architect ordinarily requires the assistance of the illuminating engineer. And, because of this complexity, the natural tendency on the part of the architect is to delegate the entire illumination problem to the engineer.

There are two hazards here. Often illumination specialists have a background in electrical engineering; they are thus all too prone to rely upon artificial light sources exclusively, paying little or no attention to daylighting. The other hazard is more subtle. Many building types have optical characteristics that are not addressed by lighting alone. For example, design decisions on questions of outlook or view, or of visual privacy versus visual access, are fundamentally architectural. Their correct solution depends upon many design decisions, often made before the illuminating engineer appears on the scene. The luminous dysfunction of much contemporary architecture, especially that involving a wide use of glass, is traceable to confusion over this critically important phase of the design process.

Orientational and Structural Factors in Daylighting

The manipulation of light falling on a building's surfaces is a function of the orientation, the geometry, and the physical characteristics of the enclosing membranes — that is, roof, walls, windows, etc. These factors may be summarized as offering various options of control (Table 5–1).

It is obvious that any building above the earth's surface is exposed to daylight, but how the building exploits this natural resource depends upon a number of variables, many of them not directly related to control of the luminous environment. Endogenous

Table 5 – 1 / *Relationships Between Buildings and Their Luminous Environment*

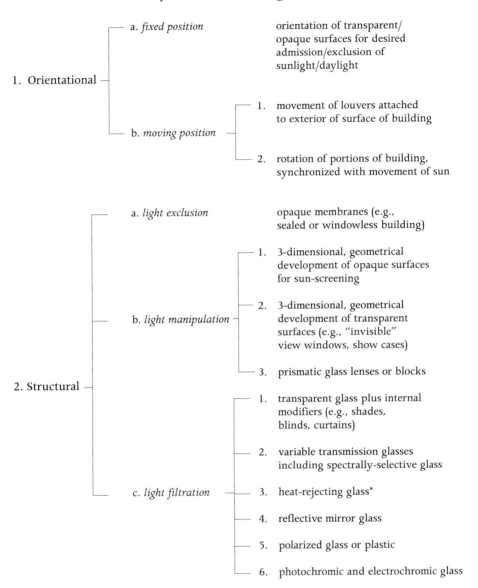

1. Orientational
   - a. *fixed position* — orientation of transparent/opaque surfaces for desired admission/exclusion of sunlight/daylight
   - b. *moving position*
     1. movement of louvers attached to exterior of surface of building
     2. rotation of portions of building, synchronized with movement of sun

2. Structural
   - a. *light exclusion* — opaque membranes (e.g., sealed or windowless building)
   - b. *light manipulation*
     1. 3-dimensional, geometrical development of opaque surfaces for sun-screening
     2. 3-dimensional, geometrical development of transparent surfaces (e.g., "invisible" view windows, show cases)
     3. prismatic glass lenses or blocks
   - c. *light filtration*
     1. transparent glass plus internal modifiers (e.g., shades, blinds, curtains)
     2. variable transmission glasses including spectrally-selective glass
     3. heat-rejecting glass*
     4. reflective mirror glass
     5. polarized glass or plastic
     6. photochromic and electrochromic glass

* Although used for thermal reasons (i.e., to reduce transmission of infrared radiation) such glasses also affect optical behavior of the wall.

Table 5-1. Energy input-output relationship between the building and its luminous environment is a function of (1) location and shape of building with reference to path of sun, (2) area, geometry, and exposure of external surfaces of building, (3) physical characteristics of these surfaces — opaque, transparent, or selective filtration.

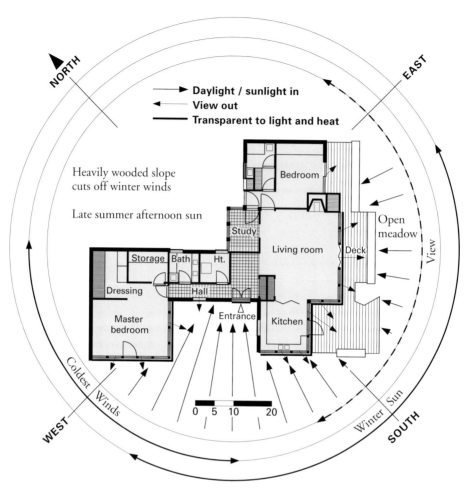

Daylight / sunlight in
View out
Transparent to light and heat

Figure 5–8 / Residence, Stony Point, New York. James Marston Fitch, architect, built in 1962. This house is oriented to take advantage of a sweeping east-to-south view. It is partially submerged in the hillside along the west-to-north perimeter to minimize impact of summer afternoon sun and prevailing southwest-to-northwest winter winds. Eighty-eight percent of all glass faces southeast, south, or southwest. Remainder of perimeter wall is designed to minimize transmission of light and heat; it is opaque and insulated.

factors (function, budget, etc.) establish the parameters of size, shape, and volume. Exogenous factors (shape, size and topography of the site, means of access, zoning ordinances, etc.) act to mold these parameters to the exigencies of the site. Each of these affect the manner in which incident daylight falls upon the various surfaces of the structure. However, except in those special building types in which good daylighting is an explicit requirement of the program, all of the above factors are too often decided before it is determined what proportion of this incident daylight should be permitted to penetrate the building (Fig. 5–8).

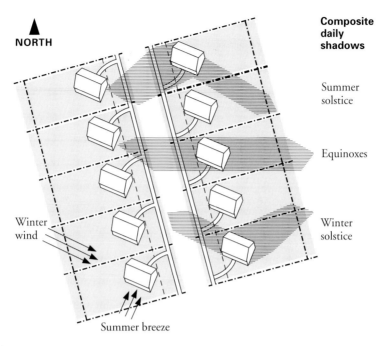

Figure 5 – 9 / Even conventional land-platting of freestanding houses on small lots can be easily manipulated so that all units get maximum exposure to sun around the year. Redrawn hypothetical study by Henry Wright for project at 40 degrees north latitude (e.g., New York, New York). Shadows shown are for shortly after sunrise and before sunset.

Some building types (theaters, department stores) have little or no need for daylight; in others (factories, warehouses) daylighting is desirable though not mandatory; in still others (office buildings, dwellings, schools) good daylighting is critically important, if only because the wall that admits light also permits outlook and view. The question of whether to admit or exclude daylight is, as we have seen, a modern paradox; it could not have arisen until reliable artificial light sources were available. Now that the alternative does exist, the problem of integrating the two sources of light into a single effective system of luminous control has become extremely complex. Failure is still more common than success; however, great advances have taken place over the past two decades. Many excellent examples of relatively new daylit buildings now exist that successfully integrate artificial lighting.

Because daylight fluctuates continuously across time in intensity, color, and direction, its precise control in even simple buildings involves the balancing of many variables — computations that, though simple in themselves, are often so numerous that computer analysis is required for any really definitive examination of alternative solutions. Perhaps because of this, and despite current energy codes and standards, all too many American architects tend to handle the problem summarily, shifting between two extremes: either to make the building windowless because daylighting is more trouble than it's worth, or

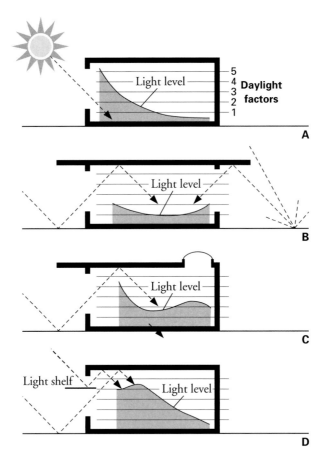

Figure 5 – 10 / Four daylighting situations: (A) A window on one wall creates strong light at one side of the room, dim light at the other. (B) Windows on opposite walls create relatively uniform light levels. (C) A skylight can raise the light level in an otherwise dim area. (D) A light shelf (a horizontal plane with a bright or reflective surface) bounces light further into a room.[8]

to sheathe the entire building in glass and leave it up to the air-conditioning engineer and interior designer to solve the problem of thermal and luminous overloads with their compressors and fans, curtains and blinds.

Because the architectural manipulation of daylight always has two components, thermal and luminous, the thermal controls discussed in chapter 3 have a certain relevance here. As in the case of thermal control, so in that of the luminous: many problems can be resolved if daylighting becomes an integral part of the design process at the early stages of site selection and development. Thus the sheer deployment of buildings on the landscape can become a tool for giving each building access to its share of sunshine as well as freeing it from the shadows of its neighbors (Fig. 5 – 9). Similarly, at this early formative stage of the design, it is easier to decide which areas require daylight or direct sunlight and to orient them accordingly. In high latitudes, where there is an absolute deficiency of solar heat and light, megastructures for neighborhoods or entire cities are the logical metabolic response to problems of energy conservation. Even here, height and density can be manipulated to give each unit its full share of winter sun as studied initially by Ralph Knowles, architect (Fig. 3−11).

The building that is properly oriented to exploit the warmth of winter sunshine is also brightly illuminated — but visual comfort is not thereby automatically guaranteed. Problems of glare, both within the room and in the landscape beyond the glass, can, under certain circumstances, become quite serious. In midwinter, one looks through south-facing glass into a low sun — an optical situation further exacerbated by snow cover. (The most comfortable view is one lighted from behind the spectator.) Thus, proposals to maximize solar heat gain also must be analyzed for their optical performance. This undoubtedly requires a further refinement of the wall membranes — more sophisticated glasses, movable blinds or curtains, etc. — and result in a more complex interface. One architectural device that has become quite popular is the light shelf, which bounces direct-beam daylight first to the ceiling; the light then diffuses deep into the occupied space. This has led to a relatively new architectural expression: low-vision glass with high glazing above to facilitate daylight entry (Fig. 5−10). Light shelves work best on the south sides of buildings in the northern hemisphere, where they also can be used as shading devices for the vision glass below (in the summer when sun angles are high).

In hot climates, where the comfort problem is one of protection against excessive insolation (Yuma, Key West, Cairo), the parameters for thermal and visual comfort coincide. There, a building that has most of its openings away from the moving sun has windows looking out upon a view lighted from behind the viewer. At the same time, a building that presents a thermally opaque wall to the tropical sun yields important economies in both capital and operating costs of cooling.

Because the sun angle changes constantly with hour and season, however, such measures can be only partially successful.[9] Theoretically, if a building were placed on a turntable and its rotation synchronized with that of the sun, luminous and thermal control would be much more precise, as azimuthal angles of incidence could be held constant. However, technological advances (particularly in glazing and lighting), when combined with careful site planning and passive solar design techniques, have obviated the need for considering such a radical approach. A simpler variant of this theoretical approach, and one presumably applicable to much larger buildings, is a tracked solar screen that rotates around the building at a rate synchronized with the sun. In climates of great seasonal or diurnal variation (e.g., New Mexico, southern Tunisia) such solar screens might be set to act as windbreaks during cold nights or cold seasons.

The most familiar form of sun shield, historically, is the *brise-soleil,* either fixed or rotating around a vertical or horizontal axis. Employing the same principle as the Venetian blind, but located outside the building wall and using larger and more stable vanes,

Figure 5–11 / Interior light shelves mounted high on the window area of the offices of the Sacramento Municipal Utility District (SMUD) in Sacramento, California. Top: Shelves are mounted in such a manner that a fire would melt the wire supports and allow for full functioning of the sprinkler system. Bottom: The light shelves bounce natural daylight further into the office space, creating more balanced light levels.

such sunscreens can be either manually or electronically controlled (Fig. 5–12). They can afford a precise means of luminous and thermal control. However, as they are exposed to the weather, they must be designed to avoid the potential problems of corrosion and freeze-up.

In certain highly specialized situations, where absolute control of all environmental factors within very narrow tolerances is mandatory, unique solutions may well be required. One of the world's largest buildings, the vehicle assembly building at the Kennedy Space Center, is the most dramatic example of this sealed container approach. Here, the very macroenvironmental factors that make for good rocketry (year-round warmth, preponderantly sunny skies) also make for difficulties in rocket assembly (intense insolation, high humidities, hurricane danger). The problem is further complicated by internal requirements for a mesoenvironment of extraordinary refinement, permitting precise manipulation of luminous, thermal, atmospheric, and biological factors. Under such circumstances, environmental discontinuities across the interface are necessarily severe and a fully enclosable vessel is the best response.

By any conventional standard, such a design program is highly uneconomical. For example, the complete exclusion of daylight from any workspace requiring high levels of illumination means its replacement by expensive lighting systems. As even relatively

Photo courtesy of Andrew Lautman

Figure 5–12 / National Education Association Headquarters, Washington, D.C. Geier Brown Renfrow, architects, completed 1990. Built in many stages, the building was completely renovated in the late 1980s when the exterior courtyard was enclosed by a sawtooth skylight. Mounted on the outside of the south-facing portions of glazing are operable louvers that close at night during the winter. During the day they are positioned to bounce daylight and prevent direct glare. Note the sunlight bouncing off the solid north wall, which performs like a large vertical light shelf.

efficient lamps are still highly inefficient in converting electrical energy into visible light, the lighting fixtures alone can come to account for a significant portion of a space's total cooling load. The vehicle assembly building is therefore a highly atypical situation.

Much more usual is the situation in which free access to daylight and view are desirable but protection against direct sunlight is required (i.e., a building wall that yields optimal transparency from the inside outward but limited or controlled transparency from the outside in).

This kind of shading can be accomplished by planar extensions of the wall surface itself—extensions whose geometry is calculated to prevent direct sunlight from impinging upon transparent wall surfaces. Modern architecture abounds in examples of this type of surface response to insolation. However, as most of them are designed on an intuitive basis—if for no other reason than that the variable conditions created by the moving sun outrun ordinary calculations—they are often more photogenic than practical.

A pioneering attempt to establish rational parameters for this problem of surface response to environmental forces is the research of Ralph Knowles.[10] Using computerized analysis techniques, Knowles demonstrated that "the mathematical derivation of appropriate surface response to selected environmental forces" is entirely practical (Fig. 3–11). In fact, he moved on to a significant extension of this same concept—namely, that the building form as well as the building surface can be allowed to "derive as a response to the combined dictates of all environmental forces—light, heat, gravity, air and sound." And, because the individual building has little or no control over these factors beyond its lot lines, he showed the need for extending the same criteria to the design of larger spatial increments—neighborhoods, districts, even whole cities.[11]

There are, of course, many ways in which light can be controlled with transparent (as opposed to Knowles's opaque) walling materials. Many types of glass and plastic can be employed to refract, focus, filter, and polarize light by modifying either the molecular structure or the physical shape of the substance. There are many special cases in architecture where such materials prove extremely useful. One form of optical manipulation of daylight is the so-called prismatic glass block. Manufactured in a range of prismatic types, these blocks are used to refract incident daylight and deliver it to any desired area of the room. Such applications are helpful in situations in which daylight is important to the visual task but outlook and direct sunlight either unnecessary or undesirable (e.g., color matching). Prismatic blocks are also useful in galleries and museums for controlled illumination of works of art, and in churches, where the architect might wish to focus a beam of sunlight on a spot that might not otherwise get it—the so-called "finger of God" effect of which baroque architects were the masters.

Ordinary sheet or plate glass can be shaped or molded to achieve certain optical effects. In situations where it is desirable to preserve a panoramic view at night, like the famous Top of the Mark restaurant in San Francisco, the glass can be angled in the vertical plane so as to minimize disturbing reflections of the room itself. A variant of this is the so-called invisible shop window; here, where the problem is to preserve transparency from the outdoors inward, the glass is curved so as to pick up no reflections from the much higher illumination levels of the streetscape. All such installations assume a single, relatively fixed observation point — that of a seated diner or a standing window-shopper.

As against a purely optical manipulation of daylight, however, quite another technique of light control has been opened up by the wide range of tinted, reflective, and spectrally selective glass types now available. In buildings glazed with these glasses, the surface response is photophysical, a function of the molecular structure of the glass rather than its geometric configuration. Such glasses have a wide range of photophysical properties that yield, singly or in combination, almost any degree of transparency for both the visible and thermal portions of the solar wave band. They afford the architect the means of filtering the daylight entering buildings to a degree that would have been impossible even a few decades ago. As we have seen, such glasses are already extremely important in very cold climates, making possible visual transparency *and* thermal opacity in a single membrane. They have a comparable significance in purely visual terms, as some of them can be used to filter the visible wave band alone, reducing the amount of visible light that enters the building as desired. Because none of these latter glasses are water clear, they modify the color as well as the intensity of transmitted light (Fig. 5–13).

The glazing choices now available to architects are many, and allow for the selection of glass types with varying properties on the different building façades. In a display eerily similar to Fig. 5–13, a wide variety of alternative glazings are available for inspection at the Pacific Gas and Electric Energy Center in downtown San Francisco. Architects can view their visual qualities, evaluate their thermal and luminous characteristics, and even take meter readings on both sides of the glass to better understand their performance.

One type of glass still commonly used to limit heat gain acts as a one-way mirror — that is, it is completely opaque when seen from the outside yet is transparent and colorless when viewed from the inside. This paradoxical effect, true only for the daytime, responds to those cases in which privacy and outlook are simultaneously desirable. It is achieved by a vacuum deposit of a very thin, evenly distributed metallic coating. (In this connection, it must be observed that most glass curtain walls act as mirrors under normal daytime conditions, as outdoor light levels are normally much higher than interior ones. Thus many buildings that aspire to easy visual access are, in reality, as opaque as though they were sheathed in polished granite!) The one-way mirror glass eliminates need for daytime use of curtains or shades, and it is highly efficient in reflecting radiant heat as well. However, when one views the outdoors through reflective or heavily tinted glass the view is muddied and dispiriting.

With today's technology, glass can be selected to satisfy almost any set of performance criteria. To minimize heat loss, double glazings with low-emissivity coatings are now readily available that perform about as well as triple-glazing. Even better insulating windows are available that perform almost like walls (see chapter 3). These windows can also

Figure 5 – 13 / Pioneering field comparison of light-filtering glasses developed by James Marston Fitch nearly thirty years ago for *Scientific American* magazine, looking towards the former Pan Am Building in New York City. Filtration of natural daylight, by admission or exclusion of ultraviolet, visible, and/or infrared wave bands, is now feasible. Shown here are four types of glass specially designed for filtration of the visible band. Top left is normal plate, almost water clear and almost 90 percent transparent. Bronze-tinted glass (upper right) transmits 51 percent of visible wave band, gray (lower left) admits 42 percent, and blue-green (lower right) 75 percent. The optical differences of the four membranes are somewhat exaggerated by black and white photography.

Figure 5–14 / John Hancock Tower, Boston, Massachusetts. I.M. Pei & Partners, architect, completed 1973. Left: Glazed, colored, and detailed to literally blend into a clear blue sky, the Hancock Tower is an example of a building using reflective glass for cooling load avoidance. Right: In this urban case, however, the term *cooling load transference* might be more appropriate, considering that the reflected light and heat now fall on the north-facing wall of neighboring buildings to the south.

come with spectrally selected tints and coatings to either welcome in or reflect away various portions of the solar spectrum. Selection of the right glazing for a particular building requires a balanced consideration of performance (i.e., thermal, luminous, and structural) along with desired appearance and initial cost.

Several types of so-called smart glazing that are emerging into the marketplace may soon enjoy increased use. They offer a whole new level of control for the designed luminous environment. *Photochromic* glass, as the name implies, has the paradoxical ability to react reversibly to the ultraviolet rays in sunlight. Because of its complex molecular behavior, it changes physically, becoming darker as more ultraviolet light falls upon it. Photochromic glass is fatigue-resistant, which means its reversibility does not diminish with time, and both the intensity of response and time lag of recovery can be controlled within narrow limits. This type of glass should prove valuable for such spaces as class-

Figure 5–15 / Buildings fenestrated with reflective glass exhibit an interesting property. Top: During the day they reveal little about their interiors when viewed from the outside. Bottom: As night begins to arrive, however, and outdoor illumination levels fall below indoor foot-candle levels, the skin of the building reverses its performance. Now from the outside one can see the interior arrangement and the work going on. Workers inside find themselves in a mirrored box, unable to see out as they could during the day.

rooms, libraries, and museums, where a stable mix of artificial and natural light is desirable but where the bother of either manually or electronically operated shades and blinds makes the mix impossible to maintain.

Changing light level is not the only activator of the smart glazings under development. Changes in temperature can change the transparency of *thermochromic* glazings. These materials, which after many years are still in the development phase,[12] are gels that switch from clear when cold to a more diffuse and reflective state when they warm to a preset temperature. Such properties may be of use in reducing solar heat gains for skylights and other glazed areas (e.g., atriums). They would not, however, be useful as vision glass as optical clarity is lost. These glasses might also be useful in passive solar-heated spaces to prevent overheating. Affecting the gel temperature are the indoor and outdoor temperatures and the solar radiation incident upon it. Such complex and changing forces may limit the applications for thermochromic glazing.

More controllable, and thus perhaps more promising, are *electrochromic* glazings now being researched, tested, and demonstrated in a number of buildings in Japan. These glasses use a low-voltage electrical charge (only 1 to 2 volts) to radically change the light transparency from quite clear (perhaps 70 percent) to quite obscure (only about 10 percent transparent) over the course of a few minutes. Such glazings could allow architects to more aggressively daylight buildings under less than optimum sky conditions if they were afforded the ability to switch off much of the glazing when daylight is abundant. The design possibilities inherent in obtaining high-quality glare-free daylit environments through use of this new glazing material are majestic.

Glazing technology has evolved mightily over the past twenty-five years. As with so many issues involving available technology, however, the architect must use considered restraint in the selection process. The primary purpose of windows, to maintain a connection with the outdoors, should not be lost in the excitement and hype of new technology. The use of advanced window technologies that interfere with fundamental human needs should be viewed with distrust.

The complex structure and optical behavior of multilayer polarizers were first described by H. R. Blackwell almost thirty-five years ago but have yet to be widely exploited.[13] The visual benefits of polarized light lie in two related areas: increased ease of seeing and economy of light required. In the natural world, surfaces are concealed behind a light veil of reflected light—a veil that tends to blur the true colors and textures of the surface. Vertically plane-polarized light, on the other hand, is absorbed by the surface and then reemitted. This is the phenomenon that permits us to see behind the light veil and perceive the true qualities of the surface with greater ease and more accuracy. This is, of course, the principle of polarized sunglasses; but these materials were not applicable to architectural illumination for several reasons: they are not equally effective from all points of the room, they absorb over 50 percent of the light, and they are unpleasantly tinted. Moreover, they are transparent and thus could not conceal the bare lamps behind them. Polarizers overcome these objections. Because they are not weatherproof, they could be used only internally and, ordinarily, in conjunction with ceiling fixtures. According to Blackwell,

[V]ertically plane-polarized light produces a fundamental improvement in the ease of seeing, comfort and pleasantness of the visual environment, with no appreciable loss in luminous efficiency. . . . No other lighting material produces a comparable increase in [visual] task detail, apparent saturation and textural richness for all materials, surfaces and viewing angles.[14]

An understanding of the above theories, techniques, and materials is essential to the correct manipulation of the luminous environment, and the scientific manipulation of daylight is an integral part of the illumination of most building types. No matter how comprehensively daylight is handled, it cannot alone meet modern requirements, either optically or temporally. The development of a satisfactory synthetic mesoenvironment is impossible without exploiting artificial light sources as well. The task of the architect is to establish a mix of the two sources, designed for specific visual tasks, with a criterion of stability in quality, space, and time.

The perfection of the dynamo in 1877 made possible the large-scale production and distribution of electricity; since then, the electric lamp has supplanted all other types of light sources. The architectural consequences of this switch from the combustion of organic materials (rush, wood, candle, oil, gas) to electrical resistance and gaseous excitation are literally incalculable. Perhaps the most obvious expression of this shift is, paradoxically, the diminishing importance of the light source itself. In historic architecture, artificial illumination was always expensive. This fact was celebrated by making the brazier, lamp, torchère, candelabra, and chandelier more important, esthetically, than the flame itself. Today many spaces are lit by ceiling-mounted fixtures that seek to go unnoticed (e.g., recessed reflectors, cove lighting). Increasingly, however, many spaces (in particular those with many computer screens) are illuminated by a task/ambient lighting scheme that provides a rather low general light level throughout and allows users to direct additional light onto the task at hand when needed.

The range and flexibility of modern sources of light make possible a whole new order of luminous control in architecture. The components can be categorized thus:

1. *type of lamp source:* arc, incandescent, fluorescent, high-intensity discharge
2. *type of luminaire/fixture:* recessed, downlight, spot, flood, pendant, track light, sconce, wall washer, freestanding
3. *type of optical accessory:* lens, diffuser, color filter, reflector, louver, baffle, egg crate, polarizer
4. *type of light source:* point, linear, planar
5. *type of light distribution:* direct, indirect, focused, general/diffuse, or direct/indirect

Dozens of manufacturers of lamps, luminaires, and controls now produce thousands of variants and combinations for commercial, industrial, scientific, and specialized uses (e.g., for hazardous and wet locations). In ordinary architectural applications, however, a comparatively limited number of lamps are used in several basic types of installations. Because these lamps vary widely in their spectra, efficiencies, and performance characteristics, some of their key architectural implications merit a brief description here.

Arcs: In these, the earliest of all electric lamps, the actual light source is the luminous bridge formed when an electric current jumps the gap between two electrodes. Their principal current applications are in movie and television studios and in searchlights, for military or maritime applications, as the light source is brilliant but very hot and inflexible. These lamps offer a point source highly suitable for focusing by reflectors and lenses (e.g., multimillion-candlepower searchlights).

Incandescents: Second oldest of the lamps, these are still the most widely used. Although their efficiency has been increased by upward of 100 percent in recent decades, they have the lowest lumen per watt (LPW) rating — less than 25. Here the light source is passed through a coiled tungsten filament in a sealed glass bulb. The principal shortcomings of incandescents lie in the low percentage of visible light produced (10 percent) and their high infrared output, which produces a lot of heat. The tungsten-halogen type of incandescent lamp uses halogens to produce a whiter light, more lumens per watt, and increased longevity. Incandescent lamps can be easily dimmed and do not require any special equipment such as a ballast to modify the characteristics of the power supply.

Fluorescent lamps: When the original edition of this book was published, fluorescent lamps were relatively new, having been introduced about a decade before at the 1939 New York World's Fair. Today fluorescent lamps are the workhorse of American industry, with some 550 million bulbs produced each year.[15] The ordinary incandescent lamp is impossible to touch while lit, whereas lit fluorescent lamps are just slightly warm to the touch. The second most common light source, their efficacy ranges from 80 to 110 LPW. They are easily distinguished by their tubular, circular, or U-bent shape 5/12 (T5), 8/12 (T8), 10/12 (T10), or 12/12 (T12) inches in diameter. Other advantages of today's lamps include their increasingly wide color range, including a close approximation of daylight. In unmodified form, the fluorescent lamp is, of course, a linear light source, but with appropriate reflectors and diffusing materials it can be made to approach a truly planar form.

The use of T8 lamps with high-frequency electronic ballasts has become the norm in 2×4 ceiling lighting and has resulted in energy savings of 30 percent or more compared to standard 40-watt lamps that by law are no longer manufactured. T8 lamps can also be dimmed easily with dimmable ballasts and are well suited for use in daylit buildings.

Alto T8 and T12 fluorescent lamps, manufactured by Phillips, have less than 11 mg of mercury per lamp — about half the industry average. These lamps contain such a small amount of mercury that they are considered acceptable for normal disposal in a landfill under Environmental Protection Agency (EPA) regulations. In an interesting move meant to broaden awareness of the product, Phillips offered (on June 19, 1997) to share the technology with its competitors.[16]

Figure 5–16 / Lighting fixtures with compact fluorescent lamps in the Library at the College of Staten Island, New York. Perry Dean Rogers, architects, completed 1993. Until quite recently, most architects insisted on using incandescent lamps in such fixtures for their improved color rendition.

Compact fluorescent lamps (CFLs): These lamps were specifically developed as substitutes for incandescent lamps and now are available in a dimmable 4-pin type. They are either integral (lamp and ballast), modular (lamp and adapter including ballast), or dedicated (hard-wired) so that they can be replaced only by other CFLs. CFLs last about 10,000 hours (10 times the life of incandescent lamps) and are generally about 4 times as efficient as typical incandescents. This means that a 60-watt incandescent can be replaced by a 13-watt CFL, assuming proper fixture optics. Their color and ability to be dimmed have now extended their use to many architectural applications until quite recently reserved for incandescent illumination. Long life is another distinct advantage of CFLs, especially in hard-to-maintain fixtures such as ceiling lights in a tall lobby.

High-intensity discharge (HID) lamps: This complex and growing family continues to be of increasing significance to architectural illumination. Each type is based on passing an electrical current through certain gases to excite them into emitting radiant energy, whose spectrum is a function of the gas employed. The family of HID sources have relatively high efficiencies and include mercury vapor (45 to 63 LPW), metal halide (about 90 LPW), high-pressure sodium (about 125 LPW), and low-pressure sodium (up to 200 LPW). HID sources produce full light output after the arc tube reaches its operating pressure (typically one to seven minutes). With the exception of metal halide lamps, most HID lamps are used outdoors for street, parking lot, and security lighting because of their poor color rendition.

Neon vapor lamps: These lamps operate on the same luminous vapor principle: variations in the gases and in the color of glass tubing yield a fairly wide range of colors. They are unsuited to general illumination, however, because of low efficiency, low intensities, and dangerously high voltages. Their architectural use is thus largely confined to outdoor signs and decorative lighting.

Sulfur lamps: This lamp is still under development and testing. The sulfur lamp is an electrodeless, high-brightness source potentially supplying over 400,000 lumens with stable color. The efficacy is similar to that of metal halide, but with a lamp size that is much smaller for similar luminous output. Its compact shape makes it ideal for precision optics. The low level of UV radiation emitted from the sulfur lamp may make it ideal for sensitive applications such as in health facilities, laboratories, and museums.

Induction lamps: This new type of lamp is a combination of electromagnetic, induction, and gas discharge lighting. It has a very long life of 60,000 hours and high LPW. It is ideal for tunnel and/or bridge lighting and hard-to-reach fixtures.

Together with appropriate fixtures, accessories, and electronic controls, these lamps offer the means for an unprecedented manipulation of the luminous environment. How this remarkable equipment is employed in a given situation depends upon what sort of environment is required and how precisely it can be described or specified. Here the architect is projected into the field of psychophysics, confronting a bewildering range of factors objective and subjective, physical and emotional. If the designed mesoenvironment is regarded as a prosthetic device and translates the eye's requirements into environmental specifications, some generalizations are possible. The first is that, within broad limits, the more light on the visual task, the easier vision becomes if there is no glare. The easier vision becomes, the less is the stress on the organism as a whole. Higher levels of illumination are a function of increased lumens from the source and increased reflectance values of all the room surfaces.

The second "law" of illumination is that the brightnesses of all areas in the room should be in balance, with no great contrasts between adjacent surfaces. For specific visual tasks, the brightness ratio between the task and its surrounding visual field should be low—not under 3:1 and not above 1:10. This topic is, however, currently under investigation (see IESNA reports RP24 and RP1). The third principle is to avoid direct and reflected glare (Blackwell's light veil on illuminated surfaces).

The recommended levels of illumination for different visual tasks rose steadily during the decades prior to the energy crisis of 1973. Since then, however, recommended illumination levels have been lowered slightly and more attention given to balancing the issues of lighting quantity and quality. Indoor tasks that in preindustrial times might have been carried out at 10-15 fc are now often recommended by IESNA for a range of 100–150–200 fc. Some tasks requiring a high degree of visual acuity (e.g., autopsies, microsurgery) may require as much as 2,500 fc. Although the relative efficiency of all light sources has been greatly increased in recent years, the ratio of visible light to infrared is relatively low even in the best of them. As a result, waste heat is a byproduct of all artificial illumination. If high illumination levels are required, this heat becomes an important factor from the standpoint of both comfort and economy. Thus, for a space with 100 fc illumination, the waste heat can account for approximately 25 to 40 percent of the summer cooling load depending upon occupancy density, equipment power density, and fenestration. When waste heat reaches such proportions, it becomes a major factor in summer cooling. By the same token, during the heating season the waste heat from lights, people, and equipment often provides much of the heat needed when a commercial building is occupied.

In response to the energy crisis of 1973, the lighting industry developed and introduced a variety of important control features. If used prudently, these controls can eliminate waste without adversely affecting luminous performance in any way. After all, if a space is not being used at all, why use energy to light it? One such development is the occupancy sensor, which turns lights off in a room (e.g., office, conference room, or classroom) if human heat and/or movement is not detected.

Figure 5–17 / The corridor of this building is daylit by the large skylight area. However, electricity is not being saved because the corridor lighting fixtures are still on. Note the white line in the skylight; this is the reflection of the strip fluorescent fixtures mounted at the top of the wall below. It appears that we have become so reliant on artificial lighting that we fail to trust daylight even when the building is designed for it.

Daylight detection and control of artificial lighting are other areas in which technology has improved tremendously, offering significant energy and environmental benefits without sacrificing luminous quality. If, for example, the task at hand requires 100 foot-candles, the worker is generally indifferent as to whether this level of illumination is provided by overhead lights or daylight. If 30, 50, 70, or 90 foot-candles of daylight are already arriving on the task, a sensor and control can dim the lights so they only make up the difference. Such is the function of continuous dimming control, now widely and reliably used for building areas benefiting from abundant daylight.

Daylighting is still, however, misunderstood by many who equate use of daylight with greatly enlarged glass areas. This misconception can lead to ill-considered architectural design decisions resulting in glare as well as greatly increased mechanical cooling requirements (Fig. 5 – 18). Proper daylighting of buildings involves intelligent selection and placement of glass along with sun control that bounces and diffuses the light into the building. Such is the task of the architect attempting to make proper use of daylight. The rewards are many, including a less artificial environment for the users and the opportunity to reduce the use (and cost) of energy.

Figure 5 – 18 / Abundant amounts of daylight and direct radiation enter through the over-glazed skylight in this atrium. In a misguided attempt to allow for daylight entry into buildings, many architects include much too much glass area, causing over-heating and increasing the required capacity of mechanical cooling systems.

Figure 5–19 / United Airlines, Terminal 1, O'Hare International Airport, Chicago, Illinois. Murphy/Jahn, architects, completed 1988. Here daylight is used judiciously to enliven heavily traveled circulation spaces. South-facing glazing is minimized.

The illumination requirements of many discrete visual tasks (precision machine work, surgery, drafting) can be defined with some degree of precision. The effectiveness of the system can be measured in terms of safety, productivity, and quality of workmanship. Such was the case for the energy and lighting retrofit of the Reno, Nevada, main post office in 1986, where the productivity of sorting machine operators is routinely tabulated (Fig. 5–20). As part of the retrofit, the building was to have its ceiling height lowered and new lighting installed. These changes were first made in one of the two mail sorting machine areas. The graph shows the number of pieces of mail sorted per hour in the 24 weeks before the retrofit and for more than a year after, in this area. In the first 20 weeks after the retrofit, productivity increased by more than 8 percent. No improvement was recorded in the area where the retrofit had not yet taken place. A year later, productivity stabilized at an increase of about 6 percent. Combined, the energy and maintenance sav-

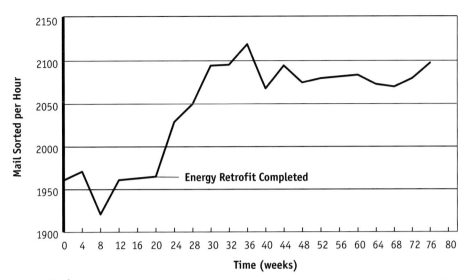

Figure 5–20 / The behavioral consequences of an improved luminous environment have been documented in numerous studies, most convincingly when the output of the particular type of work is easily measured. For example, the number of pieces of mail sorted per hour increased significantly after a lighting retrofit at the main post office in Reno, Nevada. With the new lighting design, sorting errors dropped to 0.1 percent, the lowest rate in the western region.

ings for the whole building retrofit were estimated at about $50,000 a year, but the gain in productivity was closer to $400,000 to $500,000.

But life—and, hence, architecture—is full of many other visual tasks that are subject to no such precise delineation. The illumination of retail stores and showrooms, for example, involves such subtleties as dramatizing the textures and colors of the merchandise. (Jewelry and automobiles need point sources for shine and glitter; furs and velvets show up best under floods at acute angles.) Restaurants, bars, and cafés have their own luminous criteria,* art galleries and museums have entirely different ones. Theaters and churches share special luminous requirements. The illumination of exhibition halls and botanical gardens poses other sets of problems, including the manipulation of both luminous and pigmental color. This by no means exhausts the list of architectural situations in which sheer visual pleasure may well be the end in view. In such cases, simple functional criteria may be difficult to delineate. This is probably why some of our most distinguished illuminating engineers and color specialists find it so difficult to describe or objectify the principles they follow in achieving their most striking effects. It may well be that, beyond some limit of rational analysis, intuition necessarily takes over in the cre-

---

* For some reason it is currently assumed that the proper mood lighting for such establishments involves a very low light level and the color pink. The first makes it difficult to see one's companions and the second has an unfortunate effect on the appearance of most foods. If to these we add the high noise levels common to such places, the result is often opposite to the declared aim—that of facilitating interpersonal relationships.

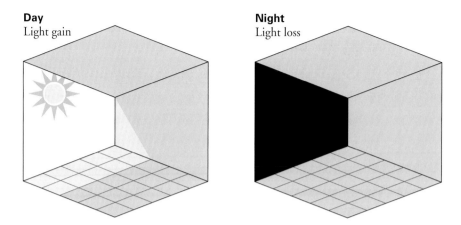

Day
Light gain

Night
Light loss

Figure 5–21 / That the optical behavior of glass is not fully understood is obvious in much current architecture. Interiors are conceived of in daylight conditions—that is, with the window glass as a source of light. But unless covered with a reflective membrane, such glass after dark becomes a light drain, destroying the luminous equilibrium of the room.

ation of these effects, just as it does in the great painter's use of pigments. But this should not become—as too often it does become—the excuse for abandoning all orderly research in this important aspect of architecture. For no matter how subtle the problems or complex the solutions, the architect must understand how such effects are achieved—if only in order to know how to replicate (or avoid) them in subsequent work.

A completely lightless room is something of a contradiction in terms (tombs and photo darkrooms are among the few exceptions). All designed spaces are conceived of in visual terms. Many of the architect's decisions as to interior proportions, colors, and textures actually deal with matters of surface response to light. They are made with an eye to how it all will look. Such a conceptual approach subsumes a stable luminous state as desirable—that is, that the room read the same way day and night, winter and summer.

In any windowless enclosure this is a simple matter, but in any room in which glass plays an important role the situation is entirely altered. Such transparent membranes are conceived of as (1) being a source of light, and (2) affording visual access to an illuminated out-of-doors. But with nightfall, both of these conditions change (Fig. 5–21). Surfaces that were a source of light become open sluiceways for its escape. The darkened outdoors is replaced by a dimly mirrored image of the room.* Historic architecture had no real difficulty with this paradox. Although daylighting was very important, the high cost of glass and of heating tended to keep windows relatively small and/or few in number. Because they were always covered at night with curtains or shutters whose reflectance

* The reflected image of a lighted room often seems so bright to the eye that it leads many designers to act as though the luminous equilibrium is not disturbed. Actually, the image is produced by about 7 percent of the incident light being reflected back into the room; the remaining 93 percent escapes to the out-of-doors. As a result, the room no longer behaves luminously in the way the architect conceived it.

value approached that of the walls, they did not seriously affect the luminous response of the walls.

But in modern architecture, with its wide use of glass walls and wide misconceptions of their optical behavior, the problem of nocturnal disequilibrium reaches serious dimensions. And not only visually: when people complain of uncurtained glass as feeling cold, they are accurately describing a combination of thermal and optical stress (Fig. 5–22). In such cases the interiors can only be restored to their daytime condition by one of two measures: by covering the glass with a reflective membrane—shade, shutter, blind (Fig. 5–23), or by lighting the outside of the building to the same level of illumination as the room itself. Both measures are technically quite feasible, though for obvious reasons the first is apt to be the simplest and least costly.

Color is another aspect of contemporary architects' confrontation with psychophysics; they seem to find it, if anything, even more confusing than light *qua* light. Part of their diffidence has historical origins. The stylistic revolution that, in the first third of this century, overthrew the dominant pseudohistorical styles, discarded their coloration as well.

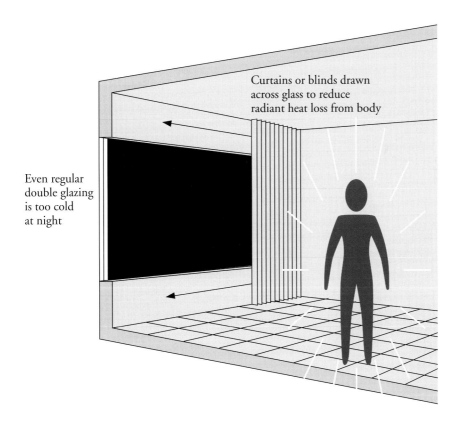

Figure 5–22 / The subjective verdict that uncurtained glass walls make a room cold after dark may derive from purely optical sensory input, but it often has a thermal component, as the body loses heat by radiation to all surfaces colder than itself.

Figure 5–23 / House at Stony Point, New York. James Marston Fitch, architect, built in 1962. Two views of living room, photographed under identical conditions of illumination. (All light sources are normal for the room, no auxiliary lights being used for photography.) Top: Note the deadening effect of uncurtained glass. The camera reveals that reflections that might seem important to the eye contribute little or nothing to maintenance of daytime light levels. Bottom: When shades are lowered, the glass wall becomes again a source of light, even if reflected, and the room is returned to its daytime "shape." The painted landscape on shades is an abstract version of the actual view.

Purity of form was to be matched by purity of color; banishment of ornament was to be paralleled by banishment of pattern. As a consequence, much of today's architecture is almost without precedent in its monochromism, and even when color is employed, it tends to be either timid or inexpert. This situation is paradoxical, for modern technology affords the designer absolutely unparalleled resources in both colored light sources and colored surfacing materials. Such developments as polarized light, black light, and fluorescent and luminescent paints and dyes offer the designer a palette of saturated colors whose range and intensity was undreamed of until modern times. Surfacing materials of every imaginable hue, texture, and pattern are available, but so far the architect has ventured to employ them extensively only in some of the big international expositions, where current standards of good taste tend to be relaxed.

The architect's hesitation to employ color more widely also stems from a justified uncertainty as to the experiential consequences of its use. Here the dilemma is partly cultural, partly psychophysiological. The physical phenomena in both pigmental and luminous color may be well understood and the conundrum of the eye's capacity to perceive them now well explored. The general laws that cover the individual's response to color are much more difficult to formulate. That different colors have different effects on different people is axiomatic. That one can generalize at all about group preferences—as consumer goods interests often do quite successfully—indicates the cultural factors involved. There is a large and growing literature on the subjective aspects of color. We are told that red is exciting, purple is stately or mournful, yellow is joyful, green is calming, etc. But these are all affective value judgments whose direct applicability to architecture seems oddly inconclusive and nonspecific.

Experimental psychologists, by observing behavioral response to luminous stimuli, are exploring such fields as the therapeutic use of color in the treatment of the mentally ill. An early researcher, Robert M. Gerard, working with normal adults, once found that submersion in red light produced more activity and in blue light less activity than normal. He found that red could lead to an increase in blood pressure, respiration, and frequency of eye blink; blue had the reverse effect. On the basis of his experiments, he proposed two laws of color dynamics: within the visible range, psychophysiological activation tends to (a) increase with wavelength and (b) increase with stimulus intensity. Gerard advanced the following general propositions:

1. The response to color is differential—that is, different colors arouse different feelings and emotions and activate the organism to a different degree.
2. The differential response to color is a response of the whole organism, involving correlated changes in autonomic functions, muscular tension, brain activity, and affective-ideational responses.
3. The differential response to color is lawful and predictable.
   a. It is related to specific characteristics of the stimulus, both physical (wavelength, intensity, number of quanta, and energy per quantum) and psychological (hue, saturation, and brightness).

b. It transcends individual differences—that is, it is shared to a significant extent by members of the same culture.

c. Individual differences in psychophysiological reactivity to specific colors can be accounted for on the basis of previous learning experience, as reflected in color preferences and color associations, and characteristics of the organism, including personality variables such as manifest anxiety level.[17]

All of this suggests that problems of architectural color, complex though they be, are susceptible to a far more systematic exploration than architects or illuminating engineers have so far attempted. Our most brilliant colorists operate largely on the basis of a highly developed personal taste. This tends to limit their effectiveness both as paradigm and as teacher, and narrows their influence. As in so many other areas of architecture, color needs to be carefully researched in holistic terms.

Exterior Artificial Illumination

Modern technology has made possible another unprecedented amenity: the nighttime illumination of streets, squares, and gardens. This has become such a basic part of contemporary life that it is no longer possible for us to imagine the crippling effect of nightfall upon preindustrial life. It brought almost to a complete halt the free movement and varied activities that characterized the daytime city. The appearance of electric lighting had two great urbanistic consequences: it doubled the time when the urban outdoors could function as a theater of action, and, esthetically, it made possible a delightful experience that hitherto only potentates like Nero or the Sun King could have afforded (and only then for a night or two)—the purely decorative illumination of the landscape.

This process of external illumination has been carried further in the United States than elsewhere; if not the best lit, American cities are the most lit on earth. They are very beautiful when seen from the air, on a clear night, their structures diagrammed by millions of lamps and signs. On the normal plane of pedestrian movement, however, both beauty and clarity disappear. Street and park lighting is strictly utilitarian, designed for economy and weather- and vandalproofness. The harsh yellow and acid blue-green of sodium and mercury vapor lamps, which looks so lovely from the air, turns out to be unflattering to the passersby and annoying to the permanent residents.

Electric signs confront us with something of the same dilemma. Seen from afar, they are often a beautiful celebration of the city's focal points. Yet, here again, the picture changes at closeup—and usually for the worse. Jostling each other in space and competing in size, color, and movement, the illuminated signs cancel out each other's information-giving function. They become confusing to the passerby, irritating to the resident, and actually hazardous to the motorist.

Yet it is possible to illuminate individual buildings, whole neighborhoods, even entire cities, in ways that better meet the requirements of spectacle and utility, tourist and inhabitant, passerby and tenant. Indeed, we can already glimpse such possibilities in London and Paris, where the monumental districts around Westminster and the Louvre are skillfully lit all summer, and in Washington and Athens, where the Capitol and the Acropolis are most dramatically illuminated. An extension of this technique for purposes of spectacle is the *son-et-lumière* technique employed in French châteaux and gardens with such touristic success.

It must be observed, however, that these examples are all buildings or districts that are either uninhabited or at least not inhabited at night. Theatrical lighting can thus be freely used for maximum impact on the spectators, who view it from established vantage points. The inhabited building confronts the illuminating engineer with a more ticklish problem. Even if building occupants have no objection to the illumination of the exterior of their buildings, their own rights to visual privacy and to outlook are jeopardized. On the other hand, if the landscape is to be illuminated for the occupants' benefit, then passersby may experience visual distress. Of course, in ordinary residential design, only

Figure 5 – 24 / Château de Chambord, France. When externally illuminated for such spectacles as *son et lumière*, uninhabited historic buildings afford an unforgettable experience. Such illuminations are designed to be viewed only from fixed vantage points, however. Exterior illumination of inhabited buildings is more complex.

Figure 5–25 / Farnsworth House, Fox River, Illinois. Ludwig Mies van der Rohe, architect, completed 1950. Top: An optical paradox: the hovering planes of cantilevered terrace and roof made for beautiful photographs, but the heat of Illinois summers made outdoor living desirable while insects made it impossible without insect screening. Bottom: In solving this problem, the owner increased habitability of the house while radically altering its esthetic impact. A subsequent owner of the house removed the screening.

Figure 5–26 / Well-integrated design tools for lighting and daylighting are now available. Shown is an image from the RADIANCE program developed at Lawrence Berkeley National Laboratory. The program can be used to assist in studying lighting and daylighting strategies, exterior horizontal "light shelves," interior shading devices, and alternate interior and furniture layouts.

the garden areas adjacent to the building are lighted; these are normally screened by walls or plantings anyway. But many urban situations demand skill and imagination on the part of the designer if everyone is to be satisfied.

From the foregoing, it is apparent that the illumination of architecture is a complex field of action. American architects have not adequately analyzed the luminous requirements of contemporary life nor mastered the technical means of meeting them. Here, as in so many other areas of the profession, the inadequacy of traditional design methods is apparent, with their heavy reliance upon taste, hunch, and intuition. Much progress has been made over the last twenty-five years in improving our understanding of the experiential relationship between people and their luminous environment, including the use of computerized design tools (Fig. 5–26). Sometimes, however, priorities are confused. Often luminous environments are compromised when energy conservation and operational economics are the focus of attention. Energy conservation decision makers often overlook the obvious: the lights are there for people and their need to function and perform comfortably and productively. While poorly conceived reductions in lighting may cut on the order of ten cents per square foot from a building's annual operating cost, they also may lead to widespread occupant dissatisfaction, which in turn may lead to reduced productivity of employees earning the equivalent of perhaps $500 per square foot. How have the economics been improved?

The lighting industry has developed many fine fixtures, lamps, and controls to handle the breadth of luminous needs. It is the duty of the architect to use them wisely and without needless excess.

Silence – Men at Work

Control of the Sonic Environment

Like the other sensory perceptual systems of the human body, that of hearing occupies its own special habitat in the external world. Like the eye and the nose, the ear scans that habitat across time and space, bringing in important information on events in that world. And submerged, like the eye, in a sea of electromagnetic energy, it perceives only a relatively small portion of the total spectrum of terrestrial sounds (Fig. 6–1). This aural habitat can be quantified and topologically described as having five dimensions: (1) a spectral or "horizontal" dimension of wavelength frequencies, (2) an energy-input or "vertical" dimension of pressure,* (3) a depth or "longitudinal" dimension, as expressed in reverberation period, (4) a dimension across time, and (5) a dimension of direction. Because many sounds can coexist in the same space at the same time, the sonic environment is very rich in aural stimulation; the ear has developed a corresponding capacity to perceive much of this complexity.

But the sonic environment differs in one fundamental respect from all the others so far discussed in this book: in its natural, unpolluted state, it is seldom, if ever, stressful to the organ of perception. The other environments may fluctuate between widely separated extremes of hot and cold, light and dark, windy and still, wet and dry. Unmodulated, these extremes carry the

---

* The magnitude of the pressure disturbance or loudness of a sound wave is measured in decibels (dB), which are a unitless logarithmic ratio of the pressure disturbance (in newtons per square meter) to a reference sound pressure (which is the threshold of hearing).

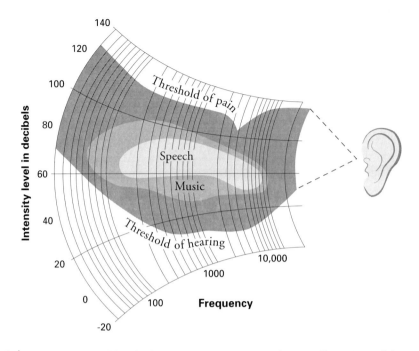

Figure 6–1 / The human ear, like the human eye, perceives only a small portion of the energy in which it is submerged. It scans this field, whose limits are defined in terms of decibels and frequencies, to pick up important information on environmental events.

threat of discomfort, disaster, death. Not so with the natural sonic environment. Here the upper threshold of human hearing is seldom crossed (e.g., the loud chatter of monkeys, a nearby thunderclap, the surge of a large waterfall, or a volcanic explosion), whereas the lower threshold (e.g., no perceptible sound at all) is commonly reckoned as restful.

Until comparatively recent times, a simple, unpolluted sonic environment was the natural state of the American. Our colonial ancestors heard few sounds, none of them physiologically stressful: conversation of neighbors or sound of church bells, song of a bird or sigh of wind in the trees, call of the plowman or blows of the blacksmith at an anvil. Many sounds might have been threatening by reason of the information they contained — rattlesnake whirring, panther crying, war whoop, or rattle of musketry — but none of them was in itself generally dangerous to health. When they did occur, loud noises often signified danger. This initiated a series of biological changes in the listener, to prepare for fight or flight.

All the more ironic, then, that manmade pollution of the sonic environment now constitutes a real and rising threat to contemporary Americans, on several counts. [1] First, evidence of the "fight or flight" response persists, even though the stimulus is no longer viewed as one requiring immediate action. Being chronically mobilized to fight off an enemy or flee can result in chronic elevated blood pressure and other stress-related conditions. In addition, the organ of hearing is often damaged. Modern industrial society created new sound to a point where sound levels in many industrial plants require hearing protection to guard against noise-induced hearing loss; where most urban areas are subject to a constant drone of traffic, screeching brakes, revving engines, blaring horns, radios, car alarms, and police sirens; where jetports and multi-lane highways are a source of constant annoyance to surrounding communities; and where supersonic jets, with their sonic booms, threaten the physical integrity of buildings, let alone the human ear.

Almost any individual human action, and all social process, has sonic consequences. New sound is produced deliberately (as when we speak to a friend, conduct a symphony, or televise a play) and incidentally (as when we accelerate a car, stamp out a metal auto body, or rivet the hull of a ship). In the first case, the new sound is the end product of the process; this might be called *productive* sound. In the second instance, the new sound is a byproduct of the process; this—which might be called *counterproductive* sound—is usually called *noise*. However, even productive sound is socially useful only as long as it is confined to the immediate environment for which it has been produced. Thus the symphony, performed in a hall designed for the purpose before an audience that has paid to hear it, has maximum cultural value. Thanks to modern electronic technology, this audience can now be enormously expanded by means of radio, television, and recordings. For this new audience, seated before millions of scattered sets, the symphony is still productive sound. But it is now amplified into spaces designed neither to receive nor to contain it; the sound escapes, impinging on countless nearby ears that do not choose to hear it but that cannot escape. For all such persons, the symphony at that time and in those circumstances is apt to be counterproductive, a nuisance—plain noise reminiscent of the pounding beat one might be subjected to from a teenager's boom box or the stereo in a passing car.

Noise is therefore seen as a social, not a physical, unit of measurement developed to describe our pollution of the natural sonic environment. This pollution corresponds closely to that of the atmospheric environment in both cause and effect. Both are an index of social waste, as both represent an incomplete or incorrect conversion of energy on the one hand and a direct threat to the health and efficiency of society on the other. This correlation has not always been so clear. All through the nineteenth century, industrially generated noise was considered a symbol of progress (the roar of the steel mills, the busy hum of the city) instead of being a certain index of waste of both human and mechanical energy. Today silence is often the symbol of efficiency in technology, with several notable exceptions (e.g., a noisier vacuum is thought by many to clean better, a noisier race car may be preferred to a quieter one). But no such criteria have as yet been effectively applied to the urban environment. Because of this paradoxical situation, in which by sheer amplification, productive sound becomes destructive noise, architects and urbanists must master two distinct scales of sonic control: the traditional one of architectural acoustics (the artful manipulation of sound within buildings) and the newer one of control of both interior and exterior environmental noise. The point of departure for both efforts must be an understanding of the requirements of the human ear.

What We Hear and How

In conventional terms, the ear is the organ of hearing. But the ear is in fact only a part of a complex auditory system that transmits vibrations (i.e., sound waves) from the atmosphere and converts them into nerve impulses. The ultimate function of this system is not merely to permit hearing but to make possible listening—a critical examination of the information picked up from the external environment.[2] For such an examination, we need two types of information: the nature of the event and the direction in which it is occurring. The binaural auditory system is nicely designed to accomplish this task. Our response to this examination of incoming auditory information is one of constant reorientation, both intellectual and physical—the more so as the auditory system also includes our balancing mechanism for spatial orientation, the vestibular apparatus. Through the brain, this system is linked to visual perception in a feedback process of marvelous sensitivity. Together they furnish the basic spatial orientation of life.

The normal ear perceives only a portion of the total sonic environment, its habitat being that described in Fig. 6–1. But within that habitat, its powers of perception and discrimination are immense. Paul E. Sabine, a professor at Harvard in the late 1930s who established the scientific basis for architectural acoustics, said:

The range of physical intensities to which the ear responds is enormous. . . . A sound so intense as to be painful is of the order of ten trillion times the minimum audible intensity. The intensity of speech is of the order of one to ten million times the minimum audible intensity, so that conversational speech falls about the middle range which the human ear will accommodate.[3]

Its powers of discrimination are, however, more limited. In theory, the human ear can discriminate among some 400,000 sounds in the sense of telling that there is a difference between any two when the two are presented in rapid succession. But in actuality, some experiments indicate that ordinary untrained people "seem unable to classify sounds beyond about seven degrees of loudness and seven degrees of pitch . . . or forty-nine tones of different pitch and loudness, hearing them one at a time. It is interesting to note that this is not far from the number of phonemes we distinguish in a language."[4]

The problem is enormously complex and still not fully understood, even among the specialists. But, in any case, the range of sonic stimuli perceived by the ear and analyzed by the brain is immense.

Unlike the eye, with its complex modulating devices of contractile iris, movable eyelid, and eyebrow, the ear has no comparable protection against environmental stress. This is probably an evolutionary reflection of the fact, already noted, that all sound in the natural sonic environment—hurricane, thunderbolt, volcanic explosion—falls well within the ear's limits of accommodation. However, the auditory system does have a subtle capacity for selective listening. In situations where a number of diverse sounds or sonic events are picked up by the ear, the brain has the capacity to tune out the unwanted stimuli—the familiar phenomenon of the cocktail party. Exactly how this process of filtering is accomplished, or at what cost in terms of energy, is not clearly understood.

According to William A. Yost, a specialist in the physiology and psychology of sound, recognizing a particular voice in a choir, distinguishing the sound of one instrument in a large orchestra, or hearing a specific conversation at a noisy party is made easier because the sound that is of interest comes from a different location from the general noise or interfering sounds in the room. The message arriving at one's ears is very complex in this situation. The voice that one is trying to (over)hear at a cocktail party has a different configuration at each of our ears than the general ambient noise alone. This subtle binaural distinction may make it easier to hear the conversation of interest. The ability for one to identify and understand a sound using two ears in the presence of other noise can occur at very low sound levels in the frequencies that contribute to the intelligibility of speech. In other words, the sounds do not have to be particularly loud to be heard. The ability to locate a sound in space is important not only as an aid for determining the position of sounds (and their sources) in space but also for listening to particular sounds in a noisy environment with seemingly competing information.

Obviously, in the cocktail situation, we supplement inadequate auditory information with visual data picked up from the facial expressions and lip movements of our conversational partners. In other situations such visual assistance is not available; at such times we describe our action as one of concentrating on hearing what we want to hear. Actually a process of filtration, it must depend upon some kind of neural action, the reflex effect of which is the contraction of blood vessels in the ear. This effect seems to take place with equal intensity during sleep and wakefulness and, as it involves energy output, cannot be accomplished without some cost to the individual. How much, and with what consequences, has been investigated by many people.[5]

The fourth dimension of the aural habitat is, of course, time. As in the case of the other systems of sensory perception, the aural stimulation of a steady sound diminishes with time—provided that the sound is not actually painful in either frequency or intensity. Sound can gradually drop below the level of conscious perception, like the white noise of a fan or window air conditioner. But this of course is a purely quantitative measure of stress. Whether we cease to "hear" the sound, whether or not we find it "endurable," depends also upon the informational content of that sound. This is one of the more mysterious aspects of listening. We can and do endure sounds of stressful magnitude if their message is important to us. As one acoustical engineer puts it:

Reasons for the difference between comfort levels and tolerance levels may be found in the information content of the various sounds. [Thus sounds that connote] "the fan is making it cool" or "the vacuum is making it clean" are usually tolerable at much higher levels than those recommended as good design practice. . . . Moreover, when a noise source is under the direct control of the listener and is beneficial to him, the allowable noise level is considerably higher than if the device were fully controlled by others.[6]

The complexities of annoyance "elude succinct definition," according to Fidell and Green.[7] Annoyance is not necessarily tied to loudness. Sometimes, sounds that are just barely heard may cause serious distraction or annoyance, such as footsteps on a floor in a room above or the dripping of water from a faucet. Fluctuations in sound level, such as the turning on and off of a neighbor's lawn equipment, while one is trying to relax and read on one's patio, or the intermittent low-level flyovers of jet aircraft that bring with them high noise levels and window vibrations, are also disturbing to many people. Indeed, variability is perhaps a key concept in the way that people react to noise — variability in whether or not the sound is annoying, in terms of what constitutes an annoying sound and how long it takes for a sound to become annoying. Here again, however, we must remember that such exposure must of necessity be fatiguing, no matter how overwhelming the motivation or concealed the physiological cost.

Because aural perception is so closely linked to vision, our eyes play a larger role in hearing than we commonly realize. Developing together over evolutionary time, the two senses have comparable scanning radii of spatial reach. The degree to which we can hear luncheon companions or actors on the stage is also a measure of how well we can see them, though the two types of sensory input are normally so blended that we are unaware of it. "I can't hear a word they say" may well be translated "I can't read a word on their lips." This symbiotic function has great significance for architectural acoustics.

The sense of acoustic intimacy is defined by Beranek as the quality that "suggests the size of the space in which it is performed to a listener."[8] An acoustically intimate room has the acoustical attributes of a small room. Beranek relates the sense of acoustical intimacy to sound reflections from room surfaces that were close to listeners. The reflections closely follow the direct sound because this is the nature of the acoustic response of a small room. In the acoustical sense of the word, even a large room can be perceived as acoustically intimate if the sound reflections follow closely after the direct sound. It has been found that many people judge the intimacy of a room based on its visual properties (i.e., how big it is or how far they are from the stage) rather than on its acoustical properties.[9]

How Sound Behaves

The behavior of sound in the atmosphere is strikingly like the sort of motion that occurs when a stone is dropped into a quiet pool. In both cases the energy is dispersed from its point of origin in successive concentric waves. The difference between water and sound waves is, as noted by Aristotle, Vitruvius, Sabine, and others, that the former move outward in an expanding circle on a single plane, while sound waves move out in an expanding sphere. In open air, this process of dispersion continues until all the energy is finally dissipated in friction with the air.

Although a sound wave displaces each air particle as it passes, setting up a characteristic vibration, the particle itself does not move forward with the wave but rotates vertically. The time required for a given particle to complete this vibration is known as the sound's *period*, the number of completed vibrations per second is the sound's *frequency*, the distance between two wave crests is called its *wavelength*, and the maximum distance between the crest and valley of the wave is its *amplitude*. The speed of sound is much slower than that of light, and varies somewhat with air temperature—at 40°F sound travels at a speed of 1,100 feet per second (fps); at 60°F, 1,120 fps. Like light, sound may be focused, reflected, and absorbed. Unlike light waves, sound waves coexist without blending.

The behavior of sound inside buildings is quite different from that in the open air. Investigation of this behavior is the basis for a whole branch of physics known as acoustics—or, when the subjective aspects are also being analyzed, psychoacoustics. The acoustical behavior of a given vessel (church, theater, living room) at any given moment depends upon a bewildering array of factors, most of them variable. The type of sonic event, its location in the vessel, the size, shape, and surfaces of the vessel itself, the number of people present—even the clothes they are wearing—all play a role in the total acoustical behavior of the volume in question. A major breakthrough in recent years that has contributed to a better understanding of the role that each of these factors plays in shaping the qualities of sounds heard in the vessel is the use of impulse response testing in rooms and models.

There has been a revolution in the design of concert halls in recent years that has several major components. First is a rigorous examination of the renowned shoebox concert halls of the late nineteenth and early twentieth centuries, such as the Grosser Musikvereinsaal in Vienna, the Concertgebouw in Amsterdam, and Symphony Hall in Boston.[10] A more complete understanding of the acoustical qualities of these halls was undertaken using a variety of techniques developed in allied disciplines. These studies identified the interactions among the architectural design features and acoustical qualities of the rooms.[11] The impetus behind this research activity in architectural acoustics was the series of questions raised by the design of several notable halls during the middle of the twentieth century that were plagued with acoustical difficulties. The techniques used in the studies are listed below:

1. impulse response testing and digital signal processing from electrical engineering
2. laboratory studies of sound quality by human listeners from psychology and neuroscience
3. advanced quantitative tests to determine primary perceptual factors, preference spaces, and correlated architectural features of rooms from statistics
4. three-dimensional computer and physical modeling of sound propagation in complex spaces from computer science and physics
5. qualitative evaluations of many performances in many rooms by researchers, consultants, and musicians
6. deliberate experimentation by consultants and architects to test emerging theories in a series of actual buildings over a thirty-year period
7. advancements in virtual acoustics, audio recording, playback, and control from digital signal processing and virtual reality

The combining of these techniques into a hybrid design and research method resulted in the development of new theories of concert hall design that center on impulse response

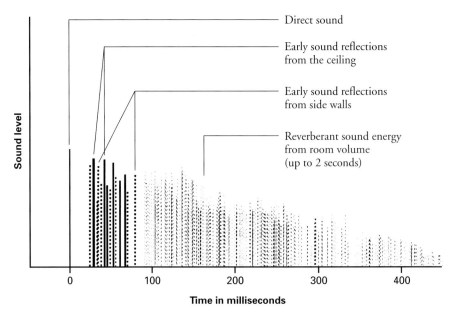

Figure 6–2 / Diagram of a typical impulse response.

test techniques. The impulse response is a physical measurement of the response of a room to a single loud sound. The direct sound and all of the subsequent reflections from the room surfaces are recorded. This is intended to represent the effects of sound reflections from the room (vessel) on a single musical note or a single syllable of speech (Fig. 6–2).

In many ways the use of impulse response tests in architectural acoustics is similar to the use of electrocardiogram tests in medicine. A doctor hooks up a series of electrodes to measure the electrical pulsing of a heart. From a visual examination of the pattern of pulsing a doctor can diagnose the condition of the heart. A series of quantitative indices, also derived from the electrocardiogram test, summarize some of the important characteristics of the heart. Likewise, acoustical consultants diagnose the acoustical conditions in a room by looking at the pattern of sound reflections in an impulse response. They can also derive a series of quantitative measures from the impulse response to summarize the complexities of the overall pattern of reflections. The impulse response is unique to each seating location in each room because it is derived from the specific paths that the sound waves take as they move from each source to each listener. Within large rooms, significant variations in impulse responses are found among different seating locations. These differences among impulse responses in a room provide physical evidence that helps to explain why certain seats are perceived as better than others.[12]

There are three primary components to the impulse response recorded at a seating location in a room:

1. The *direct sound* is the sound wave that travels directly from the source to the listener without striking any of the surfaces of the room. It is the first sound wave that arrives at a listener's location.

2. The *early sound reflections* are those waves that strike one of the room's surfaces and are reflected to the listener's location. Reflections that arrive within short time intervals after the direct sound (less than 80 milliseconds for music) are usually combined with the direct sound by our ears. These reflections add to the direct sound, increasing its apparent loudness. The suspended reflecting panels in many theaters and concert halls are carefully shaped to direct these important early reflections to listeners. Early reflections that arrive from the sides of the listener's head also contribute to sensations of envelopment and widening of the acoustic image of the sound source. This is the basic logic behind the development of stereo and surround-sound audio systems. Rooms are now designed for similar effects.

3. The *reverberant sound field* consists of sound waves that are reflected from multiple surfaces before they arrive at the listener's ears. The reverberant sound field may persist for two seconds or longer in concert halls.

In the response of any kind of vessel to any kind of sound, four physical phenomena are always to be observed: reflection, refraction, reverberation, and resonance. These also serve as objective criteria by which to measure acoustical performance. Thanks to modern physics, they can now be mathematically expressed. [13]

The *reflection* of sound is just what the term implies: when the sound wave meets a solid obstacle, it is bounced back. *Refraction* occurs when a sound wave breaks around a freestanding obstacle, such as a column. Here the action is similar to what happens when an ocean wave breaks around a pile. No surface, however, reflects all of the sound that strikes it; a portion is absorbed by the surface itself. The amount reflected and the amount absorbed depends upon the physical characteristics of the surface. Dense, smooth-surfaced materials like glass and marble reflect much of the sound energy, while rough-textured, porous materials such as fiberboard or glass wool absorb more sound.

Two other acoustical properties of closed spaces describe the response of the vessel as a whole. *Reverberation* time describes the time required, after a sound stops, for the sound intensity to fall to one millionth of its first intensity (a reduction of 60 decibels). If the time gap between the direct sound and the reflected sound is more than 70 milliseconds it is what is commonly called an echo. The other phenomenon associated with the behavior of sound in closed vessels is *resonance*. This describes the special response of a room to sounds of a certain pitch or frequency. The reaction here is identical to that which occurs when one tuning fork is set into vibration by striking another of the same pitch. When we describe a room as "brilliant" or "dull," we are describing its resonance.

The foregoing describes the behavior of sound generated within the vessel. Only a portion of the sound impinging upon the vessel walls is reflected; a portion of the remaining energy is absorbed by the wall itself, the residue being transmitted to adjacent parts of the structure and to the air beyond. The proportions vary greatly, depending upon the molecular nature of the material and the construction of the wall. Generally speaking, sheer massiveness is the most effective barrier to sound transmission through the wall. A solid masonry wall or heavy concrete floor transmits less airborne sound than a light one.

But because massive walls and floors run counter to current trends toward lightness in structural design, lightweight, absorptive insulating materials are commonly substituted, with isolation of the various wall elements as a secondary device. Thus the vessel must be visualized not as a merely inert and static container but as the active interface between two sonic environments—the internal, acoustically predetermined mesoenvironment and the macroenvironment, all too often intolerably polluted by noise.

Barriers are one form of an acoustic interface between two environments. Sometimes people like to feel a part of activity outside their immediate surroundings, so they open a window to hear the sounds of children playing in the street. In the same way, someone working in an office may like the hustle and bustle of people coming and going in the background. Yet these same sounds may be very disturbing to the same person when they are talking on the telephone, composing a letter, or trying to relax. The same person may close the door when an important telephone call comes in order not to be distracted or to maintain confidentiality. The notion of productive and counterproductive sounds flows both ways in this case, demonstrating the need for individual control over the relative permeability of an acoustical barrier at different times. [14]

The Communication Role of Buildings

As all buildings are designed to facilitate some aspect of necessary human intercourse, communication occurs in all of them. But many building types are specifically designed for communication—churches, schools, theaters, legal and legislative chambers—and they constitute, as they always have, one of the architect's most important areas of activity. This communication role has two levels, concrete and metaphysical; we are here concerned with the first: the transmission of information, by aural and visual means, between minister and congregation, teacher and class, actor and audience, judge and jury. Before the development of the electronic ear (microphone) and the electronic voice box (amplifier), all aural communication was conditioned by the reach of human energy, vocal and muscular—that is, the power of the speaker's voice box, the strength of the harpist's fingers. Before the invention of optical glasses, electric lighting, television camera, and satellite transmission, almost identical restraints were placed upon the visual component of communication—that is, what the naked eye of the spectator could perceive. The spatial parameters of all preindustrial communication were established by the scanning power of the ear and eye, organs of sonic and luminous perception, working in tandem.

These parameters, in turn, governed the development of both communication structure—that is, the formal characteristics of sermon, lecture, concert, play—and the architectural vessel in which it was projected and "consumed." Over millennia, their evolutionary development was symbiotic. Fifth-century Greek drama developed step by step with the perfecting of the roofless Greek theater (Fig. 6–3). The polyphony of early Christian church music was made at once possible and necessary by the long reverberation period of the Romanesque basilica; intelligibility being impossible, it was relin-

Figure 6–3 / Theater, Epidauros, Greece, fifth century B.C. The Greek theater was a roofless vessel of astonishing visual and acoustical effectiveness. Its shape and size were nicely adapted to the scanning range of unaided ear and eye. Because it developed symbiotically with Greek dramatic forms, it was shaped to give environmental support.

Figure 6–4 / The Bayreuth Opera, built as Margrave's Court Theater by J. de Saint-Pierre, Bayreuth, Germany, 1748. Interior by Giuseppe and Carlo Galli-Bibiena. The baroque theaters of Northern Europe, necessarily enclosed because of climate, were designed for small audiences. Wood and plaster vessels of great acoustical brilliance, they afforded lively environmental support for theatrical forms— masques, operas, and ballets— in which instrumental music had a large role.

quished as an esthetic criterion. The reverse was necessary when the evangelical necessities of the Reformation required a new vessel in which the sermon could be clearly heard, the prayer book easily read. The rise of secular music led to the courtly operas of the eighteenth century, which were predicated on the small, acoustically brilliant baroque theaters in which they were performed (Fig. 6–4).

This equilibrium between sonic form and acoustical container endured for centuries. It was anything but static, as any survey of music, theater, or dance quickly shows, but it led to a rich and stable empirical tradition that was good for all concerned. Theater lore is full of significant anecdotes, apocryphal though they may be. Thus, when he was told that he had a half-filled house in his rented London theater, Handel is supposed to have exclaimed, "Good! My music will sound the better." (Here he understood that fewer overdressed patrons would reduce the absorptive capacity, and hence extend the reverberation period, of the vessel — which, for his music, he must have considered desirable.) Richard Wagner, touring the opera houses of Europe before designing his own new vessel at Bayreuth, reportedly told an Italian impresario, "I cannot hear your chorus over the surf of your orchestra." To avoid this error at Bayreuth, Wagner both submerged his orchestra pit and pushed it well back beneath the apron of the stage. Thus he made it act as a mixing chamber to modulate the volume and direction of orchestral sound.

Electronic technology has quite truncated this long empirical tradition. Modern architects now have at their disposal the theoretical and practical tools of computers and physical models that can record impulse responses in rooms that have not yet been built. Moreover, the extraordinary audiovisual equipment of electronic technology allows the aural simulation of sounds as they would be heard in rooms not yet built. Unfortunately, it has not followed that all new buildings are better instruments of communication. On the contrary, we continue to find a disappointing record of acoustical malfunction in prestigious theaters, lecture halls, and churches. All of this suggests that architects should master the lessons of preindustrial acoustical practice before dumping them in the trash bin of history.

This is indeed happening among a group of acoustical consultants, architects, and researchers who have recently embarked on the task of designing "the concert hall of the twenty-first century," a term coined by noted acoustical consultant Russell Johnson, by studying in detail the architectural and acoustical qualities of many historic halls. They combine this empirical research with current knowledge in music, digital signal processing, acoustics, psychoacoustics, architecture, and statistics.

The concert hall of the twenty-first century has evolved as an interesting hybrid that assimilates principles of shape, proportion, material, configuration, and program from the historic precedents of the late nineteenth century.

The late nineteenth century halls were relatively narrow rooms with high ceilings and parallel walls. Several narrow balconies wrapped around the sides and rear of the rooms. The walls and ceilings were relatively hard, yet they were covered with diffusing surface textures. The halls provide a rich blend of articulate, clear sound that is simultaneously enveloping and richly reverberant.

The concert hall of the twenty-first century returns to these precedents as its basic parti. It extends the acoustic potential of performance and the architectural envelope of space by adapting the form of the precedent halls to the needs of the future. Massive, movable canopies cover the stage to improve the ensemble of performers and to provide variability in the response of the room to various types of orchestral performances. The reverberance can be increased dramatically by coupling large adjacent volumes to the hall itself through a series of operable openings. These reverberation chambers have been extremely successful in the new halls at Dallas and Birmingham. Acoustical banners are hung on the side walls of the room to allow the room to change from extremely dry to reverberant.

The result of over twenty years of work like this has been the opening of a series of highly successful halls around the world that extend the acoustical, architectural, and esthetic performance of the historic halls in innovative and creative ways. They are truly extending the architectural palette of sonic environment design. A detailed case study of the first of these rooms, the Meyerson Hall in Dallas, is presented later in this chapter.

Computer models can be used to study the progress of acoustic rays as they move from the sound source into the room. If enough rays are propagated they can be seen to approach the spherical sound waves they represent. The waves strike the room surfaces and are reflected or absorbed depending upon the sound absorption characteristics of the materials selected for the walls and ceiling. Some of the computer programs available today also represent the diffusion of sound from irregular surfaces (which are important design features of theaters and concert halls). A variety of acoustical measures can be calculated from impulse responses recorded at specific seating locations in the room.

Several programs allow auralization (or aural simulations) of the sounds in the room to be derived from the impulse responses measured from the ray propagation. The impulse response recorded at a seat is combined with music recorded in an anechoic environment.* This produces a combination of the original music with the acoustical effects of the model room (as represented by the impulse response) so one can listen to music as it would sound in the room.

It is important to note that while this technique is extremely impressive aurally and involves use of sophisticated methods, the aural simulations are just that—"sketches" of the sonic environment of rooms. Just as renderings or photographs of a building convey information about its visual qualities, they are only two-dimensional representations of our multidimensional experience. The same holds true for auralization or aural simulation.

Theater: Test Tube of Acoustic Theory

In creating vessels for the performing arts, the architect is intervening in one of the most complex of all esthetic processes. Painters and poets, for all the public nature of their cre-

---

* An anechoic environment is a room that has totally absorbent walls, floor, and ceiling. Music recorded in an anechoic environment includes no reflections from room surfaces on the recording.

ations, work in private. For this work they need one sort of environment, but the viewer of the canvas or the reader of the poem may require quite another. In the theater the work of art is created anew with each performance, right in the presence of its consumers. Live actors, dancers, musicians confront the living audience. Action and reaction are to all intents and purposes simultaneous; the contact is electric and yields an emotional climate that is specific to the theater. It is the product of a triangular relationship (not two-way, as is commonly assumed): the actor's impact upon the audience as a whole; the collective response of that audience; and the effect of that response upon the individual playgoers. This three-way feedback is what has always made the theater the most electrifying of all the forms of art.[15]

Until modern times, it had always been understood that each theatrical form—play, opera, concert, dance—had its own environmental requirements and its own inherent scale. When the Greek city of Eretria in Euboea made attendance at the theater compulsory for its citizens on certain high holidays, it was acknowledging the potency of the form. The theater was a major instrument whereby its citizens were inculcated with Greek values—where, in sober fact, they learned to be Greek. The form of the play and the form of the theater that held it had symbiotic origins in whose development the playwright and the architect took equal and mutually supporting parts. Lacking the technical means for amplification of word or gesture, the authors developed a characteristic set of formal conventions: the shouted lines and exaggerated, stylized gestures; the tragic and comic masks; and, most of all, the chorus. Placed midway between the cast on its raised stage and the audience in its roofless bowl, the chorus was a remarkable invention. It acted both as interlocutor for the audience ("*Why, oh why, must Oedipus kill his father at the crossroads?*") and as interpreter for the playwright ("*Patience, patience, you will see, the gods have willed it so*)." Pulsing back and forth between the cast and the audience, the chorus welded the two into one communion. Catharsis through pity and terror was the result.

Understanding both the importance and the fragility of this emotional climate, Greek architects exercised great care in designing the ambience in which the play was experienced. Because artificial illumination was inadequate, performances were held in daylight. With the genial Aegean climate, the roofless theater was practicable, but without technical means of visual or aural amplification, sight lines and acoustic behavior had to be exactly calculated. The Greek theater building was thus a vessel perfectly shaped to contain the Greek play.

Because of this experiential totality, its physical union of actors, audience, and individual playgoer, the Greek theater can never become obsolete. It represents a prototypal form that cannot be manipulated without fundamentally altering the theatrical experience itself. Even to enlarge the auditorium is to push the outermost seats beyond the scanning range of good vision and good hearing, thereby reducing the potency of the actors' projection. These limits are established by the physiology of the eye and the ear and cannot be violated without a qualitative diminution in the experience itself.

American architects, like Americans generally, have all too often accepted without serious challenge the proposition that technology has made obsolete or inoperative all these ancient relationships. Yet it should be obvious that when, for example, a play is transposed from the stage to the movie screen, it is divested of its most magical property: the feedback that enables the spectators not merely to receive the play but to modify the very quality of the actors' projection by the intensity of their response. In the movie, the audience no longer has a direct line of communication with the actor. Modern audiovisual technology (including home theater and surround sound) gives the audience an acceptable facsimile of the multidimensional reality of live theater; as long as it is projected before the living audience of the movie theater, it maintains some of the central elements of theatrical experience. A viable art form results. But when this same movie is projected upon an outdoor screen at one of the few remaining drive-in movie theaters, where individual members of the audience are isolated in the sealed compartments of their individual automobiles, the situation is further compromised. Perception itself is fragmented. The visual image is reduced in size, distorted by curved glass, dimmed by condensation, wipers, etc. The sound, robbed of dimension, direction, and depth, issues from one little box, heated or cooled air from another. The entire experience is converted into a travesty of the technical virtuosity which makes it possible.[16]

When, finally, that same cinematic facsimile is projected across the indecent privacy of the television screen, the process of electronic attrition is complete. With the radical alteration of the intrinsic properties of the form itself (grotesque distortions in size, scale, color, and length as well as the periodic interjection of extraneous advertising) and the radical change in the ambient circumstances under which it is projected, the play is reduced to an impoverished simulacrum of the original. Removed from its special container of public exposure, the form is mutilated and the climate demolished. Now, indeed, people are reduced to the one-dimensional role of passive spectator. Instead of being submerged in the rich and stimulating theatrical experience, a participant through all the senses, the spectator views it as if through a knothole.

It would be nonsense, of course, to argue that electronic facsimiles (films, recordings, tapes, compact discs) are without esthetic value or cultural utility. But it is equally nonsensical to argue that they are identical or interchangeable with their prototypes. Yet this is just the position assumed by many critics, including Gilbert Seldes who at the time wrote:

[A]lmost any recording studio is acoustically superior to all but half a dozen halls in which orchestral music is played to audiences; and it is preposterous to think that a third-rate orchestra in a second-rate hall is closer to the prototype (what the composer intended) than a great orchestra, using the most modern equipment, in a studio.[17]

But the conditions under which the recording is made or videotaped are not the decisive factors in the experience; these are rather the experiential circumstances under which the result is projected and received. These circumstances are literally never "superior" in the noisy bar or even the large-screen living room television, or in the parked car or the picnic grove. It is preposterous not to recognize this fact. Indeed, one could easily argue that it might be preferable actually to hear the live performance of a third-rate orchestra in a second-rate hall. (Though why must we assume, with Seldes, that we must content ourselves with third-rate musicians playing in second-rate architecture?) To insist upon these distinctions is not to assume an "undemocratic" posture, as Seldes charged; it is rather to establish and define the critically important categories of experience in a period when the tendency is to vulgarize them all. Much is made today of technologically produced "virtual reality." But such a name is folly. What is being held up as reality is reliance upon a limited use of the senses—principally visual.

Beranek asks these questions in a different way in his commentary on aural simulations. "Are the headphones and loudspeakers faithfully reproducing the concert hall experience? . . . Can simulated concert halls come even close to representing the music that is heard from a spread-out orchestra on a stage performing before a full audience?"[18]

Kidwell found distinct experiential differences between binaurally recorded simulated sound and live music performed in an actual hall.[19] In a study comparing musical recordings with live music performed in a room, large, statistically significant differences were found in the evaluation of nine acoustical qualities including loudness, clarity, reverberance, and overall impression. The differences between the scores for the live performances and the recordings was equivalent to the differences found between listening to performers outdoors and in a good concert hall![20] These studies indicate that even for acoustical aspects of the listening experience, there are distinctive differences between recorded or simulated sounds and the multidimensional sensory experience of actual performance.

It seems necessary to recapitulate some of the cultural and esthetic consequences of electronic technology because the architect has become as much disoriented by them as the public generally. This is demonstrated by the fact that many theaters and concert halls (like much modern architecture) abound in the frivolous, the idiosyncratic, and the arbitrary. When this book was last published, in 1972, it detailed the troublesome acoustical debut of the Lincoln Center for the Performing Arts in New York.

Despite the technical means at the disposal of architects in the 1960s being incomparably higher than ever before, the overall performance of new theaters was less satisfactory than that of many built centuries ago. This state of affairs was due to architects uncritically accepting the pretensions of technology on the one hand, and indulging in subjective, formalistic design decisions on the other. The substandard acoustical performance of these admittedly faulty designs spurred a thorough re-examination to determine what went wrong and why.

Since then significant progress has been made because of the collaborative efforts of architects, acoustical consultants, and researchers. These design teams have learned from selected models of the late nineteenth century. Their work is enhanced by sophisticated modern techniques that enable them to examine acoustic and architectural variables in detail. Collaboration is key to such work. The architect shares the field with a broad range of specialists—acoustical, illuminating, air-conditioning, and structural engineers. Their presence on the scene permits the architect to work in broader and more daring terms than hitherto because responsibilities formerly held alone can now be delegated.

But these experts may lack a common conceptual approach to the experiential aspects of architecture. The environmental requirements of the playgoer may have been studied, but studied piecemeal, each by the appropriate specialist. These components are sometimes not reintegrated into a satisfactory total environment.

The modern architect has a critically important responsibility here — and too often fails. One reason for this failure is that, in the work, *the appearance of things* tends to carry a weight in decision making quite disproportionate to its experiential importance. Because every architect is a visual artist, this bias in favor of vision amounts almost to an occupational disease. Whatever complex manipulation of environmental forces the architect may have in mind in a given building, the principal means of communicating these intentions is in pictorial and plastic terms — that is, by means of drawings, sketches, models, and three-dimensional computer-generated fly-through or walk-through renderings. This bends the design in the direction of *what it will look like*, to the detriment of other values equally important but much harder to visualize: what it will sound like, what it will feel like, what it will smell like.

Thus the temperature and ventilation of a theater during a performance may play a more critical role in the audience's response than the color of the walls or upholstery or the shape of the proscenium. However, it is easier to conceptualize the curve or the color than the temperature or air movement — hence theaters are full of devices aimed primarily at pleasing the eye (though not necessarily aiding it in perceiving the play itself) while other channels of perception are given only token attention: sight lines violated, ventilation skimped, acoustics poor, seating uncomfortable, etc. Computer modeling of the acoustical response of rooms and the ongoing development of the theories and technology for aural simulations will help to change this process.

There is no automatic congruity between good looks and good acoustics, any more than there is between the taste and nutritional value of a dish of food. Of course, on the other hand, there is no necessary incongruity either. Many a room that is beautiful to look at is also beautiful to listen in. But any architectural vessel designed primarily for aural communication must first comply with those factors that determine its acoustical behavior. These are the size and shape of the vessel and the physical characteristics of the enclosing surfaces. Only then, and only by respecting these acoustical parameters, can the vessel be manipulated for purely visual effects. Thus it is irrelevant acoustically whether the theater seating is upholstered in red or green, but it matters very much whether the seating is surfaced in velvet upholstery or enameled metal, or whether it is empty or occupied during any acoustical analysis.

The overvaluing of the visual and undervaluing of the aural in auditoriums was obvious in both the design and the critical reaction to the originally constructed theaters in New York's Lincoln Center for the Performing Arts. At the end of 1969, five had been completed: Philharmonic Hall, New York State Theater, Metropolitan Opera, Vivian Beaumont Theater, and Alice Tully Hall. The critical reaction to the auditoriums was most revealing. The architectural critics tended to discuss them in almost completely formal or

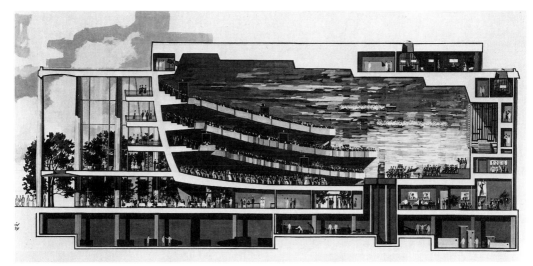

Figure 6–5 / Philharmonic Hall, Lincoln Center for the Performing Arts, Inc., New York, New York. Harrison and Abramowitz, architects, completed 1962. Cross section showing auditorium with its three shallow terraces surrounding the orchestra level. Note the reflectors, or clouds, suspended from the ceiling. They were included with the intent of providing acoustical intimacy. Instead they contributed to the acoustical deficiencies of the original hall.

esthetic terms—that is, as visual phenomena. There was some disagreement (mostly over the patent vulgarity of the interior decor of the Opera), but generally speaking, all five received favorable critiques in the architectural press.

Music and drama critics, on the other hand, were much sharper and more specific. From its opening in 1962, they pounced on the atrocious acoustical behavior of Philharmonic Hall with such continuing force that it was altered several times before being completely rebuilt in 1976 and renamed Avery Fisher Hall (see Figs. 6–6 to 6–13). While the architectural critic of the *New York Times* was rhapsodic over the white and gold color scheme of the lobby of the State Theater, the music critic of the same paper observed: "The sound is excellent in the rings and galleries but very bad in the orchestra, where a strange bounce places the sound just where the loud speakers are located in the proscenium sides."[21]

At the opening of the Metropolitan, the *New York Times* architectural critic found it to be "a curiously resolved collision of past and present . . . a sterile throwback rather than a creative Twentieth Century design." She concluded her critique by ruefully observing that: "Since the new opera promises to be an excellent performing house, with satisfactory acoustics, it may not matter that the architecture sets no high water mark for the city."[22]

The music critic, reporting the same event, reported that, because the entire stage was used without backdrops, the singers found their voices going about as far backward as

Figure 6–6 /
Philharmonic Hall
during rehearsal
week in September
1962. Note the sus-
pended clouds and
the side-wall finish.
Within days the
hall would open
and criticism of its
performance would
begin.

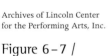

Figure 6–7 /
Philharmonic Hall,
1964. Many addi-
tional clouds were
installed in a more
random pattern in
an attempt to cor-
rect the acoustical
problems.

Figure 6–8 /
Philharmonic Hall,
1965. Clouds were
repositioned once
again. The side-wall
finish was radically
altered as well.

Figure 6–9 /
Avery Fisher Hall
(formerly Philhar-
monic Hall), 1970.
The clouds were
removed and a new
ceiling installed. A
new name, slightly
better acoustics,
but complaints and
problems persist.

forward. Reports from the upper parts of the house were favorable but the $250 ticket holders (1962 dollars, mind you) found the sound vaulting over their heads.[23] But he also added that, at an earlier preview using normal stage sets, the house "turned out to be an acoustic dream." Neither critic felt it necessary to comment upon the atrocious sight lines from the side boxes, perhaps because that is the well-known shortcoming of the traditional opera house form.

Alice Tully Hall was inaugurated in late 1969. With an emphasis on performance rather than appearance (an emphasis that architectural critics would do well to emulate), the *New York Times* music critic at the time, Harold Schonberg, wrote:

It seats 1,096, is handsome and produces a nice, clear sound. It is what can be described as a modern sound. That is, clarity rather than warmth is its main characteristic. Its reverberation period seems short and — pending further acquaintance with the hall — there seems to be a slight loss in energy from front to rear. But there is a strong bass characteristic and plenty of presence. Musicians have already reported that they feel comfortable and happy playing from the stage. They can hear one another, they say. One of the complaints about the stage of Philharmonic Hall is that they cannot.[24]

Of the five theatrical vessels at the Lincoln Center for the Performing Arts, the geometry of the Beaumont is the purest, most consistent, and least idiosyncratic. It follows quite closely the Greek parameters (diameter 130 feet, seating for approximately 1,100 people, shallow, stepped auditorium). It makes no use of the pseudohistorical decorative devices that mar the interiors of both the State Theater and the Opera (e.g., chandeliers, swags, cartouches, upholstered walls). But these visually conspicuous characteristics are only the end result that was shaped by the reach of the spectator's eye and ear. They are not decorative devices superimposed upon an abstractly conceived, anti-aural form — as is the case of the Philharmonic.

The architect of the Philharmonic is reported to have said, after the full dimensions of its acoustical dysfunction became apparent, "If we have learned anything from all this, it is that acoustics is still an inexact science." But this is to place the blame upon the acoustical engineer when, in fact, the failure seems due to fundamental architectonic misconceptions. The acoustical engineer had personally visited all the world's leading concert halls before beginning the design of the Philharmonic. That survey found their average seating capacity to be around 1,400 and their average volume to be under 600,000 cubic feet. Yet, for economic reasons, the management tossed aside these parameters and the architects agreed to double the seating capacity (to almost 3,000) and greatly increase the volume (to 850,000 cubic feet). The acoustical consultant went along, apparently feeling that such a change in size and scale was merely quantitative and, hence, subject to purely technical manipulation. This miscalculation proved disastrous; only after three renovations and then, finally, a complete reconstruction in 1976 — at a cost of $5 million — was Avery Fisher Hall brought up to a high standard of acoustical performance. It was a sad and costly confirmation of an old truism: what the trained architectural eye accepts, the musically trained ear may promptly reject.

Figure 6–10 / Avery Fisher Hall, 1976. Years and years of acoustical tinkering did not solve the problem. A total reconstruction project was completed during the summer of 1976.

The costly reconstruction of the hall in 1976 was a grudgingly reached acknowledgment that acoustical tinkering would not suffice. Instead, a major structural renovation was required to change the basic shape of the hall from Coke bottle (with concave side walls producing acoustical focusing effects) to a more traditional rectangle. The designers of the reconstructed hall were architects Philip Johnson and John Burgee in collaboration with acoustician Dr. Cyril M. Harris, who distinctly recalled his exact words when first contacted by Amyas Ames (then director of the Philharmonic) about becoming involved in the final redesign of Avery Fisher Hall. He said, "I wouldn't touch it with a ten-foot pole." His primary concern was that "the hall did not have a very happy history." He also "was not interested in becoming part of a committee of acoustical consultants." [25]

Eventually Harris relented and agreed to work on the hall. His recommendation was that another revision would be just a waste of money — a complete demolition was required. That opinion was shared by the great conductor George Szell. [26] After a time it was agreed that the hall would be rebuilt, with work actually beginning immediately after a concert on May 15, 1976. When Avery Fisher Hall opened only five months later, after an around-the-clock construction schedule, *New York Times* music critic Harold C. Schonberg wrote:

Everybody seemed to like the appearance of the hall, as well they should. The new Avery Fisher Hall is soothing, intimate, and a delight to the eye. But the sound? Everybody has been sound conscious since Sept. 23, 1962, when the word "acoustics" entered the national consciousness. That date was the opening of Philharmonic Hall. [27]

The title of Schonberg's October 24, 1976, piece, "The Verdict on Fisher Hall: Sounds of Unparalleled Clarity," sums up the acoustical rating accorded the rebuilt hall. The only substantive change since then was the rebuilding of the stage area in 1992 (see Fig. 6 – 12).

Archives of Lincoln Center for the Performing Arts, Inc.

Figure 6 – 11 / Reconstructed Avery Fisher Hall, inaugural concert, October 19, 1976. Johnson/ Burgee, architects. Dr. Cyril Harris, acoustical consultant. Finally, a design with excellent acoustics that received rave reviews. Note how the room was squared off and a totally different approach taken for the ceiling design.

Figure 6–12 / Avery Fisher Hall, 1997. The hall after modifications to the stage area. The remainder of the hall remains as it was designed during the 1976 reconstruction.

Much can be learned from the Philharmonic Hall/Avery Fisher Hall case study. Perhaps foremost among the lessons is the need to understand and abide by fundamental acoustical principles. In the more than thirty-five years since the original Philharmonic Hall was designed, the field and understanding of architectural acoustics has expanded greatly, and new tools have evolved and are available to the architect (including interlinked computer/audio programs).

Recent Acoustical Case Studies

Segerstrom Hall in the Orange County Performing Arts Center in Costa Mesa, California, was designed as an asymmetrical multipurpose hall by architect Charles Lawrence of CRS Sirrine and acoustical consultants Jerald R. Hyde, Marshall Day Acoustics and Paoletti Associates, Inc. It was completed in 1983. The acoustical challenge of designing an asymmetrical hall was increased by the large number (3,000) of people it needed to accommodate and the large variety of performances to be held in the hall. These included orchestra, solo, opera, drama, ballet, and musical theater performances.

The room became much wider than most concert halls because of the large seating capacity. However, the seating areas were divided into a number of smaller sections defined by low walls. Sound reflections from these walls provided the intimacy and envelopment normally associated with a much narrower room. A series of large sound-reflecting panels that appear to float direct early sound reflections to listeners throughout the room using quadratic residue sound-diffusing surfaces (QRDs). Floating the panels away from the structural envelope allows them to be closer to the audience; this improves the spatial qualities of sound. Gaps between the panels allow some of the sound energy to pass by and travel into the ceiling space above. The added room volume allows for the longer reverberation times (approximately 2.3 seconds) needed for orchestral performances.

The innovative acoustical and architectural design was tested using impulse response techniques in several models during the design process of the building. This was done to ensure that the theories employed by the design team would yield the acoustical qualities they hypothesized would occur in the room once completed. The room was very well received by audiences and performers. Its innovative design has been studied by consultants and researchers so they can more fully understand the effects of these unique design concepts.

Figure 6–13 / Interior perspective drawing of Segerstrom Hall, Costa Mesa, California CRS Sirrine, architects, completed in 1983. Shown: terraced seating within the asymmetrical, fan-shaped room; reflecting panels that direct lateral reflections to the audience and diffusing surfaces.

The McDermott Concert Hall in the Morton H. Meyerson Symphony Center in Dallas, Texas, is arguably the acoustical standard by which subsequent concert halls are judged. It has been hailed by musicians, music critics, audiences, and acoustical consultants as a marvelous room. It was designed by architect I. M. Pei and acoustical consultant Russell Johnson of Artec Consultants. The hall opened in 1989 to rave reviews, one of the first successful halls to be built in the latter part of the twentieth century.

Pei and Johnson took an inherently architectural approach to the acoustical design of the room. The basic acoustical design of the McDermott Concert Hall relied heavily on historic precedent. Many of the design principles were adapted from opera houses, theaters, and concert halls built in Europe between 1600 and 1910. The audience was limited to 2,065. The seats were stacked in several tiers of narrow balconies that surround the room. The width of the room was kept to 85 feet, which is relatively narrow compared to many recent halls. This allows reflections from the sides of the room to reach listeners shortly after the direct sound, contributing to a sense of acoustic spaciousness and broadening the image of the sound source. Heavy, massive finish materials that reflect all frequencies of sound were used throughout the room.

Figure 6–14 / Interior photograph of Meyerson-McDermott Concert Hall, Dallas, Texas, I.M. Pei, architect, completed 1989. Shown: multiple tiers of narrow balconies, suspended canopy overhead, and reverberation chambers surrounding the room.

Several innovative acoustical design concepts were successfully employed in the room to vary the acoustical qualities of sounds for different concert performances. Large concrete reverberation chambers surround the upper portions of the room. Sounds can enter the chambers, bounce off their walls and ceiling, and then reenter the main concert room. This creates a very long, subtle sense of reverberance in the room. Motorized doors at the chamber openings can open and close to allow more or less sound back into the room.

A large, segmented sound-reflecting canopy is suspended above the stage. This canopy can be raised and lowered by large motors to change the acoustical performance of the room. As the canopy is raised, more sound energy can enter the reverberation chambers in the upper portion of the room, which increases the sense of reverberance in the audience chamber. As the canopy is lowered it restricts the entry of sound energy into the reverberation chambers, thereby decreasing the sensation of reverberance. When lowered, it also directs strong early sound reflections into the room to increase the clarity or articulation of the sound.

A system of multilayer cloth banners, similar to heavy drapes, can be extended from storage pockets to cover much of the wall area of the room. The banners are operated by motors and are kept inside their storage pockets during most symphonic works, organ recitals, chamber concerts, and choral concerts. This allows sound to reflect off the walls of the room. The banners can be extended to cover the wall surfaces during rehearsals and also during popular music events, cinema, meetings, and other events where speech is an important activity. The room is much less reverberant when the banners cover the walls.

The Evangeline Atwood Concert Hall in the Alaska Center for the Performing Arts in Anchorage, Alaska, was completed in 1989 by Hardy Holtzman and Pfeiffer Associates, Inc., Architects, and acoustical consultant Christopher Jaffe of Jaffe Acoustics, Inc. The room is a 2,100-seat multipurpose hall with an innovative electronic architecture sound system that extends the acoustical variability of the room for a wide range of performance types, including drama, opera, symphony, and rock and roll.

The electronic architecture system adds early reflections and reverberation for orchestral concerts in a room whose volume would not otherwise provide these qualities. Three discrete electronic acoustical systems are used in the Atwood Hall. By turning on one or more of them, the acoustical qualities of the room can be enhanced subtly or changed dramatically.

The early field system provides simulated sound reflections from a series of loudspeakers located around the proscenium and in the mezzanine and balcony faces. The sound played through the early field loudspeakers is heard by listeners as early reflections arriving shortly after the direct sound, thus providing a sense of clarity and increasing the overall loudness of the sound. The late field system or warmth system is designed to provide sound reflections in lower frequencies to enhance the presence of the bass sounds in the room. The reverberant field system was designed to add almost 0.5 seconds to the reverberation time. The room was designed for the performance of opera and Broadway plays, but its volume and the corresponding reverberation time were too short for most

Figure 6–15 / Evangeline Atwood Concert Hall, Anchorage, Alaska. Hardy Holzman and Pfeiffer Associates, architects, completed 1989. A 2,100-seat multipurpose auditorium with electronically assisted acoustics. Left: View toward stage. Right: View from stage.

symphonic performances. Therefore it was desirable to prolong the reverberation time in the room during some concert performances. The multiplicity of loudspeakers provides a reverberant field that surrounds or envelops the audience with a rich, full sound.

Jaffe emphasized that the electronic architecture systems do not change the character of the sound from the source. "It is important for people to realize how subtle it is," remarked Mark Holden, one of the acoustical designers on the project. "We are providing additional reflections and additional reverberation, enhancing it by 10 or 15 percent to change the overall perception of the room's quality. . . . For the system to work well, it must be used in an acoustically sound room in the first place."[28]

Acoustical understanding has increased markedly in the nearly four decades since the acoustical failures at Lincoln Center. And, as in most fields, computers are beginning to play a larger and larger role. Today acoustic engineers are "able to listen to their designs before they're built," according to Dr. Amar G. Bose, chairman of the Bose Corporation, which developed the Auditioner™ system (Fig. 6–16). The system resulted from more than nine years of research and was validated through comparison with acoustic performance in actually built spaces where "even expert listeners describe the differences as

Figure 6–16 / The Auditioner™ system is composed of a desktop workstation, an audio computer, and audio playback apparatus. It is used to simulate the sonic environment that would be experienced in a specific location within a space. Through the use of such advanced tools, design enhancements can be studied and performance improved.

very small, as small as one would expect if one moved, for example, a few seats over in a typical auditorium."[29]

Acoustical expertise tends to be concentrated on those building types that are specifically aimed at facilitating communication: telecasting facilities, theaters, auditoriums, classrooms, etc. Little comparable attention has been paid to sound control in housing or places of work. Yet with the mechanization of industry, office work, transport, and yard work, the level of excessive noise constitutes a serious environmental hazard. It is estimated that about 28 million Americans suffer serious hearing loss, with about one third of this attributable to noise.[30] Noise-induced hearing loss is one of the most common occupational diseases, yet it is underrated because there are no visible effects and, usually, no pain. Its course is insidious, involving a gradual, progressive loss of communication, first noticed when other people do not seem to speak as clearly as before.[31] The reduction of noise in places of work and living is, technically at least, a simple problem.

It involves, among other techniques, a greatly expanded use of absorptive insulating materials and isolation devices to confine noise to its place of origin.

Pollution of the Sonic Environment

The acoustical design problem of the individual vessel (whether it be a room or an entire building) can thus be seen as entirely solvable — even though, as too often occurs, many solutions fall far short of the optimal. In any case, manipulation of the sound generated within a given building is the responsibility of the architect. But the control of noise in the environment is incomparably more difficult and complex. The sources of pollution are disparate and widely scattered; legal means of protection against them are almost nonexistent, and technical means of suppression are complex and costly. Two of the greatest sources of sonic pollution in the typical American city today are multilane highways and jet airports. Their adequate control obviously implies cooperation of many agencies at municipal, regional, and national levels.[32]

Recognition of this form of environmental degradation is rapidly growing, even though it has been slower to command professional attention than the exactly comparable pollution of air, soil, and water by chemical agents. Today there is no question but that environmental noise constitutes a major threat to health and well-being. In fact, many of the technical processes used by governmental agencies to evaluate and study the impact of environmental noise have been developed to accept increasing noise levels and result in lessening economic impact on noise makers.

The impact of environmental noise upon the individual can be observed at several levels. The most familiar one is simple interference with conversation or with purposeful activities such as studying or writing. At this level of environmental stress, we are normally aware of noise only as being an annoyance ("It's so noisy here I can't hear myself think!"). Nevertheless, even at the level of casual exposure to such noise levels as obtained on many city streets, conversation for pedestrians is difficult, if not downright impossible. Much more serious, from the standpoint of health, is exposure to noise levels high enough to interfere with rest and sleep. Such stress is now recognized as contributing to psychophysiological disturbances that, if extended across time, have a deleterious effect upon the individual's health. This is a very common form of stress for millions of city dwellers, especially in hot weather, when windows are open for ventilation. A survey of 1,400 London households revealed that sleep and relaxation of 82 percent were disturbed by noises originating outside the building and 16 percent by noise coming from adjacent apartments. Only 1 percent were disturbed by noise originating within their own apartments.[33]

Environmental medicine is now producing indisputable evidence that high levels of noise lead directly to physiological disturbance and degeneration, both of the ear itself and of the body as a whole.[34] Normal city noises not only get on the nerves but can do permanent damage to the auditory system, negatively affect the heart and blood pressure, and eventually "disturb every bodily function."[35] Loud blasts send pulse and heart-beat skyrocketing, as does the effort to talk or be heard in presence of continuous, high-level noise. A study of German steelworkers exposed to severe noise conditions showed them to have an unusually high percentage of abnormal heart rhythms. Similar studies of Italian textile workers, also exposed to high noise levels in their places of work, showed abnormal brain wave patterns, some of them actually suggestive of personality disorders. Noise-related illnesses are clearly reaching epidemic proportions, with hearing loss currently the most widely reported occupational disease.

Ear Health and Sonic Stress

Like all the organs of the human body, the hearing system deteriorates with age, but there is mounting evidence that the onset of such hearing loss occurs earlier, and is much more severe, in the noise-ridden environments of the urbanized world. To study this phenomenon, a group of specialists under the leadership of Dr. Samuel Rosen of Columbia University decided to study the hearing of a population living in a noise-free environment. The culture selected was that of the Mabaans, a people living in a remote region of southeast Sudan, some 10° in latitude above the equator and approximately 500 miles south of Khartoum.

The investigators found the natural sonic environment almost entirely unpolluted by the noises of human activity. They found that:

In general, the sound level in the villages is below the 40 dB on the "C scale" of the sound level meter except occasionally at sunrise or soon thereafter when a domestic animal such as a rooster, lamb, cow or dove makes itself heard. During six months of the year, heavy rains occur about three times a week with one or two claps of thunder. A few men engage in some productive activities such as beating palm fronds with a wooden club. But the absence of hard reverberating surfaces— such as walls, ceilings, floors and hard furniture, etc.— in the vicinity apparently accounts for the low intensity levels measured on the sound level meter: 73−74 dB at the worker's ear.

The highest noise levels encountered during our stay occurred when the villagers were dancing and singing. One recorded group consisted of ten young men and ten young women. Stanzas of a song were sung by a very soft-voiced male who also played the five string lyre. [He was] followed at the end of each stanza by the chorus of twenty. The recorded levels of 20 singers in chorus were 100−104 dB, topped by hoots and shouts at the end, yielding levels of 106−110 dB. Such festival singing apparently occurs about one to three times a week and lasts from one to three hours.[36]

This historic analysis of the sonic environment of an African village was based on studies made in 1961−1963.[37] But it could perfectly well describe that of any preindustrial village in Periclean Greece, Shakespeare's England, or the Virginia of George Washington's childhood. Existing in this largely undisturbed and unpolluted natural environment, the Mabaans were found to enjoy a hearing capacity remarkably superior to that of Americans—and this superiority increased with age (Fig. 6−17).

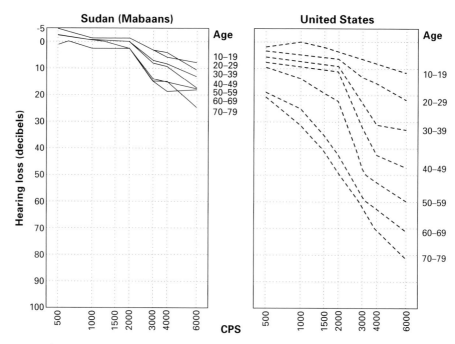

Figure 6–17 / Hearing acuity of men of Mabaan tribe in Sudan (left) was strikingly superior to that of American men of all ages (right). Mabaans spent their lives in a sonic environment that was markedly less stressful than the American.

The difference becomes quite marked in the age group 30–39 years, when the Mabaans hear better by 19.3 dB, and at 40–49 years by 29.6 dB. . . . In the 70–79 year old group, we find 53 percent of the Mabaans responding to [sounds of] 14,000 cps as compared to 2 percent for persons of the same group in New York, Cairo and Dusseldorf.[38*]

The Mabaans seemed spectacularly more healthy according to other indices as well. Blood pressures were much lower throughout life, hovering around 115 systolic from 15 to 75 years, while for Americans of that period it rose from 115 at age 20 to 160 at age 70.[39] The Rosen group also found little arteriosclerosis, greater elasticity of the small arteries, no varicose veins or thrombosis, no bronchial asthma.[40] A decrement in hearing is associated with many of these vascular conditions, as an adequate supply of blood to the capillaries of the inner ear is essential to good hearing (Fig. 6–18).

Although the exact line of cause and effect remains to be traced in greater detail, the Rosen report is epochal for establishing the fundamental relationship between environmental degradation and damages to health and hearing at an epidemiological scale. While modern industrial society cannot hope to recreate the sonic environment of a pastoral village, this relationship serves as a classic benchmark for noise-control policy in any industrialized society.

---

* Sound frequency is measured in *hertz* which are cycles per second (cps), international standard.

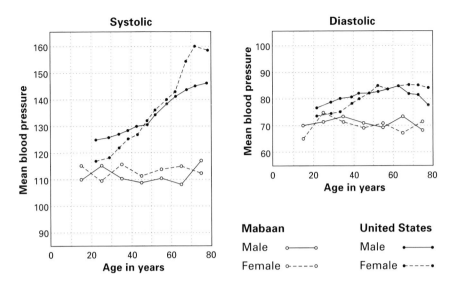

Figure 6-18 / Comparison of mean blood pressures of apparently healthy Americans with those of the Mabaans of Sudan suggests a correlation between loss of hearing and cardiovascular diseases. Many factors were probably involved in the Mabaans' better health, including diet and relaxed lifestyle, but quiet sonic environment was important.

In this country's metropolitan regions, particularly disquieting is the noise generated by takeoffs and landings at airports, as more and more Americans choose to fly. Over 875,000 people living near America's busiest airports (several of which are miles from the cities they serve) are routinely subject to excessive airport noise, defined by the Federal Aviation Administration (FAA) as an average level of 65 dB or greater.[41] Seventy-five percent of fifty airports recently surveyed indicated that they are either expanding (e.g., increasing the number or length of runways, upgrading passenger facilities, or annexing adjacent properties) or planning to do so. With such expansion, millions of Americans whose communities were originally buffered from airport operations become more and more heavily impacted.

The courts have occasionally established that noise is a *taking*, meaning that residents whose serenity has been taken by the effects of significant airport noise may receive financial compensation from the airport for their losses. Other compensatory measures include changes in flight patterns and hours of operation, soundproofing of homes or schools, and financial assistance in selling homes. Whether these measures provide more than a stopgap remains to be seen.

The entire scope of this situation bears review. Air travel is one of the most energy-intensive means of transport, and yet, because of expediency and low fares, its popularity is increasing, even with short commuter trips where other mass transit options are available. This, combined with the noise and other environmental impacts, plus the loss of land to airport expansion, leads one to question the wisdom of land use or transportation planning that led us to this point.

There are still areas in this country whose sonic environment, with minor exceptions, has remained much the same for centuries. Recent studies of sound levels in national parks have found little, if any, noise intrusion in many locations.[42] Near the highways is the roar of diesel trucks; freight (if not passenger) trains still clatter down the tracks, though most cross-country jets fly at too high an altitude to be heard. But these sounds are merely superimposed upon a natural environment that remains largely unpolluted. For long intervals and over large areas, noise levels may sink below the threshold of hearing. To the soundshocked city dweller, such a sonic environment seems idyllic. There is little doubt that these areas provide a less stressful sonic environment than that found in cities.

Because, away from the highways, the rural environment is relatively unpolluted, the problem of community noise control is still fairly simple. Modern farm equipment, for example, often comes with sound-insulated cabs. No neighbors' telvision sets or stereo systems are near enough to constitute a hazard. If the farmer owns a tractor or power tools, the chances are that the noise they make is psychologically satisfying; in any case, the farmer is seldom exposed for long periods to noise levels that are injurious to health.

There is, of course, an obverse to this idyllic condition of rural silence: boredom. We do, however, have new ways of bringing the world home and overcoming feelings of isolation and monotony. A satellite dish in the side yard guarantees access to television from all parts of the world, and world-band does the same for radio. Home entertainment centers, video stores, and compact disc players are commonly assumed to have brought to the rural areas an exact equivalent of the theater, cinema, concert, and ballet actually available to the city dweller. But, however much better than the nineteenth-century rural vacuum these audiovisual facsimiles may be, they are very much less than the multidimensional reality of their prototypes, as documented by recent studies cited above.

People living in the country may have no need for buildings that protect them against noise; what they are short of is buildings that provide them with socially productive sound. These are precisely the types of buildings they must have if they are to enjoy a civilized sonic environment—bandshells that carry the brasses to the farthest row on a hot July night, theaters that direct the undistorted lines to the balcony, opera and concert houses whose acoustical role is a part of the performance itself, lecture halls that lose not a syllable of the expert's speech, halls where a thousand can square-dance and still hear fiddler and caller. This is the sort of synthetic sonic environment that would enrich their lives.

In any case, the steady shift in population from the farms and rural villages to cities and their burgeoning metropolises, in the United States, no less than in Latin America or Africa, seems to suggest that a mere freedom from noise does not compensate for the rich and stimulating environment of the city. Once they become conscious of these urban alternatives, even the Mabaan youth are apt to set off for Khartoum or Cairo, sonic pollution or no.

In cities, sound levels run a full gamut from the absolute (and synthetic) silence of the broadcasting studio through the hubbub of street life to the concentrated clatter of a printing plant or the ear-shattering clamor of a punch press and foundry. City dwellers have lost the peace and quiet of the countryside but their sonic environment is, at the same time, infinitely more varied. They have access, at least in theory, to a range of productive sound—concert, lecture, drama. They have greater access to all forms of electronic propagation (as do, of course, their neighbors). They dwell in a sonic environment that is hostile to their physical well-being, however nourishing some aspects of it may be intellectually. They may have access to a thousand forms of productive sound. They have no refuge from noise.

A socially and physiologically satisfactory sonic environment will not be achieved in our cities without radical changes in their design and management. For here the natural environment has been destroyed. It can never be literally recreated, and it cannot be restructured along new lines until we are prepared to accept new and higher levels of controls.[43] Noise is a sign of social dysfunction; the criteria for its elimination coincide at all major points with those for the elimination of all forms of environmental pollution.

8p

The Architectural Manipulation of Space, Time, and Gravity

Human experience, through its metabolic and sensory perceptual systems, occupies its own "habitat" in the external world. Indeed, for the purposes of fruitful architectural and urbanistic analysis, each of its component systems must be conceived of as having its own separate habitat. Each of these can be described topologically in terms of modalities of stimulus and response. But each of these habitats must also be described in spatial and temporal terms as well, as all of them have dimension (height, width, length) and all of them are experienced across time.

Spatially, these habitats may be visualized as three scales — microcosmic, mesocosmic, and macrocosmic — nested one inside the other with interfaces between each. For the human body, the interface between micro- and mesoenvironments is delimited by the continuous, three-dimensional envelope of the epidermis. For architecture, the interface between meso- and macroenvironments is delimited by the walls of the room or the walls of the building. Along both interfaces we commonly install artificial membranes to modulate the flow of forces across them — clothing along the body line, insulated walls along the building line.

Though they occupy the same space, however, the spatial characteristics of the habitat of the metabolic system are quite different from those of the perceptual systems. Only the actual thermoatmospheric conditions along the body's surfaces play any role in heat exchange across the epidermis. Only the air, water, and digested food actually absorbed through the mucosa of the body's cavities afford the fuel required for the whole metabolic process. Thus we can say that, though the habitat of metabolism has extension, it has no significant depth or thickness at all. Boundary, interface, and habitat are one and the same. Heat, oxygen, water, and food may exist in plenty around us, in either the meso- or macroenvironments. Our sensory scanning systems (sight, smell, hearing) may bring us information about their distribution in space. But they have no significance for metabolic process until actual body contact with them is achieved. Moreover, such a relationship between metabolism and its habitat exists independently of any perception of it.* Thus, for example, the heat exchange across the epidermis always critically affects the body's metabolic posture, even if for some reason — sleep, coma, anesthesia — the body's perceptual systems are unable at the time to perceive it.

This dual nature of animal existence is the source of most of the fundamental paradoxes of architecture. In order for the building to be experientially satisfactory, it must afford a good fit for the body — the metabolic system and its habitat on one hand, the sensory/perceptual systems and their special habitats on the other. These latter have altogether different spatial characteristics, varying greatly in cross section: from microns (for the velvet we touch), to inches (for the rose we smell), to feet (for the painting we admire), to miles (for the church bells we hear or the distant view we admire), to light-years (for the stars we gaze at). Well-being, amenity — and ultimately, beauty itself — depend upon the architectural manipulation of all these environmental factors, with their varying scales and dimensions.

The boundaries of all architectural volumes are delimited by surfaces (floors, walls, ceilings) that constitute the second interface between people and the macrocosmic world of nature. These bounding surfaces play a decisive role in the way we respond to and behave in the spaces they enclose. Thus a wall may, at a given moment, act quite effectively to insulate us against the mechanical force and bitter cold of a winter gale. Together with the heating system, the building may thus afford optimal thermoatmospheric conditions for our metabolic well-being. But this same wall, at the same time, may have an inner surface whose color or brightness is an outrage to the eye or whose acoustical response is an insult to the ear. Similarly, a given room (intimate café, classroom) may be equipped with comfortable chairs and tables, properly organized in spatial terms to support a successful luncheon meeting or seminar — but the same room may have too low an illumination level, too high an ambient noise level, or too poor a ventilation system to permit satisfactory interpersonal communication. In short, the problem of a good fit between the occupant and the room extends from the skin right out to the walls and beyond, and implies the satisfactory manipulation of every habitat requirement simultaneously. Each habitat requirement is served by the interaction of the dynamic aspects of the built (or third) environment, as noted in chapter 1.

---

* This proposition cannot, of course, be reversed — that is, that perception cannot exist independently of its metabolic base. The metabolic process constitutes the very platform of consciousness, as explained in chapter 1.

The various aspects of the built environment are subdivided into the six *S*s by inventor/designer Stewart Brand,[1] after the earlier work of architect Frank Duffy:[2]

- *Stuff* or furnishings, which may be modified on a daily or monthly basis. Brand says, "Furniture is called *mobilia* in Italian for good reason."
- *Space plan*, or the interior layout — the walls, ceilings, floors and doors. These may change every three years or so in commercial space, or thirty years or more in some houses.
- *Services*, or the communications wiring, electrical wiring, lighting system, plumbing, sprinkler system, HVAC system, elevators, and escalators, which may wear out or become obsolete within seven to fifteen years. If the systems are outdated and too deeply embedded to be easily replaced, the entire building may have to be demolished.
- *Skin*, or the exterior surface, which in commercial buildings may change frequently — every fifteen years or so, as with "façadectomies" by developers interested in attracting new clientele.
- *Structure*, or the foundation and load-bearing elements, which to most people constitutes "the building." The life of a structure may range from thirty to three hundred years. (In some cases, as in Hong Kong, the lifespan may be far shorter, on the order of three years!).
- *Site*, or the geographical setting, the legally defined lot, whose boundaries outlast generations of buildings.

The systems for the control of atmosphere, light, heat, and sound interpenetrate each other and the structure itself to such an extent that they can be isolated only for the purpose of analysis.

The Three Dimensions of Environmental Fit

The design of any architectural component thus becomes a problem of successful adjustment between the organism and its environment: the buttocks and the chair seat, the eye and the lighting system, the student and the classroom, the pedestrian and the city street. In each case we deal with a set of spatial parameters that describe the contours of the special vessel or container. However, this vessel must be understood as not merely sustaining a given action but also as actually generating a specific mode of behavior (chair makes for sitting, light makes for reading, classroom makes for study, sidewalk makes for walking, etc.). Thus, as Professor of Man-Environment Relations Raymond G. Studer once expressed it:

The designed environment can be analyzed as a *prosthetic* phenomenon. It functions prosthetically in two distinct, but interrelated modes: 1) it is *physiologically* prosthetic in that it supports behavioral goals through maintenance of required (behaviorally correlated) physiological states, and 2) it is *behaviorally* prosthetic . . . in that it intentionally configures specific behavioral topographies.[3]

The architectural fit, in order to support or elicit the desired behavior, must therefore be analyzed from several distinct but intimately related points of view, as defined in the previous edition of this book:

1. *Ergonomics*: the study of the expenditure of physical energy by the body required to occupy space and to overcome gravity, friction, and inertia implicit in all physiological work.
2. *Anthropometrics*: the study of the spatial patterns that the body describes in the performance of work — walking, sitting, reaching, lifting, pulling, resting, sleeping, etc.
3. *Proxemics:* the study of the behavioral consequences of spatial relationships for interpersonal relationships of all scales and types.

Our understanding of these evolving fields has grown enormously since then.

Human beings have often been described — especially in the Puritan tradition — as being fundamentally lazy. The term is pejorative, involving an ethical judgment on a simple fact: humanity's compelling need to husband limited supplies of energy. There may indeed be such a thing as a lazy person, but there is no doubt at all that all animals, including us, are compelled by circumstances to expend large amounts of energy just to stay alive. Resisting the forces of gravity and inertia, of atmospheric pressure and environmental heat, is of itself stressful, as the Canadian physiologist Hans Selye's pioneering work established. All animals develop characteristic modes of behavior in response to this circumstance. Thus cattle grazing on a hillside follow the isoplethic contours so consistently that paths develop along them. In just such fashion, college students leave the formal patterns of paved walks to take diagonal shortcuts across quadrangles. Cattle or college students, the trajectory of their movement represents a resolution of all the vectors of force acting upon them at that time. Some of these forces are exogenous (change of level, choice of sun or shade, mud or dry paving, etc.) and some are endogenous (lateness for an appointment, desire to be seen or not seen, etc.). Both sets of forces are equally real, of course, and consciousness often compels people to take the less easy or more hazardous path (to jump into heavy seas to save a drowning child, to attack across an open field in battle, etc.).

Each trace or path represents the end result of a complicated process of cost accounting. It is largely an unconscious (or at least subconscious) process in which we continually weigh advantages against disadvantages, costs against possible dividends, of this or that method of achieving our objectives. Exactly how this process is effectuated in human behavior is a complex and not fully understood question. All movement in space involves work, whether physiological or societal. (A two-hour set of tennis — play — may easily involve the output of as much energy as eight hours at a computer — work.)

Because movement is costly of energy, all animals have developed monitoring systems to aid in its conservation. In all higher animals, and above all in us, this is expressed in an extraordinary capability to orient one's movements with reference to the outside world. It involves all the body's sensory perceptual systems but it clearly goes far beyond mere perception to include an ordered response. It gives the body the capacity to discriminate between movement and nonmovement, or between its own movement and that of other bodies in the exterior world. Such capacity is critically important to survival—too important, as J. J. Gibson put it, to be entrusted to any single set of sensory receptors.

There are many kinds of movement to be registered. There is articular kinesthesis for the body framework; vestibular kinesthesis for the movement of the skull; cutaneous kinesthesis for the movement of the skin relative to what it touches; and visual kinesthesis for perspective trans-formations of the field of view. In all these perceptions the sensory quality arising from the recep-tor type is difficult to detect but the information is perfectly clear. Kinesthesis is the registering of such information without being sensory; it is one of the best examples of detection without a spe-cial modality of sensations.[4]

In the psychological literature, kinesthesis is not seen as perception divorced from sen-sation. With regard to perceptual-motor processes, kinesthesis is the sensation of move-ment coming from receptors in the muscles and tendons. This is different from the sense of touch, which comes from receptors in the skin.

The operation of these various forms of kinesthesis is apparent in the behavior of peo-ple in architectural or urbanistic space. Articular kinesthesis is expressed in the way we sit in a chair or lie in a bed. If either is a bad fit, this is expressed in the way we twist and squirm in an effort to find a more comfortable resolution. Vestibular kinesthesis deter-mines our behavior on ramps and stairs. The spiral-ramped galleries of the Guggenheim Museum in New York City, for example, force a continuous disequilibrium on the visitor that stresses the vestibular apparatus. Cutaneous kinesthesis governs our response to sur-faces—for example, whether we follow the path or cut across the lawn depends upon whether the grass is dry and resilient or wet and muddy. Visual kinesthesis enables us to anticipate, and hence to avoid, hazardous discontinuities in surface. It is at the base of our tendency to draw back from floor-to-ceiling glass walls in high-rise buildings. Of course, vision overrides all other forms of perception with its capacity for transmuting other forms of sensory input into visual data. Thus, it is thanks to visual kinesthesis that we avoid mud without stepping in it, steer clear of rough walls before we scrape an elbow on them, avoid falls down unprotected changes in grade, and discriminate between soup and salad without having to taste either.

Every time architects or urban designers erect walls or pave streets, they intervene in the behavioral modes of the population of that space. As Winston Churchill once said, "We shape our buildings, and afterwards our buildings shape us."[5] The consequences of this intervention may be major or minor, benign or malignant; they are always real. Mal-function is expressed in incidents or accidents among the population—in other words, *by their not behaving the way they were supposed to.* Conventionally, these are always blamed on the individual who wasn't looking where he was going, or slipped on the pavement, or stumbled on the stairs, tripped over the chair, got dizzy and fell out the window, etc. But accident statistics alone are enough to suggest that this is a simplistic explanation of events, as different types of injuries caused by accidents are associated with *specific sets of spatial configurations*.

It is true that the inner nature of accidents connected with buildings often seems inexplicable, because they involve movement. Careful research, such as use of narrative diaries in combination with videotaping, can be useful in applications that require insight into the mental processes involved in decision making and behavior. Slow-motion photography can also be used to study activity within a space. In the context of workstation design, videotaping is conducted by ergonomists for kinetic and biomechanical analyses. Other techniques are also used to measure posture and motion, such as devices that measure patterns of motion of specific body parts, like the wrist or lower back, and infrared sensors for the motion of several body parts. These techniques are sometimes necessary to explicate even the simplest incident, as cause and effect are too entangled for the naked eye to perceive. Such research usually reveals that despite the operation of articular, vestibular, cutaneous, and visual kinesthesis, users could not adapt their actions to the spatial set involved. In other words, the architectural element could neither support nor elicit the sequence of motions it was nominally designed to expedite (Fig. 7–1).

Environmental designers must understand, far better than they presently do, the consequences of design decisions. To explore these fully requires more consistent application of ergonomic concepts, methods of measuring input-output factors, and systematic means of resolving thousands of variables into comprehensible parameters for the designer. Christopher Alexander's concerns have become all the more true today:

More and more design problems are reaching insoluble levels of complexity. This is true not only of moon bases, factories and radio receivers, whose complexity is internal, but even of villages and teakettles. . . . their background of needs and activities . . . is becoming too complex to grasp intuitively. . . . The intuitive resolution of contemporary design problems simply lies beyond a single individual's integrative grasp.[6]

In fact, many of today's design solutions appear to fail in the face of this inherent complexity. Designers tend to focus on the technology and miss the human element, as noted by University of California professor emeritus of cognitive science Donald Norman:

"I'm a rocket scientist," one engineer complained to me. "I design missile systems, but I can't figure out how to program my VCR." Why is it that we sometimes have so much trouble working apparently simple things, such as doors and light switches, water faucets and thermostats, to say nothing of computers and automated factory equipment? The answer lies not with the hapless user but with designers who fail to think about products from the operator's point of view. . . . The concepts behind their design are invisible and abstract. There may be nothing to see, nothing to guide understanding. Consequently, workers know less and less about the inner workings of the systems under their control. Such alienation has startling effects: most industrial and aviation accidents today are attributed to human error. . . . A more appropriate response would be to redesign devices in a way that minimizes the chance for error in the first place.[7]

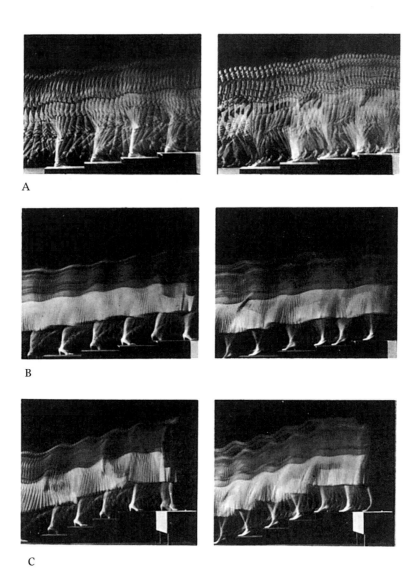

A

B

C

Figure 7–1/ Analysis of behavior-eliciting properties of stairs of varying proportions; kinesthetic research project by James Marston Fitch and José Bernardo. In an effort to isolate comfort and safety factors in different stairs, actual stairways were replicated. Male and female models, ascending and descending, were photographed in time exposures under strobe light (A) and normal light (B and C). Photographs reveal that "easy" stairs (A and B) have a spatial configuration that imposes awkward gaits upon both male and female users. Wide tread (25 inches) and very low riser (3.375 inches) impose culturally unfamiliar and kinesthetically awkward gait upon all users. Too wide for one normal male step (A) and too narrow for two female steps (B), stairs elicit erratic movement, especially in descent. Note irregular gait and arm swing. Steeper stairs (6-inch riser, 15-inch tread) elicit more-regular gait from female user in both ascent and descent (C). Males can adjust by shifting horizontal trajectory. Ascent is more comfortable despite greater energy expenditure.

Ergonomics: The Cost Accounting of Work and Fatigue

What, specifically, does the animal body require of architectural space? Not at all that it provide a controlled environment of absolutely uniform or unvarying qualities, as is so often assumed. To the contrary: the requirements of the animal body vary constantly as it goes about its various tasks. For optimal well-being, it requires equilibrium, the dynamic balance between internal needs and external means of meeting them.

Although this is true for all environmental components, it is most easily demonstrated for the thermal because, as the pioneering physiologists Winslow and Herrington put it, "The whole life process is a form of slow combustion."[8] The body is only about 20 percent efficient in the conversion of fuel into work; it must therefore always dissipate a great deal of waste energy in the form of heat. And because the body is sensitive to its accumulation, this heat must be dissipated at the appropriate rate.

In addition to its level of activity, the amount of heat generated depends on the body's basal metabolic rate (BMR) for vital functions—beating of the heart, expanding and contracting of the lungs, cleansing of blood through the kidneys, production of enzymes in the liver, digesting and absorbing of food by the digestive system, manufacturing of essential chemicals by the cells, etc. BMRs are affected by his or her sex (women have slightly lower BMRs), weight (the lighter, the lower the BMR), amount of fat (lean muscle tissue uses more calories than fat tissue, so the more fat and less muscle, the lower the BMR), age (the older, the lower the BMR), amount of sleep (the BMR is about 10 percent

Table 7–1 / *Effect of Physical Work on Metabolism*

Type of Activity	Calories per Hour	Btus per Hour
lying still	90	360
standing still	110	440
wallpapering	200	800
carpentry	210	840
scraping paint	260	1,040
sawing, power	300	1,200
plastering	320	1,280
sawing, manual	500	2,000
digging trenches	600	2,400
ax chopping, fast	1,200	4,800

Even under constant thermal conditions, heat production rises with increased activity. The caloric cost of each activity includes the BMR. Thus, trench digging burns about 600 Calories in an hour. This is not added on to the day's resting BMR; rather, this value is substituted for one hour of the BMR. The standard unit of heat energy is the *calorie*, also known as the *gram calorie*, *small calorie*, or *standard calorie*. But the unit in common use in nutrition, physiology, and medicine, and in the table above, is the Calorie (kilocalorie, kcal), which equals 1,000 calories, or about 4 Btus.

lower during sleep), and the temperature (the colder the air temperature, the higher the BMR, to maintain 98.6°F). An average male uses between 1,400 and 1,700 Calories a day just to sustain his BMR, even when "doing nothing."[9]

During activity, a person's level of conditioning, as well as the temperature and humidity of the air and how efficiently the activity is performed, affects the number of Calories expended. The rate varies with each level or type of activity — how widely is clear from Table 7-1, as presented for a 150-pound person.[10]

It is obvious that we deal here with ratios, not fixed quantities; hence, the building should be regarded as a flexible instrument for maintaining these ratios at levels established by the body. How important these ratios are not merely to human well-being and efficiency but ultimately to life itself may be seen in the pioneering work of Winslow and Herrington, in Table 7-2, showing the correlation between temperature, work, and physical condition:[11]

Table 7-2 / Effect of Temperature on Body Processes

Effective Temperature	Total Work in Foot-Pounds	Increase in Rectal Temperature Degrees F per Hour	Increase in Pulse Rate Beats per Minute per Hour
70	225,000	0.1	7
80	209,000	0.3	11
90	153,000	1.2	31
100	67,000	4.0	103
110	37,000	8.5	237

As temperature rises, the body's ability to perform work begins to drop — moderately up to 80°F effective temperature, rapidly thereafter. Such increasing stress is reflected in rising body temperatures. Pulse rates also soar as blood is rushed to body surfaces in the effort to dissipate heat.

These illustrations, drawn from the relationship between the body and the thermal component of its environment, have analogies in other areas of existence. Thus we can be sure that any task involving critical acuity in seeing (classroom study, fine machine work, microsurgery) requires a luminous environment precisely structured to that end, and we can be certain that both work and worker suffer if it is not so structured. Similarly, any activity demanding critical discrimination in hearing or communication (concert listening, airport control, radio broadcasting) requires its own special sonic environment and suffers qualitatively from the lack of it. The proper task of good architecture, in short, is to organize space and environment in which the eye, ear, tongue, or hand can accomplish its task or activity — seeing, hearing, speaking, tasting, touching, or lifting — with the greatest ease and precision, subject to the least interference or friction from extraneous factors.

Architectural "creativity" can easily subvert this intention. For example, open floor office layouts with perhaps 5-foot-high cubicle walls around individual workstations (to maximize productive use of floor area and to allow for adequate air circulation) have become the norm for lower-level professional staff in most office buildings. In this type of setting, the staff often experience a very short mean time to interrupt—that is, every ten minutes or so they may find themselves distracted (by a telephone call in an adjoining cubicle, social visits, unsolicited conversations through or over the cubicle wall). As a result, productivity suffers. The industrious among them may have to deliberately block out persistent distractions to achieve the level of focus required for the work at hand. In this case the architect has not designed a workplace free of distraction, quite possibly having been sidetracked by the visual element. This situation could have been avoided if the architect had chosen to analyze the issue of acoustics with the client and specified sound-absorbing materials.

Other factors, equally real but much harder to isolate and define, are also involved. "Work itself seldom leads to the chronic condition we call fatigue," says one researcher. "It is axiomatic that worry, not work, [is what] kills."[12] People often experience stress as a result of their own emotional reactions to work. Whether they perceive the demands of the job as overwhelming, unrelenting, or ill matched to their skills and capabilities, this state of discomfort and frustration can lead to changes in behavior and physiology. It may begin to affect their physical and psychological health.[13]

If an architect plans to intervene and improve working conditions, this intervention must be based on a recognition of the host of stressors involved—only some of which can be tackled through changes in building form and its fixtures. Additionally, while today's work may be less physically onerous in knowledge-intensive companies:

and the surroundings more agreeable, these firms typically demand *more* of their employees. . . . Employees are encouraged to use not only their rational minds but to pour their emotions, intuitions and imagination into the job. This is why Marcusian critics see in this an even more sinister "exploitation" of the employee.[14]

Moreover, there is growing evidence that the very process of living, quite apart from environment and work, produces measurable stress, which leads in turn to measurable fatigue. Though it is only under laboratory conditions that we can observe a person at rest and even partially isolated from external stimuli, it is clear that even here the body is still under stress—the heart and muscles resisting gravity and atmospheric pressure, etc. In the 1930s, the pioneering physiologist Hans Selye went so far as to try to isolate and measure such factors, giving them the status of a syndrome, "the stress of life."[15] Since then our understanding of stress has expanded. We now know that the stress response involves the secretion of perhaps a dozen hormones and the inhibition of others. Moreover, many studies have shown that chronic activation of the stress response can impair health, with some people being more vulnerable than others.[16]

In this complicated field, architects can never be more than one of many types of specialists, nor can their contribution ever be expected to solve it alone. But this is no justification for their abdicating responsibility. Indeed, by the very terms of the profession they cannot abdicate, as their every act, whether ignorant or informed, constitutes an intervention in the field of human behavior. Hence they must have a general comprehension of the problem and assume a measure of responsibility for its solution. Yet the contemporary architect displays a strange diffidence toward the whole subject. It is one of the paradoxes of American life that our architecture, like our technology, generally, has always sought to lighten human toil and ameliorate the conditions of human life, but it has simultaneously distrusted both the labor-saving mechanisms whereby this was to be accomplished and the leisure time that was to be thereby won. The Puritan ethic links work with goodness, idleness with sin. Social Darwinists, on the other hand (Puritans under the skin), equate survival with genetic superiority, a frenetic pace of work with importance or self-worth. Both thereby introduce extraneous elements (irrelevant if not fallacious) into an equation already sufficiently complex.

The Puritans' fears were, in the truest sense of the word, physiologically groundless; only in outer space will people ever confront a physical state so free of stimulus as to be degenerative. However, it is also recognized that too little stress (motion, force, stimulation) may be as detrimental as too much. The human response to stress is probably not linear, increasing with greater levels of stress, but U-shaped.

The task of architecture is not to eliminate stress or abolish fatigue. It is rather to eliminate or at least to minimize those environmental pressures that are peripheral, tangential, or only accidentally associated with the task at hand. Then stress will be the byproduct of productive work, and fatigue will come from the accomplishment of human tasks and not from mere animal exertion. Good architecture, by this standard, is that which permits us to focus our energies on whatever we are doing, whether running a lathe or listening to a concert, writing an essay or recovering from surgery. The ultimate criterion is not lack of stress but optimal well-being under concrete conditions.

It is obvious that we deal here with complex equations in which variables of time and energy are involved. As a control instrument, the building should aim at a qualitatively constant set of environmental conditions, and not some merely quantitative uniformity of temperature, illumination, or ventilation. The criteria for this constancy can only be derived from the human body itself in action. It never seeks for some abstract condition (72 degrees Fahrenheit, 50 percent relative humidity, 10 foot-candles); it always demands instead that precise balance of forces dictated by the actual task.

As we have seen (Table 7-1), a person at hard work has a metabolic rate some thirteen times as high as when he is lying still. The implications for the thermal environment of the place of work and the bedroom are obvious. Actually, for situations of protracted stress at the same task, it is likely that environmental conditions should be altered during the course of the workday. Much research continues to be needed in this area but it is clear, in any case, that the criterion of building performance is that it contribute fully to the maintenance of this dynamic equilibrium between the person and the task.

Another and most important variant in this equation is the status of individuals—their age, sex, health, and emotional and intellectual attitudes. Just as the young person at rest has different thermal requirements from the young person at hard work, so a young person at hard work has different needs from those of an older coworker at the same task. There are always idiosyncratic individuals whose requirements vary from the norm. Their variations are real and cannot be ignored in the design of buildings involving them. But this should not obscure the fact that human response to heat, cold, glare, noise, and stench is generally uniform. When plotted on a graph, all of us lie on or quite near the general curve of humanity. Architects should accept this, as physiologists and psychologists do, as the basis, the point of departure, of their designs.

It goes without saying that the degree of precision of environmental control required of a building varies with its purpose. We demand a much lower order of performance from a bus shelter than from a bus terminal, from a circus tent than from an opera house, from a hospital waiting room than from the surgical theaters of that same hospital. The margin for error in architectural design is in inverse ratio to the criticalness of the process to be housed.

Most of what we know about fatigue and employee burnout is complicated, in a sense, by the one-sided investigations of its external or objective aspects. This is perhaps the natural result of research largely subsidized by manufacturers or corporations themselves as a means of increasing productivity. However important this approach may be, it is far from complete. For one of the most puzzling aspects of fatigue is its duality: it is at once objective and subjective, physiological and psychological. Thus, if we observe and measure it from the outside only, from the standpoint of management alone, we ignore the fact that the relationship between the two halves is not merely complex: it is dialectic.

Fatigue is obviously an entirely natural phenomenon, part of the basic physiological cycle of impairment and recovery in the living organism. But that, after all, is not saying much. More specific questions remain. Precisely how does fatigue affect production? How much fatigue can one endure in a week without suffering later? How is it that the modern building, with all its laborsaving mechanization, often seems to accelerate fatigue? What is the relation between types of fatigue and health? Although an analysis of the various types of fatigue reveals a wide divergence in details, there is one fundamentally common factor: disturbance of the balance between wear and repair. We all get tired when we work. The longer we work, the more tired we grow, and the heavier the work, the less we can do of it. Like stress, fatigue is both a process and an outcome. If overwork continues beyond a certain point, it begins to affect our health. The temporary disturbance between wear and repair becomes permanent damage. Where regular intervals of rest and recreation might have cured the first, long periods of medical or hospital treatment may be necessary to undo the latter.

Fatigue may also involve both central and local processes. Psychological or mental fatigue is obviously central, involving cognitive and emotional brain functions. Physical fatigue, or exhaustion may be local—that is, limited to the capacity of a specific body tissue, like muscle and bone, or central, in the sense that it involves physiological systems such as the cardiovascular or pulmonary system.

Repetitive strain injury from working with computers is an example of the local process of tissue fatigue. The risk factors, or mechanical stressors, include repetitive motions or, conversely, constrained posture (*no* motion), that often occurs in situations where the job is monotonous (in content or pace) and affords little control. Ironically, technological marvels such as computers, if misused, rob us of opportunities to rest and rejuvenate, and, in some ways, deprive us of resources that are fundamental to our long-term well-being.

Computers allow us to work for hours without taking a break, our fingers tapping away at 240 strokes a minute. Compare this with the old-fashioned typewriter, which, by its design, required the user to pause to move the carriage, change the paper, or dab correction fluid on a mistake. In our efforts to increase productivity in the office, we have left office workers with little variation in their workday; everything—files, mail, reports, electronic messaging, and research—can be accessed through the keyboard, with little call for running to the file cabinet, or checking a dictionary or encyclopedia, or getting up to discuss an issue with a colleague.[17]

We learn (at a much slower pace than technological advancement) that the convenience of technology extracts a hefty price if human factors are overlooked. Ergonomists urge word processors to take occasional stretch breaks (even when the technology allows them to continue unbridled, with an intense focus on the work at hand) to increase circulation and relieve tension.

New theories on the origins and consequences of fatigue continue to surface. One recently completed five-year study suggests that the artificial light levels found in modern homes and offices may be having profound effects on our circadian rhythms—resetting our biological clock by four to five hours. Normally, if we bedded down at nightfall, we would achieve deepest sleep between midnight and 1 A.M. As a result of our artificially extended day, our deepest sleep occurs between 4 and 5 A.M., just before most people are forced to wake up. As a result, the theory holds, many people in industrialized countries are constantly sleep-deprived and in a permanent state of jet lag.[18]

The human nervous system, in common with the nervous systems of other animals, behaves as if it were a storehouse of potential energy. When its store becomes depleted, symptoms of exhaustion make their appearance. In a person subjected to long-continued mental fatigue, recuperative processes do not have the opportunity fully to restore the nervous energy that has been utilized, so that the person is forced to rely on a special reserve store . . . which is intended to be used only for emergency.[19]

Nor do we all tire at the same rate. Joe seems to thrive on work that would kill Jim; Joni does twice as much work as Jane in the same time. Fatigue in one industry differs sharply from that in another, while two offices doing exactly the same type of work also vary widely with respect to fatigue rates. Obviously many factors are involved in this problem and it would be an error to assume that the building and its equipment is any more important than half a dozen others. In the triangular relationship between the task, the organism, and the environment, the building affords the working conditions under which work is done. A well-designed building, unit for unit of work, causes less fatigue than a badly designed one. But the length of the workweek, the rate at which work is performed, the character of the work itself are also of decisive importance, as are the health, morale, and adaptability of the workers themselves.

Common sense should tell anybody — especially anybody who works for a living — that a 60-hour workweek is detrimental to both the individual and society as a whole. Industrial experience amply confirms this: beyond given limits, increasing the length of the workweek does not bring corresponding increases in production. Indeed, over a period of time, it results in a net drop.

Fatigue affects production in another important way: the quality of the product tends to deteriorate along with decreasing quantity. An excessively long week results in a sharp increase in rejects on the one hand and in accidents on the other. Here an interesting psychological phenomenon is observed. Toward the end of the day, after a period of declining productivity, the worker gets a second wind. From a mood of depression workers spiral into a sudden excess of exhilaration and confidence. They work rapidly again and, as it seems to them, accurately. Objectively, however, they are careless. Their judgment of dimension and timing — essential in industrial operations — is noticeably impaired. Quality of work deteriorates rapidly.

The character of a specific job has a lot to do with fatigue. Modern serial or mass production involves careful analysis of the process, breaking it down into its component parts, organizing them in efficient sequence, and assigning specially trained people to each phase. The manufacturing process is thereby atomized. This often leads to a similar atomization of the worker's movements and mental processes, as John Ruskin so shrewdly remarked over a century ago. A job may require only a portion of a person's muscular and mental capacities, but it requires that portion all the time, and with sometimes horrifying monotony. Such routines skyrocket fatigue: they can actually cause psychological trauma, as Charlie Chaplin showed with such bitter wit in his movie classic *Modern Times*. Many of the assembly-line processes so characteristic of manufacturing and service industries during Chaplin's time have been introduced into the office environment, turning them, in effect, into information factories.

Starting at least as far back as World War II, there has always been news of some new production method that cuts in half the time formerly required to make something — a house, a car, or a plane. Such advances in production efficiency do not necessarily imply an increase in the *rate* of work. (For example, a big riveted bomber has as many as 45,000 rivets, each of which takes twenty seconds to manually drive, or a total of 2,500 hours. By changing the fabrication technique to automatic multiple welding, this time is reduced by approximately 30 percent. Assuming that environmental conditions remain the same, none of these savings in time necessarily means that the workers were more fatigued at day's end, even though production per person is increased.) Incentives to increase productivity continue into the twenty-first century.

Any current setback in U.S. productivity tends to be seen in a more global economic context. Because our labor rates are high relative to other economies, there is unyielding pressure to hold on to our competitive edge by whatever means possible, whether this entails increasing the productive output of the American worker through technological change or concessions from workers, more rapid delivery of materials to the end user, or protectionism.

Since the United States is becoming more deeply embedded in the world economy, performance relative to our trading partners is progressively more important to our living standards. These trends in performance spell stagnant living standards and increasing desperation for those trapped at the bottom of the income scale.[20]

It is intense rationalization within a given process that raises the danger of the speed-up or stretch-out. These techniques are particularly endemic within certain U.S. manufacturing sectors faced with increasingly fierce global competition and lower overseas (and offshore) labor rates. Here the process itself is not altered. Instead, corners are cut, waste motions eliminated, people shifted, materials and tools rerouted.

The simple and unadorned speed-up is the most obvious and most common technique of increasing the rate of work. The work is simply piled on the workers and forced through at an accelerated rate. A high norm is established; the "best" workers hit the pace, and the rest have to keep up or else. This type of speed-up is, unfortunately, common, especially among small, technically backward manufacturers attempting to meet the competition of the great multinational corporations. It has done much to prejudice the working public against business in general and corporate America in particular. The public must understand the full significance and scope of these changes in the American workplace and demand that the changes that are entailed be democratically applied to the subjective needs of the workers (whether in manufacturing or in services) as well as to the objective requirements of the process itself.

Of course, many of these issues are altered in completely unanticipated ways by the rise of new technologies. We have witnessed the impact of mechanization, rationalization, and automation upon the building industry in the past half-century and the consequences have not always been benign. But now comes computerization, which promises more radical changes in the workplace than ever, with consequences no one can fully foresee. That they will be profound is obvious. The literature on the computer is already vast and still growing. The claims are stupefying and indeed for architecture some of them seem well founded. Thus in computer-assisted drafting we have mechanisms that can produce from the ordinary blueprint complicated perspective drawings in a tenth or a twentieth of the time required by old-fashioned manual drafting.

But at what cost to the worker in terms of energy expended? Does computerization lower, increase, or merely transfer the workload from the bicep and thigh to the eye, wrist, and brain? For example, computer operators, after steady work on the keyboard, can develop serious disability. But in heavy industry, computerization may well alter a given process so radically as to free the worker completely from hazardous work. The computer has already so radically transformed American life that its ubiquity is an established fact.

Technological advances have, by their very nature, increased our demand for skilled workers for whom learning is an ongoing job requirement, in an increasingly dynamic and unstable working environment. It is significant that, in the last few decades, there has been a steady decline in the literature dealing with fatigue, labor savings, etc., and a complementary rise in that dealing with computers, adjusting to organizational change, chaos theory, skills enhancement, achieving excellence through teamwork, seeking innovation from the plant floor up, etc. Processes that once were studied by the experts either to save the energy of the worker or to increase productivity (the two are by no means the same, as we have seen) have been leapfrogged. Now the process is automated and computerized and the worker is either transformed into a process monitor (overseeing production phases and making automatic adjustments in feed rates, temperatures, etc., based on computer displays), reduced to a minor role in production, or eliminated altogether.

None of this, of course, is an argument against the historical necessity of modern electronic technology. For the first time in human history it is possible for us to contemplate freeing workers everywhere from noisome, dangerous, or exhausting labor. (It also raises, for industrialized countries, the specter of a large and permanently unemployed body of unskilled labor.)

Though this may be a perfectly valid path of development for many linear industrial processes, it has little direct application to many complex, nonlinear activities that are little subject, or not subject at all, to such forms of rationalization. Theaters, schools, hospitals, libraries, courtrooms, and residential types of all sorts require a wide range of furniture, equipment, and tools to facilitate their respective processes. All of this could stand vast improvement in terms of both design and manufacture. But the interface between the worker and the task (teacher—teaching, actor—acting, student—studying, etc.) requires the closest and most sophisticated scrutiny if efficiency, amenity, and safety are to be improved. Recent progress has been made both in scope and quality of research in areas such as these, with attention given to functional problems in the design of office furniture and equipment.

For example, workstations and job tasks are being studied systematically by ergonomists, or human factors specialists, who focus on such issues as acceptable luminance distribution and avoidance of discomfort glare, minimization of discrete tones and narrowband noise (hums, whistles, or whines), proper back and spine support using adjustable and well-designed chairs, lift-assist devices to avoid back injuries, balanced tools that avoid kickback, adjustable-height work and keyboard platforms to position arms and hands correctly, and modified keyboard layouts (the classic QWERTY keyboard was first developed in 1872, not to facilitate typing but to slow typists down to avoid jamming the mechanical typewriters!).

While many people associate physical labor and machines with manufacturing or blue-collar jobs, and mental effort and furniture with service or white-collar jobs, process automation and computerization have, in effect, blurred the boundaries. Manufacturing now requires more judgment and vigilance, while service industries require more manual (e.g., wordprocessing) labor and office furniture is, in essence, truly office equipment.

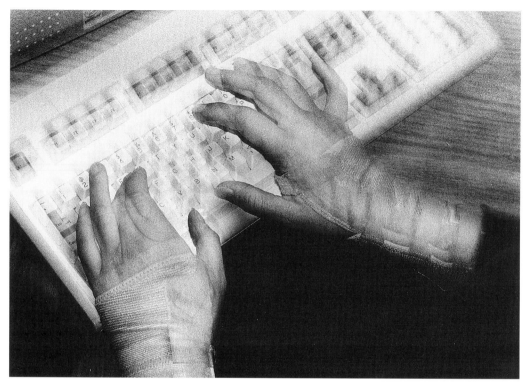

Earl Dotter, photojournalist

Figure 7 – 2 / USDA data entry clerk at work on her computer keyboard with wrist braces to alleviate carpal tunnel syndrome. Rosslyn, Virginia (1997).

Futurists Alvin and Heidi Toffler offer an interesting redefinition of the American workplace on the basis of "mind work," which they believe is the new model for all levels of employment in this country:

More and more . . . work . . . consists of symbolic processing. Farmers now use computers to calculate grain feeds; steelworkers monitor consoles and video screens; investment bankers switch on their laptops as they model financial markets. . . . [M]illions like them do nothing but move information around or generate more information. . . . Auto mechanics at Ford dealers, for example, may still have greasy hands, but they also use a computer system designed by Hewlett-Packard that provides them with an "expert system" to help them in trouble-shooting along with instant access to one hundred megabytes of technical drawings and data stored on CD-ROM. . . . When they are interacting with this system, are they "mechanics" or "mind workers"? . . . The key questions about a person's work today have to do with how much of the job entails information processing, how routine or programmable it is, what level of abstraction is involved, what access the person has to the central data bank and management information system and how much autonomy and responsibility the individual enjoys.[21]

How does the architect, understanding that places of work are places where mind work takes place, allow this to affect design decisions? With the emergence of mind work have come jobs that are no longer tethered to a conventional workplace. A common television image is people working anywhere—on the beach, in the plane, on the golf course, at the summit of a mountain. With portable laptops, satellites, CD-ROMs, and cellular technology, work is possible virtually anywhere. Additionally, this is an age where we can be instantly accessible via beeper or cell phone regardless of our activity or location on (or above, in the case of air travel) the earth, if we so choose.

What is the architect's task in this case? There is still inherent value in the formality of an office. Importantly, most innovations require teamwork and interaction—the synergy that results from simply bumping into one another at the office. The individual off working on the beach is in reality connected to an office somewhere. And while many aspects of communication have changed, face-to-face encounters are still basic to social innovation and invention.

Innovative changes are redefining the workplace as an arena for collaboration. For example, in 1989, the office furniture manufacturer Steelcase built a new Corporate Development Center in Grand Rapids, Michigan, designed by Robert Forrest of WBDC, Inc.:

[T]he new facility was conceived as a prototype facility promoting an "integrative workplace." . . . Features included areas allowing unplanned, spontaneous contacts and information exchange between disciplines; looser layouts promoting tinkering with both the physical environment and the administrative and social features of work groups; and spaces encouraging use of a collaborative and overlapping product development process instead of a linear one. Spaces are designated as "caves" for privacy, neighborhoods for related activities, and town squares for the whole community. There are marker boards at coffee-break stations so that people can sketch ideas to see what passersby think. Perhaps more practically, the facility brings together everyone involved in product development (designers, engineers, marketers) under one roof.[22]

Michael Brill, architect (of BOSTI Associates), is engaged in this rapidly expanding mode of architectural practice, integrating the workplace with technology and work processes. Brill cites research showing that the planning, design, and management of the work environment has wide-reaching effects for individuals, groups, and whole organizations. He suggests that good design (i.e., design appropriate to the work) may yield increased productivity in a range of annual benefit of 2 to 17 percent of salary. Acoustical privacy is paramount, enabling workers to focus on projects that often require a high degree of concentration. But of equal importance are serendipitous and informal interactions across teams, functions, and levels. He notes three basic strategies to "new officing:"

1. *radical redesign*, to support the intermixing of teamwork with solo work; multitasking days; rapid learning and high flexibility

2. *hotelling*, or running the office as a hotel or just-in-time workspace, for those who travel at least 60 percent of the time. These staffmembers do not own a particular workspace but always have one when they are in.

3. *work from anywhere*, which often requires use of mobile technology and remote access to networks for those who work from home (as a home base), work at home, telecommute, work from satellite space, or are virtual workers.

Anthropometry: Spatial Mensuration of Movement

Just as, in everyday experience, we equate intellectual comprehension with the sense of sight (I *see* what you mean), so emotional response is equated with the sense of touch (They have no *feeling* for the needs of others). This is no mere accident of language but describes rather a fundamental distinction. In many ways the sense of touch is the most vivid capacity the individual has for interaction with the world immediately outside his or her own body. It not only plays a central role in the satisfaction of sensual appetites (e.g., the sexual act), it is also the source of absolutely indispensable factual information about the qualities of the spatial environment. The shape, size, texture, density, and temperature of surrounding surfaces is perceived first of all by that marvelously complex system of nerve endings in the skin and muscles that furnishes us with tactile, haptic, and kinesthetic sensation.

Thus, our knowledge of the special properties of a material like marble derives largely from our tactile-haptic exploration of it. We learn its cold smoothness from touching it, its hardness from sitting on it, its density and weight from trying to lift it. Only its color and pattern are visually perceived at this initial stage of exploration and discovery. After a quite limited experience with marble, we are able to transmute this tactile information into visual terms. We say, "It looks like marble to me"; we forget that in darkness we would, each time, have to touch it, punch it, lift it before safely concluding it was marble.

This capacity of vision to metamorphose other sorts of sensory data—data which are not primarily or even not at all visually derived—is vision's most splendid characteristic. It is a great time- and energy-saving mechanism, especially in the design fields. It enables us to retrieve quickly from memory the particular combination of sense-perceptible properties that goes to make up marble. It enables us to say, "I don't need to see a sample—I remember quite clearly what it looks like."

Nevertheless, this same syncretic power of vision has inherent dangers for all designers, and most of all for architects, for in real life vision is only one channel of perception among many and often of no greater importance than others. Many architectural problems involve the manipulation of phenomena that are literally invisible (e.g., poisonous gases, high noise levels, high temperatures). Many environmental hazards are not perceptible by any sensory means (e.g., the presence of carbon monoxide, or a structural member just before collapse). But neither three-dimensional CAD drawings of a proposed building nor photographs of a finished one give any visual information about the possible existence of such factors or their relative seriousness. Because they are hard to visualize, many such problems are given low priority in relation to those that are easily visible. In short, the architect has a built-in bias in favor of the visually perceived; this bias must be rigorously examined if buildings are to be authentically successful. Nowhere is this more true than in the habitat of touch.

The sense of touch has a more complex perceptual capacity than those other scanning senses of vision or hearing, depending as it does upon several types of neural sensors in the skin and muscles. These sensors, working in various combinations, bring us an astonishing range of information on the properties of the surfaces around us. Exactly how many types is still a matter of disagreement among neurologists and psychologists themselves. For example, it appears that some parts of the cutaneous system may be better for sizing of a stimulus than others, which serve as warning areas for eliciting visual attention or reflexive action. [23]

Our current understanding is that the sensation of hot or cold is actually located in skin nerve endings, which provide thermal information by touch as well. The sensations of force or movement and acceleration are transmitted by receptors in the muscles and tendons.

As in the case of other systems of sensory perception, that of touch can thus be described as occupying its own habitat. It is bounded by a lower threshold of perception

Table 7 – 3 / *Types of Information Transmitted by Tactile Perception*

tactile information	smooth — rough blunt — sharp wet — dry
pressure information	hard — soft elastic — stiff pressure — suction
spatio-tactile information	shape volume dimension size
haptic-muscular information	weight and mass
thermal information	hot — cold (pregnant center point)

Specialized sensors in skin, joints, and muscles collaborate to pick up and transmit to the brain a wide range of critically important data on states and properties of the objects and enclosing surfaces with which terrestrial space is furnished, subdivided, and defined.

(too little stimulation to be perceived) and an upper one of pain (too much to be endured) and centered in some golden zone of satisfaction. The analogy is only approximate, however, as the properties of matter explored by this sense are not strictly comparable with the others. For the thermal sensors, the habitat extends upward (to intolerably hot) and downward (to intolerably cold) from a neutral center point, the temperature of the body itself. For the pressure sensors, the limits lie between the gentlest perceptible air movement and the crushing blow, or between the touch of velvet and the prick of a needle. Many other properties of matter produce tactile sensation without stress: a hard or a wet object is not, of itself, more stressful to handle than a soft or a dry one.

Thus, in general terms, we can describe the topography of the habitat of touch. It has upper and lower limits of stress or lack of stimulation, and some central zone of optimal stimulation. But here again, the limiting factor is that of movement and change in position across time. To discriminate between velvet and paper, it is not enough merely to touch; one must also stroke. Any tactile-haptic experience, no matter how pleasurable initially, ceases to be satisfying if extended beyond its own built-in limits. Indeed, it tends to cease to be perceptible at all. Here, as everywhere in the domain of the senses, change and variety are essential to perception itself.

An understanding of these tactile-haptic phenomena should be an integral part of the designer's expertise. The boundaries of architectural and urbanistic spaces consist of surfaces—manufactured or otherwise modified by people—that, by their very presence, affect tactile-haptic sensation in important (and often in unanticipated or ambiguous) ways. Much of the reason for success or failure of any space lies in the impact of its bounding surfaces upon its inhabitants. We have already seen how our behavior is affected by the way in which a wall rejects light or heat or sound; analogous relationships between us and the wall exist in the field of tactile-haptic stimulation and response. Surfaces that appear smooth, polished, or velvety to the eye often lead us to stroke them, as if to confirm the tactile pleasure they promise. Rough surfaces, on the other hand, cause us to shy away from them, irrespective of how handsome they may be in purely formal (i.e., visual) terms.*

The tactile-haptic properties of floors and pavements have a similarly powerful influence upon the behavior of the people who traverse them. We have already discussed the effect of gross changes in level or direction; the effect of such surface characteristics as texture, resilience, cleanliness, wetness is equally profound. Highly polished pavements (marble, terrazzo, faience tile) may be handsome visually and pleasurable emotionally because of their connotation of wealth, ceremony, urbanity. But they *look* slippery and often *are* slippery; a duller matte finish not only looks safer but actually is. Contrariwise, rough-textured pavements of gravel or cobblestones are so uncomfortable to walk on that they must be considered as nonwalkable, antipedestrian surfaces.

---

*   Thus, the corrugated, bush-hammered concrete walls of such buildings as the School of Architecture at Yale University (Fig. 7–3) are handsome indeed when experienced from a safe distance, but their rough texture is too obviously hostile to the human epidermis to make a person feel safe at close quarters. The natural tendency of persons moving along them is to maintain a safety zone of empty air between the wall and themselves.

Figure 7 – 3 / Exterior finish of Yale
School of Architecture, New Haven,
Connecticut. Paul Rudolph, architect,
completed 1964. Close-up view of
rough-textured concrete finish.

Resilience is another critical factor in paving materials, especially in buildings like
museums and art galleries, where the perambulating picture-viewer is subject to unusual
musculoskeletal stress. In such situations, marble or terrazzo flooring materials are least
desirable from an ergonomic point of view (even though, for formal reasons, they are
very commonly used). Cork or plastic is better than stone; carpeting on wood flooring
installed on wood sleepers is perhaps best of all. An inevitable experiential aspect of all
these flooring materials is their acoustical behavior. As silence is a requirement in museums, galleries, and libraries, the absorptive capacity of carpeting makes it a suitable
material. The feeling of hushed luxury of carpeted spaces is thus as much an acoustical as
a tactile-haptic phenomenon.

The exact way in which pedestrians behave on floors and pavements is subject to a
number of environmental variables. Indoors, these are subject to precise manipulation —
light, heating, air movement, humidity, noise, etc. But out of doors, a host of climatic
variables affects the comfort, usability, and safety — and hence the patterns of use — of
the pavement. While predictable, these variables are predictable only in gross terms — for
example, monthly precipitation, sun and shadow patterns, average wind directions and

velocities, mean temperatures. The maintenance of amenity in outdoor spaces is therefore complex and involves dozens of meteorological phenomena varying in intensity with time and space. The successful manipulation of these phenomena constitutes one of the most challenging and least explored aspects of landscape design. Perhaps because of its very complexity, the problem is evaded in real life; instead of designing outdoor spaces to meet at least the gross impact of the seasons, architects too often conceive of them as though for some ideal Platonic climate. Here, it is always sunny and summer; there is no rain or snow, no dust or mud, no extremes of heat or cold, no wind, no cloudy days or stormy nights, no noise or fumes from the automobile traffic that is built into the design.

This tendency to regard outdoor spaces as purely esthetic constructs, voids empty of microclimatic reality, is nowhere more apparent than in the big urban plazas that have been a feature of urban redevelopment. This conceptual error is obvious not only from their malfunction in real life; it is also revealed in the architect's presentation drawings and models, which always assume optimal climatic conditions. Obviously, it would be difficult for the sketch and impossible for the model to replicate a snowstorm or downpour, a cold wind or a blistering sun. There is nothing wrong with presenting the project under ideal conditions; the error lies in conceiving it as though such conditions were typical.

In experiential reality, there is no spot within the continental United States in which some or all of these meteorological factors do not, for some part of the year, combine to render these handsome and costly plazas literally uninhabitable. They thus fail in their central pretension—that of eliminating gross differences between architectural and urbanistic spaces, of extending in time the areas in which urban life can freely flow back and forth between the two. For much of the country and for part of the year, rain, sleet, snow, and ice are the principal obstacles to easy, urbane movement across these plazas; in any combination, they make the plazas unpretty, unpleasant, or unsafe. Soiled snow accumulates; improvised pathways, alternately icy and waterlogged and bearing little relation to the formal patterns of the plaza, are plowed or shoveled out. Trash becomes embedded in the snow and accumulates in the empty fountains. There is, in short, a great decline in overall amenity in bad weather, and the behavior the plaza elicits from its pedestrians reflects this fact.

Yet technically it is entirely possible to minimize or eliminate many of these phenomena at the microclimatic level. Computer models that allow architects to evaluate design alternatives based on the effects of changing meteorology, site conditions, etc., could lead to outdoor spaces that are more livable, durable, and real-world. Scale models could be tested for aerodynamic behavior, cumulative shade patterns for cold-weather months could be simulated, and the whole complex could be adjusted to minimize winds and shading and to maximize exposure to sun. Drainage patterns could be correlated to snowplow paths, areas allocated for mounding surplus snow. Snow melters embedded in paved surfaces would obviously be optimal. In climates without snow or ice but with heavy rainfall (e.g., Florida, the Gulf Coast, Puget Sound) the main problem is one of effective shelter and paving along the lines of high pedestrian traffic.

Figure 7–4 / Vancouver Public Library, Central Branch, at Library Square, Vancouver, British Columbia, Canada. Moshe Safdie and Associates and Downs Archambault and Partners, architects, 1995. This daylit atrium space links year-round pedestrian traffic with the state-of-the-art library (on left) and retail spaces (at right). It also utilizes an under floor air supply system that delivers more fresh air to the occupied volume of the building.

The problem of year-round viability in open urban spaces has its obverse side: protection from excessive insolation, with its resulting heat and glare, during hot-weather months. As described in chapter 9, all pavements tend to be much hotter than the natural surfaces they replace, because of their heat-absorbing and heat-holding characteristics. Unless adequately shaded and ventilated, they create desertlike microclimates, often with astonishing extremes of heat or glare. Thus, the urban plaza must be analyzed just as carefully for summertime amenity as for summer heat. Plant materials of all sorts—trees, vines, lawns—are more desirable shade makers than are architectural constructions because they maintain low surface temperatures and convert much of the solar energy that falls upon them into other forms of energy. Whatever the devices employed, however, hot-weather viability implies reduction of ambient heat and light.

It is in the highest degree ironic that contemporary design has abandoned so many of those architectural and urbanistic devices that gave beauty and amenity to earlier cities. In Piazza San Marco in Venice, a classic example of the Italian town square, formal and functional requirements were resolved to make an admirable fit with a difficult climate. The unbroken indoor-outdoor pavement plane facilitates year-round pedestrian movement and perimetric loggias provide shelter from both hot summer sun and heavy winter rains (it is, however, subject to occasional flooding). The covered sidewalk, the loggia and arcade, the courtyard and gallery — all are aimed at facilitating movement through urban space by modifying the impact of raw environmental forces upon it. The time is overdue for an objective analysis of all such features, on a functional and not merely a formalistic basis.

Proxemics: Social Consequences of Human Deployment in Space

The senses of vision, touch, and hearing bring us vital information about the objects that furnish and the surfaces that enclose terrestrial space. These sense data are so important, in fact, that we are apt to think of them as being the exclusive source of information as to where, at any given moment, we are. But our neural sensors give us an altogether different type of spatial information — that is, our kinesthetic-proprioceptive orientation in space itself. These sensors afford us a marvelous control both of our overall posture with reference to gravity and the disposition of our various bodily members in relation to each other at any given moment. This kinesthetic-proprioceptive capacity is what makes bodily movement possible in higher organisms. But it does not explain, except in purely mechanical terms, why and how we move as social beings.

Any movement in space requires an outlay of energy and we have an easily understandable tendency to conserve it. However, this energy cost is only one factor in the complex equations of our physical movement in space. The actual pattern or trajectory that we trace in any given action must be viewed as the resolution of a whole system of vectors of force acting upon us, the algebraic sum of which determines that pattern or trajectory. Some of these forces are subjective, or internally generated, and some are objective:

Psychological: the motivation of the individual, his incentive to accomplish the action in question
Physiological: the physical condition of the individual with reference to the energy required for the action
Sociocultural: the type of behavior that the space is designed to elicit (playing field, workplace, place of study or worship, etc.)
Microclimatic: the actual environmental conditions obtaining on the site (rain or snow, sun or shade, temperature, wind, etc.)
Topographic: the contours, textures and shape of the surface on which the action transpires.

The relative value of these various kinds of force, all of them simultaneously acting upon the individual, varies with circumstances. Thus a person in a desperate hurry cuts across a muddy field or runs up a steep flight of stairs which a casual stroller would circumnavigate or reject. Social convention forbids men to use the women's toilet, no matter how great the physiological pressure, just as it requires people to walk slowly and quietly in churches, libraries, and museums. A catchy shop window or an accident may pull pedestrians to the sunny side of a street, which otherwise would be deserted because of heat and glare.

The precise fashion in which architectural and urbanistic space is organized, and the way in which furnishings and equipment are deployed within it, should be determined by a clear understanding of the vectors of force described above. Unfortunately, architects and planners have had to rely upon a quite primitive theoretical approach to these complexities and a quite eclectic methodology for handling them. Now help is coming from unexpected quarters. Ecologists and behavioral psychologists have increasingly turned their attention to the study of animal behavior in its wild or natural condition. The result has been a startling increase in our understanding of the impact of spatial organization (territoriality) upon animal societies. Lessons learned here have obvious applications for an analogous approach to the more complex problem of human communities.

The behavior-eliciting function of architectural space is being explored by many investigators, from many disciplines and from many points of view.[24] For example, one group of experimental psychologists studied the effects of spatial organization of certain housing projects upon interpersonal relationships that developed among the inhabitants. The psychologists established a dramatic distinction between what they call *physical* and *functional* distance. In the projects under study, they found that two apartment houses might be only thirty feet apart (physical distance), but if their entrances face in opposite directions and give out onto different streets, the chance of interaction (and hence of friendship) between the tenants of the two houses is as radically reduced as if thousands of feet intervened. The functional distance is the equivalent of miles. [25]

Such investigations should have a sobering effect upon architects, indicating as they do the sociocultural consequences of all their spatial sets, large or small. They cannot erect a wall or enclose a room or pave a path without affecting some of those vectors of force that play a role in modifying the behavior of the occupants of the space. But there are subjective forces here too — internally generated forces over which designers have little or no control. These the architect can only try to understand and respect. The anthropologist Edward Hall explored this aspect of human behavior. He attempted to quantify the spatial dimensions of various levels of human interaction. He visualized each individual as centered in a concentric series of balloons or bubbles of private space, a sort of territorial extension of his or her own body moving through space. These concentric spheres represent optimal distances for a hierarchy of interpersonal relationships: *intimate,* up to 1-1/2 feet; *personal,* 1-1/2 to 4 feet; *social-consultive,* 4 to 10 feet; *public,* 10 to 30 feet and beyond. Any violation of these optima by other individuals, according to Hall, is reflected by a stress upon that relationship.[26]

The scale of this hierarchy is partly a mere quantification of our powers of perception — how well we can hear the words of the actor, how clearly we can see the face of a friend, whether or not we can touch the person we love. But the governing factor is not only one of acuity of perception. We want contact with the actor, the friend, the lover, but we do not want to be as close to the actor as to the friend, nor as close to the friend as to the lover. (The reverse is also true, of course: the lover wants to be closer than the friend, the friend than the actor, and so on.) Even these spaces are not absolute, according to Hall; they vary somewhat with culture, each society establishing its own norms. Thus male heterosexual friends in the Middle East want to be able to touch each other while in England such close contiguity is considered distasteful. In just such a fashion, body odors (perspiration) are considered attractive in one cultural milieu (e.g., Elizabethan England) while in another they are a social liability (e.g., contemporary United States).

Technology, too, has made it possible to modulate some of these spatial balloons. The telephone permits verbal contact between lovers across miles of space; the computer permits extensive opportunities for written communication with strangers sharing common interests as well as with family and friends; teleconferencing permits live exchanges between groups separated by geography. The footlight and the spotlight extend the radius within which we can clearly see the actor's facial expression, just as the microphone extends the distance across which we can hear the political speaker. And the airconditioned, floodlighted, and televised arena extends in time and in space the number of people who can follow a hockey game or football game within acceptable limits of perceptual acuity.*

The express purpose of many types of architectural spaces (classrooms, offices, stores, workshops) is to expedite or facilitate interactions, contact, or communication between certain groups of people engaged in certain types of activity. But privacy and isolation are desirable in other types of spaces (bedrooms, toilets, libraries). In an interesting early study of how university students actually use library reading rooms, significantly called "The Ecology of Privacy," the behavioral psychologist Robert Sommer reports: "Of those students who entered the room alone, 64% sat alone, 26% sat diagonally across from another student, while only 10% sat opposite or beside another student."[27] Sommer found that chairs at the end of the table were invariably most popular because this automatically gave the student one protected flank. Moreover, elaborate stratagems were employed to reinforce this privacy:

The seats alongside a person or directly across from him were rarely occupied except at times of high density. Individual readers marked out territories in various ways, using personal belongings (books, purses, coats, etc.) and positioning their own chair.[28]

At the same time, the students did not want absolute isolation while reading. Some felt more comfortable near people, although avoiding direct eye contact. Most of the reported distractions, however, came from human sources rather than deficiencies in the environmental control systems—illumination, ventilation, heating, etc.

---

* But as we have seen, especially in chapters 5 and 6, these attenuated spatial relationships are reflected in an analogous diminution in the experiential potency of the contact. No phone conversation or teleconference can replace the face-to-face talk; no musical form can be amplified without distortion; no cinematic facsimile is a full surrogate for the multisensory reality of the live theater.

The Sommer study indicated a number of fairly simple measures aimed at ensuring the privacy students require in library work, suggesting that attention to size, design, and arrangement of library reading tables would go a long way toward meeting these requirements.

Partitions between reading areas at a table [should] insure that no more than, for example, six individuals occupy one side of a table. These barriers [should] permit two people to sit side by side at very close distances without physical contact. By permitting greater physical closeness without psychological discomfort, barriers increase the upper limit of comfortable room density. Such barriers need not be ponderous or weighty objects. A small raised strip down the center of the table can effectively serve as a barrier and increase feelings of privacy by defining individual territories . . . it can serve as a resting place for the reader's eyes when he looks away from his books. These "study breaks" are major sources of accidental intrusion.[29]

Of course, the design and arrangement of furniture in a room can be used to bring people together as well as to separate them. In a classic study of the behavior of patients in mental institutions, Dr. Humphry Osmond found that certain seating arrangements in the day rooms tended to bring people together *(sociopetal)* and others that tended to keep them apart *(sociofugal)*. In spaces where interaction and communication were themselves therapeutic, Osmond urged the use of sociopetal designs.[30]

One factor of great significance for architecture and urbanism emerges from these studies of spatial and territorial behavior: For each type of social activity or process there are upper, lower, and optimal limits of size and density appropriate to that activity. This is partly purely quantitative, though it assumes qualitative aspects. As Osmond noted: "Among ten people there are 45 possible two-person relationships [Fig. 7–5]; among fifty

Person	Possible Unique Two-Person Relationships with These People from Among the Ten	Totals
1	2 3 4 5 6 7 8 9 10	9
2	3 4 5 6 7 8 9 10	8
3	4 5 6 7 8 9 10	7
4	5 6 7 8 9 10	6
5	6 7 8 9 10	5
6	7 8 9 10	4
7	8 9 10	3
8	9 10	2
9	10	1
		Total 45

Figure 7–5 / Diagram illustrating the number of unique two-person relationships possible among a total of ten people.

people there are 1225 possible relationships. The complexity of society has gone up by a factor of 27 at least."[31]

Four persons are required for a game of bridge—no more, no less. Easy access to and recognition of the cards dictates a table no more than 42 inches across. Tables should be at least 8 feet apart, but there is apparently no optimal number of tables. A regional shopping center also has a minimal (and almost certainly a maximal) size and requires for its economic existence 50,000 people within a radius of 20 miles. In urbanistic terms, there is clearly a critical mass below which that form of social invention and innovation that characterizes the city simply cannot occur. A village of 1,000 souls can neither produce nor support a symphony orchestra or a repertory theater. And yet, it is also clear that this state of critical mass creates only the preconditions, the sociocultural climate for social creativity; it is, by itself, no guarantee of it. Neither Periclean Athens nor Medicean Florence was as large as Chattanooga, Tennessee. Parameters of size appear to be relative, not absolute. Optima seem to vary with culture and especially with technology.

Optimal levels of density, on the other hand, appear to be relatively fixed, regardless of the size of the city. These density optima are functions of the physical limits of pedestrian range and personal contact. They have a decisive effect on the quality of life afforded by the city. The catastrophic drop in the effectiveness of American cities is due to, among other things, the fact that density has dropped in inverse proportion to increasing size. One of the major factors here is technology—specifically, mechanized transportation by rail and overwhelmingly by private automobile. The sheer presence of large numbers of autos in urban spaces that were calibrated to pedestrian speed and reach has a negative impact on pedestrian behavior. The climate of social intercourse is at once diluted and polluted by the presence of these foreign bodies; the number, ease, and frequency of face-to-face contacts is diminished; the sites of such contacts are more thinly dispersed in space; the minimal critical density necessary for self-propagating social intercourse is not achieved. As British architect Christopher Day noted:

Shops, commerce and industry are the life-blood of cities, as is the traffic which serves them. It is stopping of the traffic which caused places to start to grow. In days when it was more human-related, traffic brought into being places to stop, buy and sell. Iron wheels on cobbles, a horse for every horsepower, did not make such streets less crowded, noisy and smelly than they are today, but street life was coloured by people, not fast-moving pressed-metal containers. Conscious transport policies can—to some extent—re-apportion focus from alien mechanical things to *people*.[32]

Redesign of the Tools for a Better Fit

The building, of course, can only establish the general experiential conditions in which space, time, and gravity can be manipulated to expedite a given social process. The building affords the preconditions under which that process can occur (classroom for study, operating theater for surgery), but a range of furnishings and equipment are required to make it actually possible (desks, chairs, and blackboards; operating table, surgical instruments, oxygen tanks). A century ago a few desks, stools, and ledgers were all that was required for bookkeeping; nowadays, the volume, complexity, and speed of modern accounting demands a wide range of furnishings — electronic equipment for wordprocessing, dictating, recording, reproducing, and computing, in addition to desks, chairs, tables, filing cabinets, and shelving. For all their superficial dissimilarity, these must all be regarded as tools for manipulating space, time, and gravity in favor of the work — links in a chain for reducing the time or energy required to complete a given unit of work.

In view of this fundamental similarity of function, the disparity in design between these components is startling. The criteria that govern the design and fabrication of what is usually called furniture (e.g., the worker's chair) and those that operate in equipment (e.g., the computer) are light-years apart. Some progress, however, has begun to be made in establishing requirements for the satisfactory design of furniture. Ergonomic standards such as those established by the American National Standards Institute (ANSI) and the Human Factors Society (HFS) are being used by furniture designers to comfortably accommodate the 5th-percentile female through the 95th-percentile male. For example, the ANSI/HFS 100 standard for seated users of VDTs has dimensional requirements for seat height, depth, width, pan angle, lumbar support, seat-to-back included angle, and the width between armrests, to raise the level of comfort for a wide range of individuals.

And yet, most office workers make do with existing furniture. Office furniture is often kept as long as possible despite poor design (lack of adjustability, absence of lumbar support, etc.). By contrast, businesses scarcely hesitate before making significant investments in computing equipment that we blithely accept as obsolete on the day of sale.

It is obvious that the behavior of an electrical impulse in a circuit now seems simple in contrast to the problem of the fit between the buttocks and the chair seat. But the point here is that the behavior of electricity seemed equally obscure until scientific criteria were applied to the study of electrical phenomena. Precisely because it is incomparably more complex than electrical circuitry, the design of the worker's chair implies the highest levels of scientific theory and technological method.

Aerospace medicine is deeply involved in the investigation of weightlessness in space. Whatever the consequences for the colonization of extraterrestrial space, such investigations have profound implications for the weighted state of people on earth, for they mark the first systematic attempt to formulate a holistic concept of the optimal fit between people and their tools and equipment. As the pioneering researcher Alexander Kira succinctly put it,

The human body can be thought of as a structure composed of several masses, each with its separate weight and center of gravity, linked together by a system of joints, and held in balance with the help of muscles and ligaments. The motions of the various systems of linkages are extremely flexible and the end members or masses — i.e., the hands and feet — may assume a wide range of positions. When the body interacts with external objects (such as a tool), the system of linkages becomes increasingly complex.[33]

Just how complex these interactions are, in even a simple action, becomes clear if the action is carefully analyzed. Thus, "When a seated person operates a foot pedal, the closed chain (of the action) involves the shoe sole, the soft tissue of the foot, the foot and limb links, the pelvis, the non-rigid buttock tissues (and) the chair seat, the floor and the pedal."[34]

All furniture is, in the last analysis, a tool for intervening in this situation, for relieving the stresses of gravity on one or another of these linkages. Even in such an activity as rest-ing—that is, sitting or lying down—a number of variables are involved. If a chair were only a problem in anthropometry, for example, design would involve only adjusting all its dimensions to those of the sitter's anatomy. But physiological and physical factors are also involved. The exact degree of resistance or resiliency of the seat in response to the pres-sure of the buttocks varies with material (marble or feathers, coil springs or leather straps). Ease of movement when seated varies both with the friction between the sitter's clothing and upholstery (velvet is difficult to slide across, leather very easy) and with the shape of the seat. Thus the popular sling or hammock chairs of the 1950s tended to concentrate the body's weight in such a way as to make any change in position difficult.

Another ergonomic aspect of seating is the thermal response of the chair to the sitter. As we saw in chapter 3, the human body must dissipate about four-fifths of its heat to its environment; a large portion of its heat-exchange surfaces are in the thighs and buttocks. Chairs upholstered in conventional fabrics slow down this rate of dissipation and are thus often uncomfortably warm. Molded plastic chairs are made of materials that act as radiant reflectors; they reflect body heat back onto thighs and buttocks; the result being a hot seat in actual fact.

Today many types of specialized seating situations simply cannot be satisfied by intu-itive design: posture seating for airline pilots and bus drivers; theater seating where, in addition to normal requirements for postural comfort, the acoustical response of the chair should be identical whether occupied or empty; operating chairs for the dentist, where comfort requirements of the patient must be balanced against musculoskeletal strain on the dentist. It is significant that ergonomic principles have not been applied uniformly to solve problems of optimal fit. Automobile seats and new office furniture often incorporate ergonomic design principles. By contrast, seating in many manufacturing facilities remains fundamentally idiosyncratic and appallingly behind the times. Thus it is not uncommon for workers armed with duct tape, foam rubber, and pillows brought from home to fix their hard-backed stools in a determined if unscientific attempt to create a comfortable chair.

Much the same situation obtains throughout the furniture field—in beds and bed-ding, for example. Current research into sleep and sleeping has discredited many old the-ories. One early misconception was that a good night's sleep should be deep and dreamless, and that the proper equipment for eliciting this state was a mattress upon which one floats as upon a cloud. Clinical studies now make it clear that dreaming is a necessary function of sleep, and motion studies of sleeping subjects show that, actually to rest all its parts equally, the body must twist and turn all night! As it is a linkage sys-tem of semi-independent weights and masses, the body best accomplishes this while sup-ported by a fairly firm surface.

Similarly, it has long been held that it is healthy to sleep in a cold room with all the windows open. Proof of this was supposed to be that it led to a big appetite at breakfast.

But the accelerated heat loss from this exposure, from a metabolic point of view, is the equivalent of a night-long walk at two or three miles per hour. Conventional bedding sufficient to reduce such heat loss to acceptable levels might well be so heavy as to increase fatigue, as anyone will remember who has spent a winter night in an American farmhouse under homemade quilts.

This type of malfunction, the consequence of a poor fit between the user and the tool, has received more popular recognition since the 1970s, when journalists first reported experiencing repetitive strain injury from videodisplay terminal (VDT) use. The term repetitive strain injury (RSI) covers a series of musculoskeletal disorders involving pain, discomfort, and muscular weakness, sometimes with tissue swelling (e.g., tendinitis, carpal tunnel syndrome, muscle shortening, and nerve damage), attributed to repeated (sometimes forceful) movements (as in keyboarding or assembling small parts). These types of injuries have long afflicted jackhammer operators, meat cutters, sewing machine operators, carpenters, and musicians. Now they were affecting a wide range of office and clerical workers, including journalists, and word spread.

Musculoskeletal injuries currently rank first among job-related injuries and compensation claims in the United States. The main category of musculoskeletal injury reported is sprains and strains, the main cause is overexertion (usually lifting), and the body part most frequently reported is the back. It can be said that design and placement of equipment contribute to these injuries.

Substantial strides are being made in the design of material handling equipment that provides an ergonomic assist while increasing worker productivity.[35] For example, pallet positioners are coming into common use. These are essentially lift-tables with turntable tops that automatically position the top of the stack at a comfortable working height to eliminate awkward bending and twisting during pallet unloading. Conveyers with cantilevered, telescoping frames are being manipulated by dockworkers who are able to reach deep into trailers for automatic loading and unloading.

Vertical or horizontal carousels are being used to expedite storing and retrieving parts productively and ergonomically. In the past, parts were stored in aisles of standard metal shelving, with heavy boxes having to be retrieved and lifted from above shoulder height, in some cases. Many equipment manufacturers are beginning to study and extensively test the operation of their equipment, and to seek input from specialists in biodynamic research and functional analysis.

In some fields, such as the design of high-end office equipment, ergonomic specialists are now included in early design decisions. This involvement has led to substantial momentum in reversing the tide of forcing people to conform to technology; to a greater and greater extent, technology is being made to conform to people as obsolete equipment eventually reaches the end of its useful life.

The historical roots of some of the current research are found in the earlier work of architect Frederick J. Kiesler, who published a remarkable paper in 1939 in which he formulated a theory of the morphological development of the tool in history and presented a prototype designed according to the theory.[36] He saw the tool as the result of the continual interaction between tool and user, always strictly conditioned by the culture in which the interaction takes place. The rate and direction of this development is a function of the evolution of the culture as a whole. Thus a given tool-form might survive in a primitive culture relatively unchanged for millennia because neither the need for a change nor the means of changing it is present. Until even the comparatively recent past, the rate of change was slow, so that the basic type survived with only modest modifications. But in contemporary industrial society, with its accelerating rates of change, the life span is radically reduced. Minor modifications are no longer adequate; a new tool might become obsolete in a decade (and some are devalued much sooner). But redesign cannot be successfully accomplished without a fundamental reexamination of the problem in its context.

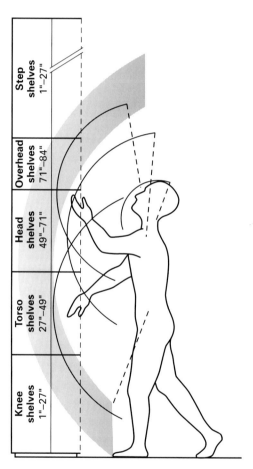

Figure 7–6 / Frederick Kiesler's formulation of user-tool relationship in book storage. Skeletomuscular access and visual recognition of people to objects in space is spheroid. Books and book storage equipment are rectilinear. Interface between user and book-storing tool is tangent, placing maximum strain upon user. To shift load, tool should be redesigned. Theoretically, user should stand in center of hollow sphere of bookshelves; in reality, tool must meet other requirements — stability, use in rectilinear architectural space, etc. Interface should therefore take the form of concave segmental arc scaled to vertical and horizontal reach of the user.

To demonstrate his theory, Professor Kiesler and his class at the Columbia University School of Architecture set to work to design and fabricate a prototype. Proceeding on the assumption that the design of even the simplest and most prosaic item of furniture was subject to radical revision and improvement, Kiesler's class chose the bookcase as a subject of analysis. It did not require much research to discover that the bookcase had reached its present form a long time ago and had seen little, if any, improvement since. How well did it meet the requirements of the user? And how well those of the books themselves? History offered little in the way of intelligent answer. More and more books were published and bigger and bigger libraries built to hold them. But if it were the task of a book storage unit to take the load off the user, then it had clearly fallen far short of its objective. If it were the task of the unit to provide the books themselves with an optimal environment, here too its success had not been spectacular (Fig. 7–6).

Beginning with the human body, where Kiesler felt all building research, to be productive, must begin, Kiesler's group came upon a major discrepancy. The first criterion of a bookcase is obviously easy recognition of and access to the books themselves. As the sweep of both the eye and the arm is circular, the limits of both recognition and access are also circular in the vertical as well as the horizontal plane. All existing bookcases were rectilinear in both planes, so between the user and the tool there was only one point of actual tangency—immediately in front of him at a point between shoulder and eye level. To read or reach any other point, the user had to stretch, squat, or move sideways.

The ideal solution, Kiesler reasoned, would be a hollow spherical bookcase, with the user at the center and the interior radius approximately that of the user's arm. Other considerations would immediately modify this initial concept. The user would not want the books directly overhead nor immediately underfoot, so the sphere would be truncated top and bottom. The center of the sphere should be somewhere near eye level, so the truncated bottom would be well off the floor. To enter or leave the unit, the user would not want to climb over or crawl under, so the unit would be built in spheroid sections, like the outer surface of the lobes of an orange, one of which would be omitted for entry. But only the inner surface of the sphere would be accessible to the user when inside it—hence each of the sections would pivot upon its vertical axis, so that both surfaces would be equally accessible. As capacity varies with the needs of the individual user, each section should be complete in itself; as the library grows, sections could be added to complete the sphere.

What of the books themselves? Had they any properties that importantly affected this schematic solution? They were, first of all, rectilinear in form, and there was little prospect of that property's being modified—hence the unit could approach the spherical only by means of small chords. Books were comparatively heavy; so construction of the case would have to be strong and the center of gravity low. They varied in size, so the shelving would have to be adjustable. The whole unit should be easy to move—hence the individual sections should be mounted on noiseless casters. Easy recognition implies good lighting—hence each unit would have its own fixture—a fluorescent tube with adjustable reflector—mounted on a universal joint.

Had books any special environmental requirements? Information was scanty here, but it was agreed that excessively dry air was as bad for paper as excessive moisture. Moving air of moderate temperature and humidity would be a satisfactory norm, so glass fronts would be omitted and the shelves slotted to permit ventilation. Dust was bad for books, however, so transparent plastic flaps would hang from the outer edge of each shelf, mounted on friction hinges that would stay put at any angle.

Only then was it possible for Kiesler's students at Columbia University to produce actual working drawings. This involved a realistic survey of industrial resources. What materials were best suited to the design? What modifications would be imposed upon it by available fabrication methods? How could cost be held to a minimum without sacrifice of quality? These and many other questions were answered in the construction of a pilot model. The result bore little resemblance to the standard bookcase because, as a tool, it was redesigned from the ground up. Its significance here lies in the methodology of its design. The user, the task, the tool: each was analyzed, free of historic precedent and prejudice, to discover the best solution in terms of modern scientific knowledge. A much

Louise Harpman, © 1995

Figure 7 – 7 / Clarendon Branch, Brooklyn Public Library, Brooklyn, New York. Stack spacing for accessibility. The Americans with Disabilities Act (ADA) requires that access to libraries be provided in a safe and dignified manner. Full compliance requires spacing of freestanding stacks at 36-inch intervals (minimum, 42-inch preferred) to allow a clear aisle for wheelchair passage. Turning clearance at the end of aisles is 48 inches. Shelf height is unrestricted, although reach range for wheelchair users extends from 9 to 54 inches above the finished floor.

more productive tool is the result. (Kiesler, incidentally, noted that knowledge had not always been stored in books. At one time we used clay tablets, at another papyrus roll, then books; now we use electronics to produce virtual magazines. The storage method for such new units requires corresponding research and revisions for the disks and tapes of word processor and computer.)

In an excellent research project completed some three decades after Kiesler's pioneering work, Alexander Kira analyzed the bathroom from much the same point of view—although apparently unaware of Kiesler's theoretical formulations.* Beginning with the notorious inadequacies of the modern American bathroom (high cost, great weight, complex fabrication, deficiencies with reference to physiological function, unsafe conditions, etc.), Kira pointed out:

The development of design criteria for the major personal hygiene activities (body cleansing and elimination of body wastes) must be based on the analysis of each of these activities in terms of: first, the complex cultural and psychological attitudes surrounding the subject—attitudes which influence our hygiene practices and our reactions to equipment; second, the basic physiological and anatomical considerations; and lastly, the physical or "human engineering" problems of performing the activity.[37]

Basing his research upon these premises, Kira first established the performance criteria suggested by medical and public health authorities. Then he photographed live models of both sexes acting against calibrated backgrounds. By this means he was able to record the anthropometrics of personal hygiene (washing the hair, face, hands, body as a whole) and elimination of body wastes (urination and defecation). This first stage employed conventional fixtures (lavatories, tubs, showers, toilets, urinals) to measure the correspondence—or lack thereof—between the activity and the fixture supposed to serve it. The second stage involved mockups of conventional fixtures, modified in size, shape, and location with reference to the floor. The final stage was the design of new prototypes whose configurations were based upon an optimal resolution of physiological, anatomical, and physical factors (Figs. 7–8 and 9).

The Kira prototypes do not depend upon radically new developments in technology; on the contrary, they could easily be manufactured with existing materials and fabrication methods. Yet they promise a whole new level of performance because of the experiential fit achieved between user and tool. The Kira study itself represents a model demonstration of how new methods of research and design can be applied to the redesign of all types of architectural furnishings and equipment.

---

* An objective analysis of the bathroom is no simple matter, as it collides with a nexus of cultural restraints and taboos. The fate of the bidet at the hands of the American plumbing industry is a case in point. Although the bidet can be merely a basin to facilitate feminine hygiene, the European form usually includes a jet of water. This jet is an extremely effective aid to cleansing the vaginal area. But it also has contraceptive potential, and this led to its being blacklisted on the American market for decades. Of course, the same jet is also a great aid to cleansing the anorectal areas of both sexes; this fact finally led the plumbing industry to place it on the open market under the name *Mister* Bidet!

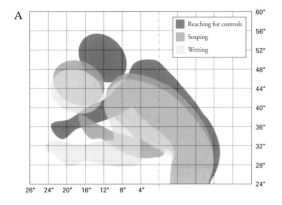

A

Reaching for controls
Soaping
Wetting

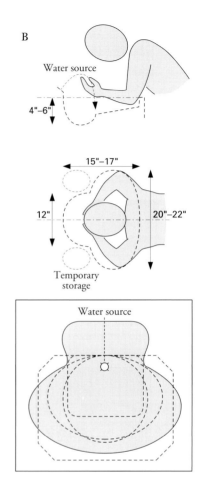

B

Figure 7–8 / (A) Ranges of body and arm movements while washing face, plotted without reference to equipment. Diagram is based on photos of models moving in front of calibrated backgrounds.
(B) Spatial balloon described in washing face, plan and section (top two illustrations). Comparison between space required and that afforded by available bathroom sinks (bottom illustration) shows wide deficiencies of models available at that time.

Through their careful and scientifically based analysis, pioneering researchers like Kiesler and Kira and contemporary architects like Michael Brill have pointed American building designers toward a better match of task with user, equipment with people. Much commendable progress has been made in the field of special design of accessible (barrier-free) environments that serve a broad range of people. It is important to realize that the early studies and designs of Kiesler and Kira addressed the need for improved functioning for all age groups. It is in this area that architects and product designers need to improve their focus and their products (Fig. 7-10). The impetus may indeed be America's large contingent of postwar baby boomers, who will become senior citizens during the first decades of the next century.

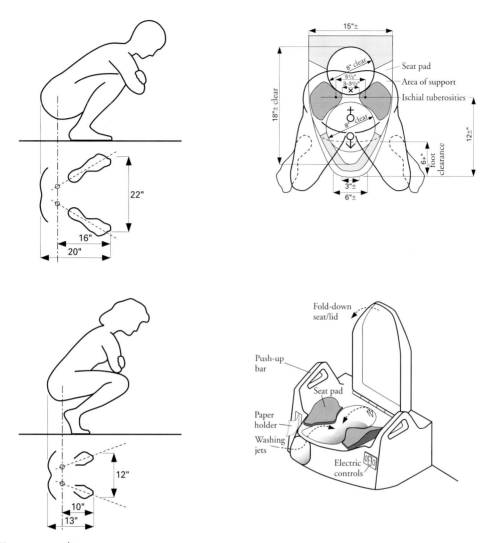

Figure 7–9 / Left: Natural postures for defecation. Right: Prototypical unit designed by Alexander Kira adds functions not normally associated with toilet use. In addition to flushing action to carry away waste, new unit has two water jets for personal cleansing. Height and configuration of seat are derived from analysis of physical and physiological aspects.

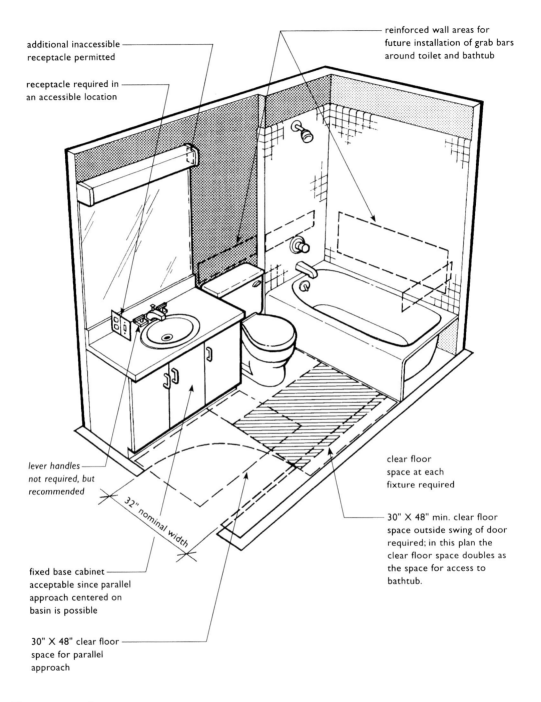

additional inaccessible
receptacle permitted

receptacle required in
an accessible location

reinforced wall areas for
future installation of grab bars
around toilet and bathtub

lever handles
not required, but
recommended

32" nominal width

fixed base cabinet
acceptable since parallel
approach centered on
basin is possible

30" X 48" clear floor
space for parallel
approach

clear floor
space at each
fixture required

30" X 48" min. clear floor
space outside swing of door
required; in this plan the
clear floor space doubles as
the space for access to
bathtub.

Figure 7 – 10 / At times, design decisions are guided by legislative mandates for the public good, such as the U.S. Fair Housing Act, which requires that new multifamily housing developments be accessible to those with disabilities. The Act's Design Manual provides optional bathroom layouts which make it possible for people using wheelchairs, walkers, or scooters to enter, close the door, use the fixtures and exit on their own—not always a simple prospect with conventional design.

Skeleton and Skin

The Morphological Development of Structural Systems

Although for thousands of years and in all parts of the world many cultures have shown a superb grasp of one or another aspect of the spectrum of structural possibilities, a comprehensive and universal—that is, scientific—theory of structure has been established and applied only in the last century or so. The marble porticoes of the Parthenon and the articulated wooden skeletons of the Ise Shrine in Japan, the plastic concrete vaulting of Diocletian's Palace and the stone-ribbed vaulting of the High Gothic in England or Bohemia, the mud-walled skyscrapers of the Moroccan oases and the monumental rubble masonry of the Mayans—each of these is the end product of a self-contained process of experimentation and refinement. Each represents a summation of one specific aspect of structural experience, developed within one specific set of objective conditions—cultural, technological, geographical. But, encapsulated by the accidents of history and lacking both the internal coherence and external applicability that only the mathematics of modern science could afford, none of these could yield a universal theory. The planned accumulation of structural knowledge, the systematic exploration and development of applied mechanics, the standardized testing of natural materials and the deliberate search for new synthetic ones—all of these essentials to a scientific theory of structure had to await the maturation of the Industrial Revolution[1] (Figs. 8–1 through 8–4).

The history of American structural development coincides with the last phases of this historic process. Moreover, this process has always been super-

Figure 8–1 / Temple of Hera II, Paestum, Italy. This fifth-century B.C. Doric temple, now roofless, clearly reveals its phylogenetic origins in articulated wooden skeletons, subsequently transmuted into marble. Most of the decorative devices of the Doric order also derive from the requirements of carpentry and joinery in woodworking.

imposed upon the special conditions of American life—a rapidly growing and polyglot population, inheritors of many specialized building techniques; a society constantly meeting new climatic and geographic conditions; a country that was, for almost three centuries, always partly settled and partly wilderness, partly agrarian and partly industrial, and, for most of its history, partly slaveholding and partly free. Under such conditions it is not surprising to find that neither our structural theories nor our structural practice has remained static for long. Rapid and violent change, uneven and undisciplined, replaced that slow, almost imperceptible accumulation of experience that characteristically preceded the sudden flowering of the great schools of building of the past. For this reason any discussion of contemporary American structural theory and practice must seem simplified, diagrammatic, and misleadingly symmetrical.

In the preceding chapters we saw something of the enormously complex problems of contemporary architecture—first in understanding and then in solving our requirements for shelter, and our need for the third environment. It must at all times be remembered that two factors in this complex equation are constants and have been throughout history: people themselves and the terrestrial environment in which they are submerged. These constants are virtually the same as they were 500—50,000—500,000 years ago.

Figure 8–2 / Hall of Rites, Kamingano, Japan. Skeletal wooden construction is raised to the highest level of sophistication in the monumental architecture of Japan.

The factors that *have* changed, and radically, are our increasing understanding of people's experiential requirements, population growth, our increasing technical ability to manipulate environmental forces, and the increasingly complex institutions and processes required to sustain social life under these new circumstances. Together these new factors have at once required and made possible a whole new order of building performance whose evolution is still in progress.

It is evident that the environmental forces that play upon a building are numerous and complex. They result in two kinds of stress upon the actual fabric or structure of the building. One set of stresses is mechanical—the loads to which gravity, wind, and earth-

Figure 8–3 / Temple of
Venus, Horti Sallustiani,
Rome, Italy. Plastic potentiali-
ties of mass masonry were
brilliantly exploited by
Roman architects after the
second century A.D., as seen
in this daring twelve-sided
segmental vaulted dome of
the Hadrianic period.

quake subject the structure. The other is chemicophysical — the remorseless attrition represented by the action of heat, light, atmosphere, precipitation upon the structure. The response that we require of the building is, of course, that it resist both these sets of natural forces. The roof must not collapse under the snow load, the walls must resist anticipated winds, the structure should not burn, rot, or rust. Expressed in purely experiential terms, however, the main requirement that we make of the structure is that it manipulate the flow of these forces between inside and out. It should act as a selective filter between the natural and manmade environments.

These two tasks are most often mutually exclusive for any single building material. That material whose molecular configuration makes it strong in resistance to tensile or compressive loads — steel, for example — by the same token offers little resistance to the transfer of heat. A vibrated concrete panel is structurally strong but acoustically poor; a foamed-concrete panel, on the other hand, makes an excellent acoustical barrier but has no load-bearing capacity. Marble floors are waterproof but not resilient; cork floors are resilient but not impervious. Glass is transparent to light, bronze opaque; one shatters, the other corrodes. And so it goes: the properties of matter are contradictory and

Figure 8–4 / Entrance hall, house in Telč, Czech Republic, late sixteenth century. The flamboyant expertise of late Gothic vaulting survived as a vernacular idiom until 1700.

intractable. The task of structural design often includes untangling and isolating them, so that they can be better exploited for the specific task at hand.

The accomplishment of this historic task, in the nearly 150 years since the Crystal Palace, led to an unprecedented flowering of structural theory and a parallel proliferation of structural systems and building materials (see Table 8–1). In most cases this specialization takes the form of a separation of structural tissue into supporting frame and enclosing membrane—that is, into skeleton and skin.* Such an evolutionary course of development has obvious analogies with a comparable specialization of tissue in the animal kingdom, a development which made possible the appearance of the higher vertebrates and of homo sapiens. As in animal evolution, it has had comparably significant consequences for architectural performance.

Modern engineering theory and technological expertise (including the immense computational power of the computer) permit us to project this process of analysis and syn-

---

* Of course, this same expertise has made possible new developments in endoskeletal structures, where the skin is at once supporting member and enclosing membrane. Such are the stressed-skin shells in metal or reinforced plastic and the tension and inflated structures whose potentials are discussed in this chapter.

Table 8–1 | Morphological Classsification of Structural Elements and Systems

Morphological Classification of Structural Elements and Systems

1. Rigid Stick (articulation)
   - beam — Truss
     - Multi-planar — Space frame — Wachsman
     - Mono-planar — Lattice frame — Geodesic dome
       - — Lamella vault
   - Column — Post & Beam
     - Rigid frame — Arch rib — Skeletal vault
       - — Skeletal dome
     - 3-D skeleton — Honeycomb — Rigid cage (skyscraper)

2. Rigid Slab (continuity)
   - Block wall
     - Block vault
     - Block dome
   - Planar slab
     - Folded plate
     - Curved shell — Synclastic — Monocoque
       - — Anticlastic

3. Flexible Filament (articulation)
   - Tensile Structure
     - Planar net — Suspension bridge
     - Single-curvature net — "Hung" skyscraper
       - — Bicycle wheel
     - Double-corvature net — (State Fair, Raleigh, N.C.)
       - — (Munich Stadium)

4. Flexible Membrane (continuity)
   - Tented Structure
     - Multimasted
     - Singlemasted (Dymaxiom house) — Denver Airport
   - Inflated structure
     - Single wall, air supported — Pontiac Silverdome
     - Dual wall, air inflated

A morphogenetic classification of structural systems. All manmade constructions can be visualized as ultimately deriving from four basic components. Modern technology has made possible an unprecedentedly wide crossbreeding and proliferation of variants.

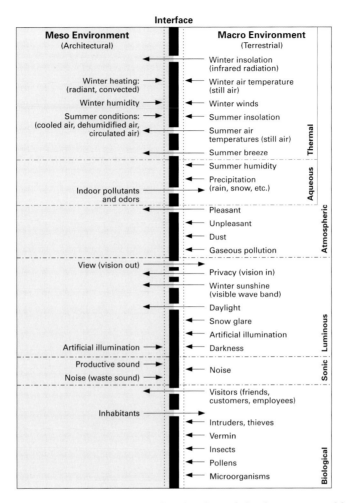

Figure 8–5 / Only with modern science and technology did it become possible to separate the load-bearing task of architectural structure from the environmental-control function of the wall as an enclosing membrane. Only then could the wall be conceptualized as a selective filter, acting as interface between natural macroenvironment and manmade mesoenvironment. This technical capacity can yield higher levels of environmental control.

thesis to levels undreamed of less than a decade ago. And yet the ultimate architectural implications of these new structural potentials are still poorly understood by many and rarely utilized. This is quite obvious from the behavior of many new buildings all around the world: employing the most advanced design and fabrication techniques and the most sophisticated materials and equipment, their overall performance often is qualitatively lower than some of their preindustrial prototypes. In fact, it is one of the paradoxes of contemporary architecture that the vernacular buildings of the folk cultures of Western civilization, not to mention the architecture of ancient, preliterate peoples, often display a more precise understanding of experiential reality than do our own.

The Function of Structure

The building is a sum total of two components: the structural elements employed to create a container for the mesoenvironment and the mechanical equipment required to hold mesoenvironmental conditions at the desired level. A building is thus a specialized instrument whose complexity may range from the comparatively simple (a bandstand, where the curved shell merely distributes the sound in the desired pattern and the sloping floor organizes the spatial relationship of the audience so that all may see) to the enormously complicated (a television studio, where the building is called upon to furnish entire environments without precedent in the natural world).

Conventionally, capacity for perceptible — or at least measurable — transfer or conversion of energy is the dividing line between structure and equipment. This is a necessary oversimplification. The compressor that removes excess heat from a room is classed as equipment. The steel truss that absorbs and then distributes the earthquake shock in such a fashion as successfully to resist it, is called structure. Yet both are engaged in a transfer of energy. In the last analysis, all of the building is dynamic. The air-conditioning apparatus that forces cool air into the room is no busier controlling its thermal environment than is the insulation in the wall, which inch by inch and molecule by molecule slows down the transfer of heat from the blistering outside. Thus the difference between structure and equipment is largely one of passive versus active function.

In previous chapters we saw how various types of equipment are employed to modulate the properties and components of the mesoenvironment. Here we are concerned with structure — that is, the physical envelope or container whose function it is to enclose, contain, support, and protect the environments so created. Contemporary structures are characterized by a high degree of specialization, usually expressed in a clear separation between skeleton and skin, framing and surfacing, support and enclosure. Nature subjects all of man's constructions to a complex process of attrition. When moisture corrodes steel, the action is chemical; when winter cold penetrates the wall, it is physical; when snow load collapses the roof, it is mechanical. Each potential type of attack requires a specialized response; the undifferentiated tissue that attempts to do everything at once often does none of it very well. Hence modern architectural design theory assigns to the skin the primary task of resisting chemical and physical attack; to the skeleton is assigned the task of resisting the mechanical forces of gravity, wind, snow loads, earthquakes, etc.

The frame or skeleton is subjected to two sets of forces:

1. *vertical*	weight of the structure itself (called dead load)
	weight of people, equipment, and goods inside it
	(called live load)
	loads from wind pressure, suction, and snow
	earthquake (vertical movement)
2. *horizontal*	wind pressure and suction
	earthquake (horizontal movement)

In its simplest terms, the task of the skeleton is to absorb these forces and convey them safely to the ground. When the house shakes before the blast of a winter gale, its frame is busily resolving such loads, breaking them down into their component parts (e.g., shear and tension) and dispatching them to the ground along the members designed to handle them. The building skeleton thus converts raw natural forces into characteristic stress patterns called normal (compression, tension, and bending) and tangent (shear and torsion).*

There are dozens of structural systems for accomplishing this load-bearing task and hundreds of permutations and combinations of these basic systems adapted to specific building materials, construction techniques, etc. But in terms of geometry, all structural elements, assemblies, and systems may be said to derive from four primary elements: the rigid stick, the rigid slab, the flexible string, and the flexible membrane.

> The *stick* is the basic element of all endoskeletal structures, from the most primitive post-and-beam trabeation to the most complex space-frame or rigid surface elements (e.g., grid domes).
>
> The *slab* (which, in geometric terms, is generated by the stick when it is moved along a given plane) is the basic element of all exoskeletal structures, from the rubble masonry vault to the most complex reinforced-concrete folded plates or shell structures.
>
> The *string* is the basis of all net like structures, from the rope ladder to the suspension bridge to cable-net roof structures.
>
> The *membrane* (which is generated when the string or filament is moved along a given plane) is the basic element of all endoskeletal tensile structures, like the tent, and of all exoskeletal pneumatic structures, like the balloon.

In recent decades, thanks to the rise of structural science and technology, these have been cultivated and refined, crossed and recrossed into a whole spectrum of specialized systems, each with its own inherent advantages and inherent limitations. Generally speaking, they can be classified morphologically as lower or higher forms, as indicated in Table 8-1.

Historically it was possible (indeed, before modern mathematical physics, inevitable) that the building wall be conceived of as a barrier pure and simple — an element that held up the roof, kept out the cold, and offered maximum resistance to the attacks of rot, rust, rodents, and robbers. But modern scientific knowledge forced the modification of such concepts in many fundamental respects. In the first place, to raise the efficiency and

---

* In another type of loading — vibration — the critical factor is time and not force. Certain types of vibration can alter the crystalline structure of metal and radically modify its properties. Sound waves at a certain pitch set up vibrations in a water glass that can shatter it. Soldiers marching in lockstep across a bridge can set up an oscillation that can literally destroy the structure, though the same soldiers walking out of step or standing still would not approach its load capacity. The dramatic failure of the Tacoma Narrows suspension bridge in 1940 demonstrated the dangers of aerodynamic instability in structures that were very strong from any conventional point of view.

performance levels of the building, clear distinctions had to be made between the functions of *support* and *enclosure*. This was necessary first of all for analytical purposes: because environmental stress is manifold and complex, structural response must be correspondingly specialized. Then it became clear that barriers are only relative, not absolute; no single material is literally impervious to all environmental forces. Finally, it became clear that all concepts of permanence are relative; no material is permanently resistant to all forms of chemical, physical, and mechanical attrition.

Specialized structural forms are thus to be understood as the direct response to the above discoveries. They represent the invention and exploitation of whole species of means of structural support; the enclosing function is largely incidental to most of them. But, as we saw in preceding chapters, there has been a comparable florescence in means of enclosure. The selection of any one structural support system for any given project is generally be determined by the given requirements for enclosure. Thus, for building types in which transparency or permeability to environmental forces (heat, light, sound, breeze, etc.) is a desirable quality, endoskeletal support systems are apt to be most suitable — for example, shops, houses, schools, office buildings. If, on the other hand, maximal opacity or resistance to movement of environmental forces across the interface is desirable, then exoskeletal support systems are more suitable — for example, concrete shells for exhibition halls, museums, warehouses.

All of our constructions are peculiarly vulnerable to another form of attrition: fire. In a certain sense, fire merely telescopes the ordinarily slow and often imperceptible processes of physical, chemical, and mechanical attack into a single cataclysm — a process that makes up in intensity for what it lacks in time. With its threat to life and property, fire has always been an important consideration in building design. But with the growth of modern urban society, the demand for fire resistance (the term *fireproof* is seldom employed now because the genuinely unburnable building is almost an impossibility) has increased.

The first iron-framed buildings were widely hailed as fireproof, but a few disastrous fires sufficed to prove the fallacy of this assumption. Metal frames were then encased in concrete and ceramic sheaths, thus making possible the multistory skyscraper. But this did not prevent a series of terrible conflagrations. Thus, the La Salle Hotel in Chicago was a "fireproof" building on the June night in 1946 when fire swept through it, taking the lives of sixty-one persons, and it was probably structurally as sound the day after as it was the day before. Actually, the fire fed upon the contents of the building, not the building itself — curtains, carpets, furniture, even the accumulated paint on the walls and the grease in the elevator shafts. As a result of these varied combustibles, the smoke from the fire was complex and toxic, so that many of the deaths were due to asphyxiation, not burns. This was true, to an even more marked degree, in the famous Cocoanut Grove nightclub fire in Boston in 1942, in which 492 persons died. Subsequent investigation revealed that the principal cause of death was the presence of noxious fumes from the flammable artificial shrubbery. Deaths directly due to flame and trampling were secondary — that is, had the victims not been overcome by the gases, they would have been able to escape unharmed.

Other deadly fires in recent years pointed out design and construction inadequacies. In 1980, 84 people were killed in the MGM Grand Hotel in Las Vegas, which had enough rooms for 3,500 guests but nary a smoke alarm. Then there was the fire in 1985 that Philadelphia police set by firebombing a house in an attempt to dislodge members of MOVE, a black separatist organization. That fire quickly spread through the cocklofts of the adjoining dwellings, killing 11 people and leaving approximately 200 homeless. And then, in 1993, to further underscore the tinderbox nature of many buildings, the horrific fire instigated by authorities at the Branch Davidian cult compound in Waco, Texas, resulted in 72 deaths. Terrible mistakes, accidents, explosions, and terrorist attacks *do* happen. Therefore, architectural design should serve to minimize the extent of the potential damage.

Hundreds of thousands of building fires occur in this country each year (614,000 in 1994[2]), mostly in structures that, being wholly or largely of wood, are as flammable as their contents. In 1994 there were 4,275 civilian fire deaths, of which about 80 percent occurred in the home. Moreover, for 1994 the property damage for all structural fires was estimated at $6,867,000,000.[3] Despite their magnitude, these recent statistics indicate significant progress in preventing and limiting fire damage in buildings when inflation is considered. For example, in 1969, some 12,100 persons lost their lives in fires, and property losses ran to $1,952,000,000* for the year.

Much of the progress in reducing fire damage in commercial buildings can be traced to codes requiring noncombustible construction. Yet the fires that occur in "fireproof" buildings indicate that the problem is only partially a matter of structure. As long as the contents are flammable, a fire hazard exists. Realization of this factor has served to widen greatly our concepts of fire prevention and control. The field now covers a range of measures in planning, building codes, firefighting equipment (both inside the building and out), and the training of building inhabitants in fire safety precautions. Only by the most careful control of all these factors can the incidence of fires be measurably reduced.

Over the last few decades, the statistics of the National Fire Protection Association (NFPA) clearly show that fire incidence and severity in commercial buildings has significantly decreased, with particular credit due automatic sprinkler systems.

A recent ten-year NFPA study (for the years 1985–1994) reports that the reduction in deaths because sprinklers were in place varies by building type: 83 percent for hotels and motels, 59 percent for selected health care properties (for the sick and aged), and 30 percent for manufacturing facilities. Sprinklers are not yet common, however, in other building types where the potential for loss of life in fires is substantial. These systems are rarely found in homes, schools, low-rise apartments, dormitories, barracks, stores, and smaller offices. Ironically, most fires occur in the types of buildings that typically do not have sprinklers, even though "when sprinklers are present, the chances of dying in a fire and the average property loss per fire are both cut by one-half to two-thirds, compared to fires where sprinklers are not present."[4]

---

* The 1969 figures do not include losses in U.S. government properties.

The retrospective study by the NFPA offers powerful evidence for the performance and effectiveness of sprinklers in extinguishing fires in their incipient stage, saving precious time, lives, and property. Obviously there is considerable potential for expanding the use of automatic suppression systems to a wide range of building types.

Many purely architectural problems remain to be solved, as well. For example, current trends in open planning reinforce the natural tendency of halls, stairways, and shafts to act as flues that can rapidly fan a small fire into a disastrous conflagration. (The fire that all but wrecked the building and threatened the collection of the Museum of Modern Art in New York in 1966 was of this type.) Hazards like these are implicit in modern buildings and it is difficult to see how they can ever be completely eliminated. One need only think of the bomb explosion at New York's World Trade Center in February 1993 that sent black smoke through the 110-story twin towers, killing ten, injuring hundreds, and causing approximately 100,000 panic-stricken people to evacuate. The bomb blast itself was, of course, an out-of-the-norm event. However, the disaster was exacerbated by the design shortcoming that allowed such free flow of deadly smoke. To minimize such smoke spread, many codes now require fire-safing of joints and openings in fire-rated construction assemblies, often using intumescent materials that expand when subjected to fire and heat. Interestingly, the World Trade Center was built and is operated by the Port Authority of New York and New Jersey, a bistate entity whose construction project did not have to meet the codes of either state.

Hence, even the most advanced buildings must be assumed to have some hazards and to require secondary lines of defense. Fire extinguishers, sprinkler systems, and alarms all have inherent limitations. For example, fires originating in concealed wall spaces or in adjacent properties may grow to proportions that cannot be managed by the time the sprinkler system is activated. As a result, perhaps the most important single advance has been the development of extremely sensitive electronic detection and alarm systems; these are designed to react to tiny rises in temperature or to increases in smoke or gases in the atmosphere and thus summon firefighters at a very early stage in the fire.

Steel: The Mathematician's Material

From a purely structural point of view, the walls of the pyramids are the least efficient structures in the world, occupying all but the tiniest kernel of the total space they displace. From the same narrow viewpoint, the molded plywood or laminated fiberglass boat hull is probably one of the most advanced, surpassed only by large open roofs using tensioned fabric membranes. *Efficient* and *advanced* are, however, relative terms; that structure is most advanced or efficient that most closely corresponds to the configuration of its own stress patterns. To put it another way, that structure is best which does the most work with the least material—or, as the engineers put it, whose strength-weight ratio is highest.

Among the first great demonstrations of this principle were the Crystal Palace, the Brooklyn Bridge, and the Eiffel Tower.[5] All three were remarkably efficient structures.

A

Figure 8 – 6 / San Francisco Main Library, San Francisco, California. Pei Cobb Freed & Partners and Simon Martin-Vegue Winkelstein Moris Associated Architects, completed 1996. (A) The technology of designing buildings to prevent fire damage and remove smoke has evolved tremendously. To prove that the sophisticated smoke exhaust system designed for the atrium was adequate, an actual fire was set once the architectural construction was complete. (B) A view toward the top of the daylit atrium. (C) To provide seismic protection in this earthquake-prone area, the building's structure rests on base isolators made of rubber layers laminated between stainless steel and stiffened with an internal lead core to dampen vibrations and provide resistance to earthquakes with a magnitude of 8.3.

B

C

But two of them are not buildings at all, and the Palace was a very special sort of show-case, with few of the complexities of plan or function that characterize the ordinary five-room house. Of greatest significance is the fact that all were built of iron. The historic accomplishment of their designers was their demonstration of a new structural concept: the achievement of strength through precision instead of sheer mass. To accomplish such a task it is necessary to analyze the problem of structural efficiency theoretically—that is, mathematically. Only thus can one determine in advance precisely under what circumstances a given amount of a certain material supports the greatest load. The application of such theoretical investigations was scarcely possible until the development of structural iron and steel. Steel is a mathematician's material because it is almost perfectly isotropic and elastic—that is, its physical characteristics make it react identically in all directions from a given point of stress and that strain is related linearly to stress. Natural materials such as timber or granite do not react in this fashion because of their cellular, crystalline, or fibrous construction, nor do they react with predictable consistency, because of their natural flaws and impurities. Steel was the first building material to display the fabulous potentials of isotropism and linear elasticity.

Structural theory fed chiefly on steel during the latter half of the nineteenth century. Because it is equally strong in compression and tension, it can be fabricated in either stick or string form. The tower and the bridge gave dramatic evidence of the structural implications of this fact. For the American experience, the steel stick and steel string had a special appropriateness. The primeval forests of North America made it inevitable that our construction would be primarily wooden. Thus, when steel structural shapes began appearing in quantity around 1850, the transition from wooden to metallic members was rapid and easy. Heavy mill construction of timber, the wooden truss, and the frame house, with its light skeletal cage and thin stiffening membranes of sheathing and plaster, were established basic structural forms. They had channelized American building technique and it was entirely logical that iron or steel columns and beams first be treated as stronger and more fireproof replacements for their wooden prototypes. Gradually the concept of a complete metal skeleton evolved and the skyscraper could appear. Even here a great debt was owed the earlier wooden structures, for it was in such systems as the balloon frame that a clear differentiation had been made between supporting skeleton and enclosing skin.

Once this distinction had been made, the wall ceased to have much structural significance, despite its visual importance. The sleek walls of Chicago's Monadnock Building gave it the appearance of a true skyscraper. By dint of solid masonry walls, seven feet thick at the sidewalk, it reached sixteen stories and visually challenged the genuine steel cage of Le Baron Jenney's Home Insurance Building nearby. In reality, there was a great morphological gap between the two: the Monadnock was the old, exoskeletal masonry pushed to its uttermost limits; the Home was the newer, articulated endoskeleton with its more highly specialized tissue. As with the evolutionary appearance of the higher vertebrates, the endoskeleton was the precondition to higher levels of performance.

The other great forcing bed for structural advance was transportation—first the canals and then the railroads, with their requirements for bridges and terminals of

Figure 8–7 / John Hancock Tower, Chicago, Illinois, completed 1970. Skidmore, Owings and Merrill, architects. High-strength steel made possible skyscrapers such as the Hancock Tower, rising one hundred stories or 1,127 feet. Note the diagonal wind bracing expressed on the façade. Nothing underscores the brute strength and braggadocio nature of the structure more than the location of a large swimming pool on the forty-fourth floor.

unprecedented clear spans. Here again, the metallic stick and string took over from their vegetable predecessors. It will be recalled that it was to produce stronger, more uniform, and longer-lived cables (than hemp and sisal ones) that John Augustus Roebling developed his first machinery for weaving steel cables. After their successful use on the Pennsylvania Canal, he quickly went on to apply them to structural uses, producing the spectacular series of suspension bridges that culminated in the Brooklyn Bridge (begun in 1868). With few exceptions (e.g., Figs. 8–8 through 8–10) the enormous structural potentials of steel in tension (as in tensile or suspension structures) has yet to be fully exploited in architecture proper.

Of course, the steel cage was an important development for architecture, as the great skyscrapers of today bear witness. Yet the sheer overpowering mass of hundred-story towers like the World Trade Center in New York or the Hancock Tower in Chicago (Fig. 8–7) is apt to obscure the fact that, from a purely structural point of view, the first skyscrapers and

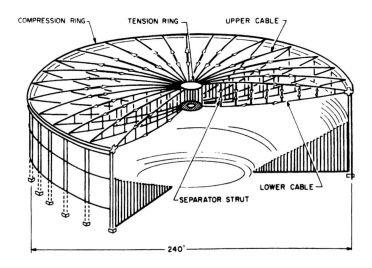

Figure 8–8 / Cable-suspended roof, Municipal Auditorium, Utica, New York. Lev Zetlin and Associates, structural engineers. A two-layer prestressed cable-suspension system yields a 240-foot clear span, with a minimum of material doing maximum work. The system is entirely free of flutter despite the dynamic and vibratory forces to which it is subjected. The entire roof was pre-fabricated and erected in three weeks from one central scaffold.

Figure 8–9 / Madison Square Garden, New York, New York. Severud Associates, structural engineers. Top: the radial cable system in place during construction (in 1962) formed a reverse dome hanging from a circular ring beam with a 450-foot diameter. Bottom: the completed arena.

Figure 8–10 / Cable-net tensile structures utilize steel cables and opaque roofs to create exciting structural forms in architecture. Top: Yale Hockey Rink, New Haven, Connecticut, completed 1958. Eero Saarinen, architect. The roof consists of two saddle surfaces spanning three arches, with the cable nets covered with wood decking. Bottom: Olympic National Stadiums, Tokyo, Japan. Kenzo Tange, architect. Completed in time for the 1964 Olympiad, the stadiums show an understanding of traditional tents and appreciation of Saarinen's work.

Figure 8–11 / Lightweight steel space frames can be used to span large distances and address a variety of architectural design issues. Top: Jacob Javits Convention Center, New York, New York, completed 1988. I. M. Pei & Partners, architect. Here the space frame encloses a main hall that is 160 feet in height. The longest clear span is 270 feet. Bottom: Baltimore-Washington Airport, Main Terminal Building, completed 1979. Peterson & Brickbauer, architect. Although more modest in scale than the convention center, here the space frame extends beyond the exterior wall to provide shelter for passengers arriving or departing via ground transportation. Among the ground transports are shuttle buses to the nearby commuter and northeast-corridor train station, which encourages efficient travel independent of the individual automobile.

the most recent ones follow the same basic structural theories. As a matter of fact, articulated stick constructions, which are morphological developments of the simple truss, represent a far more advanced exploitation of the metal, whether they assume a monoplanar form, like the Lamella vault or Fuller's geodesic dome, or multiplanar forms, like some of the recent great space frames. In all such cases we find steel operating most efficiently in fundamentally compressive applications. In the one case, the lattice gets its great stiffness from being curved into a vault (Lamella) or a dome (geodesic). In the other case, the lattice is developed three-dimensionally; this gives the structure as a whole the stiffness that permits it to be used in a single plane for enormous spans and cantilevers (space frame).

Two environmental hazards—fire and corrosion—still restrict the use of exposed steel in most architectural applications. Building codes require that, in multistory buildings, all steel members be wrapped in a fireproof casing; this is bound to lead to reductions in the flexibility and efficiency of the steel skeleton. One obvious way to get around this limitation is to move the skeleton completely outside, and free of, the enclosed space. This device is being increasingly employed in low-rise buildings. Nearly thirty years ago the architects of the 64-story office building for U.S. Steel in Pittsburgh went much further. Not only did they place all columns outside the building envelope, but the columns themselves were converted into hollow tubes filled with water. The design assumption here is that heat from a conflagration inside the building would dissipate up and down the column of water so rapidly that it could not accumulate in the metal tube itself. An interesting concept, perhaps, but not adopted by any other known American building in the many years since. Also innovative, but more widely utilized, is the design concept of flame-shielding exterior exposed horizontal members, as at One Liberty Plaza in New York (Fig. 8–12).

In the future, more and more construction now made of steel is likely to be fabricated of aluminum and composites. One reason for this is availability—approximately 1 percent of the earth's crust is iron (steel is an alloy of iron and carbon), compared to 4 percent aluminum. Another reason is the lighter weight that aluminum and composites impose on the other members in the structure.

Corrosion is the other limiting factor on the exterior use of unprotected steel. Until recently, the only solutions to this problem were stainless steel or repeated painting—but stainless steel is difficult to fabricate, expensive, and, in many locations, objectionably shiny; painting is costly, messy, and seemingly an endless undertaking unless very high-quality paints are used. An alloyed steel called Cor-Ten was developed with the property of quickly establishing a solid, permanent coat of rust. As this coat is chemically stable and physically unchanging, it affords permanent protection to itself thereafter. The final surface is a handsome red-brown matte finish that requires no subsequent attention. This new steel made possible the exposed frames of both the Mt. Sinai Hospital in New York and the U.S. Steel building in Pittsburgh. Today, many buildings and structures in marine and industrial environments utilize Cor-Ten steel for corrosion protection. Often, however, the Cor-Ten steel is painted for additional protection and to minimize staining of surrounding materials.

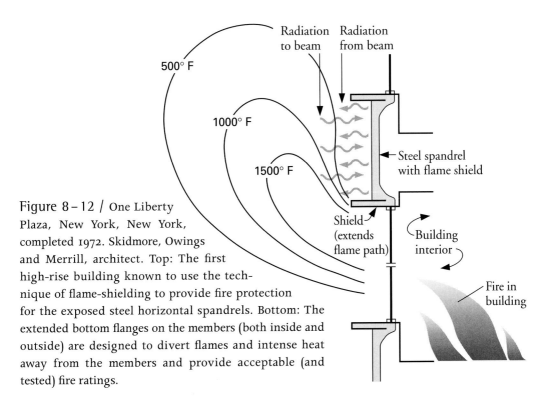

Radiation to beam   Radiation from beam

500° F

1000° F

1500° F

Steel spandrel with flame shield

Shield (extends flame path)

Building interior

Fire in building

Figure 8–12 / One Liberty Plaza, New York, New York, completed 1972. Skidmore, Owings and Merrill, architect. Top: The first high-rise building known to use the technique of flame-shielding to provide fire protection for the exposed steel horizontal spandrels. Bottom: The extended bottom flanges on the members (both inside and outside) are designed to divert flames and intense heat away from the members and provide acceptable (and tested) fire ratings.

Concrete: The Original Plastic

Metals dominated the field of large and complex structures from the 1850s on, capturing the imagination of designers and public alike by the remarkable bridges, towers, and skyscrapers they made possible. Concrete construction, once a specialty of the ancient Romans and then a lost art, reemerged toward the end of the nineteenth century and followed a line of morphological development analogous to that of steel and iron.

The manufacture of true Portland cement preceded that of steel, as it was produced in large quantities, in both France and England, before 1850. But the concept of reinforcing concrete with steel, uniting the compressive strength of the former with the tensile strength of the latter, was later in its appearance and slower in its spread. The actual invention is attributed to a French gardener, Joseph Monier, who in 1867 hit upon the idea of embedding small steel rods in concrete fishponds he was building. Making reinforced concrete possible, of course, are the relatively equal coefficients of thermal expansion for concrete and steel; thus the bond is maintained under all thermal conditions from very hot to very cold.

Prior to Monier's discovery, and for decades thereafter, the chief use of cement was as the binding element in masonry mortars when used in lieu of the more common lime mortars. Perhaps because of this, the real identity of concrete as a distinctly new material was overlooked. Even after reinforced concrete emerged as a structural medium, it was for a long time regarded as a purely utilitarian material—ugly, gross, and inaccurate. Under the conditions of empirical design and on-the-job mixing, it was in fact often both ugly and inaccurate. But, once begun, the technology of reinforced concrete was rapidly perfected, especially in Europe. In the present century it is unchallenged in such constructions as highways, dams, and harbor works. Indeed, such masterpieces as the Tennessee Valley Authority system of locks and dams are inconceivable without it.

Concrete is by definition a plastic material during construction: poured into any mold, it assumes that form and permanently holds it. It is all the stranger, therefore, to see how seldom this property of plasticity was exploited by American designers before World War II (bridge and hydraulic engineers always excepted). In architecture, its principal use was in rectilinear skeletal structures—that is, as a competitor of wood and steel. Even then it had certain advantages: it was its own fireproofing; it required somewhat less skilled labor; it could be used for floors, walls, and foundations that were impracticable in wood or metal.

Yet all such structures failed fully to exploit concrete's peculiar properties. The mere fact that it could be poured into any shape or form did not mean that it was equally appropriate for all of them. Europeans were much quicker to grasp this than Americans. In his now famous bridges in Switzerland, the engineer Robert Maillart displayed a totally different conceptual approach to the material. By an exquisitely detailed knowledge of reinforced concrete, Maillart was able to achieve forms that bore no resemblance to their steel and masonry prototypes. Basically, he used the reinforced slab and beam (or arch), but he used them in a revolutionary manner. He saw that because of its homogene-

Figure 8–13 / The bridges of Swiss engineer Robert Maillart became art by making visible the way loads are carried across the span. In his Schwandbach bridge, for instance, two main elements stand out: the thin, folded-plate arch, shaped like a reversed free-hanging cable to guide the weight of the bridge in the most direct way toward the supports; and the substantial roadway girders, which through beam action, balance the loads from unsymmetrical traffic. Light vertical web plates connect the two in a composition of comforting elegance and simplicity.

ity he could thin the member without reducing its strength. In fact, to all intents and purposes, he reduced both slab and beam to two-dimensional planes, which he stiffened by folding or bending—sometimes vertically, sometimes horizontally, or sometimes both. In a series of brilliant bridges Maillart isolated and exploited the special plasticity of the material in such a way as to indicate wholly new levels of structural efficiency.

There was little American work before midcentury to compare with Maillart's. The monolithic buildings so widely publicized by the Portland Cement Association were not significant structurally. They were derivative forms, absurdly imitating the mass-masonry baroque of the Spanish-American Southwest or late medieval English Gothic, where reinforced concrete vaulting was sheathed in a thin limestone veneer to imitate the original. Frank Lloyd Wright was one of the few Americans to use concrete as an architectural material—that is, one with authentic esthetic qualities that put it on a par with marble or brick. But even he, in his early buildings, used it in fundamentally mass-masonry forms—for example, Unity Temple. Later, of course, Wright more fully exploited the potential of concrete in projects such as Falling Water (see Fig. 1–2) and the Guggenheim Museum in New York City.

Fortunately, this unhappy phase is long past and concrete is used in a bewildering range of applications. In fact, the new concrete technology is now brilliantly employed not only where one might expect it (in plastic architectural forms like shells, domes, vaults, and paraboloids) but also in most of the stick- and block-derived forms. Here, thanks especially to prefabrication and prestressing, one finds structural shapes (columns, beams, panels) as strong and as precisely dimensioned as any steel equivalent. Concrete has even been used in a suspension form by Eero Saarinen in the great catenary roof of the Dulles Air Terminal near Washington (Fig. 8–15B). Such virtuosity in a material so long assumed to be clumsy and inert is due to a wide range of technical developments: the use of computers in the design of complex, hitherto incalculable structures; precision control of chemistry, aggregate size, and vibration of mixes; chemical additives to control setting time; prestressing; etc.

Figure 8–14 / Marina City, Chicago, Illinois. Bertrand Goldberg architects, completed 1964. These circular towers captured much attention for their expressive use of reinforced concrete. A negative feature, however, is the conduction of heat through the uninsulated concrete slab edge leading to energy loss and cold feet.

In these varied forms, modern reinforced concrete has most of the attributes of steel construction and lacks two of steel's weaknesses: susceptibility to fire and corrosion. Concrete as a material is inherently watertight and even has been used for the hulls of ships. Heinz Isler, a Swiss engineer, built more than 1,500 thin-shell watertight concrete domes whose concrete was carefully mixed and placed. (It must be observed, however, that many other designers are not so bold or confident, especially in the so-called temperate climates that subject concrete to severe attrition by repeated freezing and thawing, wetting and drying, expansion and contraction. In all but warm, dry climates, concrete shells and domes are often covered with weatherproof membranes for protection.) Moreover, because of its versatility, concrete makes possible a wide range of structural systems, from trabeation to shells, which would be almost inconceivable in any other building material.

Aside from this astonishing versatility, which makes possible the fabrication of almost any structural form in concrete, it has another fundamental advantage: abun-

Figure 8–15 / The airport terminal is a building type that requires large, flexible spaces. Reinforced concrete has been successfully employed using various structural techniques to create exciting and efficient architectural enclosures. (A) Trans World Airlines (TWA) Terminal, John F. Kennedy International Airport, Queens, New York. Eero Saarinen, architect. The complex concrete shell building was started in 1956 and completed in 1962. The structural virtuosity of the birdlike thin-shell concrete form of the terminal is familiar to most American architects and millions of international travelers. Many critics, however, failed to notice or appreciate the building's naturally daylit environment. (B) Main Terminal Building, Dulles Airport, Chantilly, Virginia (west of Washington, D.C.), 1962. Eero Saarinen, architect. The draped one-way concrete slab hangs between two rows of concrete piers and is put under compression by post-tensioning with high-strength steel strands. (C) New Terminal Building, Newark International Airport, Newark, New Jersey, completed 1973. Designed by the Port Authority of New York and New Jersey. Here reinforced concrete was used to create the large clear spans needed in an airline terminal through the use of hyperbolic concrete shells approximately 90 feet square.

dance. The cementitious soils, sands, and gravels out of which it is fabricated are available everywhere on earth. This fact has long dominated the building picture in wood- and metal-poor countries and explains why concrete technology has reached such high levels in Japan, Brazil, and Italy. The continued depletion of iron ore deposits may make concrete (especially prestressed concrete) increasingly dominant in the United States in coming years.

Wood: The Universal Material

Wood has always been America's favorite building material. In some respects, it still is; the great majority of the nation's dwelling units are wholly or substantially built of wood. The reasons are not far to seek: on one hand, wood's unique structural and esthetic characteristics; on the other, its abundance and relatively low cost, although it has risen steeply in price recently (1997). Wood is strong in compression and effective in tension and shear. Easily worked, even by unskilled workers using simple tools, it can be sawn, drilled, turned; mortised, nailed, glued, bolted; sanded, planed, polished, painted. Esthetically, it is one of the most ingratiating of all materials—endlessly varied in color and pattern, warm and silken to the touch, in many cases even fragrant (Fig. 8–16). Such properties made it the almost universal building material of preindustrial America. In the form of sawn lumber, it lent itself naturally to skeletal use, either in trusses or in cages. Thus, for popular building, it was ideal—plentiful, easily worked, yielding relatively efficient structures with low costs. This made it applicable to simple domestic structures;

Figure 8–16 / The potential for exciting, lightweight wood structure is perhaps best exemplified in the work of architect Fay Jones. Through careful spatial manipulation, combining large glass areas with special framing details, Jones creates exciting and spiritual spaces bathed in abundant daylight. Thorncrown Chapel, Eureka Springs, Arkansas, completed 1980. Fay Jones & Associates, architect. Left: Exterior view. Right: Interior view.

it was also used in fairly large and complex structures like the great New England churches with their trussed roofs and daring steeples, in many remarkable covered bridges and railway trestles, and in heavy mine and mill construction.

For nonresidential construction, wood began to be eclipsed by metals only after the Civil War, when the whole scale and complexity of American life began to escalate. This eclipse was due to wood's inherent limitations. Although relatively strong (allowable bending strength of about 1,400 psi for sawed lumber), it can not compare with steel (24,000 psi and upward). Wood is combustible. Being a natural cellular material, it is not isotropic and hence its behavior cannot be accurately predicted. Wood is not uniform in texture and strength, and, being organic, it is subject to attack by insects and fungi. Finally, wood is a lively material, responding quickly to changes in the moisture content of the atmosphere.

Nevertheless, significant new potentials lay hidden in wood, for nineteenth-century technology had neither the theoretical nor the technical means of isolating them. But with modern methods of manufacturing plywoods, particle board, oriented strand board (OSB), and laminated structural members, wood reappears in forms so novel as to be almost a new material. In multi-ply laminations, the characteristics as well as the form of wood are radically altered. It becomes relatively isotropic for, if the grain is placed at right angles in successive plies, tensile strength is equalized in both directions. By the same token, plywood is much more stable and uniform than natural wood, flaws or expansion and contraction in one layer being largely corrected by the other plies. The weakest aspect of earlier plywoods (they have been mass produced for a century) was the animal glues used as binders; soluble in water and subject to fungal attack, they held plywood to the level of an interior finishing material. But with the development of synthetic resins as binders, plywood emerged as a structural material. These new resins have great adhesive strength (under test, the individual plies rupture before the joints between them). In addition, they render plywood resistant or immune to moisture, fire, fungus, and insect attack. However, a new area of concern regarding these manufactured wood products is the potential impact of the adhesives and resins (e.g., urea formaldehyde resins) on indoor air quality (see chapter 11).

From a purely structural point of view, the most significant development is the perfection of plastic resins that permit the molding of all types of curved shapes under heat or pressure. Shells such as speedboat hulls, when molded in this way, have a very high strength-weight ratio, especially in resistance to impact blows and vibration. But the greatest significance of lamination is in the fabrication of skeletal elements such as hinged arches and rigid bents. Laminated-wood elements of this type are in many ways superior to comparable ones in steel or concrete — especially in single-story buildings of large span, such as churches or clubhouses, where the color and texture of wood are desired.

There have been considerable advances in fabrication methods of conventional wood framing — for example, so-called engineered nailing in light frame structures, timber connectors in heavy mill construction, etc. Many of today's homes are built with prefabricated members such as 14-inch truss-joists that can span more than twice the distance

A

B

C

Figure 8–17 / Timber frame house under construction, Bucks County, Pennsylvania. Donald Prowler, architect, completed 1998. (A) View of the timber frame roof structure. (B) Structural insulated panels (SIPs) await hoisting to infill timber frame. (C) Panels are hoisted into place, as shown here on another project.

of 12-inch solid joists and also are less likely to cause squeaking floors as a result of warping. In addition, the exterior walls and roofs of many homes are now constructed of structural insulated panels (SIPs) that are premanufactured, delivered to the site, and then hoisted into place (Fig. 8–17). Such technical improvements extend the structural use of wood products.

Over the years many informed persons have argued that, with the nation's forests in danger of exhaustion, structural use of wood is barbarous; because of its unique esthetic characteristics that its use should be confined to purely decorative applications in furnishings and interior design generally. Pulp and paper technologists make the same sort of argument against the structural use of wood but for quite different reasons. From their point of view, wood is a chemical treasure trove of raw materials (resins, lignin, alcohol) and finished products (paper, rayon, film). However, the danger of forest exhaustion appears to have been avoided with current forest management practice. Through the 1980s and 1990s over two million acres of trees were planted annually in the United States. Moreover, the world's leading timber producers (the United States, Russia, Canada, and Western Europe) all have more net growth than removal.[6] Additionally, the growing popularity of engineered wood permits use of farmed, fast-growing, small peeler trees. These trees are harvested, peeled, cut in strips, mixed with adhesive, extruded, and milled into timber, which can be used for long-span, high-strength, large cross-section members for roof framing. Gone are the days of harvesting long, large boards from old-growth forests for these purposes.

Perhaps confusing the issue are the rapidly dwindling acreage of tropical rain forest in South America and Asia. In response to rain forest destruction, efforts to discourage the marketing of tropical lumber are gaining strength. Indeed, the states of California, New York, and Arizona and the city of Minneapolis are considering prohibiting the use of tropical timber in public construction projects.[7] There also are efforts to promote the use of lumber produced in a sustainable manner through labeling of wood products. Ultimately, such efforts should lead to improvements in the way future rain forests are harvested or transformed and result in a less damaged global environment. If sustainable forest management practices can indeed be realized, the supply of wood for America's buildings is assured. In addition, wood can now be milled more efficiently through the use of computer-guided saws to maximize the amount of lumber obtained from a log.

The Role of Masonry

Though brick and stone constructions have always dominated the urban landscape, there has never been an authentic masonry tradition in the United States. The masonry surfaces that seem so important on the landscape are preponderantly enclosures stretching around endoskeletal structures. The reasons for this historical anomaly are peculiarly American. They are complex and interlocking, but the central reason is the abundance of skeletal materials—first wood, then iron and steel. Even in its heyday, the masonry building relied upon wood and metal for the framing of floors and roofs. Our genuine masonry vaults can almost be counted on two hands. Even our most famous dome, that of the U.S. Capitol, is fabricated of cast iron and steel.

Nevertheless, as surfacing materials, stone and ceramic materials still have great merits. They are all relatively inert and stable and hence much less vulnerable to rot and rust than either steel or wood. They are nonflammable and their resistance to climatic attrition is relatively high (though marble and some stones are attacked by atmospheric pollutants). Masonry has other merits of both functional and cosmetic nature. Brick, tile, stone, and marble offer a matchless range of colors, textures, and integral patterns; these can be used in almost limitless combinations. They assemble into a surface of many joints, which gives the surface as a whole a fluidity that is missing in sheet and panel materials. In climates with wide diurnal or seasonal temperature fluctuations, the masonry wall has less crazing and cracking; such imperfections are largely confined to the joints and hence less obtrusive. Because of matte finishes, natural irregularities, and generally darker tones, small failures — which, in smooth materials like stucco or glass, would be disastrous esthetically — are effectively masked in masonry. Moss and lichens, capillary action, and coal smoke have little cosmetic effect on most masonry surfaces. The capacity to absorb thermal shock has functional significance as well. In far northern cities like Moscow, for example, it is notable how much better medieval brickwork has survived climatic attrition than either the stucco of baroque times or contemporary reinforced concrete.

Synthetic Strings and Membranes

The extraordinary development of the chemical industry during the past few decades has produced an enormous range of new synthetic fibers, fabrics, and extruded membranes. Used singly or in combination, they display an equally wide spectrum of performance characteristics: high tensile strength, flexibility and elasticity; resistance to fire, intense cold, and many chemicals and gases; immunity to attack by animal pests, fungi, and microbes; transparency/opacity to light, heat, and other forms of electromagnetic energy; permeability/impermeability to fluids and gases, etc. The availability of such materials has, in turn, brought to the fore the increasingly utilized family of suspended, tented, and pneumatic structures.

Some of these forms, like the tent, have only in the last few decades been widely used by the urbanized Western world. Some of them, like the suspension bridge and the dirigible, have had great significance for transportation and the military. But, until recently, none of them has played any significant role in architecture proper — and this despite the fact that they are all extremely efficient structural forms. Part of this neglect was no doubt due to simple prejudice; traditionally, Western society has equated strength with rigidity. With its great emphasis on stability and permanence, it has relegated tented structures to carnivals and nomadic peoples generally.* But neglect of these tensile-stressed structural

Figure 8–18 / U.S. Pavilion, Expo '70, Osaka, Japan. Davis, Brody and Associates, architects; David Geiger and Horst Berger, structural engineers. This air-inflated dome, 262 feet wide by 460 feet long, is held in shape by an internal pressure differential of only 0.03 psi. Yielding 100,000 square feet of unobstructed floor space beneath a roof of unprecedented lightness, the structure consists of a diamond-pattern lattice of steel cables stitched to the vinyl-coated fiberglass membrane; this lattice is in turn anchored to a perimetrical concrete compression ring that rests on an earth berm. Designed to resist earthquakes and winds of 125 miles per hour, the structure is safe even with air-pressurization (fan) failure, as it cannot sag low enough to injure visitors.

types has been fundamentally due to the very real limitations of the fibers, fabrics, and membranes hitherto available. Exclusively organic in origin, they were all too vulnerable to all forms of environmental attrition. The appearance of new synthetics is changing all this. Tensile, tented, and pneumatic buildings are now appreciated as offering some of the most promising developments in the entire field of structural engineering.

Pneumatic structures promise unprecedented means of enclosing very large areas. The first large pneumatic structure was the U.S. Pavilion at Osaka, Japan, completed in 1968 prior to the 1970 Expo. The design combined a hanging cable system with the desired form of a dome that was high in the center and low along the elliptically shaped edge. The structural forces were resolved through use of a two-layer diagonal cable net and PVC-coated fabric that weighed less than 1 pound per square foot (Fig. 8–18).

---

* Suspension bridges, of course, have flourished ever since the perfection of the steel cable by Roebling in the mid-1840s, but there has been no comparable flowering of suspended structures in architecture proper. This paradox was no doubt due to the fact that steel in trabeated forms was so cheap and abundant that no economic drive for its maximal exploitation in tensile structures developed. There are now signs that this is changing and we begin to see the principle applied to buildings.

Figure 8–19 / Pontiac Stadium (the Silverdome), near Detroit, Michigan, completed 1975. The design team included O'Dell/Hewlett & Luckenbach, Inc., architect, Kivett & Myers, consulting architect, Geiger-Berger Associates, structural engineers. This air-supported pneumatic structure spans an area 722 feet by 552 feet. Soft vertical panels hang from the cable grid to absorb crowd noise. Daytime events are brightly daylit due to the translucency of the Teflon-coated fiberglass covering.

The Osaka project successfully demonstrated the use of lightweight pneumatic structures to enclose large spaces such as sporting areas. In the 1970s and 1980s domed pneumatic stadiums were designed for various cities including, most notably, Minneapolis (the Metrodome), Detroit (the Silverdome [Fig. 8–19]), and Indianapolis (the Hoosier Dome)—three colder cities that can experience significant snowfalls. Although these pneumatic structures have served well, their use in such cold climates is problematic. Construction economy, indoor conditions, and operational cost concerns all serve to limit air pressures to below 10 pounds per square foot, even in locations where significantly heavier snowfalls are quite possible. As a result, under heavy snow loads structural collapses have occurred. Air-supported domed stadiums have been designed with mechanical systems that can be activated to direct warm air to the roof membrane, to melt the snow as it falls. In general, this approach works. However, sometimes snows are too heavy and wet, or they arrive unexpectedly. The solution of last resort, the employment of emergency crews with warm-water hoses on the roof, has fallen out of favor, and several air-supported structures in cold climates are being replaced or retrofitted to correct this deficiency.

Tented tensile structures represent an excellent design solution for large-span spaces such as airline terminals (Fig. 8–20) and stadiums. However, architects should also investigate their design potentials for a wide variety of other building types.

The Line of Increasing Efficiency

Structural theory did not develop and could not exist in a cultural vacuum. In the light of the past century's accomplishment, however, it is possible to formulate the laws of structural development. All of our structural forms, like those of organisms generally, belong morphologically to two broad genera: endoskeletal and exoskeletal. Within these two categories, some species are more advanced than others, either relatively (because of more intensive cultivation by a given society) or absolutely (because of inherent static characteristics). Finally, there has been an evolutionary progression toward more efficient forms—often, as in organisms, as a result of hybridizing and crossbreeding. Historically this development has been largely unplanned, pragmatic, and hence asymmetrical. This is by no means a purely technological phenomenon; on the contrary, controlling factors have often been economic, geographic, even political or military. Thus the formulation of reinforced concrete theory was largely the byproduct of the great burst of dam and highway construction in the early twentieth century. Similarly, the intensive cultivation of the steel truss and the steel cage was the consequence of the great periods of railroad building in the last half of the nineteenth century and skyscraper construction toward its end.

Each material has its characteristic potentials, each has its limitations. As a result, each becomes associated with certain types of structural forms or systems. This parallelism between form and material served to accelerate the development of some aspects of structural theory, but by the same token it often served to distort or stultify the development of other aspects equally promising. Here three factors are in constant interaction: structural system, material, and production or fabrication method. A change in one inevitably affects the other two and, consequently, the entire equation. But contemporary technology is dissolving most of these parallelisms, often with startling effect. By means of the fabrication method of thermopressure molding, an existing material (plywood) can appear in a radically new structural form (semimonocoque and stressed-skin shells). Materials traditionally thought of as sticks are now the basis of latticed spheres (Fuller's geodesic dome). A plastic material like concrete, once thought uniquely appropriate for curved shells and vaults, is now prefabricated into skeletal components as precisely dimensioned as steel or wood sticks. Such a state of affairs makes possible an unprecedented hybridization of structural systems.

But as this very plenitude of structural means has also led to unprecedented confusion in the selection of structural systems for various plan types, it might be appropriate to recapitulate their essential characteristics. Structural systems derived from sticks, such as two-way grid domes (Fig. 8–21) or string, such as cabled nets, lead to articulated constructions, while those derived from slab or flexible membranes employ the principle of surface continuity. In the first case, the integrity of the walling membrane can be interrupted at almost any point, as it is merely hung on the outside of the skeleton and contributes little or nothing toward resisting the mechanical loads of gravity and wind. Surface structures, on the other hand, employ a shell that is at once enclosing and

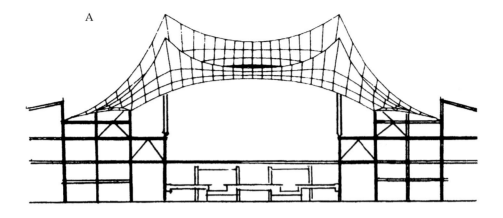

A

B

Figure 8–20 / Main Terminal of the Denver International Airport, Denver, Colorado, completed 1994. W. C. Fentress, J.H. Bradburn & Associates, architects; Severud Associates, structural engineer, Horst Berger, principal consultant. The potential snow problem with pneumatic structures precludes use of lightweight, large-span designs in cold climates. While pneumatic systems can be thought of as active membrane structures requiring operation of large fans to maintain the air pressure and the intended architectural shape, passive tented structures that require no continuous expenditure of energy can be designed. The Denver International Airport is such a structure, designed to withstand the snowfall so common in its cold climate. (A) The first sketch of the proposed tent roof configuration (by Horst Berger). (B) The masts were constructed first, followed by the top ring and mast cover assemblies. Valley cables were then strung across and the fabric installed a bay at a time.

C

D

(C) The completed, daylit terminal space with its translucent membrane covering rows of arching valleys. The significant lighting savings should more than offset the heating costs for this continuously occupied building. (D) The membrane roof is in place for the main terminal building. Parking structures are in the foreground, the snowy Rocky Mountains in the distance.

Figure 8–21 / Garden Exhibition, Mannheim, Germany, 1967. Frei Otto, architect; Ted Happold, engineer. This organic structure was generated from a square grid of continuous wood struts covered with translucent fabric.

supporting; its physical integrity cannot be violated without serious or even disastrous consequences.

The significance of this for architecture should be obvious. Those activities that involve a great deal of traffic, movement, exchange across the interface between meso- and macroenvironments are apt to be most easily contained in the exoskeletal structural systems, where nonstructural skins hung on load-bearing frames make provisions for penetration at any point a simple matter. In those types of buildings (or building sections) where movement across the interface is regular, limited in space, or periodic in time (e.g., theaters and stadiums of all sorts, warehousing, and storage facilities) the endoskeletal structure is more appropriate. This congruence of structural system and societal use is all the more marked because large and unobstructed spans are also indicated for spectator sports and theatrical performances.

Today structural designers and theorists have computerized design tools that allow them to quickly and accurately evaluate whatever alternatives their imaginations propose. No longer does intuition have to govern in the design of structures requiring many, many equations. The computer programs now available allow architects and engineers to achieve purity of form with unprecedented confidence and curiosity. As Horst Berger writes in *Light Structures—Structures of Light,*

Common to all of my structures is an attempt at purity of form. Some critics may read this as a sign of the narrow mindset of the "engineer." Yet I believe that clarity of purpose, simplicity of form, and directness of expression can be solid foundations for an architectural design philosophy in which the quality of its art is tested by the criterion that "nothing needs to be added and nothing can be taken away."[8]

The Integration of Environmental Control Systems

The optimal control of all environmental factors within a given building, in the interests of the persons and processes housed in that building, is today technically more feasible and socially more imperative than ever before. Yet by and large, contemporary architecture does not succeed in discharging this task. The reasons for this failure are to be found in many different domains. There is, first of all, the architect's difficulty in formulating the program—in conceptualizing the exact behavioral topography that the building is supposed to elicit and support. Even when this part of the task is properly done, the architect faces the task of effectuating it—of reconciling the many contradictory requirements of the various control systems that must be employed. Thus a problem in acoustics may render more difficult an optimal solution of the illumination system. Or a mandatory requirement for ease of access or exit may complicate the design of wintertime weatherstripping and thermal insulation. Or some local condition, such as an earthquake or hurricane hazard, may dictate a structural system that is far from ideal for the plan suggested by the program. Finally, almost all buildings are expected to satisfy the often divergent environmental requirements of the people and the processes they shelter.

Such contradictions must be resolved at the highest possible level, yet they involve factors that are at once disparate and variable, biological and mechanical, subjective and objective, poetic and practical. Nevertheless, such considerations are endogenous to the design; as such, they are subject to a fairly high degree to rational analysis and design control. In meeting them, the building becomes both the container for and the creator of the third environment, or mesoenvironment. But the contradictions between this contained mesoenvironment and the natural macroenvironment in which it stands submerged can be only partly resolved at the wall line, no matter how sophisticated the design of the walling membrane may be. The qualitative fluctuation of the macroenvironment across both time and space is immense and only in gross terms predictable. Such exogenous forces must therefore be dealt with by means of other techniques of environmental manipulation—that is, landscape architecture and city planning.

Unfortunately, the coordination between these three scales of environmental design is ordinarily poor or nonexistent. As a result, the individual architect, acting for the individual client, is compelled to adopt a defensive design policy. For example, the buildings that surround the one being designed obstruct the prevailing breeze. Unable to exploit this natural resource, ventilating fans must be installed. Neighboring structures not only make no intelligent use of their own share of the sun's heat and light, they also prevent a normal distribution of sunlight on the plot. Thus, for all too many architects, insolation and daylighting remain academic questions; space heaters and fluorescent tubes must be installed instead. Surrounded by paved courts, masonry walls, and traffic-crowded streets, the plot is flooded with noise; sound insulation is required to make the building tolerably quiet. Having access only to polluted "outside" air, as opposed to "fresh" air (in all too many locations), the architect must rely upon filters to cleanse it. The building is thus doubly on the defensive—against nature and against human beings. It has to overcome the natural deficiencies of its external environment without being able to exploit those features that are favorable. As if this were not bad enough, it must also overcome the cumulative damage its neighbors may have already wrought upon the natural environment.

The ingenuity that American buildings display in overcoming such peripheral obstacles is little short of miraculous. By mechanical means, we can now create any set of environmental conditions we desire. Important as they are, however, the wide use of these techniques and equipment has inherent dangers. The contemporary designer runs the risk of accepting treated air that has passed through filters or electronic air cleaners as a satisfactory substitute for clean, fresh air; of feeling that electronically operated louvers are preferable to natural foliage; of preferring sound insulation to plain, ordinary silence. In many specific situations our synthetic environments are superior to nature's. But this is no adequate basis for the mechanistic conclusion that we don't need nature any more. On the contrary, with the complexity of modern building we need nature more than ever before. It is not a question of air-conditioning versus sea breezes, of fluorescent tubes versus the sun. It is rather the necessity for integrating the two at the highest possible level.

On Understanding the Terrestrial Environment

To intervene effectively in the situation in which we find ourselves—that is, to construct a truly effective third environment for individual and social life—both architect and

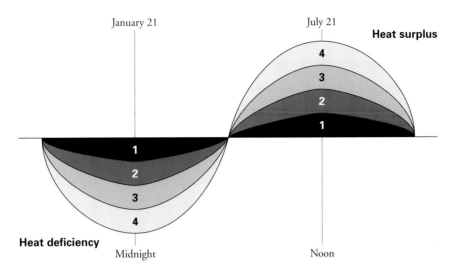

Figure 9–1 / Four stages of optimizing thermal fit between building and its environment (after Victor Olgyay). Instead of employing transparent walling membranes and then relying upon complex mechanical systems to compensate for high rates of energy transfer across interface, the design process should begin at other end of the design option spectrum: (1) Mechanical systems can then operate more effectively, yielding better comfort conditions. (2) Enclosing membranes should be selected for transparency or opacity to specific environmental forces. (3) Building's exterior surfaces should be shaped and oriented to maximize desirable, minimize negative forces. (4) Site should be selected for microclimatic advantages and then landscaped to maximize them.

urban designer require a much deeper understanding of the terrestrial environment than they commonly display. For the quality that continues to characterize the majority of contemporary architectural and urbanistic activity nearly everywhere in the world today is a profound misunderstanding of ecological realities. This misunderstanding is, in turn, characterized by two sorts of error. One is a lack of comprehension of the absolute inter-relatedness of all the component elements of the natural environment—an interdependence that makes it impossible to manipulate one factor without setting in motion a complex chain reaction that usually extends far beyond the individual designer's sphere of action. Twenty-five years ago this volume noted that it "seems possible that gaseous wastes from two centuries of fossil fuel combustion, accumulating in the upper atmosphere, may irreversibly alter the climate of the entire world." This prophetic warning is taking on new meaning in today's world (see chapter 4). The other professional error is the consistent tendency of modern architects and engineers grossly to underestimate the magnitude of the natural forces of the environment—or, contrariwise, grossly to overestimate the magnitude of manmade capacities at their disposal. (Recent spectacular failures of the electrical power grids, including a July 2, 1996, event that resulted in the loss of power to fifteen Western states and parts of Canada and Mexico, are examples of such faulty estimates.)

The natural world in which we live and move is the result of the interaction of a vast number of forces acting upon the earth and upon each other. A bewildering network of relationships, primary and secondary, causal and resultant, interact to produce those conditions that we call *climate* and *weather*. While we cannot expect architects and urban designers to be also meteorologists and climatologists, we might at least demand that they have a general understanding of the ecological systems that they are constantly called upon to manipulate in one way or another.

For the purposes of our analysis, the principal environmental factors may be summarized in this decreasing order of magnitude (not of decreasing importance):

1. *meteorological*	a. solar radiation
	b. air masses
	c. precipitation
2. *geographical*	a. latitude
	b. land mass-water surface ratio
	c. terrain
3. *topographical*	a. elevation
	b. orientation to sun, prevailing winds
	c. soil structure
4. *biological*	a. fauna (including microorganisms)
	b. flora

While the scale of these factors varies enormously—the first being cosmic, the latter quite local in extent—they interact with each other at every level. A forest, for example, is the result of a given temperature and precipitation regime. This regime may be regional or subcontinental in extent. But this same forest, by its very presence, in turn modifies the regime that makes it possible in the first place. Every local factor acts upon regional norms to create local variations. Often these variations assume quite astonishing magnitudes and compel us to make the distinctions we do between *macro*climates and *micro*climates—the distinction being all the more important because the locus of all individual experience is, obviously, always the microclimate.

The sun is the prime mover of the entire terrestrial system. All meteorological phenomena—wind, rain, clouds, temperature; night and day, winter and summer; gravity, magnetism, the movements of the earth itself—are the results of the sun's actions upon the solids, fluids, and gases of our planet. In addition to being the generator of all terrestrial activity, the sun is a prime factor in the climates of the world. Insolation, the amount of solar energy falling upon the earth as a whole, is relatively constant. Its variable impact is due to the complex motions of the earth itself, including constant rotation, a tilt on axis of 23-1/2 degrees, and yearly revolution in a slightly elliptical orbit (Fig. 9–2).

On the winter solstice, December 21, the earth-sun distance is 91.4 million miles. On the summer solstice, June 21, the earth-sun distance is 94.5 million miles. The elliptical

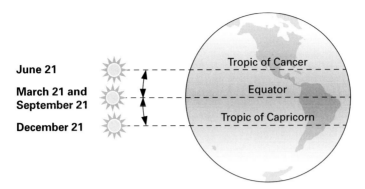

Figure 9–2 / Solar energy received annually at any point on earth's surface is a function of angle of incidence times exposure length — hence higher latitudes have colder climates than low ones.

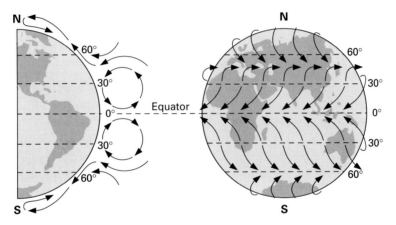

Figure 9–3 / The sun as prime mover of the terrestrial system. All meteorological phenomena, including wind patterns, cloud cover, and precipitation, are the consequences of the sun's irradiation of the solids, fluids, and gases of our planet.

orbit, with its varying earth-sun distances, accounts for the more extreme climates in the southern hemisphere (e.g., hotter summers and cooler winters). The earth is always tilted on its axis at an angle of 23-1/2 degrees. What changes is the effect of the tilt, also known as *declination*. Thus, when it is summer in the northern hemisphere, the earth is tilting in toward the sun, and when it is winter in the northern hemisphere the earth is tilting away from the sun. On the equinoxes (March 21 and September 21), neither hemisphere is tilting toward nor away from the sun, which is directly over the equator.

Insolation sets in motion the great global system of air circulation. From this solar action upon the earth's atmospheric envelope comes the movement of equatorial and polar air masses, whose collisions over land and sea bring the whole train of clouds, sunshine, winds, and precipitation that make up local weather (Fig. 9–3). At both these levels, insolation is the most important factor in the thermal environment.

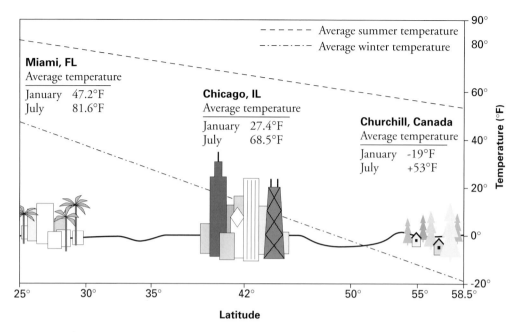

Figure 9–4 / Temperature change with latitude. The earth's temperatures drop roughly in proportion to distance north or south of the equator—however, the hottest spots on earth are found not at the equator, which is often cloudy, but around 20 degrees north and south of it, where skies are clearer and the sun is overhead for a longer period in the summer. Above the Tropic of Cancer, the annual average mean temperature is about 5°F lower for each degree of latitude, but the actual differential between two points can vary widely. Latitude is, at most, only a rough guide; many other factors, including altitude, distance from the sea, ocean currents, vegetation, and amount of clear sky, also play a role.

The principal geographical factor in environment is expressed in latitude, for it is distance from the equator that determines the amount of solar energy received at any given point (Fig. 9–4). (Longitude has no comparable significance; it is merely an index of location, never of climate.) Were the surface of the globe absolutely uniform in profile and material, the correlation between latitude and climate would be absolute. However, because the earth's surface is so widely varied, the climates along any given latitude vary also. Thus Pompeii and Samarkand lie on the same latitude as Beijing and New York; St. Petersburg, Russia, is as far north as Churchill, Manitoba, while St. Augustine, Florida, and Lhasa in Tibet both lie near 30 degrees N.

The main reason for climatic anomaly along a given latitude lies in the differing heat-holding capacities of water bodies and land masses. Primarily because water has much the higher specific heat, temperature accumulation and decay is much slower in water than on land. Thus the effect of any body of water upon its immediate environment is to reduce diurnal and seasonal temperature extremes; the larger the water body, the more pronounced this stabilizing effect. Honolulu, at 19 degrees N near the center of a great warm ocean, sees very little temperature variation between midnight and midday, and between January and July. Tombouctou (Mali), in Africa, at approximately the same latitude (17 degrees N) has much higher temperatures and much greater diurnal and seasonal variations because it is embedded in the center of a great arid land mass.

Land masses themselves have vastly different heat-holding capacities. Partly these are due to the physical characteristics of the earth itself — that is, whether it is sand, silt, rock — and partly to the overlying ground cover or lack thereof. Thus the sands of the Sahara and the snows of Antarctica are the result of a set of primary climatic factors — very dry air and intense insolation in the one case, very cold air and weak insolation in the other. But the two materials are, at the same time, the cause of secondary climatic characteristics. Sand is a good absorber of solar energy, while snow is a good reflector of it. Thus each tends to exacerbate the climates that caused them, rendering the desert still hotter and the Arctic tundra yet colder than they otherwise would be.

It is also apparent that the ratio between land mass and water body at any given point has a characteristic impact on the climate of that point. For this reason, continental land masses produce wide regional variations even along the same latitude (Oregon and Maine, Copenhagen and Omsk in Siberia) and wide seasonal extremes within a given region (e.g., the climates of the American Canadian prairies and the Russian steppes). Peninsulas and isthmuses tend to yield climates strongly influenced by adjacent water bodies (Mexico, Italy), while islands always show the steadiest climates and the least deviation from the norms of their latitudes (the Azores, the Galapagos, Madagascar).

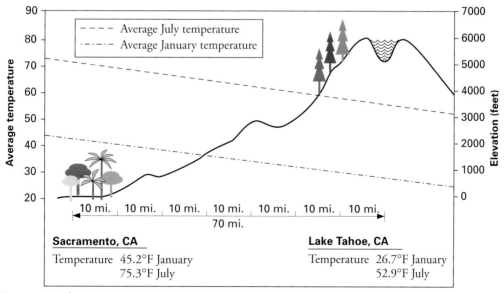

Figure 9–5 / Temperature with altitude. Air temperatures drop in inverse proportion to altitude at an average rate of 3.6°F per thousand feet. Local conditions can modify or even reverse this (temperature inversion), but only for limited periods of time.

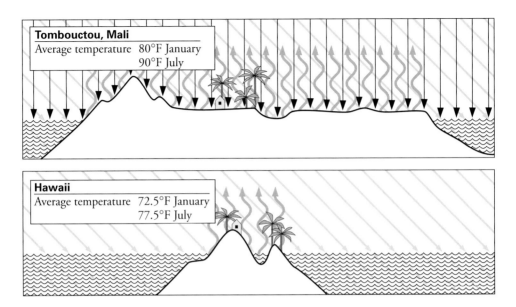

Figure 9–6 / Temperature change with land mass. Due to differing heat-holding capacities of land and water, higher temperatures develop and greater diurnal and annual temperature extremes occur in large land masses than in large water bodies.

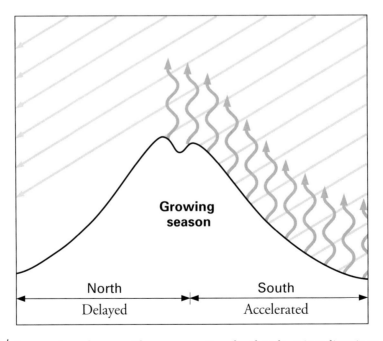

Figure 9–7 / Temperature change with exposure. On a local scale, microclimatic variations due to different exposure to sun can be as significant as if separation were by hundreds of miles instead of a few feet.

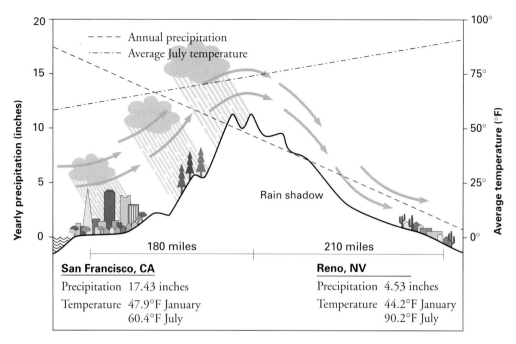

Figure 9–8 / Temperature and precipitation changes due to orographic uplift. Large climatic variations can occur within relatively short distances when precipitation falls on windward side of mountain ranges. When this drop in precipitation on leeward slopes is severe, as in American Southwest, desert conditions can result.

Elevation above sea level acts to modify climate in two important ways. The first effect is due simply to air temperatures dropping at a constant rate as one ascends — that is, inversely with altitude. This temperature lapse rate amounts to 3.6°F per thousand feet of altitude. A 1,000-foot rise in altitude is equivalent, on average, to a horizontal displacement or change in latitude of approximately 450 miles to the north or south of the equator. This elevational effect is what leads to such climatic anomalies as the Peruvian Altiplano or the Mountains of the Moon in East Africa. Despite an almost equatorial location, their altitudes (10,000 and 16,795 feet respectively) give these regions the icy fogs and alpine flora of the tundra instead of the tropical rain forest normal to such low latitudes (Figs. 9–5 through 9–7).

High elevations also have an important climatic impact upon the lower lands around them. Thus the mountain ranges along the west coast of North American force the moist air masses coming in off the Pacific to rise. In the process this air is chilled and condensation takes place. As a result, the air mass discharges most of its moisture (in the form of rain, hail, sleet, or snow) on the upper weather side of the mountains. This effect, called *orographic uplift*, produces a so-called rain shadow on the windward slopes and an aridity shadow to the leeward. In the American Northwest, this finds classic expression in the cool, rainy climates of coastal California, Oregon, and Washington and the semiarid regions of Wyoming, Nevada, and Utah (Fig. 9–8).

The Microclimate as Human Habitat

Such meteorological and geographical factors as the above are decisive in establishing the climatic regimes of continents and large regions, the macroclimates of the world. But for the average person, as for the average building, they are largely statistical abstractions. They bear little relation to the experiential reality in which individuals are, at any moment of their existence, immersed. The microclimate — the milieu of the yard, the street, or the neighborhood — is the only true measure of this level of human experience. Here, the play of larger forces upon the local landscape produces the weather in which people actually live.

The perspiring person in the street who doubts the Weather Bureau's 88°F when a private thermometer shows 103°F in the shade, the irate citizen who chases a hat down a roaring streetwide gale while the instruments at the airport blandly register an eight-mile breeze, the gardener whose seedlings on the north side of the house freeze despite an official low of 39°F, the puzzled writer whose radio proclaims a visibility of nine miles when outside the window the smog is so thick that it is impossible to see across the street — all these people are the victims of experiential contradiction. There is nothing wrong either with their powers of observation or with the instruments at the weather station. It is merely that the same climate is being measured at two entirely different levels. The Weather Bureau is reporting on the macroclimate while the citizens are feeling on their own backs the effects of the microclimate.

Meteorology has reached a high level of proficiency in this country, but so far it has worked largely on a macroscopic scale, dealing in terms of continents and regions inside of which important variations go largely unobserved. Historically this emphasis is not difficult to understand. Meteorology got its earliest impetus from such activities as agriculture and maritime shipping. In recent decades, aviation and satellites have enormously extended both its coverage and its accuracy. This is essential knowledge, but of scant use to the designer or consumer of buildings. For the rude and pressing needs of the individual deal with the immediate environment — conditions within the apartment, block, or place of work. Until quite recently, detailed knowledge at this scale was almost totally lacking in this country.

When homely observation christens a certain intersection "the coldest corner in town," chances are that a check with instruments would confirm this as fact. Moreover, intensive research along accepted meteorological lines would reveal *why* it is the coldest corner and how it might be redesigned to correct the situation. The character and juxtaposition of air masses determines the weather in a given locality at a given time. The local behavior of these air masses is in turn affected by the particular configuration of the land: the height and depth of its hills and valleys; the shapes, sizes, and densities of the buildings upon it; its bodies of water, groves of trees, parks, and paved streets; and, finally, by the way the sun falls upon the whole.

It thus follows that every change we make upon the landscape — every house we raise or tree we cut down, each field we plow or street we pave — affects the microclimate.

This change may be small; it is certainly definite. It may be for the better, but chances are that, with our appalling ignorance, it is for the worse. We cannot say, with Mark Twain, that everyone talks about the weather but no one does anything about it. As a matter of fact, we talk about the weather all the time and are never conscious of how importantly we are changing it. The microclimate of a given site is largely determined by small-scale variations in the topographical features of the site:

1. elevation above sea level
2. exposure to sun and prevailing winds
3. size, shape, and proximity of water bodies
4. soil structure
5. vegetation — trees, shrubs, meadows, crops
6. manmade structures — buildings, streets, parking lots, etc.

It is imperative for us to remember that, although the spatial extent of these factors may be quite limited, their physical magnitude with reference to the people in that space may be very large. For example, a building may at noon cast a very small shadow on the adjacent sidewalks, but if the location is Miami and the month July, the condition of pedestrians in that shadow is dramatically different from the condition of those in full sun a few feet away. From an experiential point of view, hundreds of miles and not dozens of feet might separate these two microenvironments.

We have seen the macrocosmic effect of elevation upon climate. Architects and urban designers seldom realize that changes in elevation play a comparably important role in the microclimate. Such phenomena are well understood by farmers and orchardists, who know that a rise of a few feet may render the higher elevation frost free. In some marginal areas, like the northern edge of the Florida citrus belt, elevation is so important that weather forecasts and frost warnings are issued in terms of feet above sea level. (Incidentally, the heat-holding capacities of the many lakes and ponds in this district are apparent after a night of frost: there is always a band of undamaged vegetation around the edges of each water body.)

Orientation has comparably important consequences for the microclimate. A north-facing slope (in the northern hemisphere) may have a growing season shorter by several weeks than a southern slope at the same elevation on the same mountain. Knowledge of this phenomenon would be critically important to developers of a ski trail, who would find longer and more severe winters on the northern slopes. The vineyardist or orchardist would seek a southern orientation for the opposite reason — that is, shorter, less severe winters and a longer growing season. Colorado potato growers exploit this phenomenon at the smallest possible scale by planting the tubers along the southern base of east-west furrows cast up by special plows.

By themselves, then, minor changes in elevation or orientation can produce significant variations within even small horizontal distances. Combined, the two effects can produce spectacular climatic anomalies. The Italian lakes (Como, Garda, Lugano) afford classic

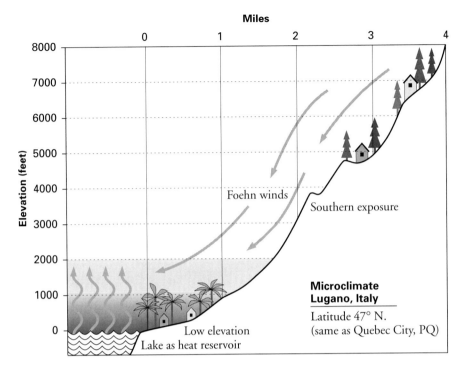

Figure 9–9 / Several meteorological and geographic phenomena coincide to produce microclimates around north Italian lakes that are much warmer than Alpine hinterland: (1) foehn winds warmed by orographic air coming over the Alps, (2) low elevation of lake shores, (3) maximum exposure of northern shores to low winter sun, and (4) thermal reservoir of lakes, with their slow rates of temperature decay. Result: semitropical microclimates in close proximity to true Alpine climate regimes.

examples of this. The shores of these lakes, on the same latitude as Minneapolis (44 degrees N), enjoy a subtropic climate complete with bougainvillea and palm trees, yet only a mile or two inland and several thousand feet higher, the climate is literally Alpine. This anomaly is the composite result of several factors. One is a location at the southern base of the Alps, which exposes the lakes to low winter sun and protects them from the cold winds of Western Europe. Superimposed upon these warming effects are two others: the warm foehn winds, which slip down the southerly slopes in winter, and the heat reservoirs represented by the lakes themselves (Fig. 9–9).

In varying degrees, such anomalies are to be found everywhere; architects and planners should be much more attentive to them than they commonly are. This example is typical:

Tremendous microclimatic temperature differences [have been found] within the Neotama Valley of Central Ohio, based on four-year studies of 100 to 300 observational points within one square mile. The number of frost days varied from location to location between 124 and 276 per year; the dates of the last Spring frost from March 9 to May 25; those of the first Fall frost from September 11 to December 13. Differences between temperature minima amounted to about 40°F and those between maxima seem to be even higher.[1]

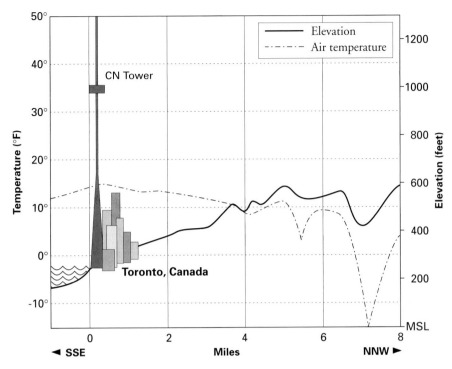

Figure 9–10 / Temperature distribution on a January night across Toronto, Canada. Warming effect of lake added to metabolism of heated urban fabric renders temperatures in central city some 30°F higher than those seven miles inland. Note sharp drop in temperatures along floor of inland valley, into which cold air of slopes has drained.

Nothing in the city layout or architecture of Toronto, for example, reflects the climatic realities shown in Fig. 9–10. Here, on a typical clear winter night, it may be 30 degrees or more colder seven miles inland than downtown at the lakefront. This radical difference is due to three factors: (1) the heat-holding capacity of the lake, (2) the heated masonry fabric of the city itself, together with the haze hood of atmospheric pollution, which prevents much of the heat from escaping into outer space, and (3) the frost-pocket effect of the little valley seven miles north-northwest of the city.[2]

Superimposed upon natural microclimatic variations are an increasing range of man-made effects, the scale of which is rapidly approaching geographic or geological dimensions. The most important of these, from the standpoint of architect and urbanist, is the process of urbanistic development itself. By its substitution of a masonry landscape of paved streets and heated buildings for the vegetable cover of the natural landscape, it automatically substitutes the microenvironment of the desert for whatever it replaces. This is characterized, first and foremost, by disturbances in the normal thermal cycle of the day—a disturbance due to the heat-absorbing and heat-holding capacities of masonry materials as compared to vegetal ones. Thus urban tissue absorbs heat all day and reradiates it all night. This thermal effect is further accentuated by heat loss from

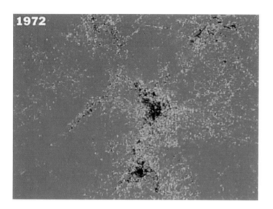
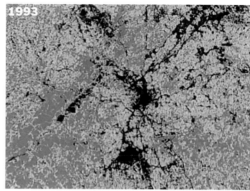

Figure 9–11 / The effects of urbanization in creating an urban heat island effect can be vividly seen in these graphic images for Atlanta, Georgia. Left: Landsat satellite imagery of the Atlanta region taken in 1972. Dark sections are areas of urbanization, with downtown Atlanta near the center and Hartsfield airport near the bottom. Right: This 1993 satellite image indicates the dramatic spread of urbanization that has engulfed 60 percent of the region.

millions of cubic feet of heated building space and by the haze hood to which we have already referred. For these reasons, the city is always warmer than its surrounding countryside, day and night, winter and summer (Fig. 9-11). This situation is commonly much more exaggerated than Weather Bureau data indicate, as their measurements are made inside instrument shelters and take no account of radiant temperatures, which play a critical role in human comfort. Indeed, this phenomenon has now become so marked that it is necessary to regard the city as an organism with its own peculiar metabolism.[3]

Even agriculture, in replacing virgin ecologies with plowland, alters preexisting climatic conditions in real and significant proportions.[4] Indeed, it can be said with certainty that every time someone plows a field or erects a building or paves a road, the microclimate of that spot is altered. Always, until relatively recent times, the architecture of each region displayed characteristic responses to the special climatic regimes with which it had to cope.[5] Indeed, this is the origin of many of the most distinctive features, in both plan and structure, of American regional architecture. A close scrutiny of the meteorological data for these regions shows that preindustrial architecture was often more scientific than our own in its method of handling environmental stress.

Because the animal body is first and foremost a heat machine, the primary task of all building everywhere is always the control and manipulation of the thermal environment in our favor. In a highly advanced technological society like our own, one might expect that contemporary American architecture would be characterized by a precise and elegant response to thermal stress. Unfortunately, this is far from true. American technology produces a splendid range of heating, cooling, and ventilating equipment as well as a wide array of thermal insulation materials. These make possible a level of thermal control that would have been inconceivable until the recent past — exemplified, of course, in rocket and space-vehicle technology. But, in normal architectural practice, this equipment and material is often less efficiently designed and more wastefully used than were the much more limited resources available to our ancestors. The result is that our buildings yield far less satisfactory thermal environments than we have the right to expect, and they cost far more to install and to operate than they would if we paid as close attention to microclimatic reality as our ancestors were compelled to do.[6] It is a vulgarization of technology to argue that, with modern potentials, such factors do not matter anymore. The fact is, they matter more than ever: to function well, the air conditioner needs a cool roof to provide comfort for the persons whom it serves.

In an exemplary examination of actual American climates, one striking characteristic emerges: the enormous variations in thermal regimes between one region and another and the large seasonal and diurnal fluctuations within a given region[7] (Fig. 9–12). Such wide variations are characteristic of continental climates, and they subject all structures to enormously unequal stresses in both time and space. Minneapolis, for example, has a recorded range from 107°F down to −45°F; the city commonly sees a range of from 90°F down to −20°F (Fig. 9–12D). Spatially, the discrepancies are equally dramatic: on December 21, the south wall of a building located at 40 degrees receives approximately 15 times as much solar radiation as the north wall of the same building. Annually, the differential amounts to about 5 times as much insolation on the south as on the north walls.*

The architectural consequences of such asymmetrical thermal stresses is expressed at two different levels: (1) wear and tear on the actual fabric of the building — nothing is so destructive of building materials as alternate freezing and thawing, wetting and drying, expanding and contracting, and (2) wear and tear on heating and cooling equipment to meet fluctuating external conditions. Such conditions clearly make the design of a building in Minneapolis a more difficult task than in Miami (Fig. 9–13). In the former instance, the building budget must be spread equally over a wide range of heat-generating and heat-dissipating devices, with redundant capacity inevitable in both. In Miami, on the other hand, the budget can be largely concentrated upon heat-dissipating devices and equipment. For this reason, also, a truly effective wall in Minneapolis is not likely to resemble a comparable one in Miami.

In light of such considerations, the tendency toward standardization of building form and building fabric to conform to a few international stereotypes does not represent a truly scientific exploitation of modern technology. The visual poverty and monotony of the resulting architecture is merely one expression of overall dysfunction. Contrariwise, an esthetically rich and sensuously satisfying architecture can only be derived from the closest attention to and respect for its actual terrestrial environment, especially at the microclimatic scale.

* Diagrams showing the average monthly solar radiation (in Btu per square foot per average day) transmitted through double glazing with external shading are published in the Solar Radiation Data Manual for Buildings available from the National Renewable Energy Laboratory, Golden, Colorado.

A – Miami, Florida

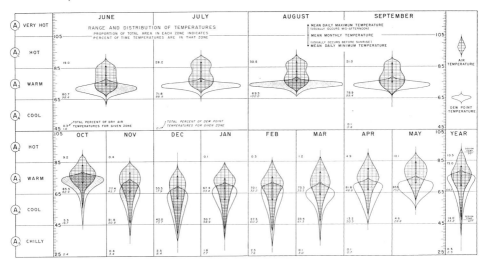

B – Phoenix, Arizona

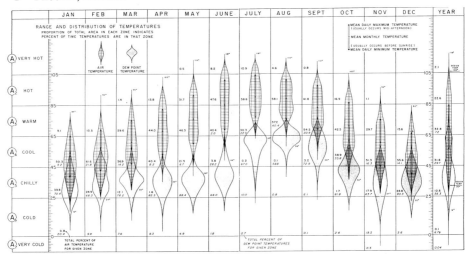

Figure 9–12 / (A) Temperature regime of Miami, Florida. A semitropical climate characterized by moderate air temperatures, high relative humidity, and intense insolation. Because of its low latitude (26 degrees N) and location on a peninsula surrounded by warm seas, there is a comparatively small diurnal or seasonal variation in temperature. Somewhat amazingly, the air temperature in Miami has never risen above 100° F, due to the thermally stabilizing effect of the water and very high humidity in the air. (B) Temperature regime of Phoenix, Arizona. A true semiarid climate characterized by high ambient temperatures, very high radiant temperatures due to the intense radiation and very low humidity. Because of clear skies and sparse vegetation, both diurnal and seasonal temperature variations are large.

C – Portland, Oregon

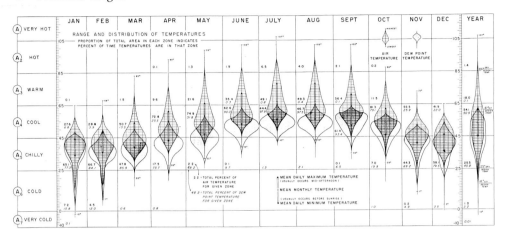

D – Minneapolis, Minnesota

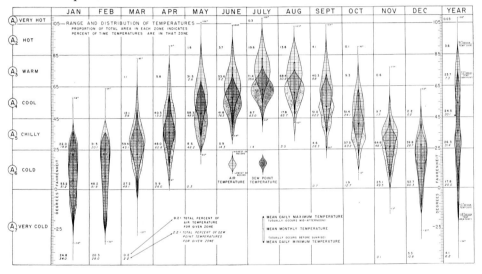

(C) Temperature regime of Portland, Oregon. A truly temperate climate characterized by moderate temperatures and modest diurnal and seasonal extremes. Because of prevailing winds off the Pacific Ocean and high mountain ranges to the east, Portland is in a rain shadow, with high precipitation, fog, and cloudiness year round. (D) Temperature regime of Minneapolis, Minnesota. Located at the downwind rim of a continental steppe, this city has one of country's most difficult climates. Extremely cold winters, with high winds and heavy snow cover, alternate with hot, humid summers to make difficult a good fit between environment and architecture.

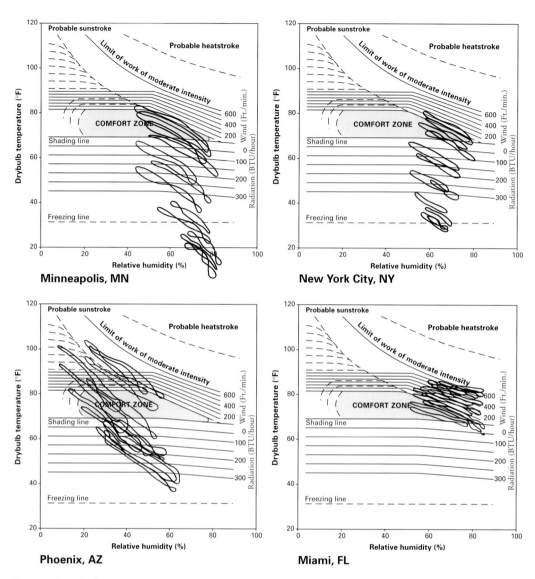

Figure 9–13 / Evaluation of four American climates relative to human comfort (adapted from Victor Olgyay). By plotting average monthly temperatures on a bioclimatic chart two facts emerge: (1) none of these climates would be fully habitable without architectural intervention, and (2) an architecture truly responsive to the environmental reality of each would of necessity be very different, in both performance and appearance, from the limited stereotypes currently used by American architects.

Architectural Response to Climatic Reality

To minimize stressful fluctuations across the interface between the building and its immediate environment, manipulation of all physical factors must be extended far beyond the building wall. This is carried on at two scales—that of the landscape architecture and that of urban design. Manipulation of the landscape has obvious significance for the performance of the building, yet recognition of the importance of landscape design to overall architectural amenity is, even today, of a peculiarly limited kind, being justified (even by landscape designers themselves) in largely esthetic terms. Streets planted with trees are now generally recognized as being more attractive than streets without them. Buildings are no longer considered complete until their surroundings are landscaped. Open areas add to the beauty of a neighborhood. Parks and playgrounds are important to the health of growing children. All of this is true. Yet it does not convey an adequate picture of the complex relationship between individuals, building, and landscape. It does not describe the real physical impact of the landscape upon us and upon the microclimate, nor of our every action upon it. Today, however, if a development is planned without proper consideration of ecosystems this is not because of the absence of information or computer analysis tools. Incredible software, such as the CITYgreen™ program by Washington, D.C.-based American Forests can now be used to evaluate the benefits of tree canopy, including stormwater reductions, cooling energy savings, and carbon sequestration (Fig. 9–14).

Figure 9–14 / Site analysis can now be improved by computer software such as CITYgreen™. Here the program is used to analyze ecological impacts of two scenarios for a residential development in Tucson, Arizona. The images for these views are produced with the assistance of aerial photography. Left: A development with a tree canopy of only 8 percent. Right: The same development with a tree canopy of 42 percent, with significantly reduced stormwater runoff, substantial summer (mechanical cooling) energy savings, and much improved carbon sequestration.

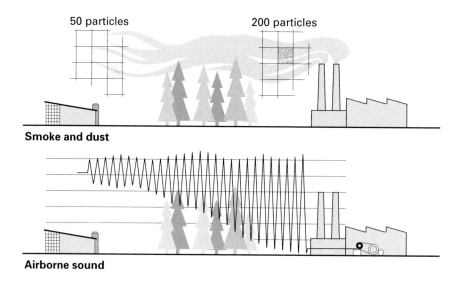

Figure 9–15 / Reduction of atmospheric and sonic pollution by trees and turf. All foliage acts as an impingement filter, trapping airborne particulates until washed away by rain. Trees, shrubs, and turf are also highly effective absorbers of airborne sound, although they also generate potentially stressful particulates in the form of pollen.

Certain aspects of the landscape are susceptible to wide and flexible manipulation, the health and comfort potentials of which have scarcely been tapped by contemporary architects and landscape architects. Two examples suffice: the functional use of trees and lawns in urban areas. Above and beyond their esthetic contribution, which is, of course, generally recognized, the scientific use of deciduous trees accomplishes the following environmental desiderata: (1) deflect, absorb, and reduce solar heat, (2) reduce free air temperatures, (3) filter the atmosphere of particulates, (4) reduce light levels and glare, (5) increase visual privacy, (6) reduce transmission of airborne sound (Fig. 9–15) .

In general, trees have a stabilizing effect upon their immediate surroundings, reducing all environmental extremes. Rudolph Geiger, in his pioneering study of the microclimate, found that mixed forest growths of spruce, oak, and poplar cut off 69 percent of the sun's heat from the ground. He found that forests are cooler in summer and warmer in winter than cleared land, and that a belt of trees reduces wind velocities in its lee by as much as 63 percent. In this country, measurements show that a shelter belt of trees reduces wind velocities by 50 percent and reduces heat loss in houses thus protected from infiltration of cold air by as much as 30 percent[8] (Fig. 9–16).

Much the same result flows from the intelligent use of lawns and dense ground covers. Temperatures are reduced by them. Because of its rough texture and low color value, a grass surface absorbs more sunlight and reradiates less heat than any paved or masonry surface. Because of transpiration, a lawn converts a large portion of the heat it absorbs into other forms of energy. In general, both air and radiant temperatures are much lower above a grass plot than over a paved area of similar exposure. Observations in Texas on an

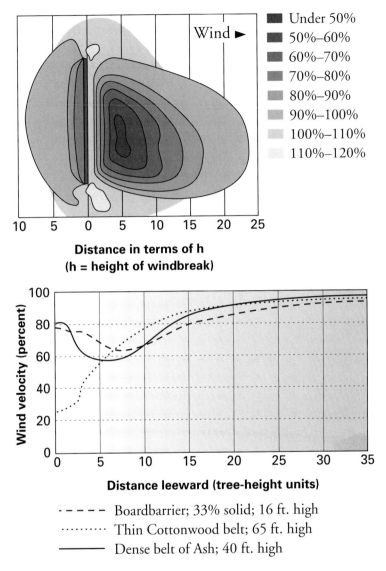

Distance in terms of h
(h = height of windbreak)

Distance leeward (tree-height units)

- - - - - Boardbarrier; 33% solid; 16 ft. high

············ Thin Cottonwood belt; 65 ft. high

———— Dense belt of Ash; 40 ft. high

Figure 9–16 / Reduction of wind velocities by barriers. The percentages shown are expressed as a percentage of an unobstructed wind. In cold climates, where an absolute deficiency of heat is a prime environmental problem, wind chill is an important cause of thermal stress. Thus all types of windbreaks, whether natural or manmade, should be considered integral components of overall thermal control systems.

August afternoon revealed a temperature immediately above an unshaded asphalt pavement of 124.7°F; above a shaded grass plot 30 feet away the temperature was 98°F—a differential of almost 27 degrees.[9]

In his pioneering research, Geiger cited significant temperature differentials of various surfacing materials, made under similar conditions of exposure on a day in June. He found asphalt paving twice as hot as the grass it replaced.[10] The microclimatic conse-

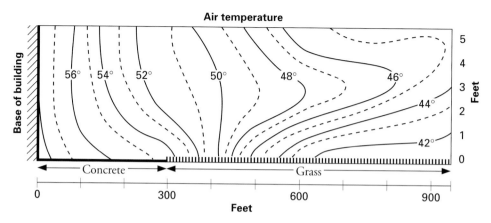

Figure 9–17 / Turf as a thermal modifier. Both ambient (shown in degrees Fahrenheit) and radiant temperatures are reduced by turf in two important ways: (1) it acts as an evaporative cooler as a side effect of the process of evapotranspiration, and (2) in the process of photosynthesis it absorbs solar energy, reflecting much less heat or light than any masonry surface.

quences of such local overheating are significant, as the measurements cited by Jeffrey Aronin clearly demonstrate[11] (Fig. 9–17). Moreover, current research in this area by Baruch Givoni and others corroborates the basic findings of Geiger and Aronin. In view of the enormous expansion of paved surfaces (and especially asphalt and blacktop surfaces), the importance of data like these is obvious. They suggest the importance of shading the paved surfaces that surround most buildings—and shading them, where at all possible, with either trees or vines.

> *Glare will be eliminated.* Grass presents a glare-proof texture. Despite immensely higher illumination levels outdoors, glare on a natural landscape occurs only over water, snow, or sheets of rock.
>
> *Dust will be reduced.* Obviously, a healthy lawn can be the source of very little dust; in addition, its grass blades catch and hold a large amount of airborne dust.
>
> *Noise will be reduced.* A grass surface offers an effective surface for the absorption of airborne sound.

From facts such as these it is apparent that the landscape is an immensely important factor in building design—a factor that no architect can intelligently ignore. Trees, shrubs, sod, and ground cover must be viewed not as luxuries, not as ornaments, but as actual items of equipment, as essential to the efficient operation of the building as its furnace or lighting system. Their selection, disposition, feeding, and watering need not be charged off to overhead or justified as pleasant hobbies; they are serious matters of maintenance. Such an evaluation of the landscape implies new concepts for the landscape designer as well; designs must recognize new disciplines. Purely visual considerations of composition, proportion, vista, and balance must be subjected to the acid test of environmental control. Landscaped areas must then be judged by their actual performance as well as by their beauty. No more than in architecture are the two contradictory; on the contrary, such an integration will yield new and higher esthetic standards. And they have begun to, in neotraditional developments such as Kentlands (see chapter 10). Here, and in similar developments, paved areas are kept to a minimum and removed from primary views whenever possible. Also kept to a minimum, however, are areas of grass in front of houses, which would require regular mowing.

Toward a New and Higher Level of Synthesis

The meteorological features of the natural environment—the path of the sun, of prevailing breezes, the patterns of rain and snowfall—are not subject to facile manipulation. Of course, in any densely built-up area even these forces are modified, sometimes importantly. The way in which the sun falls upon a given building depends upon the size, shape, and proximity of its nearest neighbors. Similarly, the play of wind or the drifting of snow is modified by the actual topography of the area, just as drainage patterns are radically altered by grading, earth-moving, and paving.

More often than not, however, the consequences of such microclimatic manipulation are unfortunate precisely because they are not anticipated and, hence, not controlled. We have already seen the need for intensive studies of the aerodynamic behavior and surface-solar response of individual buildings, such as the pioneering work of J. Douglas Balcomb, first at Los Alamos Laboratory and currently at the National Renewable Energy Laboratory (NREL) in Golden, Colorado. But it is obvious that, in any urban situation, the isolated individual building can seldom achieve even tolerable control in such matters. What is urgently required is a new sort of environmental zoning that would establish areawide or citywide norms of orientation, density, and height. Such norms would establish an overall topology to which the individual building could conform. They would give the fabric of the city as a whole the type of surface response dictated by the actual climate of the area. In a region of overheating (e.g., Miami, Tucson), this topology would aim at minimizing solar heat gain and maximizing natural ventilation. In an underheated area (e.g., Fairbanks, Calgary), the surface response would be designed for maximum protection from winter winds and maximum exposure to winter sun. In response to the energy crises of the 1970s, the concept of *solar access* or *solar rights* enjoyed much debate in zoning circles. In general, solar rights zoning has not yet become a reality, mainly because the short-term economics have not been shown to be compelling. However, such analysis is shortsighted. Buildings last fifty to one hundred years or more. If new buildings are allowed to be placed where they block access to sunlight, such blockage will persist long after advanced solar technologies (e.g., photovoltaics) become more cost-effective and widely available.

The potential economies of such environmental zoning would be real in terms of both capital and operating costs. It would certainly yield a far higher general level of amenity

Figure 9–18 / Hunan Province, China. These settlements represent an adroit response to environmental stress. To combat high winds and low temperatures of the steppe winter they are built subterraneously, thus minimizing the wind chill of inhabited spaces and utilizing the comparatively high temperatures of the subsoil.

than is common in most built-up areas today, where the negative climatic factors are exaggerated and the positive ones canceled out. Nor need such environmental norms impose any great restrictions on the design of individual buildings—no greater, certainly, than those of normal American land-plotting practices in which the arbitrary gridiron is the normal pattern. On the contrary, the esthetic quality of the whole townscape would be enhanced, if we are to judge from folk practices in such matters around the world.[12] Thus in the loess lands of western China, where bitter winter cold is aggravated by high winds, the peasants build entire villages below ground. Literally carved out of the loess, each house consists of submerged rooms opening into a sunken courtyard (Fig. 9–18). This environmental response has two great virtues: it takes advantage of relatively high subsurface soil temperatures while escaping the chilling effect of the wind. In addition, the courtyards are shaped, sized, and oriented to permit penetration of low winter sun. Such an urban topology would be eminently appropriate for residential communities in the Great Plains of the United States and Canada. Modern technology could easily solve problems in waterproofing, daylighting, and drainage that are beyond the technical capacity of peasant society.

In the deserts of Northern Africa and the Middle East one can observe another instance of canny folkloristic response to thermal overloading. Here an architecture of mud brick masonry — ideal for the great diurnal fluctuations of hot days and cold nights — is combined with a dense urban texture of narrow streets, inward-facing buildings, and highly compartmentalized courts and gardens. Often the streets are continuously shaded with awnings and vines, and often the entire village is shielded from the sun by a high, continuous canopy of nut palms. Such principles of environmental response could well be applied to the American Southwest, where real savings in air-conditioning costs would be matched by a real increase in amenity for the townscape as a whole (Fig. 9–19).

Figure 9–19 / Mud masonry megastructures in the Moroccan desert. Here the village is built to act as metabolic unit; high heat capacity of mud masonry plus self-shading effect of intricately subdivided ground plan acts to ameliorate intense heat and glare of daytime. The same configuration acts to cushion the abrupt temperature drop after sunset.

Precisely because of the spectacular development of environmental technologies in heating, cooling, and illumination, we tend toward an extravagant reliance upon them, to the almost total neglect of other possibilities. Contemporary architects and urbanists have shown little interest in a systematic exploration of such problems. Many years ago, under the editorship of the principal author of this book, the climates of fifteen American cities were analyzed and a series of climatic specifications for domestic architecture were evolved and published.[13] Almost forty years ago, the architects and brothers Victor and Aladar Olgyay published a series of papers and books dealing with architectural climatology, especially the manipulation of sunlight.[14] Ever since, this pioneering work has provided the solid foundation upon which solar and environmentally sensitive "green" design has been built. And, as we saw in chapter 3, an adequate technical literature has been developed on solar orientation, calculation of solar heat gain through various wall materials, etc. Over the years, most of these studies have dealt with the design of individual buildings and not with that of neighborhoods or towns as a whole. Now, however, more integrated approaches to community are being adopted by spirited advocates such as the New Urbanists (see chapter 10).

We have already seen that even with freestanding houses on narrow lots, it is still possible to locate the houses in such a fashion that each would have an optimal orientation with respect to winter sun and summer breezes (Fig. 5−9). This is a simple illustration of a profoundly important principle—namely, that the voids between buildings are just as important to the overall amenity of built-up areas as are the enclosed volumes of the buildings themselves. Knowles, in his theoretical works, extended his research on surface responses of individual buildings to a study of the metabolic response of whole neighborhoods to the environmental forces that play upon them.[15] These studies emphasize the obvious but often forgotten fact that topography, whether accepted as given or radically altered by the designer, is a critically important factor in the viability of the completed settlement. With modern capabilities in mechanized earth-moving, it is no longer necessary to fit a new development to existing contours; if necessary, the landscape can be remolded to act as a new element in the final urban fabric. But the ultimate consequences of such radical interventions must be carefully studied if ecological disaster is to be avoided.

The Viability of Preindustrial Practice

An understanding of folk and primitive practice is of more than academic interest to today's architect because, with the growing industrialization and urbanization of the Western world, all too many architects continue to ignore or minimize the importance of the natural world and the precariousness of humanity's position in it. Not only are modern architects largely insulated from any direct exposure to climatic and geographic cause and effect; many of them also seem persuaded that it no longer affects them. We saw the disastrous consequences of this attitude in the preceding chapters. The central reason for this failure is lack of an adequate theoretical—one might properly say philosophical—

apparatus. This is expressed in the architects' consistent underestimation of the magnitude of the environmental forces that play upon their buildings, in their failure to grasp their ineluctable unity, and in their persistent tendency to overestimate their own technological capacities for overriding or ignoring them.

The primitive builders never work under such misapprehensions.* In all their structures, they always face one supreme and absolute limitation: the impact of the environment in which they find themselves must be met by their own efforts, using the building materials which that environment affords. The environment itself is scarcely ever genial, and the building materials available seem appallingly meager in quantity or restricted in kind. The Eskimo (or Inuit) had only snow and ice; the Sudanese, mud and reeds; the Siberian herdsman, hides and felted hair; the Melanesian, palm leaves and bamboo. Yet the vernacular architecture of these peoples reveals a sophisticated grasp of the problem, not only within its own terms but even when analyzed in the light of modern scientific knowledge. Primitive practice reflects a precise and detailed understanding of local climate on one hand, and a remarkable grasp of the performance characteristics of local building materials on the other.

It happens, coincidentally, that the forms of primitive architecture, like those of primitive artifacts in general, have esthetic qualities that make them attractive to modern urban dwellers. House or totem pole, war canoe or wooden bowl, these artifacts display a harmony, a clarity, an integrity of form and function that represents high levels of artistic accomplishment. But it would be a serious error to assume that these forms can simply be appropriated, imported, like tea or nutmeg. One must not oversimplify the cultural processes that endow primitive art with its attractive qualities. Spiritually and psychologically, a primitive culture is no less complex than our own. The exact path of the primitive artist, from aspiration to artifact, is equally obscure and mysterious. Primitive architecture, like primitive agriculture and medicine, often has a magical-religious rationale that only anthropologists or psychologists can understand. But primitive practice — that is, how things are done as opposed to the reasons given for doing them — is often astonishingly sensible and perceptive.

Primitive builders are captives of an economy of scarcity, their resources in energy, time, and materials being severely limited. At the same time, their conditions of life allow little margin for error in coping with environmental stresses; disaster lurks behind even small miscalculations. Both theories and practice are strictly disciplined by these circumstances. Without the formal knowledge of literate civilization to rely upon, practice is always subject to check and modification by direct, sensual experience. Thus primitive practice offers many examples that contemporary architects can study with profit, but two will suffice. These are buildings designed by "architects" of the dim past — the Eskimo (or Inuit) igloo and the mud-walled houses of the American and African deserts.

---

* As used here, the term *primitive* describes a preliterate culture, whether historical or contemporary. In such cultures knowledge is transferred verbally, training is by apprenticeship, industry is handicraft, tools often pre-Iron Age.

Of all environmental components, heat and cold are the two that confront the primitive architect with the most difficult structural problems. Because (as we saw in chapter 3) thermal comfort is a function of four separate factors—ambient and radiant temperatures, air movement and humidity—and because all four are in constant flux, any precise manipulation requires real analytic ability on the part of the designer. The Eskimo displayed it in the design for the igloo; from a purely theoretical point of view, it would be difficult to formulate a better scheme for protection against the Arctic winters. Its performance is excellent; with no mechanical equipment, the igloo achieves a performance that modern engineers might envy (Fig. 9–20); this performance is a function of both its geometry and its material. The hemispherical dome offers maximum resistance to winter gales from all points of the compass while exposing the minimum surface to their chilling effect. The dome as a form has the further merit of enclosing the largest volume with the least material, and it also yields that shape most effectively heated by the radiant point source of a blubber lamp. To this day, research scientists who venture to the South Pole are taught during orientation exercises how to construct their own igloos in the event that they become stranded from the remote outposts of civilization that serve as their home base. Credit is due the Inuits of the past for this survival safety net.

In terms of thermal response, the intense and steady cold of the Arctic dictates a wall of the lowest possible heat-transfer capacity. Dry snow meets this criterion most admirably, though at first glance it might seem the least likely structural material imaginable. The Eskimos unlocked the paradox by constructing a dome of snow blocks (18 inches thick, 36 inches long, and 6 inches high), laid up in one continuous in-sloping spiral. The finished dome is made both stronger and more windproof by a glaze of ice on the interior surface. When, finally, the interior is draped with skins and furs, thereby preventing body chill from either radiant or conductive heat loss to cold floor and walls, the Eskimo architect completes a most admirable instrument for thermal control.

For the non-Eskimo nostril, olfactory conditions are said to be less than optimum, but odors are highly subjective in their impact, and ventilation inside the igloo is entirely adequate to supply oxygen needs of family and fire alike. Space inside the dome is certainly limited, but historically the Baffin Island Eskimos built igloos of several units, connected by barrel-vaulted snow-block tunnels and air locks, to house dog teams, extra food, and equipment. Such igloos have a short life, collapsing when outside temperatures rise above freezing. Like most primitive building, igloos sacrifice durability in favor of performance, and they lasted exactly as long as the seasonally nomadic Eskimo required them.

If we turn to another thermal regime, that of the great deserts of the lower latitudes, we find another type of architectural response equally appropriate to radically different conditions. Here the problem confronting the primitive designer is one of extremely high daytime temperatures and intense insolation alternating with much lower temperatures at night. Sometimes, as in the Algerian mountains or the American Southwest, the diurnal fluctuations are superimposed upon comparably severe seasonal ones. The main requirement for thermal comfort in this situation is a building material with a very high heat-holding capacity—that is, one that absorbs solar radiation all day and releases it

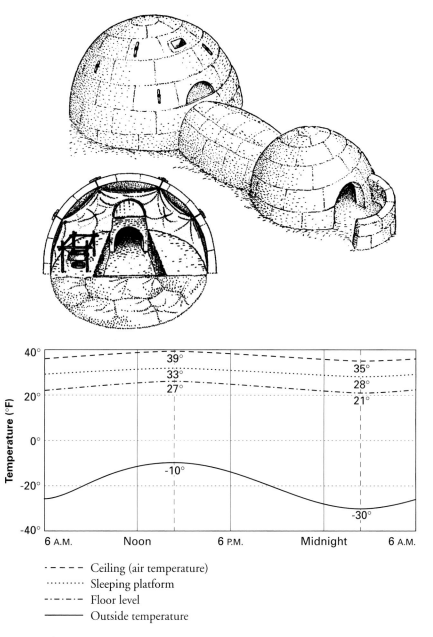

- – – – – Ceiling (air temperature)
- ·········· Sleeping platform
- – · – · – Floor level
- ——— Outside temperature

Figure 9–20 / Top: Historical design for the Eskimo igloo, Baffin Island, Canada. In shape and material the igloo represents high-level environmental response. The shape offers maximum resistance and minimum exposed surface to wind while enclosing the most volume with the least material. The thermal efficacy of the snow wall is increased by a draft-reducing inner glaze of ice. Draped furs act as insulation against radiant heat loss from the bodies of the family. Bottom: Thermal performance of the igloo. With no mechanical aids and no heat source beyond a small blubber stove, internal air temperatures are held at tolerable levels. The chart plots only air temperature; radiation from the stove and bodies keeps effective temperature so high that the family needs to wear few, if any, clothes for comfort.

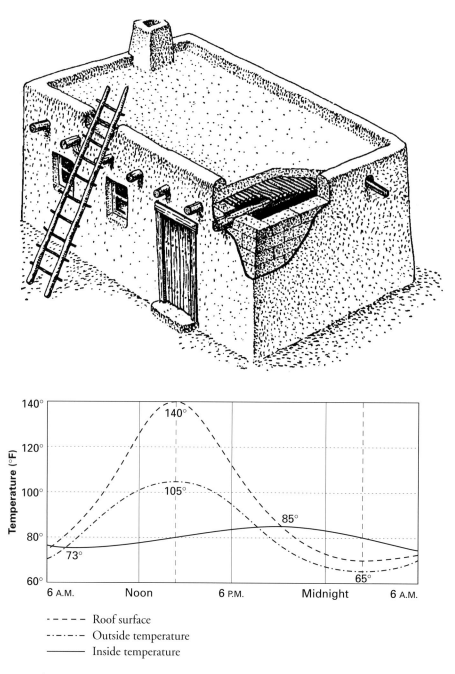

Figure 9–21 / Top: Mud masonry Indian house, American Southwest. The high heat capacity of mud masonry, well suited to the great temperature fluctuations of the desert, is cannily exploited in primitive housing. Because the air, though dry, is very hot, ventilation is not desirable. Native Americans build freestanding brush-covered arbors for daytime shade, using houses for storage and cold-weather sleeping. Rooftops are used for summer sleeping. Bottom: Thermal performance of mud masonry house. High heat capacity of thick adobe walls and mud roof acts to flatten out stressful thermal curve of desert climate.

286

Figure 9–22 / San Francisco de Asis Church, Ranchos de Taos, New Mexico. This heavily buttressed Spanish church is a fine example of a massive adobe structure. It was built in 1710 and completed in 1755. One of the most recognizable buildings of the Southwest, it has been depicted by painters Georgia O'Keeffe and John Marin and photographed by Ansel Adams and Paul Strand.

slowly all night. The mud-walled, mud-roofed constructions that desert peoples all over the world evolved accomplish this task most admirably (Fig. 9–21). As humidities are low, cross ventilation is not mandatory; indeed, at midday in midsummer, air temperatures are so high that a breeze passing across the skin adds more heat by conduction than perspiration can dissipate. Thus, the typical desert form is closed, centripetal, and uses a limited number of small openings in order to cut down heat and glare.

In some arid areas, like those around the Persian Gulf, where diurnal fluctuations are reduced by water bodies, nighttime temperatures do not fall appreciably and ventilation is necessary. To meet such a contingency, the native architects evolved a fantastic family of wind scoops, as handsome as they are effective, to force night breezes down into the interiors (Fig. 9–23). Thus two quite contradictory tasks are accomplished: a closed vessel with a high capacity to resist intense insolation at one time of day is combined with a forced ventilation system with a high capacity for admitting the breeze at another.

We have already seen how this principle of controlled surface response, as a means of governing the building's metabolic relationship with its environment, was demonstrated by Knowles (Fig. 5–11). The same principle can be applied to the design of entire human

Figure 9–23 / Rooftop wind scoops, commonly seen throughout the Middle East and Southwestern Asia. A rare climatic circumstance — high humidities superimposed on desert temperatures — makes ventilation mandatory. These wind scoops are oriented to prevailing breezes.

settlements — villages, cities, whole regions — as the more advanced architectural theoreticians are coming to realize. Indeed, we will be compelled to apply this principle if current metabolic dysfunctions are to be corrected, especially in stressful climates where there is either an absolute deficiency of solar energy (northern Canada, Siberia) or an absolute surplus (the Sahara, Arizona). Much air pollution is, to a large extent, due to the misapplication of enormous amounts of energy required to maintain our cities — to heat, cool, ventilate, and illuminate them at even minimal levels of amenity. This energy is largely derived from the combustion of fossil fuels, whose energy conversion produces large quantities of noxious wastes which, when discharged, lead directly to pollution of air, land, and water masses. It is technically possible, of course, to improve the efficiency of both conversion and waste disposal methods and thereby reduce the soaring rates of environmental attrition.

Reluctantly and belatedly, Western technology has begun to face the fact that much of this pollution is the consequence of a fundamental misunderstanding of the proper allocation of energies of all sorts to the problem of environmental manipulation. These consequences are especially significant for architecture. Despite the existence of energy codes and standards (e.g., ASHRAE/IES 90.1), many contemporary buildings continue to employ walling membranes that are overly transparent to most forms of energy. Complex and delicate mechanical systems for compensating for this high energy exchange across the interface then become mandatory. The amounts of energy required to maintain this balance are often exorbitant. Moreover, most buildings are designed as discrete, free-standing structures whose ratio of enclosing surface to enclosed volume is very high.* Obviously, important reductions in energy input and pollutant output would result if this ratio were reversed.

Here again, the folk practice of preindustrial societies offers astonishingly effective paradigms. The pre-Columbian builders of the great pueblos of the American Southwest built in a climate with high insolation and great diurnal and seasonal variations in ambient temperature. They employed the mud masonry house (Fig. 9-21) but used it as the basic module of a megastructure. Heat loss through the exterior walls was thus reduced by some 60 percent, and these exposed walls were carefully oriented. Thus the overall heat exchange was manipulated to minimize summer surpluses and maximize winter deficiencies. The high energy costs of constructing the settlement were offset by the low energy requirements for maintaining it. Such allocation of available energy (whether animal or solar) is characteristic of folk practice. It yields a far more favorable balance than such putatively modern cities as Albuquerque and Phoenix.

Theoretical Approaches to Architectural Form

These are some instances, out of hundreds around the world, of the brilliant ways in which indigenous builders responded to environmental stimuli. The body of conventional wisdom that such practice represents should be carefully scrutinized by architectural science — not brutally plowed under, as is so often the case, only to be replaced by some international methodology that is often grotesque in the coarseness and insensitivity with which it responds to local, microenvironmental conditions. Fortunately, there is growing recognition of this in the urban cultures of the West. Two historically remarkable studies by American architects — *Architecture Without Architects* by Bernard Rudofsky and *The Significance of Primitive Architecture* by Ernest Schweibert are symptomatic of this interest.[16]

Rudofsky's study (the byproduct of his spectacular exhibition of the same name at New York's Museum of Modern Art in 1965) approached the subject from a frankly esthetic point of view. He was interested in demonstrating the enormous range of beautiful solutions that craftspeople are able to produce. They were and perhaps are more fortunate than us. Although they lacked the formal theoretical training that we value, these artisans were able to master design by apprenticing to elders who held years of practical experience in observing the play between structure and the raw elements of weather and

---

* This reaches unprecedented proportions in the typical middle-class American suburb of single-family detached houses standing in large lots. Never before in history have as many units of energy been required to supply a family life-support system.

climate. Rudofsky selected his examples with an eye to their visual effect, but he recognized that the effect did not result from an arbitrary act like that of the contemporary avant-garde artist in search of novel forms, but from the dictates of local conditions. Schweibert, in an eloquent foreword, gave his reasons for study: his dissatisfaction with the formalism of current architectural theory and his dismay at the dysfunction it leads to in some of our most prestigious buildings. His material was similar to Rudofsky's but his approach was from a functional point of view—that is, analyzing the derivation of the forms in terms of response to climate, materials, techniques. But the inescapable conclusion of both studies is that, for architecture, the solution of experiential problems is the only source of valid form.

Such works as those of the American architect Ralph Knowles or the Anglo-Swedish architect Ralph Erskine fully confirm the rich possibilities of this approach to structural design.[17] Even where there are no indigenous folkloric prototypes (as in Knowles's studies on the skyscraper), or where the existing prototypes are only obliquely applicable (as in Erskine's new towns north of the Arctic Circle), the environment becomes the fundamental generator of the building form.

Of course, the demands of modern urban life are much more rigorous and complex than any that preindustrial builders confronted. Study and analysis cannot remain purely pragmatic, learning can no longer be transmitted by apprenticeship nor design carried on by sheer intuition. Indeed, as Christopher Alexander pointed out, the many variables involved in contemporary architectural decision making simply outrun the capacities of even the finest minds.[18] Under such circumstances, the computer has inevitably become an important new tool. Twenty-five years ago the computer began to be used for purely structural computations, but Knowles's work indicated a much broader, and possibly even more significant, application. Describing his method as "the mathematical derivation of surface response to selected environmental forces," Knowles said that "while it is true that design depends on imagination, imagination itself depends on the terms of reference given to it. These should be in the form of the most reliable knowledge available."[19] Today computers enable us to answer the most complex what-if questions our imaginations can conjure up. If used properly, design can be optimized for improved environmental performance, comfort, and maintainability.

It is apparent that Knowles and structural engineers like Horst Berger (see Chapter 8), employing the resources of a most sophisticated technology, arrived at substantially the same conclusion as the Eskimo designer. The parameters of the experiential problem remain the same; only the methods of analyzing them and the technical means of resolving them are enormously expanded. It should also be apparent that this is no vulgar proposal for instant or automatic design. To the contrary, the aim is a methodology for establishing objectively valid reference frames for esthetic decision making—that is, for describing the variables in any given problem, for isolating the acceptable alternatives, and for assigning them a hierarchy of objective values. Such a reference frame, far from restricting the freedom or independence of the architect, affords a greatly broadened field of choice across which the architect's creative capacities can play, secure in the knowledge that the risks of frivolous or idiosyncratic solutions have been eliminated.

There are, of course, more pragmatic ways of approaching the same problem, and the work of Ralph Erskine is significant in this connection. An architect who contributed to both town planning and architecture in the Swedish Arctic, Erskine worked in this extraordinary environment at two distinct levels of design. As a town planner he was compelled to study the problems of founding modern urban communities in an environment that had never before supported any society more complex than the reindeer economy of the Laplanders. This led him to formulate some far-reaching propositions for a long-range solution to the problem of inhabiting the Arctic.

As Erskine analyzed it, the long, dark, severe winters of the far north subject human societies to severe stress, with psychological and social consequences that have only begun to be explored. He realized that the notorious alienation of many Swedes may well be related (culturally, not genetically) to the physical isolation that the northern winters impose upon the Swedish countryside and, to some extent, even the towns. This environmental load is so enormous in extent, so pervasive in psychosomatic effect, that it cannot be successfully ameliorated with individual buildings, no matter how well designed or built. What is needed in addition is a kind of townwide megastructure specifically designed to handle the grossest environmental stresses—intense, steady cold, high winds, heavy snow cover, long periods of darkness. By thus lightening the environmental load, such a megastructure would make possible the year-round continuity of social life at optimal levels. It would guarantee that pedestrian circulation, for example, would be no more inhibited in January than in June.

One of Erskine's prototypical designs for urban form in the Arctic represents a rigorous application of conventional orientational theories. Here the entire town is built as a series of concentric interlocking terraces to form a south-facing hemicycle. Situated in this shallow bowl, the town is tilted toward the south and protected to the north by a continuous wall of multistory housing. This great enclosure lifts the grossest environmental loads—low temperatures, high winds, heavy snow, and darkness—off the entire urban tissue. Within this mesoenvironment, streets, buildings, open and closed spaces can have normal configuration. Circulation is at two levels—above ground for good weather, below ground for bad. The traffic pattern combines circumferential and radial roads with mountain tramways for all-weather transit. Interior pedestrian streets, both concentric and radial, facilitate movement in bad weather.

Another of Erksine's more radical proposals goes further; here the entire town is built inside a great dome, the function of which is to absorb the most severe meteorological forces—primarily wind and snow—in order to create a mesoenvironment for the town as a whole. Within this context of ameliorated conditions, individual buildings of more normal design provide the more precise environmental control required. Both Erskine variants employ a wide range of communalized facilities—car-wash stations, laundries and drying yards, kindergartens and parklets — which at once facilitate and compel a wide movement of all family members outside the individual dwelling unit.

In one of the British "new towns" built after World War II, Cumbernauld, near Glasgow, we see something of the same philosophy of environmental response. The climate is, of course, less stressful than the Swedish far north, though the winters are characterized by much wind, rain, fog, and short days (the area lies at 56 degrees N latitude). Only the town center employs the megastructure principle; the residential units are quarters based on a conventional cul-de-sac layout. The center, a large articulated structure, is organized along a multilevel east-west spine of vehicular and pedestrian traffic ways. It incorporates a full range of activities normal for a town of its size — department stores, cinema, shops, pubs, a hotel, garages, an elementary school, and a range of apartments. All living units face south, overlooking a series of landscaped areas whose microclimates are importantly modified by the sheer mass of the center behind them to the north. The result is a new kind of experience for Scottish townspeople — a dry, all-weather promenade that is rain-, snow-, and wind-free, with a small-scale coziness welcome in this kind of climate (Fig. 9–24).

On another side of the world, across the Nile from the Tombs of the Nobles at Luxor, the Cairene architect Hassan Fathy employed this same environmental response approach in the model town of New Gourna.[20] The climatic and cultural conditions are about as far removed as possible from Sweden and Scotland, and the technical means available to Fathy (himself a thoroughly cosmopolitan architect) were both primitive in kind and limited in extent. But he deliberately used traditional building methods (load-bearing masonry of sun-baked brick) and village planning principles (narrow, curving streets, walled yards, rooftop sleeping terraces) to demonstrate the continuing viability of folkloristic practice. New Gourna was built by the local peasantry, using only materials at hand and employing techniques that are millennia old. Despite its many attributes, the promising town of New Gourna was soon abandoned as the relocated villagers (whose move was not motivated by their own needs or desires) returned to their old homes across the Nile — apparently drawn at least in part by the valuable antiquities in the ancient Tombs.

The most suggestive American demonstration of environmental manipulation on a townwide scale can be seen in the early development at Sea Ranch, California, a residential community up the coast from San Francisco.[21] The original Sea Ranch condominium is considered possibly the most influential American building of the 1960s, designed by the architectural firm of Moore Lyndon Turnbull Whitaker and landscape architect Lawrence Halprin. It was the winner of the American Institute of Architects 25-Year Award in 1991.[22] This small town was built on a great natural meadow atop a range of bluffs overlooking the Pacific Ocean. Its natural assets are magnificent scenery, luxuriant flora, a moderate thermal regime (no frost or excessive heat), and an above-average number of days of sunshine. The single meteorological liability is the wind — so strong and so persistent that it has sculpted the native cedars into the typical Monterey deformation.

Figure 9–24 / Model of the town center in Cumbernauld, Scotland, a "new town" designed by the city architect after World War II. The main environmental problems—long, wet, windy winters, cool summers with clouds, fog, and rain—dictated an all-weather enclosed pedestrian circulation route along multilevel malls containing stores, shops, pubs, library, meeting halls, cinema, schools, and a hotel. All vehicular traffic is confined to the lowest level.

The problem facing the designers was how to intervene urbanistically and architecturally in such a way as to create a truly pleasant outdoor environment. The central issue was the wind. To have developed the area with conventional detached single-family houses or isolated high-rise apartments would not only not have improved matters, it would have made a bad aerodynamic situation much worse. Taking his cue from the great cedar windbreaks used by the sheepmen who had grazed the meadows for a century, Halprin decided to cluster his houses in much the same fashion. By massing them as windbreaks (with, incidentally, much the same cross section as the cedar hedges), he created microclimates in their lee; as these areas faced south, they made possible warm, sunny, wind-free patios in a landscape that had previously resembled a Scottish moor.

Thus was confirmed Rudolph Geiger's prescient observation of decades earlier that in building a house, the architect makes a number of separate climates out of the single one existing near the ground above the building site. On the south wall, the microclimate is so favorable that fruit, perhaps even grapes, can be grown. This gain is at the expense of the north side, which is dark, cold, damp, and raw. Still different are the microclimates of the east and west sides. The climates of the various rooms are modifications of these four outdoor climates. In addition, there are the climates of the cellar and the attic.[23]

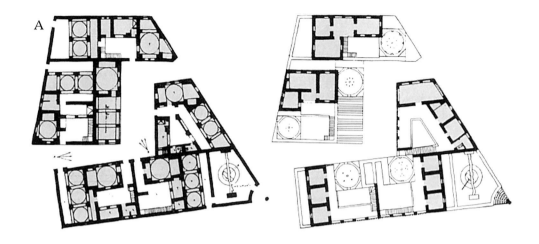

A

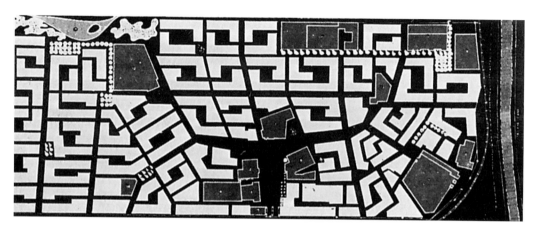

Figure 9–25 / New Gourna, Egypt. Hassan Fathy, architect, completed 1948. Located across the Nile from Luxor, this village was planned by the architect as a demonstration of the continuing validity of the traditional theories and techniques of town planning, architecture, and construction of the Egyptian peasant. Mud masonry was used both because its thermal performance makes it ideal for desert climates and because it required no cash outlay. Fathy taught peasants ancient techniques of mud-brick vaulting without scaffolding. House plans provide walled living quarters at street level for cool weather and roof decks for hot-weather sleeping. The street layout is aimed at creating shade and privacy, discouraging outside traffic through extended family enclaves. (A) Unit house plans (above) and town plan (below) reflect the desert climate and the Muslim population of peasantry organized into extended families. (B) Roof deck of peasant house. (C) Courtyard of boys' school.

As development proceeded since the 1960s, however, the early planning principles were eroded to a degree. In particular, development on the north end of Sea Ranch no longer hugs the hedgerows, nor does it follow the natural topography; instead, it more closely resembles a conventional suburban layout, with cul-de-sacs in the meadows and house lots lined up along the bluffs. Additionally, the meadows are reverting to forest without the manicuring of the sheep. The original Sea Ranch style has been duplicated in other locales without regard to the specifics of site and climate. "I wish people had paid more attention to the *siting* than to the *siding*," laments architect Donlyn Lyndon.[24] The graceful integration of the original houses into the landscape still serves as a powerful lesson in quality design.

Limited and disparate as are these examples, they are enough to indicate the possibility of reaching new levels of environmental amenity in human settlements. Though they aim at exploiting a range of phenomena in the natural environment, they by no means imply a rejection of scientific method or modern technological systems. To the contrary: to adequately master these subtle and intricate interrelations between people, buildings, and the natural environment requires the highest level of scientific thought. They involve such a bewildering array of variables that they will certainly depend upon the collaboration of the computer and the human mind for solution. Rather than aiming at the elimination of such basic elements of modern architecture as air-conditioning and artificial illumination, they aim at creating the environmental conditions in which such systems are able to operate at optimal levels of efficiency, economy, and safety.

Figure 9 – 25 B

Figure 9 – 25 C

Figure 9–26 / Sea Ranch, California. Lawrence Halprin and Associates, planners and landscape architects, completed 1966. Top: Panoramic view of original site plan looking north from Conference Hill shows existing cedar windbreaks. Bottom: View of Esherick cluster shows how profiles conform to cedar windbreaks. Framed of wood and sheathed in plank and shingle, the original houses resemble buildings of earlier ranchers.

Table 9 – 1 / *Major Input-Output Mechanisms of Cities*[25]

input (fuel) per day		*output (waste) per day*	
water	625,000 tons	sewage	500,000 tons
food	2000	solid wastes	2000
fuel		air	
coal	3000	particles	150
oil	2800	sulfur dioxide	150
natural gas	2700	nitrogen oxides	100
motor fuel	1000	hydrocarbons	100
		carbon monoxide	450

In view of the depletion of energy resources to power our cities, on one hand, and the rising tide of environmental pollution from the waste products of this application of energy on the other, the question of a new environmental policy is no longer hypothetical. It is a matter of burning immediacy, as figures on the metabolism of cities clearly prove.[25]

Table 9–1 is Abel Wolman's depiction of some of the metabolic requirements and waste products of an American city of 1 million in the mid-1960s. He argued that, while there are countless inputs and outputs in cities, three inputs—water, food, and fuel—and three outputs—sewage, refuse, and air pollution—are common to all. His analysis begins with a statement as relevant today as the day it was written: "As man comes to appreciate that the earth is a closed ecological system, casual methods that once appeared satisfactory for the disposal of wastes no longer seem (so)."[26]

However, the transition from a consumer society to one that truly integrates environmental principles cannot be expected to be easy or smooth, until the evidence becomes incontrovertible. Even then, the counterarguments will be fierce, and even those who agree it must be done may argue over the means by which it will be accomplished.

During Wolman's time, the evidence that air pollution was a human health hazard was considered inconclusive, and so Wolman questioned the wisdom of requiring what he regarded as substantial expenditures to control it, despite the recent enactment of an early version of the Clean Air Act. And although California was starting to reduce carbon monoxide and hydrocarbon emissions from new cars, Wolman argued that this approach did not serve as a particularly useful model for the nation. The benefit for American cities other than those like spread-out and growing Los Angeles did not appear to outweigh the added expense to society ($40 to $50 per car, or a total of $300 million per year).

Wolman showed that water, "which enters the city silently and unseen," overshadows other inputs and most of it soon returns, contaminated, to the city's sewers. Now, thirty-five years later, city planners are just beginning to consider water conservation as seriously as energy efficiency, primarily when limited availability or high costs demand it. As the crises foreseen by Wolman materialize thirty-five years later, his concluding remarks can be appreciated anew:

One must also recall that when large scale changes are contemplated, the whole spectrum of society is involved. Rarely do all forces march forward in step, particularly where public policy and scientific verity are not crystal clear. Competitive forces delay correctives until public opinion rises in wrath and pushes for action on an *ad hoc* and intuitive basis . . . as has happened so often in the past, we may find action running ahead of knowledge. This is not necessarily to be deplored. My own view coincides with that recently expressed. . ." We are not yet qualified to prescribe for the . . . welfare of our grandchildren. . . . I should say that present skills are sufficient for present ills."[27]

In our time, we are seeing the first signs of a more ecologically aware and responsible view for our cities, exemplified by initiatives in such cities as Austin, Texas, and Boulder, Colorado. Even the megalopolis of New York City, through the Department of Design and Construction, began in 1998 to consider the implementation of environmentally responsible design guidelines for the city's capital construction and renovation projects. During that same year, national teams from Austria, Canada, Denmark, Finland, France, Germany, Japan, Netherlands, Norway, Poland, Sweden, Switzerland, U.K., and U.S.A. convened at the Green Building Challenge '98 in Vancouver, Canada. Presented at this conference were the results of an ambitious two-year process to develop and test an international method for measuring building performance, considering life cycle impacts and emphasizing energy, environmental, and other global priorities. They plan to meet again, hopefully with even more countries participating, in Amsterdam in the year 2000.

Plan: The Instrument of Policy

A plan is many things, depending upon how one looks at it. From the point of view of society as a whole, a plan is an instrument of policy, a means of facilitating a certain line of action. Thus the plan of an American city, or entire metropolitan area, or region, may be regarded as an instrument of socioeconomic policy for the production and exchange of goods and ideas. The plans of individual buildings of which the city, or suburban satellite center, is composed are likewise expressions of smaller, individual policies. From the standpoint of the architect or physical planner, however, a plan is a representation of a horizontal plane passed through a building, city, or community. In this sense, a plan is a *solution* for a given line of action. It inevitably reflects the designer's concept of how — within the limits given — a certain amount of space may be best organized for the specific operation to be housed. For the people who live or work in the completed building or city, a plan is something else again. It is the *schema* of a control mechanism that, to a large extent, determines how happily they live or how well they work together.

Planning may therefore be analyzed at many different levels and from many points of view. Our concern in this book is with physical planning — the system of spatial relationships created by real buildings in actual cities and communities. Here again, the most illuminating approach is from the point of view of the health of both the individual and society as a whole. The primary function of all plans — architectural, urban, and regional — is to produce that specific organization of space that simultaneously elicits and supports the specific modes of behavior desired. (See discussion in chapter 7.) A successful plan maximizes the social productivity and individual well-being of the people whose energies it channels.

In a limited, technical sense, to plan is to manipulate space. A set of building plans has only, so to speak, a potential energy, but once the building is up and people are using it, its plan ceases to be an abstraction and becomes instead a real and dynamic force. The building modifies importantly the social relationships of the people who use it. Thus it may be said that planning is the manipulation of physical relationships for the purpose of facilitating social relationships. There is, of course, no metaphysical significance to what a plan can accomplish. A family can be forced to live in a school or a church or a factory instead of in a house. Its relationships will be adversely affected, its well-being and productivity diminished, if it is forced to operate in a plan not designed for it. But as a social unit it will remain recognizably a family. It will not become either a history class, a church congregation, or a trade union. From this it is apparent that each social unit (class, congregation, work crew) and each social operation (study, worship, industry) has its own private set of spatial requirements.

Indeed planning and discussions on building typology have been the source of much dialogue and debate since the first publication of this volume over fifty years ago. In this chapter we will discuss how plans and building types have evolved—often for the better when well-established historical and environmental forces are respected.

The Classification of Plan Types

It is characteristic of the emergence of any field of human endeavor into an independent status that it attempts two things: to define its area and to classify its content. It is ironic that John Ruskin should have been one of the first to do this in the field of planning. He was the first to recognize the growing specialization of Victorian building and to attempt to set up a system of categories for its planning.

Architecture proper naturally arranges itself under five heads:
  Devotional—including all buildings raised for God's service or honor.
  Memorial—including both monuments and tombs.
  Civil—including every edifice raised by nations or societies for purposes of common business or pleasure.
  Military—including all private and public architecture of defense.
  Domestic—including every rank and kind of dwelling placed.[1]

This was an ethical critique of English building—a sermon on what Ruskin thought it should be rather than a description of what it actually was. He established a separate category for monuments and tombs while blandly ignoring all the new plan types that were so important a part of contemporaneous life. He saw no distinction between the plan of the Crystal Palace and that of the Houses of Parliament, and nothing to distinguish either of them from the great railway stations designed by Phillip Hardwick at Euston Square (1839) and by Francis Thompson at Derby (1839). The factories that had already made England the leading manufacturing nation in the world cannot anywhere be crowded into Ruskin's list. Clearly, when he provided for "private military architecture of defense," he had in mind the England of Walter Scott's novels and not that of Darwin's essays.

The truth is that an accurate classification of the buildings of a given era is determined not by abstract systems of ethics but by the character of the society itself. The more advanced the society, the more numerous and specialized becomes the range of building types required to house it. (It has been estimated that American society today requires more than three hundred distinct types.) And no juggling of types according to some preconceived scale of ethical values can conceal the fact that social process is the determinant of plan. Moreover, it must be observed that there is an internal relationship between each form of social process. These relationships mesh and interlock to form a closed cyclical system. In theory, this cycle may be entered at any point, but because industrial production is the most decisive of all contemporary processes, it seems logical to classify plan types in relation to it. Historically, the factory has been the crucial cornerstone building of our society.

The factory at once makes possible and necessary all the rich variety of American building. If old types, such as the livery stable, disappear, it is because of the factory, and if new ones, like the airport, appear, this is also due to the factory. It is the factory again that is responsible for the astonishing specialization in the dwelling houses — the self-contained suburban homes, the towering apartment houses and hotels, the tourist motels, the trailer parks, and the resort hotels. There is not a single building type that does not — in its structure, equipment, and plan — reveal the impact of the factory and its products. Indeed, our very history would be unintelligible without an understanding of this relationship. Industrial production is the nodal point of our society. Thus, any classification of modern American plan types must be of the order given above.[2]

There is, naturally, some deviation from such a schematic classification as this in real life. Some of the simpler building types may serve more than one process or operation without adverse results. A movie theater built for entertainment may be used for certain types of visual education, an auditorium may serve for both a church service and a bingo game. Again, a given plan type may in one situation form a complete building while in another and more complex project it may be only a small unit. From biological necessity, some types are more or less constant in all buildings. Washrooms, which require only a small corner of an airplane, grow into large and complex buildings at the pithead of a mine.

Functionally, each of these specialized plan types can be viewed as a unit in a subsystem that, in turn, is a component of larger local, regional, and national systems. Locked together vertically in hierarchical order, each system supports some social processes — for example, communications, health, education. Of course, each of these systems coexists and intermeshes with other types of systems on a horizontal basis to form villages, towns, and cities. This leads necessarily to the development of two distinct scales of planning: (1) architectural (the design of the discrete building or complex), and (2) urbanistic (the design of districts, communities, whole towns).

Table 10 – 1 / *Classification of Plan Types*

Social Process or Operation	*Corresponding Plan Types to Facilitate It*
1. production	industrial or manufacturing facilities, smelters, mills, mines, factories, etc.; agribusinesses, dairies, greenhouses, food processing plants, abattoirs, etc.
2. power	dams, hydroelectric and steam generation plants, nuclear plants, electrical distribution systems, wind farms, photovoltaic arrays, etc.
3. transportation and communication	airports, railroad and highway systems, heliports, bridge and tunnel authorities, marine, bus and rail terminals, etc.; telephone, radio, television, cable, and postal systems; overnight courier centers; broadcasting centers, computer telecommunications centers, recording studios, multimedia centers, newspaper and publishing plants, visitors' bureaus, travel centers, etc.
4. storage	warehouses, refrigeration plants, grain elevators, oil tank farms, vaults, etc.
5. exchange	shops, department stores, malls, shopping concourses, markets, restaurants; banks, financial institutions, commodity exchange centers, stock exchanges, etc.
6. administration	capitols, courthouses, city halls, etc.; offices, headquarters, etc.
7. protection	jails, police stations, fire halls, etc.
8. dwelling	houses, apartments, cooperatives, condominiums, townhouses, hotels, resorts, tourist and trailer camps, dormitories, etc.
9. education and research	nurseries, schools, universities, academies; laboratories, libraries, museums; zoos, botanical gardens, planetariums, science centers, aquariums, galleries, experimental stations, convention centers, exhibition halls, nature centers, etc.
10. recreation	stadiums, swimming pools, sports centers, gymnasiums; theaters, concert halls, auditoriums, performing arts centers, music

Social Process or Operation	Corresponding Plan Types to Facilitate It
	halls, video arcades, cinemas; racetracks, ball grounds, parks, playgrounds, etc.
11. repair and reconstruction	clinics, health centers, hospitals, hospices, sanitariums; salons, rest and old-age homes; orphanages, reformatories, and asylums, etc.
12. religious worship	churches, synagogues, mosques, cathedrals, chapels, etc.
13. elimination and conservation of waste	cemeteries, crematoriums, etc.; water and wastewater treatment plants, incinerators, resource recovery facilities, etc.
14. war	military installations of all sorts (there are few buildings that do not automatically become military under total war)

Classification of plan types relative to six-phase production; modification and update of original formulation by Knud Lonberg-Holm and C. Theodore Larson. The six phases are (1) research, (2) production, (3) distribution, (4) consumption, (5) obsolescence, (6) elimination.

Evolutionary Process and Architectural Plan/Building Types

A formal classification that groups buildings according to type and relates them to social process is necessary to an understanding of the planning field. But building activity is in constant flux, subject to the impact of social, economic, and technical developments. Our society is fertile in invention and architecture is quick to reflect each innovation. Thus the automobile made obsolete the horsedrawn buggy; coincidentally, the garage replaced the feed store and blacksmith, the giant traffic interchange replaced the dusty crossroads, and the regional shopping center replaced the crossroads' general store. Movies and radio supplanted the legitimate theater and vaudeville house; sound stage and broadcast stage appeared in their stead. Then television appeared—and under its remorseless advance, all other theatrical forms began to decline. The focus for the family at home shifted from the dinner table and the radio to the more intrusive and absorbing television.

Home entertainment gained in stature with, at first, three major networks sharing a nationwide audience. Beginning in the 1980s, the market share of these individual television networks dwindled as choices expanded to perhaps sixty or more cable television channels and the potential for many more via satellite dish. Plus, the typical American was offered many hundreds of movies at the local video store, and a host of entertainment and communication exchange options through the computer, often set up in a home office. In effect, the home became a multimedia domain to a degree never before imagined.

Figure 10–1 / Representative of one of the newer building types, the Liberty Science Center is located in Jersey City's 1,114-acre urban-based Liberty State Park, in view of the New York City skyline, a short ferry ride from the Statue of Liberty and Ellis Island. Liberty Science Center has an 11-ton geodesic dome that houses one of the country's largest IMAX™ theaters, a tower with a glass observation deck to view Manhattan, and an exhibit hall with hundreds of interactive exhibits, including a darkened 100-foot Touch Tunnel for exploring the tactile sense. Separate floors are devoted to the subjects of environment, health, and invention.

At the same time, the entertainment consumer, bombarded with all of these ways to be entertained at home, was being enticed to visit increasingly sophisticated learning-centered facilities. For example, interactive science and technology centers gained wide appeal. These centers represent a completely new concept for which the museums of the past were barren forerunners, not unlike yesterday's city zoos in comparison to today's wildlife conservation parks. The learning centers are focused on the user, allowing visitors to explore basic concepts of physics, chemistry, biology, and mathematics; learn about information-age technologies, fiber optics, microelectronics, and computer software; view exhibits on robotics and artificial intelligence; don virtual reality eyewear; and experience multiscreen, multisensory films. The emphasis is on active participation, learning by doing, in stark contrast to the passive, isolating experience of television viewing. Often, these centers support other nearby activities. Liberty Science Center in Jersey City, New Jersey (Fig. 10–1), for example, is located near a ferry terminal for passage to Ellis Island and viewing the New York City skyline and Statue of Liberty.

With such an interplay of forces, the individual plan type is anything but static. There is a steady obsolescence in all types, so no plan of thirty years ago is apt to be satisfactory today. And yet, there are occasions when "outmoded" ideas resurface and are found to hold merit. Sometimes the life cycle of a plan is brief. Thus a scant four decades encompasses the rise, dominance, and decline of the tuberculosis (TB) sanitarium. In the 1930s there were more than 500 TB sanitariums across the country. The sanitarium appeared in response to a certain theory of combating the disease by sunshine, fresh air, and quiet. It flourished in the desert and the mountains. Once medication with appropriate drug regimens became the accepted treatment, the sanitarium slipped back and was abandoned, beginning in the 1950s. By the 1970s, after rates of infection had declined for more than half a century, the U.S. Surgeon General declared that it was time to close the book on infectious disease. But this proved premature with the resurgence of tuberculosis in the 1990s, particularly in urban centers, among the poor, and among those afflicted with HIV. Some have argued that the sanitariums should be recreated to ensure that the full course of drug treatment is completed under adequate supervision or to isolate those who have developed drug-resistant forms of the disease.

These developments are not as aimless or unpredictable as they might seem at first. They appear as surface disturbances, so to speak, and long periods may elapse between the first wave and a deep tide of change. Such lags are especially characteristic of the building field, for buildings are hard things to liquidate, either physically or financially. Some types respond to change much more readily than others—thus the backwardness of housing is notorious while the rate of change in commercial building types is quite rapid. This unevenness of development is even more noticeable in city planning than in individual buildings, for here the lag is cumulative in both time and space.

Nevertheless, standards in planning do change, and along fairly definite lines. Beginning in the era of modern architecture in the 1950s, several characteristics are notable in most building types:

1. multiple use of space
2. flexibility
3. mechanization

The multiple use of space is characteristic of many modern plans. One has only to compare contemporary plan types to those of a century ago to realize the extent to which we have specialized the use of enclosed space. Though by no means the most spectacular example of this trend, the evolution of the American home is the most familiar example. A century ago the parlor was used only for company, weddings, and funerals; if the home had any pretensions, it boasted two parlors, the front one being opened only for the most formal occasions (i.e., weddings, funerals). Today, at the same socioeconomic level, there is likely to be only a single living room, and this a space used all the time, by all the family, every day in the week. One corner is often used for eating, another as often as not for sleeping. The dining room of a century ago has all but disappeared, and despite the fact that the kitchen has absorbed this function also, it is apt to be only a fraction as large as its early Victorian progenitor. This compression of a given range of activities into a limited number of rooms has occurred in most building types. While it is a form of overcrowding, it differs from the procrustean congestion of poor urban neighborhoods in this important respect: it is a designed compression, with the introduction of all sorts of structural and mechanical devices aimed at compensating for the lost space.

A multiple use of space may flow from physical or mechanical necessity, as in the case of a trailer or an airliner. Here weight and bulk must be held within fixed limits, yet the resulting space must provide facilities for a fixed number of operations (lounging, sleeping, cooking, eating, defecation). Because these cannot occupy the same space at the same time, the areas allotted to each must be compressed to the minimum and the space, wherever possible, organized so as to permit different uses at different times.

The same tendency appears in buildings, but usually as the result of economic forces. Rising land values, construction costs and taxes, and a demand for high return on capital investment also tend inexorably toward compression of plan. In commercial buildings, where street frontage is at a premium, shops that thirty years ago would have been cramped with fifty feet are today able to manage with ten. In office buildings, the cubic space per worker has been reduced by perhaps two thirds since the days of H. H. Richardson. In theaters and auditoriums of all sorts another expression of the same tendency is apparent. A movie theater may occupy a relatively large amount of expensive space, but this space is used twelve hours a day, seven days a week. A legitimate theater occupying the same amount of space is used only twenty-four hours a week, seldom as many as twenty-six weeks per year. This uneconomic use of space has already forced the disappearance of many such theaters. But there is another possibility, one that is increasingly apparent in auditoriums: the tendency to extend the working day of the building by providing for a greater range of activities. This leads to large auditoriums that can be subdivided into smaller ones, to seating that can be shifted or removed altogether, to floors that can tilt to create proper sight lines, rise to form platforms, or sink to form pits. Here the intense use of time is made to compensate for the comparatively lavish use of space.

It is, of course, in the efficiency or studio apartment that most Americans have become acquainted with the multiple use of space. Here, because of economic (not physical or mechanical) limitations, the processes of living are compressed into steadily dwindling areas. A multiplicity of devices and equipment make it possible and simultaneously make it tolerable. Tables fold out of the walls, sofas pull out to become beds, lofts contain sleeping areas overhead, kitchens fit into ventilated closets, and futons double as couches and beds. Soundproofing, lighting, and elevators are added to compensate for increased densities. These apartments are often economically organized in terms of space, but it does not necessarily follow, as is so often assumed, that they are also efficiently organized from the standpoint of the human user.

An economical organization of space may result in a plan that, objectively, makes work easier — in other words, channels the energies of its tenants effectively. But an economical plan is only truly efficient if the internal requirements of both the process and the worker involved in the process are carefully considered and substantially met. Modern kitchens can sometimes be marvels of compression. Old equipment has been radically improved, new labor-saving equipment has been added (dishwashers, microwaves, frost-free refrigerators), and all of it has been organized into a space only a fraction as large as its prototype of a century ago. Insofar as the new model cuts down waste motion on the part of the cook, economy may coincide with efficiency. But there is a point beyond which a multiple use of the same space makes work harder and not easier. If the family eats in a small kitchen with limited counter space, the chances are that more energy is required to prepare the meal, serve it, and clean up afterward than would be required in an old-time layout of large kitchen, pantry, and 18-foot dining room. As a consequence, at the upper end of the residential market the trend is away from compact design toward large, roomy kitchens that open into the dining/living room area in a way that encourages guests to interact with the cook during preparation of the meal. The kitchen has, in some families, become the most popular room in the house, and reflects this popularity in its size and lay-out. New home designs often integrate kitchens with the family room and sometimes even the laundry room in an open plan. All of these uses are combined in a multipurpose living center. While highly versatile, this space requires some coordination and cooperation among family members, as sound travels freely throughout. Open plan designs are highly popular; a recent survey indicated 78 percent of prospective homebuyers preferred the kitchen next to the family room with either a half-wall or no wall in between.[3]

The paradox of compression versus efficiency holds true for much more complex social operations and much larger buildings. It holds true for the city as a whole. For example, the compression of a range of cultural and entertainment activities into a single building might give a community a more satisfactory solution than a series of single-purpose buildings. There is no merit to wasting space. But, generally speaking, the tendency to scrimp on urban space, inspired as it is by economic pressure, should not be raised to the level of a principle. The criterion of physical planning must be the space the process requires for its fullest development, not merely how much of such-and-such process can be crammed into a given area.

Flexibility is the natural result of the rapid rate of change that obtains in industry, commerce, and all urban institutions in general. In some production fields the rate of change in technique is very rapid. Industrial processes and operations are constantly revised in the light of rapidly broadening knowledge. New ones appear and old ones drop out, and the ones that persist undergo steady modification. This flux exerts great pressure upon both structure and plan. The total amount of enclosed space necessary to house a given operation is changing; the fashion in which this space is subdivided and organized by the plan changes likewise. Buildings designed along conventional lines, built of conventional materials, are thus apt to be technologically obsolete before they are completed. Unpredictable changes in production techniques occur, rendering all but the most flexible and farsighted plans prematurely out of date. Thus there is a real point to the apocryphal tale of the manufacturer who, when asked to describe the best type of building for his needs, responded: "None at all." He meant by this that changes in the

Figure 10–2 / Chan Centre for the Performing Arts, University of British Columbia, Vancouver, British Columbia, Canada, 1997. Bing Thom, architect. The Centre is a highly versatile complex of three facilities incorporating academic space for UBC's music, theater, and film students as well as formal space for public performances for the city of Vancouver.

manufacturing processes were so continuous and so profound that any layout would be soon outdated. He meant that most buildings are so planned as to make radical spatial reorganization both time-consuming and expensive. And he meant that most structural systems are so unsalvageable as to make it more economical to build a completely new structure than to try to reuse the old components.

The multiple use and flexible organization of space are, at the contemporary scale, inconceivable without a high degree of building mechanization. If space is at such a premium that it must be intensively used, then it must be flexibly organized, readily convertible from one use to another. To make conversion easy or at least tolerable, the process must be mechanized. The municipal auditorium of the average town offers a typical illustration of this problem. To be of maximum effectiveness, it must be adaptable to a wide range of uses. To be economically operated, it must be intensively used. Thus, an auditorium seating five thousand is desirable for large political rallies, whereas a room seating only two hundred might be needed for chamber music. A level floor is essential to basketball, while a sloping one is desirable for stage performances. For a boxing match, a raised platform is required; for theatrical performances, an orchestra pit may be needed. For dancing, a waxed hardwood floor must be furnished; for hockey, a sheet of smooth ice. And each of these activities has its own requirements in terms of illumination, acoustics, ventilation, temperature, etc.

Years ago, separate structures would have been required for most of these activities. Because it takes a comparatively large group of people to support most of them, adequate provisions were seldom found anywhere but in the largest cities. Thanks to our technical development, all such facilities can now be housed in a single building. The changes they imply often can no longer be made manually, however. The scale of the elements is too large, the time available for change too short, the cost of manual labor too high. Hence the structure is mechanized. Motor-operated walls, floors, seating, and partitions rise, drop, slide, or fold at the touch of a button. Lighting, sound, and air-conditioning systems can be designed to serve the large cheering crowd of a basketball game or the smaller, more sedate group at a lecture. Sometimes, however, the specialized demand for optimum building performance leads to the construction of separate, and less utilized, single-purpose structures.

New performing arts centers are often designed for flexibility of use. Included in the Chan Centre for the Performing Arts in Vancouver, Canada is an experimental theater of approximately 250 seats, a 1,400-seat concert hall, and a 150-seat cinema (Fig. 10–2). Within the Chan Center, the BC TEL Studio Theatre, designed by Theatre Projects Consultants of London, incorporates a series of twelve portable towers with seating on three levels. The towers, together with a demountable main audience floor, can be reconfigured for up to twelve distinct theatrical settings, from cabaret to thrust to proscenium layout. The acoustical shape and properties of the Concert Hall were developed by ARTEC Consultants of New York and include a series of convex, curved walls inside an elliptical hall, with a 37-ton canopy suspended over the stage and a series of absorbent sound banners that can be adjusted for a wide variety of performance requirements and audience sizes. The Royal Bank Cinema was designed for academic film, video, and lecture presentations and has the latest in audio, visual, and surround-sound equipment.

Such mechanization of buildings is quite feasible; there is scarcely a conceivable problem that is not technically soluble. Nor is there any doubt that mechanization can greatly increase the productivity of enclosed space. But mechanization has its own problems. The more sophisticated the apparatus, the more vulnerable it is to systemic dysfunction and to external exigencies, such as regional power failures. With today's advanced computers, problems such as those arising from the year 2000 (Y2K) issue complicate the picture in ways previously unimaginable. Moreover, the social desirability of highly mechanized buildings should be measured against a larger reference frame. Such intensively exploited spaces may lead to needless congestion, wasteful travel for the users, and a concentration of facilities in locations that are detrimental to the overall well-being of the community.

Dialectics of City Planning

City planning in the Western world has been the exclusive province of architects and civil or military engineers from the Renaissance until the very recent past. This has had important consequences for the development of both theory and practice. Few urban designers had any background in what today would be called the environmental sciences; the Frenchman André Lenôtre and the American Frederick Law Olmsted, with their backgrounds in horticulture, were exceptions. Because of this tradition, it was easy to regard the city as a sculptural or stereometric construct. In addition, until recent years most urban designers came from upper-class backgrounds and hence were indoctrinated with academic preconceptions of formal order and monumental form. Given these two tendencies, the city was considered as a work of art.

The great era of urban expansion in both Europe and the United States was dominated by such conceptions. Baron Georges Eugène Haussmann, the military engineer, was responsible for the reconstruction of central Paris between 1853 and 1870. Here, a geometry of radial and intersecting boulevards was dropped like a cookie cutter upon the medieval street pattern of Paris. Onto the exposed faces of the intersected tissue was grafted a new streetscape of standardized Renaissance façades. This conception was imported to America, with the Chicago Columbian Exposition of 1893, by a triumvirate of powerful designers: the architect Daniel Burnham, the landscape architect Olmsted, and the sculptor Augustus St. Gaudens. The astonishing popular success of this project led to their being named as the planners of the national capital by the McMillan Commission of 1901. They thereby established the City Beautiful movement, which dominated American city planning almost until World War II.

Given such a historical background, it is not surprising that urbanistic theory developed in isolation from environmental and ecological considerations, on one hand, and from social and economic theory on the other. Nevertheless, in the period between the two world wars, many new movements growing out of the crisis of the rapidly expanding cities were gaining great momentum. The new field of social work was symbolized by the pioneer Jane Addams; the slum clearance and housing movement was led by such figures as Edith Elmer Wood; and the Garden City concept was imported from England by Clarence Stein, Charles Harris Whitaker, and the elder Henry Wright. By the time of the Great Depression and the New Deal, the theoretical propositions of these movements had been fairly well absorbed into academic city planning theory. But, unlike the physical planners with their Beaux-Arts idiom, these new social forces were without any special interest in esthetics. They were generally content to accept the Roman Renaissance vocabulary of the architects or the English Cottage bias of the British town planners.

Beginning with the New Deal, however, architects and city planners became more and more anxious to give their theory an esthetic dimension appropriate to their changing social and political goals. They derived this new esthetic idiom from two main sources: the utopian schemes of Le Corbusier for rebuilding Paris as a skyscraper-studded park (1921–25) and the utopian decentralist plans that Frank Lloyd Wright set forth in his Broadacre City (1935). Although they occupied opposite poles of urban theory—Le Corbusier for urban concentration, Wright for decentralization—both men discarded the discredited eclectic idiom in favor of their own private vocabulary of form. Since in visual terms their work was so radically new, it was easy to assume that all necessary modifications had been made to American planning theory to bring it into line with contemporary reality.

Opportunity to apply these new theories on a wide scale did not occur until after the end of World War II. Immediately thereafter, a series of huge federal programs for housing and for urban renewal and redevelopment gave planners their first major opportunities. The next quarter of a century afforded ample opportunity to measure the efficacy of the city planning theory of the time and to demonstrate that, even with the additional input from the economists and social scientists, it showed deficiencies that led to serious dysfunction in completed projects.

The most devastating critique of orthodox city planning theory came almost forty years ago in 1959 with the publication by Jane Jacobs of her book *The Death and Life of Great American Cities*.[4] The arguments in this epochal work are too dense and intricate to permit easy summary, but her thesis was, in substance, that architects and planners were actually killing the cities that they were in the process of "renewing" and "redeveloping." This was the inevitable consequence, Jacobs argued, of the origins and formalistic education of the planners themselves. They might have relinquished the neoclassic iconography of the City Beautiful for the avant-garde idioms of Le Corbusier and the Bauhaus. They might even be liberal in their attitudes toward the explosive social and political issues that were convulsing American cities. But they still clung to a fundamental fallacy: that the city was a work of art and that their task was to make the city beautiful.

It was not that beauty was bad — it was that it was completely irrelevant. Jacobs's model of the city was a living organism responding to its own ineluctable requirements in both its form and its development. The true measure of urban success was therefore viability, the quality of the life the city elicited and supported, and not mere surface appearances. Moreover, her book challenged the competence of middle-class white professionals even to conceptualize, much less adequately to house, the varied lifestyles of all the ethnographic components of the American city: European immigrants like the Jews, Italians, and Middle Europeans; displaced populations like the African Americans, Latinos, Native Americans, and Mexican Americans.

As specialists from the social sciences were attracted to the planning field, they began to scrutinize the city from vantage points quite outside the scope of architects, landscape architects, and civil engineers. The critique of the economists was especially relevant, and perhaps no one analyzed the economic functions of the city more eloquently than Louis Winnick in a remarkable paper, "The Economic Functions of the City Today and Tomorrow." He saw the city as "a mammoth labor-saving innovation for which no patent has been issued and no inventor honored. The primary economic function of the city is to lighten the toil of mankind, to make more effective use of its productive capacity." Humanity, Winnick went on to point out, is the victim of two inherent limitations: the "friction of distance" and the "affliction of uncertainty." The city overcomes these two disadvantages by the physical organization of space in such a way that people are placed close to other people, workers to employers, producers to consumers, establishments to establishments.[5] The city thereby affords three economic advantages, critically important and nowhere else available: proximity, predictability, and, hence, choice.

Viewed as an economic invention, the city constituted a common reservoir of raw materials and finished goods, of manual and intellectual skills, upon which everyone engaged in production could draw. This reservoir was of absolutely incalculable value, one that no single individual could conceivably afford to maintain alone. Its concentration in space guaranteed that all producers had proximity to the various goods and services upon which they depended, as well as to those that, in turn, depended upon them. Because there was always duplication of every type of skill, goods, and service, there was always predictability of supply. And, finally, because of these factors, the city offered that last essential ingredient of the marketplace: option—a range of choice within any given category.

Jacobs continued her examination of the city in her second book, *The Economy of Cities*. Essentially an investigation of urban morphology, this was mainly an attempt to discover the laws that govern the growth and development of the cities. Why do some cities languish while others flourish? Her model of the economic city is like a kind of engine for the performance of work. It is a reciprocating engine, absorbing imports, turning out exports, but in the process yielding an "awesome force," what she calls "new work." This latter byproduct is the index of the city's health and viability. But if this is a general law that governs their development, each city must be studied as a living organism, bedded in a specific environment and always delicately balanced between growth and decay. To understand the city, Jacobs argued, one must study it like a biologist who knows that, while all members of a given species display common characteristics, no two individuals are identical. Such a study reveals unexpected (and, in her argument, almost *unexpectable*) possibilities inherent in each city—hence the danger of abstract formalistic plans. Manchester, the widely hailed model city of the nineteenth century, turned out to have far fewer developmental potentials than "inefficient" and "unplanned" Birmingham, and Los Angeles, so impractically located far from transportation centers and sources of raw materials, turned out to be far more viable than Detroit, ideally placed with reference to both.[6]

Jacobs argued that the city is uniquely valuable precisely because of its "inefficiencies" and "impracticalities":

Cities are indeed inefficient and impractical [when] compared to towns . . . but I propose to show that these grave and real deficiencies are necessary to economic development and are thus exactly what makes cities uniquely valuable to economic life.[7]

This being the nature of the city organism, its physical form must at all times allow for the fullest, freest interplay of economic forces. Its development must not be hampered by arbitrary or formalistic physical configurations imposed upon it by professionals who do not understand its inner, ineluctable demands. In essence, Jane Jacobs argued for the purest laissez-faire, the socioeconomic Darwinism so popular earlier in the twentieth century.

It would be difficult to formulate a theory more directly contrary to most assumptions of orthodox planning theory or more outrageous to professional planners. And yet, as

Christopher Alexander pointed out in "*A City Is Not a Tree*," another truly significant paper,[8] contemporary experience in city building seems to confirm Jacob's diagnosis. What he calls "artificial cities"—Brasilia, Chandigarh, the new towns of England and Sweden, as well as the Levittowns and Restons and Columbias of this country—have not lived up to all expectations. Despite the fact that they often offer high levels of visual beauty and physical amenity, they have not all succeeded in generating the self-supporting life expected of them, particularly in the United States. In Britain, most of these relatively young "new town" communities (built between 1946 and 1991) are highly self-contained, with the majority of their residents working locally. In the United States, the most self-contained places (with low transportation fuel use rates per capita) are not its planned communities but its densest urban centers, Manhattan and San Francisco.[8]

Some critics charge that artificial cities have failed in America because social engineering and physical determinism are unpalatable to most Americans. Our social myths are based on rugged individualism, which runs contrary to what is perceived as voluntary subjugation to planned community life. Superficial appearances to the contrary, this country is probably the most intensively planned area on earth. Visible and invisible, local and national, public and private, mesh after mesh of plan is thrown across the nation. Interlocking, overlapping, contradictory, or mutually irreconcilable, their effect is everywhere apparent. It is argued that the pattern of urban-suburban development that resulted from federally subsidized highways and home mortgages was yet another step in the continuing evolution of planning in this country.

Since the early 1980s, a town planning movement called New Urbanism has developed in the United States—to, in essence, replicate old-style neighborhoods—in recognition of historically valued concepts in city planning. The New Urbanists formed in direct response to what they saw and experienced: undifferentiated suburban sprawl predicated on unlimited access to the automobile (or, increasingly, the family van). Modern suburbia, with its separation of housing (which is segregated into distinct enclaves based on income, housing type, and race) from shopping centers, recreational facilities, government buildings, and business parks, is navigable only by car. This type of growth is viewed by the New Urbanists as a prescription for isolation, waste, and malaise.

Peter Calthorpe of San Francisco and Andres Duany and Elizabeth Plater-Zyberk of Miami are at the forefront of this movement. The foundation for their "new towns" is the creation of pedestrian-based neighborhoods, with ready access to mass transit. Low-traffic streets (with wide, tree-lined sidewalks) are set in a grid network. Stores (including the corner convenience store), workplaces, and public transportation are within walking distance. Calthorpe's Laguna West is a transit-oriented, 1,000-acre development near Sacramento, California, with shopping, child care, and other services concentrated in the town center, within walking distance of home.

The layout of such neighborhoods is of higher density than that typically permitted in conventional subdivisions and includes a variety of rowhouses, apartments, townhouses, big and small houses, and studios above garages and stores to accommodate a wider range of income and age groups. The typical yards are small, but public facilities, including parks and walking trails, encourage interaction. Cars are parked using a variety of methods, including detached garages in alleyways between buildings to avoid the large expanses of asphalt so commonly seen. The development itself builds on the past and the region's history rather than being of standardized design. This layout closely describes Duany Plater-Zyberk's 352-acre Kentlands community in Gaithersburg, Maryland.

Reviews on these types of new developments have been mixed. Architectural critic Ada Louise Huxtable finds new towns like Kentlands and Seaside, Florida,

a conscientious contradiction in terms. By reducing the definition of community to a romantic social aesthetic emphasizing front porches, historic styles, and walking distance to stores and schools as an answer to suburban sprawl—that post-World War II domestic American dream that has fallen out of favor as suburban problems have multiplied—they have avoided the questions of urbanization to become part of the problem. Only now are the proponents of a nostalgic regionalism beginning to focus on the revitalization of older communities in the inner city.[9]

The New Urbanists, to their credit, do not create their traditional neighborhood developments (TNDs) in isolation, but stage charrettes—collaborative efforts between design professionals and public and private sector leaders, community activists, and other citizens in the building of communities. Often, the integration of land uses they espouse requires fundamental changes to conventional zoning and planning guidelines in order to accommodate a greater diversity in building types and to create public spaces. The street layout may include small blocks, sometimes in an orthogonal or rectangular grid, sidewalks, and alleys for parking and utilities. A code is established to protect the structure of the community.

The New Urbanists' charter indicates a focus on the challenges of disinvestment in central cities, the spread of placeless sprawl, increasing separation by race and income, environmental deterioration, loss of agricultural lands and wilderness, and the erosion of society's built heritage.[10] Indeed, the Congress for New Urbanism was instrumental in formulating design guidelines for HUD's Homeownership Zone program, which will rebuild sizable areas (ranging from 100 to over 400 acres) in the inner cities of Baltimore, Buffalo, Cleveland, Louisville, Philadelphia, and Sacramento.[11] The urban designs that emerged included creation of town greens surrounded by civic buildings, Olmstedian boulevards, and distinct urban villages within the larger city.

Then there are sustainable or low-impact developments, such as that on Dewees Island, a barrier island near Charleston, South Carolina, governed by a detailed package of covenants, restrictions, and development guidelines. The state-approved master plan for the island allows a maximum of 150 houses to be built on 1,200 acres, with 65 percent permanently protected open land. Property owners must agree to restrictions related to site impact and landscaping, building size, construction materials, and construction waste recycling. Building materials prohibited because of scarcity, esthetics, or environmental concerns include large-dimension solid lumber (greater than 2 x 12), aluminum and vinyl siding, composition asphalt and fiberglass shingles, unsealed particleboard, fiberglass insulation, HCFC-blown insulation (polyisocyanurate, extruded polystyrene,

A

B

Figure 10-3 / (A) Seaside, Florida. The
precedent-setting community designed
by town planners Andres Duany and
Elizabeth Plater-Zyberk, Architects, Inc.
(DPZ), built in the early 1980s and based
on the principles that governed the planning of traditional cities such as
Charleston, South Carolina. (B) Seaside
incorporates pedestrian pathways to
facilitate errand-running and to encourage residents to leave their cars at home.

and most polyurethane), and paints and stains with high VOC content.[12] Only indigenous plants or those native to the South Carolina coastal plain are permitted, and roadways are constructed of sand, shells, or wood chips to allow stormwater infiltration. No gasoline- or diesel-powered vehicles are permitted except for safety and maintenance purposes; residents use electric carts or bicycles. The island has a central water system with reverse-osmosis equipment to remove minerals, and only rainwater can be used for irrigation, pools, and spas.

Others have built based on the concept of cohousing, which originated in Denmark. These developments, such as EcoVillage in Ithaca, New York, offer shared dining and cooking facilities, home offices, play areas for children, and guest quarters. The community shares tools such as lawnmowers and laundry facilities, and adjacent units have common heating systems. These types of developments, while still on the fringes, appear to be attracting wider audiences as the post-baby-boom generation matures and acquires their own homes. Builders are slow to embrace these new concepts, especially because of the continued success of most typical suburban developments and the absence of side-

Figure 10–4 / Habitat preservation and destruction. View of the Atlantic City skyline in the distance (11 miles south) from the 20,238-acre Brigantine National Wildlife Refuge in Oceanville, New Jersey. Southern New Jersey is a welcome stopover point for millions of migratory birds, lying as it does between the Atlantic Ocean and Delaware Bay. The need for habitat acquisition and regulation in the area is becoming increasingly understood by the Nature Conservancy, the Cape May Bird Observatory, and wildlife agencies in New Jersey, Virginia, Delaware, and Maryland.[13]

by-side comparisons. Typically, these developments are governed by an overall plan or code that provides continuous structure to the pattern and nature of growth.

Meanwhile, Jane Jacobs's diagnosis of the organic complexity of the city made almost forty years ago may indeed have been valid, but her proposed therapy overlooked a central fact: a city is not composed of living tissue, with its properties of cellular subdivision and genetic memory. All environmental manipulation is the consequence of deliberate human action. All city building proceeds according to someone's plan, whether that of a national government, a county school board, or the corner grocer. Moreover, the complexity of modern life makes it impossible that the implementation of these plans not be in the hands of trained specialists — architects, planners, environmentalists.

Failures in city building do imply that planning theory must be completely restructured to accommodate totally new levels of complexity. Moreover, there are serious students of the city who question the ability of the human mind to handle these problems unaided. Just as space travel became possible only with the appearance of advanced mathematical theory, and actually solvable only with computer technology, so too with the planning of the modern metropolis. Christopher Alexander dealt with just this conceptual problem. Himself an architect and mathematician, Alexander pointed out that the "process of thought itself works in a tree-like way, so that whenever a city is 'thought out' instead of 'grown,' it is bound to get a tree-like structure . . . [F]or the human mind, the tree is the easiest vehicle for complex thoughts. But the city is not, cannot and must not be a tree."[14]

What is the nature, the inner ordering principle, that distinguishes the "natural" cities (London, Boston, Istanbul) from the "artificial" cities of the world (Chandigarh, New Delhi, Canberra)? Alexander found it in their fundamental structure: the natural city has the organization of a semilattice but the artificial city has the structure of a tree.

Within the tree-like structure, no piece of any unit is ever connected to other units except through the medium of that unit as a whole. The enormity of this restriction is difficult to grasp. It is a little as though the members of a family were not free to make friends outside the family, except when the family as a whole made a friendship.[15]

Conventional subdivisions often emerge as treelike forms, with cul-de-sacs fanning out from a main central thoroughfare (Fig. 10–5). This layout, while expediting vehicular traffic, is winding and indirect for those wishing to walk to other houses in the development. One might say that this development pattern impedes commerce by serving the one-dimensional, dead-end function of getting each resident home.

The greater structural complexity of the semilattice yields an enormously greater range of overlap, ambiguity, multiplicity of aspect. This is clear from the fact that "A tree based on 20 elements can contain at most 19 further subsets of the 20, while a semi-lattice based on the same 20 elements can contain more than 1,000,000 subsets."[16]

Necessarily, those who design and plan new cities, or remodel old ones, manipulate a range of sets, subsystems, and systems of material elements — people, blades of grass, cars, bricks, molecules, houses, gardens, water pipes and the water that flows in them. But

Figure 10–5 / Aerial view of a conventional subdivision showing cul-de-sacs and an indifference to solar orientation.

what they ultimately manipulate are invisible, immaterial relationships and processes. The simplistic tree structure makes no physical provisions for this complex overlap.

In every city there are thousands, even millions, of times more systems at work whose physical residue does not appear as a unit in these tree structures. In the worst cases, the units that do appear fail to correspond to any living reality, and the real systems, whose existence actually makes the city live, are provided with no physical receptacle.[17]

A city is a receptacle for life. But if the city has a tree-like form, it severs the overlap of the multiple strands of life within it, "like a bowl full of razor blades on edge." Only the semi-lattice, Alexander argued, with its thicker, tougher, more subtle, and more complex structure, can support life. As Kenneth Jackson, history professor at Columbia University and author of *Crabgrass Frontier: The Suburbanization of the United States*, remarked:

[T]he same catalytic mixing of people that creates urban problems and fuels urban conflict also spurs the initiative, innovation and collaboration that taken together move civilization forward. Quite simply, metropolitan centers are the most complex creations of the human mind, and they will not easily yield their roles as marketplaces of ideas.

Cities are places where individuals of different bents and pursuits rub shoulders, where most human achievements have been created. Whereas village and rural life, as well as life in the modern shopping mall, is characterized by the endless repetition of similar events, cities remain centers of diversity and opportunity. If they express some of the worst tendencies of modern society, they also represent much of the best.[18]

Modern society has experienced a sea change in how and where people shop, work, and socialize. Megamalls, discount centers, strip malls, and factory outlets proliferate outside city limits, and the great downtown department stores have for the most part closed for good. Downtowns are no longer dominant. Many residents of metropolitan areas are proud that they never go downtown anymore; even the tourists are being drawn first to the "edge cities" located convenient to airports and highways. In 1990 there were 280 discount megamalls (each with a million or more square feet of retail space) in the United States, with sales estimated as high as $18 billion.

Northwest Airlines has "Shop Till You Drop" package tours that fly Britons and Japanese with empty suitcases to the Mall of America, conveniently located next to the Minneapolis-St. Paul International Airport (on the stadium site where the Minnesota Vikings and Twins played before moving on to Minneapolis) and hemmed in on all sides by highways. This mall, a complex of 4.2 million square feet, attracts 40 million visitors annually to its 420 stores, restaurants, sports bars, and nightclubs, 78-acre entertainment center, and 18-theater movie complex. The mall shields visitors from the often harsh Minneapolis weather (at no small energy expense). For those coming from Great Britain, it is possible to board a plane in London late Friday afternoon, get to the mall Saturday morning, shop all day, and arrive back in London early Sunday.

Ironically, in addition to impacting the downtown retail centers of Minneapolis and St. Paul (and other shopping areas within a 150-mile radius), the Mall of America has had a big influence on Southdale, a shopping mall five miles away in Edina, Minnesota.[19] Completed in 1956 and designed by Victor Gruen, Southdale was the country's first enclosed shopping mall. Its appealing, thermally controlled environment spurred the construction of the skyway system in downtown Minneapolis. Now Southdale is threatened by one of its own offspring. And what lies ahead for the Mall of America? Will the awe of a first-time visitor be replaced by familiarity and boredom? And of what use will the behemoth be if it fails? Surely it is not of such a form and scale that reuse is assured. Might it someday simply become a sprawling white elephant?

Business failure and property abandonment are not unknown to the American experience, and are not without social consequence. Abandoned, deteriorating factories in older industrial sections of most of our cities once supported vital neighborhoods and employed hundreds of workers. These buildings lie dormant on sites that are almost always contaminated by industrial operations of the past. They have either been mothballed by their owners or reverted to the public domain. The property owners may have chosen abandonment, the path of least resistance, avoiding the specter of daunting financial liability and regulatory delay, should the property come to be classified as a hazardous waste site.

Because of the strict joint and several liability provisions of the federal Superfund law (Comprehensive Environmental Response, Compensation, and Liability Act), the financial risk for the owner of a hazardous waste site, as well as for the buyer, regardless of fault or level of responsibility, is often perceived as being greater than the value of the site's best use. As a result, an urban brownfield site (the name given to underutilized or vacant urban land with industrial soil or water contamination that inhibits redevelopment) is at a tremendous economic disadvantage when compared with a rural or suburban greenfield site (typically, an untouched, undeveloped tract of farmland). Additionally, lenders may simply brownline industrial companies seeking to reinvest, screening out undesirable borrowers categorically, such as by industrial classification (e.g., metal fabricators, semi-conductor facilities, utilities, tool and die shops, bottling and canning plants), to avoid assuming more than conventional economic risk.

These individual, private actions have larger social impacts, indirectly leading to development ever outward, and removing valuable real estate from commerce — properties that are still served by networks of streets and utilities, on public transportation routes, near transit facilities, schools, churches, parks, downtown business centers, universities, hospitals, and cultural institutions, and that are accessible to urban residents. Instead of imposing costly cleanup standards that are often unrelated to the site's intended use, environmental agencies are beginning to apply more reasonable standards to sites with low or moderate levels of contamination. Engineering and institutional controls over alternative uses of the properties are implemented through deed restrictions. In the case of building-related conditions, like asbestos or lead-based paint, sale and use or reuse of an industrial property is not normally impeded to the same extent as occurs with site contamination. The market value is simply discounted for the estimated cost of the remedy and the property transaction proceeds.

Although far too many of our cities and suburbs appear virtually lost when it comes to fitting into their natural environment or stimulating fruitful social exchange, several notable planning efforts are countering this trend. Of particular note is the revitalization of the waterfronts of such cities as New York, Boston, Baltimore, and Chattanooga. The improvements in New York include the World Financial Center (and Wintergarden), housing and recreation at Battery Park City (on land reclaimed from the Hudson River), the nautical museums and culinary experiences of South Street Seaport (Fig. 10–6), and diverse entertainment and recreational activities at Chelsea Piers (renovated after years of underutilization and decay). Waterfronts offer many exciting possibilities — and these types of projects have proven successful. Many unmet opportunities for urban revitalization remain. To bring such projects to fruition requires vision and political commitment, often to reverse longstanding impediments to constructive change.

Another project that demonstrates foresight and determination is the Riverwalk, or Paseo del Rio, in downtown San Antonio. Historically, the San Antonio River continuously overflowed its banks; a flood in 1921 resulted in 50 deaths and millions of dollars of property damage. A bypass channel and two dams were constructed to control flooding. This system also allows the river to be drained, and every January, the cleaning of the

Figure 10–6 / South Street Seaport is a restored nineteenth-century twelve-block historic landmark port district on the lower east side of Manhattan between South, John, Pearl, and Dover streets. Top: View south on Fulton Street showing Schermerhorn Row. Cobblestone pedestrian streets link shops and restaurants in the Fulton Market and along the Schermerhorn Row and Museum Block. Bottom: Historic ships line the waterfront piers. New York's maritime heritage is celebrated in such attractions as the Boat Building Shop, the Maritime Crafts Center featuring maritime artisans, the Fulton Market Building, and the Norway Galleries. Replica nineteenth-century riverboats and an 1885 schooner leave here for tours of New York Harbor.

Figure 10–7 / Baltimore's Inner Harbor. The decaying docks and warehouses of Baltimore's waterfront were transformed into a busy retail and entertainment district combining old and new buildings. Attractions include Harborplace, two glass-enclosed shopping malls opened in 1980; the tent-roofed Columbus Center, a marine biotechnology research institute; the World Trade Center, a thirty-two-story pentagonal building with an observation deck on the twenty-seventh floor; and the Maryland Science Center and IMAX™ Theater. In the planning stages is a retail and office center to be housed in the massive brick Power Plant complex, originally used to provide power for the city's trolley system.

river bottom is a civic event. A 2.5-mile tree lined park trail (Riverwalk) was constructed along the banks of the river through the business district, twenty feet below street level. The Riverwalk has become San Antonio's premiere draw, offering opportunities to dine, shop, or listen to live music at restaurants, sidewalk terraces, craft shops, outdoor cafés, galleries, and jazz clubs along the way.

The City as a Prosthetic Instrument

Critiques of traditional city planning such as those originally put forth by Jacobs, Winnick, and Alexander cannot be lightly dismissed. The new levels of complexity they describe undoubtedly do run far beyond traditional parameters. New modes of mathematical logic and a new computerized technology are essential to meet them. But more is required than merely new techniques; planners must also resolve a number of internal contradictions in their own relations to society. Because they can, at best, implement only the social, economic, and political policies of their society, it is obvious that their powers are strictly limited. Nevertheless, within the limits of a given policy, sheer professional competence plays an important role. Lack of it too often vitiates many a valid project. Too often merely visual criteria are applied to the solution of complex problems in which overall amenity is the desideratum. This amenity is a difficult quality to describe in positive terms. Although formal esthetic qualities—proportion, balance, harmony, rhythm, etc.—do play a role in achieving amenity, they are by no means decisive. We have had ample opportunity to see in this volume that architecture engages people at every level of their existence—psychic and somatic, subjective and objective, individual and social—and that these levels have their own hierarchy of importance.

These hierarchies are apparent in the behavior of city dwellers in response to various aspects of the city. Thus many visually beautiful areas—plazas, malls, civic centers—are empty, neglected, and unused while many areas nominally ugly and unkempt support an active life. Pedestrians vote with their feet. Though the reasons for their behavior may often be obscure (even, on occasion, to themselves), the controlling factors are real. They are almost always experiential: a slight change in level, a better-lighted block, sun as against shade, a choice between mud and pavement, the visual interest of shop windows as against a blank wall. Such factors often override a subjective opinion that the chosen path of movement or locus of action is "beautiful" or "ugly."

Certain streetside attractions or distractions—a political speaker or a traffic accident—can of course attract people to the sunny side of the street, even on a blistering day. But the gawkers do not stay there very long; all things being equal, they return to the shade in hot weather or to the sunshine in cold. It takes a fairly strong motivation to draw a pedestrian up three steps into a shop, as any retailer can tell you. A climb of three or four flights is the upper limit of normal motivation and muscle power alike. In much the same fashion, it takes either an obstacle or a cop to make pedestrians turn at a right angle when a diagonal cutoff is possible.

The same behavior can be observed inside buildings. Almost every house has elements of which it is said, "We never use it—I don't know why," or "People are always tripping over that step," or "Don't sit there—there's a draft or something." These are judgments based upon observed experience. They outweigh formal value judgments as to the beauty of the stairway or chair. Yet they are seldom consciously analyzed by architects or urban designers.

Many amenities—and many nuisances and hazards, too—are the result of relationships between buildings rather than of the individual buildings themselves. They thus fall into a kind of terra incognita for which the individual architect is not responsible and about which the urban planner is either unaware or unable to act. An active shopping street is one such construct. Smog is another. Both are the result of urban concentration. One is a major amenity of civilized life, the other a cause of lung cancer and emphysema. The cause and effect of one is immediately perceived; the other is never even sensed by the victim. Both phenomena are integral aspects of the urban experience, yet neither are encompassed by conventional definitions of beauty.

If the amenity of our cities is to be raised above the lamentably low current level, the vantage point from which architects and planners approach them must be radically altered. The required change in perspective is both technical and cultural. Technically, we must shift our attention to actual city dwellers in their life zone six feet (or so) above the earth. Culturally, professionals must recognize their middle-class mores and esthetic standards as being of limited validity for their own milieu and often ridiculous when applied to working-class groups and ethnic minorities.

Comprehensive planning, at a regional and metropolitan level, is obviously an indispensable step if we are to restructure our urban environment along more satisfactory lines. But such plans, even when completely elaborated, are far from actual, human-scaled designs. These must be developed on a microenvironmental scale, where a six-inch change in level, or a ten-degree change in temperature, or a difference of a few foot-candles of illumination is an important consideration.

This does not mean the abandonment of larger-sized (or smaller-scaled) concepts. It does mean that, once clearly formulated, these concepts ought to be temporarily put to one side while subplans are developed for the microenvironment. At this stage, we should proceed from the bottom up, from the particular to the general. Most large models of small scale (e.g., 1 inch equals 100 feet) are not only of limited informational value — they can actually be dangerous to the design process. Decisions affecting 68-inch tall people are, in effect, made from an altitude of 3,500 feet — a distance too great to permit real discrimination in matters of great experiential significance. Whether a parent is to be separated from a three-year-old child in a sandbox by a horizontal distance of 30 feet or a vertical distance of ten floors is a spatial decision of vital importance to the well-being of both. But, at the scale of most architectural models, such distances seem merely matters of formal composition.

The time scale of the pedestrian's movement, no less than the pedestrian's actual size, is crucial to truly satisfactory urban spaces. Few modern streetscapes and traffic schemes recognize this, hence they do not hesitate to introduce into the microenvironment scales of movement and rates of speed that are literally hostile to urban life, not to mention urban well-being and amenity. Yet conflicts of this sort can never be discovered, much less resolved, at the scale at which most urbanistic studies are carried on.

Historically, most architects and planners have been middle-class in origin. (The sheer cost of professional education takes it beyond the reach of many low-income and minority groups.) From this education, if not from their familial backgrounds, they develop characteristic modes of life and typical attitudes toward esthetic matters. Though they are apt to think of them as absolute and universal, these modes and attitudes are actually highly localized, even in American culture. Whether these are "better" or "higher" than mass taste is not at all established, either, though professionals would like to think so. In any case, the tendency to reorganize the urban scene along middle-class lines of beauty, tidiness, order, etc., often creates tensions as serious as those it seeks to alleviate. Public hous-

Earl Dotter, photojournalist.

Figure 10–8 / Federally financed low-income housing renovation in New Haven, Connecticut. Increasingly, existing residential buildings are being salvaged and renovated rather than bulldozed to rubble and replaced with monolithic towers.

ing and urban redevelopment projects afford ample evidence of this danger. If "depressed" and "substandard" neighborhoods are going to be salvaged instead of simply bulldozed, designers are going to have to display more imagination than they have as yet. And this act of imagination can only come from an authentic shift in their conceptual vantage point. Such a shift may indeed be forthcoming from the increasingly international group of architectural students now attending universities and entering the profession.

In modern America the real client of the environmental designer is less and less the legal client. The white-collar office manager in the big skyscraper, the worker in the big plant, the family in the housing project, the child in the big consolidated school—these are the people for whom the architect works and to whom the architect is ultimately responsible. They are the contained for whom the building containers should be accurately and sensitively designed. Yet these are the people whom the architect or planner no longer sees. They deal instead with their agents—those corporate or institutional entities who commission the projects. Instead of firsthand observation of real people and their needs and aspirations, the architect is given statistical data with which to work—peak loads, median incomes, average family size, minimum floor areas, etc. These data, of course, may be essential for the establishment of the broad lines of policy, but they are no more a substitute for firsthand detailed knowledge of the actual consumers of the building than statistics on the incidence of cancer are to a physician with an actual patient.

Nor can it be assumed that these corporate or institutional clients, acting though they may be as agents for the consuming public, are always to be relied upon to represent its best interests or requirements. In a profit-motivated society, criteria for actual architectural projects are all too apt to drop to the minimums permitted by building codes or by the law of supply and demand. Of course this tendency varies from field to field. The speculative builders of tract housing are notorious for the venality of their design and construction policies. On the other hand, a life insurance company planning a big housing project for long-term investment purposes may, out of sheer self-interest, follow more enlightened policies. The demand for maximum economy in public projects can often prove quite as limiting a factor as the demand for maximum profit in a private one. Naturally many public builders with specialized requirements, such as hospitals and schools, must meet factual standards determined by the uses themselves. American public housing, on the other hand, has been permitted to slip to the lowest levels of mediocrity of any country in the West, to the point where the very agency that had them constructed is now financing their demolition.

Without the input of the real client in the design process, we may be doomed to repeat the design miscalculations of the past. In December 1996, a two-day planning session (proposing thousands of new mixed-income housing units as well as new schools and parks and a relocated police station) for the troubled 3,200-unit Cabrini-Green public housing complex in Chicago was not open to the public, and no residents participated. [20] The charrette was reportedly primarily a physical planning exercise, borrowing from the principles of the New Urbanists, replacing superblocks with street grids. The closed nature of the process fueled residents' suspicions that the neighborhood would be gentrified and they would be displaced. Resident leaders filed suit in federal court to block further demolition of the high-rise buildings there.

It is obvious that physical manipulation of bricks and mortar alone will not fix America's ills. As award-winning low-income-housing architect Christine Killory stated, "We are firmly committed to the proposition that architecture can change people's lives, but not everybody's and not immediately and not on its own.[21]

The now well-established popularity among many architects and planners of so-called advocacy planning is a response to this unhappy state of affairs. The advocacy concept abandons the idea of the planner as a kind of Olympian agent who accurately weighs the needs of all the diverse elements of the community and doles out environmental justice on an evenhanded basis. The advocate planner recognizes that conventional practice has not met the burning needs of the nation's minorities, the poor, the sick, and the aged. The advocate planner therefore argues the need to intervene directly on their behalf, arguing correctly that the better-off sections of any community find adequate spokespeople for their needs. In a narrower, more technical sense, the advocate planner also argues that to work directly with actual clients, instead of the usual legal surrogates, is the only way to improve the experiential quality of our cities.

Advocacy planning is thus a professional recognition of this chain of cause and effect. The sheer complexity of modern technological society makes inescapable the development of comprehensive planning at all levels, but it also makes inevitable a bureaucratic apparatus to prepare and administer them; this, in turn, raises the problem of democratic control over the inertia that all bureaucracies develop. Although confrontation politics are always distasteful to the bureaucrat, they often seem to the disadvantaged the only way of persuading a bureaucrat to respond effectively to their needs. In the process, better plans and better planners appear.

Indeed, they have appeared in the years since this book was last published. In addition to advocacy planning, special open forums at the beginning of the design phase were developed to generate plans for new (and, one hopes, better) communities in the thick of discussion and debate. For example, the New Urbanists routinely open their charrettes to the public. The architectural and town planning firm of Duany Plater-Zyberk uses intense weeklong charrettes—bringing together disparate constituencies such as interested citizens, investors, architects, planners, engineers, public officials, and environmental consultants—to generate the conceptual plans, drawings, renderings, and technical documents needed to go forward.

There has been considerable ferment since the 1970s in all aspects of planning, not least of which are the issues of severe economic and social inequity and the isolating effects of suburban life. Between 1950 and 1990 the suburbs gained more than 75 million people, and by 1990 there were more people living in the suburbs than in cities and rural areas combined. Northern industrialized cities like Detroit and Cleveland lost over 40 percent of their population, while others, including Baltimore, Philadelphia, Chicago, and Boston lost over 20 percent.[22] These are not simple times. As jobs and higher-income people move outward to the so-called edge cities, with intersuburban commutes to work becoming more and more the norm, inner cities and their nearby suburbs are decimated.

In addition, new immigrants are more frequently bypassing the cities to settle in the suburbs where the jobs, whether in service or manufacturing, are located. The result is that single-family neighborhoods are sometimes transformed seemingly overnight into multifamily communities with quite different modes of operation. The suburbs are, of necessity, becoming more heterogeneous in terms of cultural diversity and economic strata.

This is in the context of a world in which more than half of us live in urban areas with at least 1 million or more in population; it is projected that there will be 27 megacities (10 million or more in size) by the year 2015.[23] For the first time on earth, more people now live in cities than in rural areas. It is clear that monumental changes are occurring globally, in citizens' awareness of other cultures, in expectations and goals for oneself and one's family, and in the nature of work and the ability and desire to travel and emigrate. As Robert Kates indicated in his essay "Sustaining Life of the Earth,"

I believe the world of the next century will be warmer and more crowded, more connected but more diverse. . . . Goods, information and people are generally drawn to places of wealth or opportunity, which can make such areas more diverse. And strong counter-currents that emphasize ethnic, national and religious distinctiveness may create eddies and whirlpools where differing currents can mix and clash. At the opposite extreme from the currents of certainty are the undertows, riptides and storm surges that batter our conventional expectations, leaving us only with the wisdom to expect surprises. National boundaries that had seemed immutable for decades have been swept away in a matter of months.[24]

It is clear that the challenges that confront the architect of today require a higher degree of global awareness than in the past, as travel from one country to another, communications, and technology transform the world into a much smaller place.

However, the essential principles of human habitation and sound architecture remain unchanged. And fundamental human needs change slowly, if at all.

Toward Sustainability

When first published in 1948, this book was predicated on the assumption that wise use of energy is basic to good design. However, energy conservation per se was then a minor consideration in the text. This remained true in the revision published in 1972, immediately preceding the energy crisis. That was a reflection of the times; with heating oil retailing at 11 cents per gallon, energy shortages seemed hypothetical at best. This situation is reversed today; the conservation of energy is a central concern for many serious architectural theoreticians, including such specialized groups as the green architects.

For historic preservationists, their concern with energy conservation is admittedly coincidental. In the past, many reasons have been advanced for the preservation of old buildings, but the conservation of energy has not commonly been among them, historical association or esthetic significance being the most usual.[1] Obviously, the energy embodied in any artifact is conserved when the decision is made to preserve it and put it to new or extended use rather than to throw it on the junk pile. If our attitude toward this conventional behavior is now changing this is due, among other things, to our new capacity to quantify the actual amount of energy embodied in any manmade artifact and to express that value in objective terms — that is, British thermal units (Btus). This capacity is due to the appearance of the computer, with its fantastic ability to complete complex calculations in a fraction of a second — operations that might have taken days, weeks, or even months for the old mathematician.

Thus we can compute the amount of energy that goes into the making of a brick, a brick wall, or a brick house, tracing the operation from the clay pit and cement mill right down to the last stroke of trowel and mortar. Because these energy inputs are expressed in Btus rather than dollars and cents, they are absolute, not relative, values.* This new ability to quantify the energy in manmade artifacts gives us an awesome tool for establishing new attitudes toward evaluating the built world.

Consider the potential. There are 4.8 million commercial buildings now standing in the United States. They contain 67.9 billion square feet of floor area,[2] and many of these buildings are relatively short-lived. If this space was on one floor, it would cover about 75 percent of the continental United States! Not only the embodied energy but the enormous investment in resources that so-called obsolete buildings represent offers architects an opportunity of staggering proportions.

Embodied energy computations permit great refinement in the contemporary design and construction process. For example, we know that the production of aluminum in structural shapes is much more energy-intensive than that of steel, even though the manufacturers have managed to market it so that, pricewise, aluminum is competitive with comparable structural steel sections. Thus, in competitive bidding on standard construction that can be satisfied by either material, the dollar cost of aluminum may bottom out as equal to that of steel, even though the embodied energy content of the aluminum members may run from 30 to 35 percent higher than that of the steel.

Of course, historic buildings will continue to be preserved irrespective of how many Btus they happen to embody. But this method of assessing the energy content of old buildings may serve to increase the number of them deemed worthy of preservation, whether historic or not.

Embodied energy estimates summarize the total energy expended, animal and mechanical, during the life cycle of the product, including the energy to run the various processes and transport the raw and intermediate materials as well as the final product. These estimates also include the inherent energy of the natural resource, or its energy value if it were used as a fuel source rather than as a raw material (e.g., when petroleum, natural gas, or coal is used for chemical production). Energy is but one input that is considered; demand for material resources is another.

A third component might be investment in labor. This is especially significant in a culture like the American, where raw materials have always been abundant and labor scarce. This historic condition seemed to generations of Americans to lead inevitably to the conclusion that the conservation of an old building was inherently foolish—hence the motto, "It's cheaper to tear it down and start over." Complete building renovations are likened to open heart surgery in requiring careful dismantling and reconstruction techniques typically foreign to demolition contractors, implying higher labor costs.

---

*   To keep such calculation within manageable proportions, we must obviously trace the energy investment in the individual brick no further back in time than its production in the clay pit and kiln, as each of these facilities represents in turn other investments in energy, ultimately going back to the dawn of history.

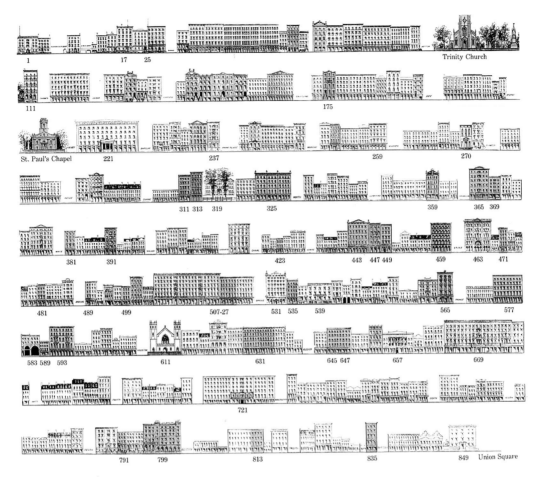

Figure 11–1 / From the base of Broadway in New York City to Union Square, sixty buildings from 1865 were still standing in 1990, as indicating by those shaded. The west side is depicted here, along with the addresses of the survivors. In some cases longevity has had less to do with a preservation ethos than with narrow lots that are viewed as uninviting to new development.

Many of the grand buildings constructed near the end of the nineteenth century were rudely treated by history. Some, like Frank Lloyd Wright's Larkin Building in Buffalo, were demolished. Others continue their existence in our great older cities, but are shabbily maintained and often the site of sweatshops and other marginal occupancies.

And then there are the lucky buildings—those that, after falling into disrepair, experience a renewal and regain their prominence. One such building is the former Schermerhorn Building on lower Broadway in New York City, now the headquarters of the National Audubon Society. This eight-story building, which opened as a fashionable department store in 1891, is a classic example of Romanesque Revival architecture (Fig. 11–2). When the Schermerhorn Building was purchased in 1990, the $10 million price tag was primarily for the land. Apparently, the conventional wisdom in real estate was that

Figure 11–2 / The Schermerhorn Building was designed in 1891 by architect George Browne Post, who also designed the New York Stock Exchange and the Williamsburgh Savings Bank in Brooklyn. Left: The exterior view is distinguished by soaring arches and a cornice that features a series of grimacing terra-cotta gargoyle masks. Right: Interior view of skylit top-floor reception area of National Audubon Society offices.

the building itself lacked value and that if a building on that site were to thrive (as had the Schermerhorn Building in earlier days), it would be a modern one. Perhaps that would have been true if other forms of conventional wisdom were applied during the building's restoration. Fortunately, they were not.

After many years of underutilization, and during its hundredth year, the building was purchased by the National Audubon Society to serve as its new headquarters. It provided an ideal site for the Society to demonstrate its environmental commitment and leadership. After all, it was originally built with large operable windows for light and air at a time when fluorescent lights and modern air-conditioning had not yet been invented. It was built before architects, along with most of our society, became addicted to technology and the notion that mechanical and artificial environments are superior to the natural atmospheric conditions with which we are blessed. All of the basic functions of a modern office were met. Most fundamentally, floor space was adequate, and the environmental

Table 11–1 / *Approximate Amounts of Embodied Energy in Various Building Materials (Btu/lb unless otherwise indicated)*

steel framing	19,000
wood framing	92,000 Btu/ft^3 or 30,000 Btu/8 ft. 2 x 4
fired clay brick	4,000 (or 14,000 Btu/brick)
concrete masonry	700–1,000
mortar in portland cement	2,400–4,000
Ready–Mix concrete	1,100,000–2,600,000 Btu/yd^3
glued laminated timber	6,000 (or 160,000 Btu/ft^3)
self-sealing asphalt shingles	30,000 Btu/ft^2
flat glass	6,800–7,500
polycarbonate glazing	68,000
gypsum board	3,000 Btu/ft^2
ceramic tile	25,000 Btu/ft^2
linoleum flooring	7,500
vinyl flooring	23,000–28,000
vinyl composition tile	6,000
nylon carpet	64,000
interior oil-based paint	1,000 Btu/ft^2
2-inch (Schedule M) copper pipe	32,000 Btu/ft

This table contains rounded data extracted from the AIA's *Environmental Resource Guide* (ERG) now published by John Wiley & Sons. It provides embodied energy equivalents for some common construction products.

conditions (thermal, luminous, auditory, etc.) to perform work comfortably, if not ideal in the old building, could readily be brought up to contemporary standards.

The Society decided to seize the opportunity to recycle the building while incorporating concepts of energy efficiency and environmentally responsible design, construction, and operation. The architect chosen for the project was the Croxton Collaborative. This was one of the first prominent examples of a process that incorporated the concepts of embodied energy and the use of "green" building materials (another being the Natural Resources Defense Council building in Washington). It was by no means the last. With time, the roster of successful, sustainable building renovations has multiplied.

The decision to reuse the Schermerhorn Building rather than to demolish it and build a more modern structure in its place saved approximately 9,000 tons of masonry, 300 tons of steel, and 560 tons of concrete (Table 11–1). Materials for the interior were selected based on performance (i.e., energy conservation, reduction of polluting gas emissions, resource conservation, and indoor air quality) and tested against three broad criteria:

1. Is it good for the environment?
2. Is it cost effective?
3. Can it be achieved through methods readily available to everyone?

Under the restoration process, the walls and roof were insulated in excess of code requirements. Window sashes were equipped with heat-mirror glazing that has a thin polyester film suspended within the airspace of conventional double-glazing. Applied to this suspended film is a low emissivity (low-e) coating, which blocks a significant portion of the radiant heat transfer. As a result, during the heating season, the glazing performs better than triple-glazing by reducing heat loss from the building; it thereby permits use of a smaller-capacity heating system. During the cooling season the spectrally selective coating admits a large portion of light in the visual spectrum while blocking out most of the heat over the longer wavelengths. The windows are, of course, openable and thus allow for locally controlled cooling during moderate days from spring to fall.

Lighting is typically the greatest energy-related expense in commercial buildings. An approach combining task and ambient lighting allows for a generally low lighting power density of less than one watt per square foot, yet individuals can raise light levels locally when required for a particular task. The renovation reactivated a fundamental design strategy of the Schermerhorn Building, namely the purposeful use of its large windows and high ceiling heights to bring in natural daylight. As the daylight streams in, automatic controls dim many of the artificial light fixtures. Moreover, the architectural design includes the use of glass partitions to bring daylight through perimeter spaces and into circulation and work areas, providing light and a visual connection with the outdoors.

The investments made in improving the thermal envelope of the building, and in reducing the lighting loads, are returned in several ways. Over time the operating expenses have proven to be far less than for similar office buildings. The reduced loads also facilitated the installation of much smaller and less costly heating and cooling equipment than usual. Gas-fired heating and cooling equipment was employed, avoiding the use of CFCs (or replacement refrigerants, widely used) that are damaging to the ozone layer and are now subject to strict regulation.

Even a recycled structure like the Schermerhorn Building generates a significant amount of waste in the course of restoration. On typical construction projects most of it is simply carted away and landfilled (Fig. 11–3). During the Schermerhorn renovation, concrete, glass, wallboard, bathroom partitions, masonry, roofing felt, and fluorescent tubes containing mercury were separated for recycling.

Construction materials with recycled content were incorporated into the renovation: ceramic floors of recycled glass, drywall from recycled newsprint, and countertops made of recycled plastics. No endangered woods were specified.

To avoid indoor air quality problems, attention was paid to selecting nontoxic building materials and furnishings, including non-CFC-based insulation materials and batt insulation without toxic binders, low volatile organic compound (VOC) water-based paints, and formaldehyde-free carpeting installed over 100 percent jute padding. Many common building materials such as plywood and particleboard (materials that use formaldehyde binders) were not employed and the surfaces of manufactured wood products were sealed with plastic laminate. Similar attention was given to the selection of other finishes and furnishings to minimize offgassing.

Figure 11 – 3 / Increasingly, building demolition projects no longer entail simply scooping up large piles of debris and transporting them to a landfill. Site recycling procedures are becoming standard practice for sustainable building projects. Salvageable scrap metal, brick and concrete, and wood are separated and reclaimed by recycling centers, and mercury is recovered from fluorescent lamp ballasts off-site. Sustainable new buildings are being designed with recyclable, replaceable, or biodegradable components to eliminate future waste. By contrast, many manufactured homes are assembled with adhesives, making it difficult to separate materials into component parts for reuse.

The renovation of the Schermerhorn Building provides a good example of how sensitive, ecologically informed design can be employed in restoring a fine old building to extended useful life. It was not accomplished through rocket science, or the use of technologically advanced materials. Instead, it simply incorporated off-the-shelf products and readily available design principles.

In the five years or so since the building renovation was completed, much progress has been made on a larger front. Markets for recycled materials have greatly expanded, and many manufacturers have introduced low-toxicity products. The EPA is developing guiding principles for federal agencies to support Executive Order 12873, on Federal Acquisition, Recycling, and Waste Prevention, to maximize procurement of recycled content and other environmentally preferable products and services, from small purchases to major acquisitions.

Many architects have learned from the Audubon renovation and environmentally responsible design solutions have increased dramatically in the past several years. For example, features of the planned energy-exporting Environmental Studies Center at Oberlin College include passive solar design, massive walls, a glass membrane, a thermal

Figure 11–4 / Completed in 1996, the Natural Resources Defense Council's 20,000-square-foot office in Washington, D.C., was designed to showcase state-of-the-art environmental and energy-efficient features. One of the more innovative products selected was a wall system, pioneered by Stramit International, made from compressed agricultural waste wheat straw. Although used in a number of applications overseas, NRDC's office was the first application of this technology in a Class I commercial project in the United States.

Figure 11–5 / Model of the Environmental Studies Center, Oberlin College, during design in 1997. William McDonough + Partners, architects. The objectives for the new center included creating a building that would at times be a net energy *exporter* by transferring watts of electrical energy back into the utility grid.

storage cistern, an exterior brise-soleil calibrated to block high summer sun angles, photovoltaic panels for electricity, and a desiccant dehumidification system (Fig. 11–5). The building will have a Living Machine to process sewage waste. Building materials are categorized as either consumables or products of service. Consumables are goods or materials that decompose safely after their use, becoming nutrients for other living organisms. Wooden post-and-beam frame and straw bale insulation are biodegradable consumables. Other building systems, as products of service, are removable for refurbishing or recycling. Flooring consists of carpet squares that can be removed individually and returned directly to the manufacturer for recycling. All materials, finishes, and systems were evaluated on the basis of embodied energy, life-cycle costs, and toxicity.

Sustainability features of the SCJ World Wide Commercial Markets Division Headquarters Building include the integration of daylighting, indirect electric lighting with dimmable ballasts, a raised floor for air and telecommunications distribution, and personal environmental controls and occupancy sensors at each workstation. Energy consumption

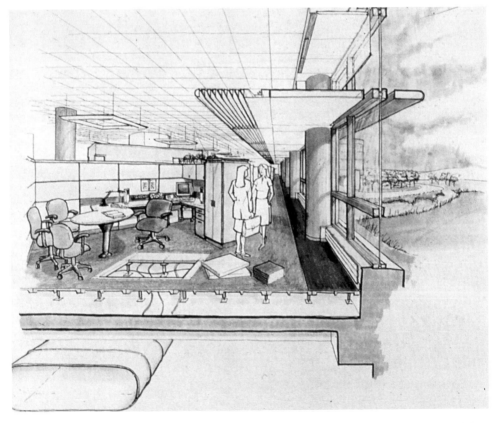

Figure 11–6 / The SCJ World Wide Commercial Markets Division Headquarters Building in Racine, Wisconsin, completed 1997. Design team: HOK Architects, the Zimmerman Design Group, and Fladd Associates. This 250,000-square-foot laboratory and office facility achieved substantial environmental gains and energy savings within a tight construction budget. Photo courtesy of HOK.

Figure 11–7 / C.K. Choi Building for the Institute of Asian Research and the Centres for China, Japan, Korea, India and South Asia, and Southeast Asia Research, University of British Columbia, Vancouver, British Columbia, Canada, completed 1994. Matsuzaki Wright Architects. Top: The building's undulating façade admits cool northern light into the interior space. The curved roofs were designed to receive photovoltaic panels in the future. Bottom: Recovered old-growth timbers from a nearby demolition site were used after the weak end portions were trimmed.

is only 40 percent of that consumed in a building of comparable high-quality new construction, while higher levels of user comfort and control are also achieved (Fig. 11−6).

Four key design goals have been met on the C.K. Choi Building in Vancouver; another very interesting North American project. First, water consumption was substantially reduced — composting waterless toilets are used throughout, saving over 1,500 gallons of potable water daily. Second, attention was given to embodied energy in construction — red-brick cladding and heavy timbers were reclaimed from other locations and used. Third, operating energy was cut — daylighting, daylight dimmer controls, and natural ventilation (operable windows and fresh air vents) were used and fourth, air quality was improved through careful selection of materials, including use of formaldehyde-free millwork, solvent-free finishes, and carpet installation without the use of adhesives (Fig. 11−7).

Renovations like that of the Audubon Society and other energy-efficient projects reduce the growth in demand for purchased electricity for lighting and other uses. Some new projects, like the Oberlin College Environmental Studies Center, seek to be net energy exporters, and others are beginning to use on-site geothermal energy for space heating and cooling. This ultimately results in lowered need for generating power (with its associated damaging effects of carbon dioxide, carbon monoxide, nitrogen oxides, and sulfur dioxide emissions from power plant smokestacks). However, for the foreseeable future, power plants with smokestacks will continue to meet most of the electricity needs of our existing and new buildings.

Gone are the once optimistic expectations for nuclear power due to fundamental economics and vivid recollections of Three Mile Island and Chernobyl (Fig. 11−8). Instead, we as a society face the daunting prospect of dealing with spent nuclear fuel and the remains of nuclear accidents. It was not until early 1997 that 150 tons of damaged fuel rods and other radioactive debris resulting from the 1979 accident at the Three Mile Island reactor in Harrisburg, Pennsylvania, were removed and taken to a temporary underwater storage area in Idaho, to remain until at least 2010, when it is expected that safer, more permanent quarters will be located.* According to Eric Epstein, chairman of the group Three Mile Island Alert, "At this point, it's waste without a return address."[4]

In 1993, nuclear power supplied about 7 percent, or 334,000 megawatts, of the world's electrical demand. In 1995, just thirty-four reactors, representing 27,000 megawatts, remained under construction, the fewest in nearly thirty years, and no government began construction of a new reactor. In the United States it has been estimated that twenty-five reactors will close prematurely by 2003 because of high costs and accelerated aging. New nuclear powerplants are rarely proposed because of the legacy of Three Mile Island, Cher-

---

* The Department of Energy (DOE) states that a permanent nuclear waste storage dump will not be ready until at least 2010, or twelve years later than required by law. DOE has yet to complete feasibility studies for the underground site being planned at Nevada's Yucca Mountain, about one hundred miles from Las Vegas. Thirty-six utility companies and thirty-three states are suing DOE for failing to meet the January 31, 1998, deadline. Currently there are approximately 30,000 tons of spent nuclear fuel in the United States, an amount estimated to double by the year 2010.

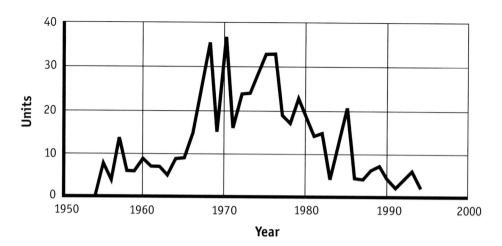

Figure 11–8 / World nuclear reactor construction starts, 1960-94. Reprinted with the permission of The Worldwatch Institute.

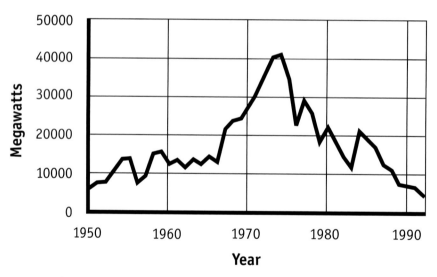

Figure 11–9 / Additions to U.S. generating capacity by utilities and independents, 1950-92. Additions have slowed following the energy crisis of 1973. Independent producers are beginning to contribute measurable capacity, a result of impending deregulation. Reprinted with the permission of The Worldwatch Institute.

Figure 11–10 / Worldwide wind power generating capacity was at 4,880 megawatts in 1995, equivalent to the electricity needed to light 122 million 40-watt lightbulbs, or less than 1 percent of the world's electricity. In the United States, most wind power development supports wind farms—groups of twenty to a hundred turbines; installed capacity from these farms was 1,650 megawatts in 1995.[6] Shown above are a few of the wind turbines installed in the Altamont Pass east of San Francisco.

nobyl, and lesser-known events like the explosive sodium leak from the secondary cooling system of the Monju fast breeder reactor in Japan in December 1995 (see Fig. 11–8).[5]

From 1950 to 1990, worldwide hydroelectric generating capacity increased tenfold, from about 60 to over 600 gigawatts. Although hydropower is often considered less damaging to the environment than nuclear, specific projects such as HydroQuebec's plans to dam major rivers in the James Bay region have spurred major controversy over destruction of river systems and permanent loss of habitat.

Environmentally Preferable Materials

Since 1990, the American Institute of Architects, with support from the U.S. Environmental Protection Agency, has endeavored to provide mainstream architects with tools enabling them to make environmentally informed choices when they select and specify building materials. This effort has resulted in the publication of the *Environmental Resource Guide* (ERG), which is housed in a large three-ring binder to accommodate periodic updates. The ERG represents a Herculean effort to come to terms with all of the rea-

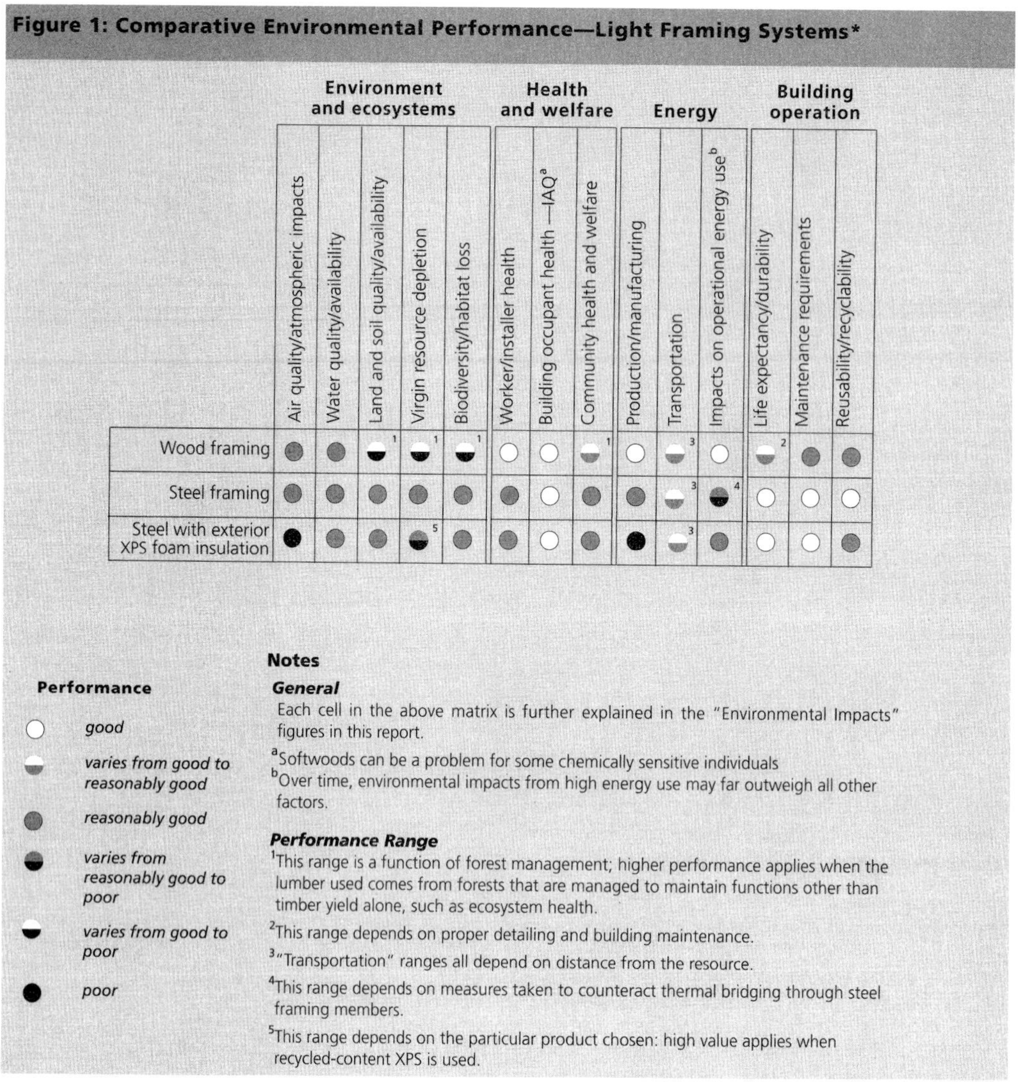

Figure 1: Comparative Environmental Performance—Light Framing Systems*

	Environment and ecosystems					Health and welfare			Energy			Building operation		
	Air quality/atmospheric impacts	Water quality/availability	Land and soil quality/availability	Virgin resource depletion	Biodiversity/habitat loss	Worker/installer health	Building occupant health —IAQ[a]	Community health and welfare	Production/manufacturing	Transportation	Impacts on operational energy use[b]	Life expectancy/durability	Maintenance requirements	Reusability/recyclability
Wood framing	◐	◑	◑[1]	◑[1]	◑[1]	○	○	◑[1]	○	◑[3]	○	◒[2]	◐	◑
Steel framing	◐	◑	◐	◐	◐	◐	○	◐	◐	◒[3]	●[4]	○	○	○
Steel with exterior XPS foam insulation	●	◑	◐	●[5]	◐	◐	○	◐	●	◒[3]	◐	○	○	◑

Performance

○ good

◒ varies from good to reasonably good

◐ reasonably good

◑ varies from reasonably good to poor

◒ varies from good to poor

● poor

Notes

General

Each cell in the above matrix is further explained in the "Environmental Impacts" figures in this report.

[a] Softwoods can be a problem for some chemically sensitive individuals

[b] Over time, environmental impacts from high energy use may far outweigh all other factors.

Performance Range

[1] This range is a function of forest management; higher performance applies when the lumber used comes from forests that are managed to maintain functions other than timber yield alone, such as ecosystem health.

[2] This range depends on proper detailing and building maintenance.

[3] "Transportation" ranges all depend on distance from the resource.

[4] This range depends on measures taken to counteract thermal bridging through steel framing members.

[5] This range depends on the particular product chosen: high value applies when recycled-content XPS is used.

Figure 11–11 / Typical excerpt of information from the American Institute of Architects' *Environmental Resource Guide* (ERG) including the graphical rating scale popularized in Consumer Reports Magazine and an overview of categories analyzed for light framing systems.

sons why such a guide would be impossible to write: conflicting information, data gaps, variability in product formulation, and trade association pressure, to name a few. Each product or process is weighed in terms of its relative environmental burden in energy consumption, waste generation and disposal, and natural resource use and depletion, from raw material acquisition and processing through manufacture, fabrication, and use to final recovery, reuse, recycling, or disposal. Consideration is given to each stage of building including design and construction, use and operation, renovation or demolition. Also included are environmental issues involved in transportation and packaging.[6]

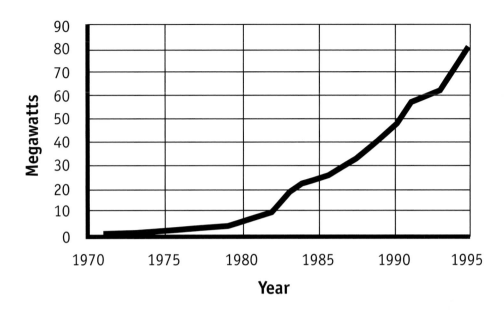

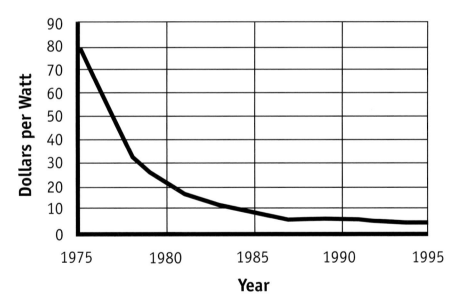

Figure 11-12 / Production and cost of photovoltaic module. The cost to produce photovoltaics (solar cells that generate electricity) continues to fall while their use is rising dramatically. Top: By 1995, the cumulative global output of photovoltaic cells approached 600 megawatts; the United States was the major producer. Bottom: Wholesale factory prices in 1995 were about $4 per watt. Reprinted with permission from The Worldwatch Institute.

A

B

C

D

Figure 11–13 / Photovoltaics (PV). The use of solar cells to produce electricity is growing rapidly, as indicated by the statistics in Fig. 11-12. Of particular importance to the field of architectural design is the evolution of building-integrated photovoltaics (BIPV), where the panels are used to perform additional functions such as being the roof itself, or providing shade for windows below. Significant American building-integrated photovoltaic projects include: (A) Carlisle House, Carlisle, Massachusetts, completed 1980. Solar Design Associates, architect and photovoltaic consultant. The first building in the United States to feature a photovoltaic array integrated into the architectural expression (although not serving as the actual roof). (B) Intercultural Building, Georgetown University, Washington, D.C., completed 1984. Solarex & Hughes, PV design. When built, it was the largest system in the United States, providing 325 Kilowatts. (C) Entrance canopy to the natatorium at the 1996 Olympics in Atlanta, Georgia. Rosser Fabrap, architect; Solar Design Associates, PV design. A case where the economics of the installation are enhanced because the photovoltaic panels serve as the actual roof of the structure. (D) Solarex Manufacturing Plant, located in Frederick, Maryland, completed 1983. Solarex, PV design. One of the leading manufacturers of solar cells created a solar breeder, as energy from PV panels is used in the manufacture of more PV panels.

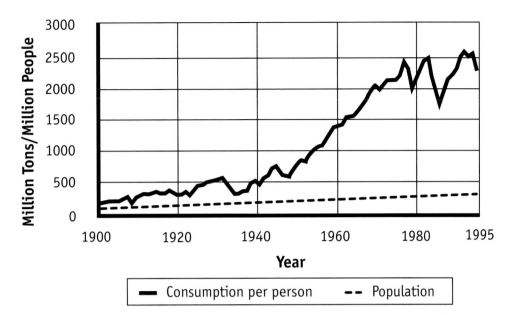

Figure 11–14 / U.S. material consumption and population. In comparison to population growth, the U.S. rate of material consumption rose precipitously from World War II to the early 1970s. That our per-capita resource use has begun to level off is hopeful, yet in the context of historical precedent and the world at large, this plateau is far too high, making us arguably the most wasteful society on earth. Reprinted with permission from The Worldwatch Institute.

AIA's ERG contains a growing roster of case study buildings that incorporate environmental concepts and technologies. Included are descriptions of design goals, strategies, construction issues (e.g., special bidding and negotiation to manage construction waste and use recycled materials), and a profile of performance (energy use, lighting levels, water consumption, and indoor air quality) during building use and operation. Perhaps most instructive are the candid observations of the architects in evaluating the buildings once they are open and occupied, and their descriptions of the difficulties encountered during construction. This is, after all, an emerging practice, requiring many changes and accommodations.

The methodology behind the ERG is life-cycle assessment (LCA), which has most often been used in the environmental/energy arenas to assess cradle-to-grave or cradle-to-cradle impacts of new or existing products. LCA provides a wide tracking perspective useful in accounting for the value of pollution prevention initiatives or product stewardship campaigns.

The streamlined LCA methodology used in AIA's process is qualitative in some aspects; it also considers factors that are important to the client, designer, or builder—that is, how the material performs (its energy efficiency, thermal performance, lighting load), its impact on indoor air quality, its durability and useful life, and its availability both globally (e.g., does its use deplete finite resources?) and locally (e.g., is transportation an issue?).

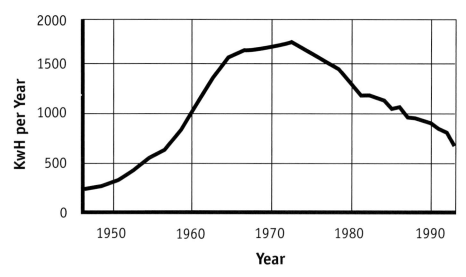

Figure 11–15 / Annual electricity use in average U.S. new refrigerator. Sustainability results from the additive benefit achieved by many seemingly small technological improvements, along with sensible decision making. Without compromising performance, refrigerators have achieved remarkable energy savings since the 1970s. Reprinted with permission from The Worldwatch Institute.

While no doubt an imperfect document, the ERG promises nonetheless to be a powerful agent for change. By transforming what was marginalized to part of the general practice of architecture, multiple benefits may be anticipated, including, one hopes, better, more reasoned architecture.

There are growing signs that this practice is becoming mainstream. For example, the American Society for Testing Materials (ASTM) drafted a Standard Practice for Green Buildings (ASTM Standard E-50.06.1) to address the design, construction, operation, and demolition of commercial buildings that promote environmental and energy efficiency and performance. This is based on ASTM's finding that there is "a national consensus for consideration of energy, natural resource usage and conservation, and occupant health in the design, construction, and operation of buildings."[7]

All of this promising news should be seen in the overall context of our technological society. Our capacity to manipulate our physical environment was enormously extended in recent decades by advances in science and technology. We made huge strides, particularly in the area of energy efficiency. Excellent examples of improvements arising from technological ingenuity include heat-reflecting windows, electronic ballasts for fluorescent lights, and variable-capacity supermarket refrigeration systems. Efficient windows, ballasts, and refrigerators already sold in the United States are projected to save $8.9 billion in fuel cost over their lifetimes![8] Market penetration of energy-efficient refrigerators (see Fig. 11–15) was also enhanced by groups such as the Natural Resources Defense Council that have worked to have them installed in new and renovated housing projects.

Also, since 1996 manufacturers have been producing CFC-free models, with completely new compressors, refrigerants, and insulation.

The growing industrialization of many developing countries presages greater rates of consumerism and resource depletion globally. This is coincident with the introduction of "earth-friendly" products and services in North America and western Europe, whose impact has yet to be determined. One fourth of all new household products introduced in the United States in 1990 were advertised as "ozone-friendly," "biodegradable," "recyclable," "compostable," or something similar. It is healthy to view the rise of green consumerism and green architecture with a healthy measure of skepticism. At worst, they are simply marketing ploys, allowing us to continue business as usual while feeling virtuous about "saving the earth." At best, these initiatives begin to move us as a society toward sustainability, curtailing our use of resources by shifting to high-quality, low-input, durable goods and encouraging us to seek nonmaterial venues for happiness and fulfillment.

And yet, in the midst of our current resolve to build frugally and responsibly, we would do well never to lose sight of rare and truly elegant engineering feats. The Gateway Arch in St. Louis, Missouri, looms above the city and the mighty Mississippi River to a height of 630 feet, an imposing monument to the vision of Thomas Jefferson and the pioneers who settled the western frontier (Fig. 11–16). Its shape is a catenary curve, the form assumed by a freely suspended chain. The lean line and strength of the arch is achieved by a stressed-skin design (similar to aircraft), using double-walled construction with poured concrete and high strength steel rods. The cross section of each leg is designed as an equilateral triangle whose shimmering stainless steel sides are 54 feet wide at the base. Nearly 26,000 tons of concrete was used in the foundation. The entire arch—steel and concrete—weighs an extraordinary 16,678 tons, including 900 tons of 1/4-inch stainless steel on the exterior and 2,200 tons of 3/8-inch carbon steel plate for the interior walls. A squandering of resources? Or a soaring cultural achievement?

Advances in technology have not been uniformly benign, in our favor. Partly this is due to the deliberate abuse of the new technologies, their application to malign ends—as in the application of the mastery of nuclear fission to the production of the atomic bomb. More often, it is due to sheer ignorance of the long-range consequences of the new processes—as in the cumulative effect of the burning of fossil fuels upon the atmospheric envelope that makes the world habitable. Our resolve to significantly minimize future damage is still being tested, although the means to do so are growing in sophistication daily. As William McDonough remarked:

[W]e live in a profound historical moment. We have created a culture of waste which cannot be sustained. Our situation is daunting and alarming, but we view it above all as an opportunity to develop models embodying higher goals and principles, including those of justice and ecological stability.[9]

Of course, the cataclysmic effects of the abuses of science and technology have not gone unobserved, nor have remedies failed to be prescribed for their cure. But each of these remedies reveals its own inherent limitations—that is, the special interests of its

Figure 11–16 / The Gateway Arch in St. Louis, Missouri, Eero Saarinen, architect. Completed 1965. Where do engineering feats such as this fit in the realm of environmental responsibility?

proponents: architects, planners, developers, politicians, etc. Actually, the people least heard from, the people least queried as to their environmental needs, are the tenants of the earth and its buildings. Yet it is clearly from their vantage point that the crisis in architecture and planning — indeed, in environmental management itself — can be most fruitfully analyzed. Then we can see people in the light of modern knowledge of their actual experiential situation — not in the Renaissance concept as the masters of creation, but in the more modest but more noble concept as once the highest form of life on the planet whose existence is umbilically tied to its lowest forms.

Prospects for the Democratic Esthetic

The pace of technological change that is being experienced in architecture is worldwide and profound, but it is fundamentally no different from that which invests other fields of activity, such as medicine or agriculture or art. Originally the pace seemed more rapid in the United States than elsewhere, but this is largely due to the historic process we loosely term the scientific technological revolution flowering here earlier and more extensively than elsewhere. But currently, on the international front, initiatives in other countries—particularly in Europe and Scandinavia—bear watching.

Quite literally, in both its scope and its profundity, the need to properly utilize technology is without historic precedent, as was noted in the earlier edition of this book, when such tumult was first apparent. For that very reason it will not be resolved by traditional means. New tools will be required, and it is the fundamental thesis of this book that these tools must be theoretical—in the fullest sense of the word, philosophical. Architecture today, no less than cosmology, needs a unified theory, a system of postulates that fully explicates the principles that cause, control, or explain facts and events.

Clearly, no such system is in common use today. We have, instead, a profession that cultivates technological perfectionists (at best) or technicians (at worst) focused on limited aspects of the profession in order to keep pace with short-term demands. With the need never greater, there are fewer and fewer truly knowledgeable generalists capable of integrating principles from many fields. In order to create buildings and communities that are a delight to inhabit, we need intelligent design. Nowhere is evidence of this more obvious than in the unyielding sprawl of suburbia beyond our major cities, while large portions of our core cities continue to lie abandoned and ignored.

The evolution of esthetic standards in American architecture over the nearly four centuries of its history can be understood only when seen in relation to the underlying technical, economic, and cultural forces that conditioned their development. *American Building: The Historical Forces That Shape It*, published in 1972, traced the main lines of development of these forces, indicating how they interacted to produce the significant stylistic patterns of the nation's architectural history. From such a survey, we are able to see esthetic standards as the end result of an enormously complex social process.

In this edition we studied in some detail the experiential relationships between human beings and their environment. We concentrated upon the material aspects of these relationships because this is most urgently required. But this by no means implies that the esthetic experience is negligible. On the contrary, as was pointed out in the opening chapter of this book, esthetic judgment constitutes the quintessential level of human consciousness. Thus, it is obvious that a building can meet all objective criteria of physical performance and still be esthetically unsatisfactory to a given person or group of persons. It is likewise apparent that a building can be hopelessly obsolete when judged by such criteria and yet be esthetically satisfactory to many people. This is merely another way of saying that, to be genuinely effective, a building must conform to esthetic as well as physiological standards of performance.

To formulate these esthetic standards we are forced to consider a range of social, cultural, and ideological phenomena. We are forced to examine not building but humanity. The whole tradition of architectural criticism in this country, like criticism in other fields, is permeated with metaphysical abstraction. Consistently the attempt was made to divorce esthetics from life, to emphasize only its metaphysical aspects. This tradition led to a paradox: while consistently overemphasizing the importance of beauty in architecture, it was stubbornly insisted at the same time that beauty was not and could not be subject to an orderly, scientific investigation. On one hand we were told that a thing of beauty is a joy forever, on the other that beauty lies in the eye of the beholder. According to dicta like these, beauty is simultaneously a property of (1) the object and (2) the beholder. Yet the whole history of art exists to prove both propositions fallacies.

Most art forms once considered beautiful have outlived that prestige, to fall ultimately into disuse and obliquity, while disagreement in any mixed group as to the esthetic value of a given object is axiomatic.

Culture, Class, and the Esthetic Process

The esthetic process in architecture must be discussed at two levels: the reaction of the individual and the standard of the group. The reaction is not a property of either the individual or the building but of the relationship between the two. As a process, it is the result of the individual's intricate psychological and physiological response to external stimuli. It varies with objective circumstances—whether the individual is hot or cold, rested or tired, hungry or well fed. Within these physiological restraints, the individual's evaluation of the reaction—the sense of satisfaction (beauty) or dissatisfaction (ugliness)—is largely conditioned by social and cultural background. Agreement between individuals as to the esthetic merit of a given building is therefore largely a matter of similar social and cultural background. From this it follows that esthetic standards are expressions of social agreement, of a common outlook or attitude toward this particular aspect of human experience. These standards vary from one period to another, and in any given period they may vary somewhat between this class and that, although the relation between the popular taste and the dominant high style is intimate. The folk arts echo the idiom of the fine arts. The latter are, in turn, the distilled expression of the outlook, ambitions, and prejudices of the dominant social classes of the period.

The process is firmly rooted in social reality and operates in American architecture as in every other phase of American life. Yet in architecture the problem is complicated by special factors that prevent a mechanical comparison between buildings and other art forms or artifacts. The field as a whole is lethargic in responding to changes in esthetic standards. Because buildings are large, expensive, and durable things, the field at any given time shows stratum upon stratum of conflicting styles. Their sheer physical persistence is reflected in subsequent standards, so that both high style and popular taste are full of echoes and repercussions of the past, which, in any other medium, would have long since died away.

It is this confusion of cause and effect that has troubled every critic since Ruskin. The esthetic standards of architecture, when measured against the great periods of the past, are demonstrably low. What caused this? How can the process be reversed? In its most familiar form the problem was reduced to a hen-and-egg conundrum: which came first— bad design or popular taste that sinks to the lowest common denominator? As the discussion is almost exclusively the property of specialists in esthetics—architects, editors, and critics—it is perhaps not surprising to find that the verdict is against the people. Low popular taste is responsible for bad building design. Yet the question is actually meaningless, for it ignores both the constant interaction between popular taste and high style and their joint subordination to the exigencies of our society as a whole.

Under handicraft methods of production for use there is no such thing as bad taste; popular standards cannot be corrupted or debased. Modern scholarship established this beyond question, both in the folk arts of preindustrial Western civilization and in the great primitive cultures of Africa, Asia, and the South Seas that continue to some extent even today. This is not due to any moral or artistic superiority but rather to the simple fact that, in such societies, esthetic standards are constantly disciplined by the production method itself. Here design is so intimately linked to execution as to make any divergence between the two most difficult. Designer, producer, and consumer are one and the same person. There is consequently neither much incentive nor much opportunity for adulteration of workmanship or design. It would, of course, be absurd to hold that even in primitive cultures every individual is able to make every item he or she needs, or that everyone is equally skilled or gifted in making them. Even here there is specialization. Yet all members of the community remain close to actual production, can from their own experience judge what the craftspeople or artists are trying to do and how well they succeed in doing it. This creates a situation in which the average level of esthetic judgment is extraordinarily high — a fruitful environment for both artist and consumer. It also makes possible the striking unity of primitive art wherein there is no qualitative difference between the design of a simple wooden bowl and an important ceremonial canoe. It creates a situation in which popular taste and high style are one and the same.

Much the same forces operated to create the folk arts of precapitalist, preindustrial Europe and America. Here too handicraft production, despite a relatively high degree of specialization, involved a large part of the community in the actual work of design and fabrication of buildings and artifacts. Here, too, was production for use, with its inherent resistance to adulteration of workmanship and corruption of design. This folk art coexisted with the high style of the ruling classes, to which it loaned and from which it borrowed liberally. Despite this continuous interaction, however, folk art preserved a large measure of independence. It was slow to respond to the abrupt changes of upper-class taste. Indeed, until production relations were altered by the capitalists, it could not change. As a result, the folk arts were expressions of popular taste of an uncommonly high average level. They may never have reached the pinnacles of achievement of the high styles, but they always avoided their disastrous collapses. It is this quality that, beginning with Ruskin and Morris and continuing to the present day, holds such fascination for modern artists and architects. They might, like Ruskin, fail to understand the material conditions that produced these esthetic standards. They might have romantic ideas as to how such conditions can be recreated. But they recognize that until the nineteenth century popular taste always proved itself sound.

Under modern industrial capitalism, this relationship was disrupted. The design process was separated from that of fabrication. It was put into the hands of a small group of specialists who, by the same token, were isolated from the work and the workers. Because production is no longer for use, the entire production process is subjected to the remorseless pressure of the profit motive. This makes possible an unprecedented advance in technical standards and increases in productivity. At the same time, however, it introduces the motive and the opportunity for deterioration — adulteration in workmanship and materials at the level of fabrication, artificiality, irresponsibility, and vulgarity at the level of design.

The paradox hinges upon the new position of the common individual under the new system. For taste is the product of experience, both as consumer and producer. The good taste the individual once displayed in what was bought under earlier systems of handicraft production was of a piece with the good sense required in what was made; indeed, the two are only different aspects of the same thing, as is clear enough in folk art. Here the confrontation of the consumer with the producer is of the most direct sort. Folk artists work by themselves and for themselves, on artifacts of their own design, intended for their own and their neighbors' use.

The industrial system of serial production acts in precisely contrary fashion: the industrial worker labors with others, for others, on artifacts designed by professionals with whom there is no contact, for ultimate uses of which he or she often has no comprehension. Divided and particular production on the assembly line robs the work of both significance and intelligibility for the individual worker placed somewhere along it. The good sense that is the basis of good taste cannot derive, as it always had in the past, from the world of work. And any specialized knowledge or skills have little application to the act of consuming, in which the worker as consumer is forced to judge the values of artifacts of increasing complexity. The result for ordinary people is a steadily declining capacity for mature and satisfying esthetic decisions.

The Changed Relationship Between Architect and Client

The consequences of this historic process can be clearly seen in the history of American architecture. For the first two hundred years or so, American architects and builders were guided by a fairly effective body of theoretical postulates, however unsophisticated or unformulated they often were. These principles derived in about equal parts, as shown in *American Building: The Historical Forces That Shaped It*, from folk experience and formal scholarly knowledge. They began to collapse only in the nineteenth century, under rapidly developing science and technology, on one hand, and the unprecedented proliferation of new social, economic, and industrial processes and institutions on the other. At any time prior to the death of Thomas Jefferson in 1826, both the architect and the building would have been disciplined, structured, held in shape, by a clear and comprehensible reference frame of needs and means. The size, shape, and contours of this reference frame were established by two sets of complementary but opposing forces, endogenous and exogenous.

The endogenous forces, those representing the client's minimal requirements, pressed outward from the center. These minimums varied with culture and class. The ethical standards and ceremonial apparatus of the Roman emperor required quite different architectural accommodations than those of President Jefferson, just as Jefferson's minimal requirements as president were quite different from those of his slaves at Monticello. Both emperor and president had at their disposal the most advanced theories and technical means afforded by their respective societies, and they employed them architecturally to win optimal amenity, not mere physical survival.

Nevertheless, objective conditions sharply restricted the ambitions of even the mightiest, establishing the limits of satiety and survival alike. The exogenous, inward-pressing forces were six in number: (1) the impact of the climate, (2) a limited range of building materials, (3) a lack of mechanical prime movers, (4) limited means of transport and communication, (5) a slow rate of cultural change and technical invention, and (6) a well-informed but extremely conservative clientele.

Modern science and technology disrupted this balance of forces by reducing the magnitude of exogenous forces and increasing man's capacity for environmental manipulation. Paradoxically, in most new buildings no new equilibrium has appeared. Despite the many inroads made throughout the twentieth century, our society continues to produce millions of buildings and thousands of communities that fall below optimal standards of efficiency, health, and safety.

By contrast, Preindustrial building developed with a strictly balanced set of forces, endogenous and exogenous. As a life-support system, it could not drop below fixed experiential thresholds. It did not often reach optimal levels of amenity, but it did produce furnishings, buildings, and communities of great esthetic consistency.

The formal consequences of such an equilibrium of forces are obvious in the buildings of both folk and primitive cultures. Under such circumstances, the architect's margin of error was sharply curtailed; personal idiosyncrasy was disciplined by external limits upon freedom of action, and the possible solutions to any given problem were restricted in range and number. Under such preindustrial conditions, an architect like Jefferson could encompass both the poetic and the practical requirements of the day by employing the formal and folk knowledge of the times. Jefferson designed both the curriculum and the campus of his beloved university and then moved on to supervise the making of the bricks and nails required to build it. Concept and campus display an elegance and balance, in both formal and functional terms, that we must still admire today.

But the balance of forces that established the reference frame of a Charlottesville has been radically altered by the intervention of science and technology. Either by removing or by greatly reducing the magnitude of the inward-pressing limitations upon building, a complementary expansion of the outward-pressing demands of appetite and ambition has been encouraged. Technology has enormously extended our capacity to manipulate the natural environment, so that habitable structures anywhere become a reality, not only in the Arctic but in outer space as well. This has been accomplished by an unparalleled fluorescence of new methods and materials, of new prime movers and sources of energy. The cultural expression of all this has been an accelerated rate of invention whose ultimate consequences none can predict but whose negative impact upon the esthetic standards and inherent good sense of both architects and their clients is all too clear to see.

The beginnings of this crisis in architectural esthetics did not appear—indeed, *could not* appear—until around the end of the nineteenth century. It was not until industrialization had successfully infiltrated the major fields of production that design began to be removed from the hands of millions of anonymous, independent artisans and put into the control of a handful of specialized designers. Whatever else it accomplished, this process of centralization automatically isolated design from the healthy democratic base of popular participation. A new esthetic idiom began to emerge, leaving its subtle imprint upon every article of daily use—art forms, buildings, clothes, china, furniture, and trains. It was the idiom of the Victorian mill and factory. Whether it was better or worse than its predecessors might have been subject to some argument, but there was no need for confusion as to the responsibility for the change. It was the Victorian entrepreneur, not the consumer, who brought it about.

Under this new system, the entrepreneur took over some of the functions of the earlier consumer—those of ordering and paying for production. The independent master artisan became a professional designer whose orders came from a faceless management, not a specific customer. And the customer, who could only accept or reject the finished product, was reduced to the truncated function of simple consumption. Both architect and client suffered under this new arrangement.

As a result, the nation's physical plant, whether analyzed from a functional or from an esthetic point of view, falls grotesquely short of national capacities. This is in large part due to the inability of the building consumer to understand or implement a range of demands, requirements and expectations. The result of the architect's isolation from the real client has been the increasing prevalence of the abstract, the formal, and the platitudinous in architectural and urban design. This changed relationship is not only expressed in the architect's personal life, whose fortunate position in J. K. Galbraith's economy of abundance insulates him or her against the squalor and discomfort of Michael Harrington's culture of poverty. It is also expressed in subtle but definite changes in cultural orientation.

It is true, of course, that from the very nature of the work, the architect has always stood closer to the upper classes than to the common person, although the profession today increasingly draws from all classes and cultures and both sexes. For ordinary people the architect's services are always much more rare and much less imperatively required than those of lawyer or doctor. Nevertheless, the tradition of the socially conscious, intellectually committed architect has a long history in the United States. One might say that the leading spokespersons of the profession in each generation have been of this persuasion: Jefferson, Latrobe, Greenough; Sullivan, Wright, Gropius, Neutra. This tradition reached its apex during the days of the Great Depression and the New Deal, when unemployment in normal channels forced approximately three quarters of the architectural and engineering professions into government-sponsored projects of one sort or another. This switch from the private to the social client gave architects an exhilarating sense of identification with society. It shifted their attention, if not allegiance, toward social architecture.

To a certain extent the sustained afterglow of this Rooseveltian liberalism still diffuses the profession, giving a more liberal aspect to its posture, perhaps, than to those of the American Medical Association or the American Bar Association. But increasingly, since the 1950s, the profession returned to "normal." Architects were reabsorbed into the world of private enterprise. Some of them became leaders in the world of big business. Ironically, this general prosperity led, in some quarters, to the impoverishment of intellectual speculation and invention. And yet, the utopian element in architectural thinking is alive and well in other quarters, spurred largely by the environmental movement and a growing frustration with business as usual. The people whose polemics (whether in print or in stone) once galvanized the Western world—Wright, Mies van der Rohe, Le Corbusier, and Gropius—are gone. Few younger people aspire to their prophetic role, as they struggle to simply maintain a foothold in the profession of their choice. The dominant attitude is one of complacent laissez-faire whose esthetic expression is a genial eclecticism. The result is a body of work as antipopular and aristocratic in its general impact as anything ordered by Frederick the Great or Louis XIV.

This aristocratic esthetic of many of our leading architects is evident in the most prestigious buildings of the day, such as those in Manhattan that come immediately to mind: the AT&T Building, the Trump Tower, and even the new "green" skyscraper (if that is not an oxymoron) at 4 Times Square. It is dismayingly apparent in our ostentatious "gated" suburban communities, with their pretentious, architecturally eclectic "mansions" and three-car garages. The urban redevelopment schemes that convulsed the centers of many American cities, although nominally aimed at radically altering the physical appearance of the central city, almost without exception ended by evicting the poor, the disadvantaged, the ethnic minorities. The poorer workers, the racial minorities, the small merchants and tradespeople, were replaced with upper-middle-income groups. The result is some of the most candid class planning since Baron Haussmann remade central Paris. Designed in the self-styled modernist manner, these projects are often handsome from a purely formal point of view. But this should not blind us to the fact that this particular mode of expression has been largely emptied of its original functional-democratic connotations. Its main components were formulated decades ago, under conditions quite different from those which obtain today. The spacious and humane character of New Deal architectural programs is today being put to quite other uses. Whatever one's personal estimate of this transformation of the modernist esthetic, it remains the outward evidence of an internal involution: the abdication by the profession of its claim to be the architect of the whole people, to become instead the agent and spokesperson for the elite.

How the profession will extricate itself from this cul-de-sac is a knotty problem, though it is evident that a committed minority are beginning to pave the way. Because of its default, the profession as a whole probably faces that sort of socialization that has overtaken the medical profession, and for many of the same reasons; just as millions of Americans lack good medical care, so are the same millions deprived of good housing, good schools, good hospitals. The satisfaction of this need undoubtedly implies the increased intervention of governmental agencies, and this probably implies an increase in the bureaucratic architecture so abhorred by the profession. But—aside from the fact that big private firms are quite as bureaucratic as any counterpart in local or national agencies of government—this socialization of architecture will not, of itself, guarantee qualitatively superior architecture and town planning. Only a greatly improved system of education and training, together with a new kind of functional rapport with the building consumer, can accomplish this goal.

Training the Architects of the Twenty-first Century

The historical origins of architectural education lie much closer to engineering and dentistry than to those of medicine and law. This is because competence in the former could be acquired through apprenticeship exclusively, whereas theoretical training was of critical importance to the latter. Thus, until the opening of the twentieth century, the vast majority of building was in the hands of those whose origins were closer to the craftsmanship of millwright and mason than to academic scholarship. Professional education at the university level has been a commonplace requirement in medicine and law for centuries. But the first professional school of architecture in the United States was established only in 1865, at the Massachusetts Institute of Technology. The American Institute of Architects itself had been formed only eight years before in an effort to establish professional standards of training and competence. It was decades before the various state governments, acting under the public health and welfare clause of the Constitution, could be persuaded to pass legislation establishing a system of examination and licensing procedures (Illinois was the first in 1897, Vermont the last in 1951). Only in the last century, then, has the training of architects been put upon an equal academic footing with the older professions.

But preindustrial architecture had one anomaly that it shared with no other profession: the presence in its midst of the amateur and the connoisseur. (Both terms, in those days, had the favorable connotation of a disinterested love of the field.) From the Renaissance onward, the architect's patron often crossed the line to become, in actuality, an architect too. But whether these amateurs remained passionate and tireless patrons, like Horace Walpole or the Earl of Burlington (or, more recently, Prince Charles of the United Kingdom) or became actual designers of buildings, like Jefferson at Charlottesville, they established the other polarity of preindustrial architecture. As opposed to the direct economic incentive of the gifted artisan, they entered the arena from many other lines of approach: from an enthusiasm for literature, especially the classics; from antiquarianism; from political commitments (Jefferson saw the Roman basilica as the only fit container for his new Republic); even from religious conviction (the Gothic Revival was above all the vehicle for nineteenth-century religiosity).

In view, then, of their widely divergent cultural milieus and their disparate motivations, it must be reckoned as extraordinary that these early architects managed to resolve the contradictions between craftsmanship and scholarship, poesy and practicality—in short, the contradictions between the formal and the functional—to the extent they did. Nevertheless, the fundamental tensions remained; in fact, they grew steadily sharper with the rise of industrialism, and they are accurately reflected in the curriculums of our schools today. The effort of the schools to resolve this contradiction has been, generally speaking, to move toward increased emphasis on the academic and technologically advanced. This is the case for increasing dependence on computerized design. But it is always at the expense of the craft elements of the field. From one point of view this is both inevitable and desirable. Modern architectural problems can no more be solved by carpentry than can spacecraft be built by village blacksmiths. However, the shift in training away from craftsmanship is more toward the mastery of computer tools than toward a truly scientific investigation of architecture as a whole.

There can be no denying that the price paid for this new professionalism was high. It played an important role in the extinction of the conventional wisdom of the entire preindustrial field. Few contemporary architects have firsthand knowledge of actual construction methods and techniques. Simultaneously, and by the same process, the craftspeople were robbed of their historic competence and wisdom. What with the factory production of building components and the mechanization of the construction industry itself, there is less and less need for intelligent, well-trained artisans. Indeed, the modern CADD working drawings from the architect's office objectively tend to remove the process from experiential reality, or, at minimum, to blur the lines between what is real and what can be simulated and imagined as real. Project architects are consumed by minutiae as they struggle to create perfect documents. In effect, the architect has become a skilled laborer; the product is not the building but its computer facsimile. More and more, the building process is reduced to one of mere assembly, it implies the headless hand of the assembly line. This disastrous process of impoverishment is then reinforced by the disappearance of the individual patron of architecture and his replacement by faceless consumers who have no real voice in, or control of, the buildings in which they are born, live, and die. Market research informs the developer and guides the design.

Both the incentive to, and the opportunity for, adulteration of material quality and debasement of design appear to increase in direct proportion to the increasing centralization, mechanization, and automation of design. This specialization of the worker and the parallel atomization of the work, this isolation of the policy making from product making, this dwindling of the power and authority of the actual designer—all of these seem to be corollaries of modern production. All of them inhibit the creativity of the worker, whether manual or intellectual. Of the worker is demanded a precocious knowledge of a chosen field while sheer illiteracy is permitted in other fields of knowledge or experience. One sector of the worker's capacities will be enormously developed while the others are permitted to shrink or ossify. The very conditions of modern work act to limit generalized experience, to inhibit spontaneity, to restrict the play of intuition. The result is that esthetic standards, like those in other areas of judgment, are stultified.

Artifacts themselves become increasingly complex, involving a constantly expanding range of processes and materials. Less and less able to encompass the complexity of modern technology, the architect's function is truncated. The designing becomes more and more a process of assemblage, more removed from functional necessity and therefore more susceptible to the pressures of fad and fashion.

Meanwhile, the consumers of the architect's production, the actual inhabitants of the buildings, are removed by this same process from any possibility of firsthand knowledge of what they are buying (or renting). The consumer can only express satisfaction (or dissatisfaction) by buying (or refusing to buy) from among the range of artifacts offered by mass production. In real life, it is difficult for this consumer to refuse for long to buy essentials—a house, a bed, a car. So the consumer is compelled, ultimately, to make a choice from a range of products, some or all of which may be unworthy or unsuitable. In accepting this situation, the consumer largely abdicates power—first a voice in the design process, then capacity for coherent judgment of design. It is true, of course, that this same consumer can sometimes drive a given product off the market by simply refusing to buy it. (The quick demise of the Edsel automobile, produced with such fanfare by the Ford Motor Company decades ago, is one of the most notorious demonstrations of this power; New Coke is another more recent example.) But this is a clumsy and socially extravagant method. Because the consumer can never tell the designer which features are objectionable, the designer cannot profit from the experience. Instead, the rejected model is abandoned and another one — also based on statistical data — is rolled out onto the market in its stead. Only the fantastic fertility of modern technology conceals the fundamental wastefulness of this process. And while it may succeed in meeting our gross material needs, it does so with artifacts whose esthetic quality is ordinarily quite low.

We may, however, be on the threshold of change. Under today's demanding circumstances, a broad educational program in both architectural and environmental design is delivered by programs that have adopted holistic architectural design principles. Many universities now have innovative programs with advocacy for energy efficiency, sustainability, and community-based planning. Indeed, the University of California at Berkeley has developed a "Vital Signs" summer workshop program through which technology professors learn to use diagnostic tools to evaluate how real buildings function (by checking their "vital signs" of temperature, luminous quality, acoustical performance, etc.). The professors then return to their universities and introduce these tools and concepts into the architectural curriculum.

Architectural programs should include both architect and layperson, as no professional field can reach a higher level of competence than that demanded by its clientele. Where the formal education of architects is concerned, their entire curriculum should be infused with a truly scientific (as opposed to a merely technical) approach to environmental and ecological problems. Such enriched and reoriented curriculums should be supplemented by internships in three distinct areas:

1. office experience in architectural firms
2. construction work on actual building projects (e.g., carpentry, masonry, mechanical equipment)
3. staff and maintenance work in functioning institutions (e.g., housing projects, hospitals, schools)

These kinds of experience would help give the young architect a multidimensional grasp of how buildings are actually designed, how they are put together, and how they affect the lives of the people who ultimately inhabit them.

At the same time, the layperson requires a broad program of consumer-oriented education in architecture and environmental design. This should be a structural part of a primary and secondary education, like physical education. While the traditional art history and art appreciation courses for laypeople are useful, they should be considered supplementary to a factual, concrete, and user-oriented curriculum. This should aim at giving the individual a clear understanding of all experiential requirements a human being has, a general concept of what levels of amenity and well-being to expect as a citizen in a democracy, and a grasp of what standards of performance and appearance to demand as a consumer of the world's most advanced technology.

American building as it stands today is far too broad in scope, complex in function, and rapidly changing in both form and material to be easily encompassed by any private set of esthetic standards. It may well be true, as is often charged, that the average American has a low level of taste. But there are historic reasons for this situation, one of them being architects themselves. For it is also true, as we have had occasion to see, that the esthetic standards the architect is advancing are all too often incorrect in the light of experiential reality. In the last analysis, the current dichotomy between esthetic and technique, between high art and popular art, is an expression of deeper conflicts in society itself. To free American building from the contradictions that for the most part continue to stultify it today, building designer and building consumer must join with all Americans of good will to build a sustainable and more environmentally sound society. Thus, perhaps, will they lay the objective basis for an ever increasing flowering, both rich and wide, of a truly democratic esthetic.

Notes

Chapter 1

1. Walter B. Cannon, *Science and Man* (New York: Harcourt Brace, 1942), 290.

2. R.P. Clark and O.G. Edholm, *Man and His Thermal Environment* (London: Edward Arnold, 1985), 135.

3. Edward T. Hall, *The Hidden Dimension* (New York: Doubleday, 1966).

4. George E. Ruff, "Psychological Stress," *Program*, (School of Architecture of Columbia University, spring 1962): 66–79.

5. Philip Solomon, "Sensory Deprivation and Psychological Stress," (lecture at the School of Architecture of Columbia University, November 12, 1963).

6. Woodburn Heron, "The Pathology of Boredom," *Scientific American*, 196 (January 1957): 56.

7. Ibid.

8. Hannah Arendt, *The Human Condition* (New York: Doubleday, 1959).

9. Turpin C. Bannister, ed., *The Architect at Mid-Century: Evaluation and Achievement* (New York: Reinhold, 1954), Table #57, Appendix.

10. Ernst Fischer, *The Necessity of Art* (Baltimore: Penguin Books, 1963), 17.

Chapter 2

1. World Resources Institute, *World Resources: A Guide to the Global Environment—The Urban Environment 1996-97* (New York: Oxford University Press, 1996), 192–193.

2. National Safety Council, *Accident Facts, 1996 Edition* (Itasca, Ill., 1996).

3. Ibid.

4. Ibid.

5. Ibid.

6. "Asthma: New Understanding Can Help You Gain More Control Over Your Symptoms and Lifestyle," *Mayo Clinic Health Letter* (February 1996): 1–8.

7. U.S. Department of Housing and Urban Development, *Guidelines for the Evaluation and Control of Lead-Based Paint Hazards in Housing* (Washington, D.C.: GPO, 1995).

8. Evan J. Ringquist, "Environmental Justice: Normative Concerns and Empirical Evidence" in Norman J. Vig and Michael E. Kraft, *Environmental Policy in the 1990s: Reform or Reaction?* 3rd edition. (Washington D.C.: Congressional Quarterly, 1997), 231–254.

9. World Resources Institute, *World Resources*, 179.

10. Lester Brown, Christopher Flavin and Hal Kane, *Vital Signs 1996: The Trends That Are Shaping Our Future:* A Worldwatch Institute report. (New York: W.W. Norton, 1996), 130.

11. Britten, Brown and Altman, *Certain Characteristics of Urban Housing and their Relation to Illness and Accident* (New York: American Public Health Association, 1941), 178.

12. World Resources Institute, *World Resources*, 180.

13. Al Gore, *Earth in the Balance: Ecology and the Human Spirit* (Boston: Houghton Mifflin, 1992), 150.

14. Linda Ross Raber, "EPA's Air Standards: Pushing Too Far, Too Fast?" *Chemical & Engineering News* (April 14, 1997): 13.

15. Alan Durning, *This Place on Earth: Home and the Practice of Permanence* (Seattle: Sasquatch Books, 1996), 71.

16. Ramin Jaleshgari, "Long Island Asthma Sufferers Question Air Quality," *New York Times*, 24 September 1995, Long Island Weekly Desk, 13LI.

17. Lester R. Brown, *State of the World: 1997* (New York: W.W. Norton, 1997), 47.

18. James Marston Fitch, *American Building: The Forces That Shape It*. (Boston: Houghton Mifflin, 1947); James Marston Fitch, *American Building: The Environmental Forces That Shape It* (Boston: Houghton Mifflin, 1972).

Chapter 3

1. A classic exposition of our relationship with our thermal environment was presented in *Temperature and Human Life*, by C. E. A. Winslow and L. P. Herrington (Princeton, N.J.: Princeton University Press, 1949). Also of particular note, and of more recent vintage, is *Man, Climate and Architecture*, by B. Givoni (New York: Van Nostrand Reinhold, 1981).

2. John M. Kinney, "Energy Metabolism: Heat, Fuel and Life," in Jeejeebhoy, Hill and Owen, *Nutrition and Metabolism in Patient Care* (Philadelphia: W.B. Saunders, 1988), 12.

3. National Safety Council, *Accident Facts, 1996 edition*, Itasca, Ill. National Weather Service, 1996, as cited in. "Hot Spell Gives Cities Chance to Prepare for Sizzlers to Come," *New York Times*, 27 May 1996.

4. Ibid.

5. C. E. A. Winslow and L. Harrington, *Temperature and Human Life* (Princeton, N.J.: Princeton University Press, 1949), 255.

6. Thomas Tredgold, *Principles of Warming and Ventilating Public Buildings* (London: J.Taylor, 1824).

7. U.S. Bureau of the Census. *Current Construction Reports—New Housing: 1995, C25/95-A* (Washington D.C.: U.S. Department of Commerce, 1996).

8. Richard G. Stein, "Architecture and Energy," in *Architectural Forum* (July/August 1973): 38–58.

9. Richard G. Stein, *Architecture and Energy* (Garden City, N.Y.: Anchor Press/Doubleday, 1977).

Chapter 4

1. F. W. Wendt, David B. Slemmons, and Hugo N. Mozingo, "The Organic Nature of Atmospheric Condensation Nuclei," proceedings, National Academy of Sciences, vol. 58, no. 1, 71.

2. William Cookson and Miriam Moffatt, "Asthma: An Epidemic in the Absence of Infection?" *Science*, 275 (January 1997): 41–42.

3. Pam Belluck, "As Asthma Cases Rise, Tough Choices and Lessons," *New York Times*, 29 September 1996, sec. 1, 39.

4. "Asthma: New Understanding Can Help You Gain More Control Over Your Symptoms and Lifestyle," *Mayo Clinic Health Letter* (February 1996): 1–8.

5. Cookson and Moffatt, "Asthma," 41–42.

6. S. Findlay and J. Silberner, "Allergy Warfare," *U.S. News & World Report* (February 20, 1989): 69.

7. "Asthma: New Understanding," 1–8.

8. Cookson and Moffatt, "Asthma," 41–42.

9. Betsy Wade, "Practical Traveler: Tracking Down Disease on Ships," *New York Times*, 14 August 1994, sec. 5, 4.

10. A useful reference on this subject is Joseph Lstiburek and John Carmody, *The Moisture Control Handbook: New Low-Rise Residential Construction* (Oak Ridge, Tenn.: Oak Ridge National Laboratory, 1991).

11. National Institute for Occupational Safety and Health, *Biological Hazards Health Hazard Evaluation: Cleveland Area Homes*, HETA 95–0160–2571, (Washington, D.C.: GPO, 1996).

12. Robyn Meredith, "Infants' Lung Bleeding Traced to Toxic Mold," *New York Times*, 24 January 1997.

13. W. A. Croft, B. B. Jarvis, and C. S. Yatawara, "Airborne Outbreak of Trichothecene Toxicosis," *Atmospheric Environment* 20 (1986): 549–552.

14. J. Kay et. al., *Indoor Air Pollution: Radon, Bioaerosols, and VOC's* (Chelsea, Mich.: Lewis Publishers, 1991).

15. Harriet Burge, "Health Effects of Biological Contaminants," in Richard B. Gammage and Barry A. Berven, eds., *Indoor Air and Human Health* (Boca Raton, Fla.: CRC Lewis Publishers, 1996), 171–178.

16. Kay et. al., *Indoor Air Pollution*.

17. R. Berkow, ed., *The Merck Manual of Diagnosis and Therapy*, 15th ed. (Rahway, N.J.: Merck Sharp & Dohme Research Laboratories, 1987), 171.

18. Ibid, 169.

19. L. Hines et. al., *Indoor Air Quality and Control* (Englewood Cliffs, N.J.: PTR Prentice-Hall, 1993).

20. Lester Brown, Christopher Flavin, and Hal Kane, *Vital Signs 1996: The Trends That Are Shaping Our Future*. A Worldwatch Institute report. (New York: W.W. Norton, 1996).

21. Lester Brown, Christopher Flavin, and Hilary French, *State of the World 1997: A Worldwatch Institute Report on Progress Toward a Sustainable Society*. (New York: W.W. Norton, 1997), 102.

22. Ibid.

23. Ibid.

24. John C. Ryan and Alan Thein Durning, *Stuff: The Secret Lives of Everyday Things* (Seattle: Northwest Environment Watch, 1997), 22.

25. Al Gore, *Earth in the Balance: Ecology and the Human Spirit* (Boston: Houghton Mifflin, 1992), 83.

26. See papers read at Smithsonian Institution Symposium, *Quality of Man's Environment*, Washington, D.C., February 17–19, 1967. Especially relevant: Rene Dubos, "Destructive and Creative Consequences of Adaptation;" Baron Bertrand de Jouvenal and Ian L. McHarg, "Values, Process and Form"; Lew Marx, "Pastoral Ideals and City Troubles."

27. This change in perspective is readily apparent in the first edition of this book, *American Building: The Forces That Shape It* (Boston: Houghton Mifflin, 1947), 219–222.

28. Leonard Greenberg, technical paper no. 65–4, read at the Air Pollution Control Association conference in Toronto, Canada, 1965.

29. James G. Townsend, "Investigation of the Smog Incident in Donora, Pa., and Vicinity," *American Journal of Public Health* 40 (February 1950): 183–189. See also Berton Roueche, "Eleven Blue Men," *New Yorker* 26 (September 30, 1950): 33ff.

30. The epidemiological character of London's smog-related deaths has been investigated at length. See, among others, J. Pemberton and C. Goldberg, *British Medical Journal*. 2 (1954): 567; R. E. Waller and J. Lawther, *British Medical Journal* 2 (1955): 1356; D. J. B. Ashley, *British Journal of Cancer* 21 (1967): 243.

31. Leonard Greenberg, "Air Pollution, Influenza and Mortality in New York City: January–February 1963," *Archives of Environmental Health* 15 (October 1967): 430–438.

32. Study developed jointly by Division of Air Pollution, U.S. Public Health Service, and School of Medicine, Vanderbilt University, Nashville. (Reported by Walter Sullivan, *New York Times*, 12 November 1968.)

33. Gladwyn Hill, "Los Angeles: A Model for the Nation," *New York Times*, 26 September 1966, 36.

34. Ibid.

35. Amory Lovins and L. Hunter Lovins, "Reinventing the Wheels," *Atlantic Monthly* (January 1995): 75.

36. Keith Bradsher, "Start Expanding That Garage for Detroit's Next Generation," *New York Times*, 17 June 1997, 1.

37. U.S. Emissions of Nitrogen Oxides and Sulfur Dioxide, 1940–92: Council on Environmental Quality (Washington, D.C.); U.S. Environmental Protection Agency, Office of Air Quality Planning and Standards, National Air Pollutant Emissions Trends (Research Triangle Park, N.C., 1993).

38. Andrew Wright, "Tall Order in Arizona," *Engineering News Record*, 10 March 1997, 30.

39. Lars O. Hedin and Gene E. Likens, "Atmospheric Dust and Acid Rain," *Scientific American* (December 1996).

40. Odil Tunali, "Global Temperature Sets New Record," in Brown, Flavin, and Kane, *Vital Signs 1996*, 66–67.

41. "26th Environmental Quality Index," *Time*, February/March 1994.

42. Nicholas Kristof, "In Pacific, Growing Fear of Paradise Engulfed," *New York Times*, 2 March 1997, sec. 1, 1.

43. Hilary F. French, "Learning from the Ozone Experience," in Brown, Flavin, and French, *State of the World 1997*, p 151–171.

44. Ibid, 153.

45. Nadav Malin, "The Refrigerant Revolution: Cooling Buildings . . . But Warming the Earth?" *Environmental Building News* 6, no. 2 (February 1997): 1.

46. French, "Learning from the Ozone Experience," 152.

47. "26th Environmental Quality Index."

48. Henry Ford, *Today and Tomorrow*. (Cambridge, Mass.: Productivity Press, 1988), 94. Earlier edition (New York: Doubleday, 1926).

49. "26th Environmental Quality Index."

50. "The Recycling Bottleneck," *Time,* 14 September 1992, 52.

51. Andrew Yatrow, "Company Drops a Plan to Build Brooklyn Plant," *New York Times,* 5 October 1991, A25; Steven Lee Myers, "Judge Rebuffs Opponents of Incinerator in Brooklyn," *New York Times,* 25 December 1992, B2.

52. Todd Wilkinson, "Why Megadump May Be Neighbor of a Desert Park," *Christian Science Monitor,* 25 February 1997, 3.

53. Attributed to Henry David Thoreau.

54. Michael Lieberman, Bernard DiMuro and John Boyd, "Multiple Chemical Sensitivity: An Emerging Area of Law," *Trial* (July 1995): 22.

55. Ibid.

56. K. Kizer, *Using Ultraviolet Radiation and Ventilation to Control Tuberculosis.* (California Department of Health Services Indoor Air Quality Program, Air and Industrial Hygiene Laboratory, and the Tuberculosis Control and Refugee Health Programs Unit, Infectious Disease Branch, Sacramento, CA, 1990); J. Macher, "The Use of Germicidal Lamps to Control Tuberculosis in Healthcare Facilities," *Infection Control and Hospital Epidemiology* 14 no. 12: 681−685.

57. American Society of Heating and Ventilating Engineers, *1966 Guide,* ASHVE, New York, 123ff. See also William F. Wells, "Sanitary Significance of Ventilation," *ASHVE Transactions* 54 (1948), 275−290.

58. Jon Ruth, "Odor Thresholds and Irritation Levels of Several Chemical Substances: A Review," *American Industrial Hygiene Association Journal* 47 (March 1986): A−142−A−151.

59. Richard Axel, " The Molecular Logic of Smell," *Scientific American* (October 1995): 154−159.

60. C. McCord and W. W. Witheridge, *Odors: Physiology and Control* (New York: McGraw-Hill, 1949), 15.

61. Axel, "Molecular Logic of Smell," 154−159.

62. Edward T. Hall, *The Hidden Dimension* (New York: Doubleday, 1966); Roy Bedichek, *The Sense of Smell* (New York: Doubleday, 1960).

63. Hans Kalmus, "The Chemical Senses," *Scientific American* 198 (April 1958): 97ff.

64. J. Enrique Cometto-Muniz and William S. Cain, "Physicochemical Determinants and Functional Properties of the Senses of Irritation and Smell," in Richard Gammage and Barry Berven, eds., *Indoor Air and Human Health* (Boca Raton, Fla.: CRC Lewis Publishers, 1996), 53.

65. Susan C. Knasko, "Human Responses to Ambient Olfactory Stimuli," in Richard Gammage and Barry Berven, eds., *Indoor Air and Human Health* (Boca Raton, Fla.: CRC Lewis Publishers, 1996), 107.

66. McCord and Witheridge, *Odors,* 15.

Chapter 5

1. Hans Blumenfeld, "Integration of Natural and Artificial Lighting," *Architectural Record* 85 (December 1940): 49ff.

2. Edward T. Hall, *The Hidden Dimension,* (New York: Doubleday, 1966), 40.

3. H. Richard Blackwell, "Specifications of Interior Illumination Levels," *Illuminating Engineering,* 54 (June 1959): 320.

4. John Lott Brown, "Afterimages," in Clarence H. Graham, ed., *Vision and Visual Perception,* (New York: Wiley, 1965), 497.

5. H. C. Weston, *Illuminating Engineering Society Transactions*, vol. 18, (London: 1953), 39−66.

6. Samuel H. Bartley and Eloise Chute, *Fatigue and Impairment in Man* (New York: McGraw-Hill, 1947), 34.

7. George C. Brainard and Craig A. Bernecker, "The Effects of Light on Human Physiology and Behavior," proceedings, International Commission on Illumination, vol. 2, 23rd session, 1996.

8. Donald Prowler, *Modern Mansions: Design Ideas for Luxurious Living in Less Space* (Emmaus, Pa.: Rodale Press, 1985), 137.

9. The wealth of literature on the general subject of architectural orientation includes many mathematical and graphic systems for computing sun angles for time, season, latitude, etc., building on the classic work contained in *Solar Control and Shading Devices* by Aladar and Victor Olgyay (Princeton University Press, 1957) and *Design with Climate* by Victor Olgyay (Princeton University Press, 1963).

10. Ralph Knowles, "The Derivation of Surface Responses to Selected Environmental Forces," *California Arts and Architecture* (June 1964): 21−24.

11. Ralph Knowles, "Form and Stability" paper presented to the Building Research Institute, National Academy of Sciences, Washington, D.C., April 23, 1968.

12. H. Richard Blackwell, "Visual Benefits of Polarized Light," *Journal of the American Institute of Architects* 40 (November 1963): 87−92.

13. Ibid.

14. Ibid., 92.

15. Claudia H. Deutsch, "Phillips Concession on Bulbs May Have Political Motive," *New York Times*, 19 June 1997, D6.

16. Ibid.

17. Robert M. Gerard, "Differential Effects of Colored Lights on Psychophysiological Functions" (thesis, University of California, Los Angeles, 1958).

Chapter 6

1. Alice H. Suter, "Hearing Conservation," in E. H. Berger, W. D. Ward, J. C. Morrill, and L. H. Royster, *Noise and Hearing Conservation Manual* (Fairfax, Va.: American Industrial Hygiene Association, 1986), 9.

2. See James J. Gibson, *The Senses Considered as Perceptual Systems* (Boston: Houghton Mifflin, 1966), especially for his clear and cogent description of the process of listening. Also see William A. Yost, *Fundamentals of Hearing: An Introduction* (New York: Holt, Rinehart and Winston, 1985).

3. Paul E. Sabine, "Control of Sound in Buildings," *Architectural Record* 85 (January 1940): 69.

4. Van Bergeijk, Pierce and David, *Waves and the Ear* (New York: Doubleday, 1960), 74.

5. John D. Dougherty and Oliver L. Welsh, "Community Noise and Hearing Loss," *New England Journal of Medicine* 275 (October 6, 1966): 759−765.

6. Lewis Goodfriend, "Sound or Fury: Man's Response to Noise," *Architectural and Engineering News* 7 (April 1965): 43.

7. Cyril Harris ed., *Handbook of Acoustical Measurements and Noise Control* (New York: McGraw-Hill, 1991) 23.1.

8. L. L. Beranek, *Concert and Opera Halls: How They Sound* (Woodbury, N.Y.: Acoustical Society of America, 1996).

9. Richard Cervone, "Subjective and Objective Methods for Evaluating the Acoustical Quality of Buildings for Music" (master's thesis, University of Florida, Gainesville, 1990).

10. R. Johnson. "Reflections on the Acoustical Design of Halls for Music Performance" (V. O. Knudsen Lecture; a paper presented at the 120th meeting of the Acoustical Society of America, San Diego, November 1990).

11. G. W. Siebein, "Acoustics in Buildings" (paper presented at the 127th meeting of the Acoustical Society of America, Cambridge, May 1994); W. Chiang, "Effects of Architectural Parameters on Six Acoustical Measures in Auditoria," (Ph.D. diss., University of Florida, Gainesville, 1994); Beranek, *Concert and Opera Halls*.

12. Siebein, "Acoustics in Buildings."; Chiang, "Effects of Architectural Parameters"; Beranek, *Concert and Opera Halls*.

13. A standard, classical text on the subject is *Acoustical Designing in Architecture* by V. O. Knudsen and Cyril M. Harris (Woodbury, New York: Acoustical Society of America, 1978).

14. A detailed analysis of the acoustical behavior of building materials is found in David Egan, *Architectural Acoustics* (New York: McGraw-Hill, 1985).

15. A fuller theoretical development of this material was originally published in the James Marston Fitch paper, "For the Theatrical Experience, An Architecture of Truth," *Arts in Society* 4, no. 3 (1968): 491–501.

16. H. Kuttruff, *Room Acoustics*, 3rd ed., (London: Elsevier Applied Science, 1991).

17. Gilbert Seldes, "Communication." Columbia University Forum 6 (Fall 1963): 44.

18. Beranek, *Concert and Opera Halls*.

19. John Kidwell, "The Subjective and Objective Comparison of Acoustical Modeling and Full Size Rooms." (master's thesis, University of Florida, Gainesville, 1995).

20. Gary W. Siebein, Martin A. Gold, Mitchell Spolan, and Christopher R. Herr, "Evaluating the Acoustical Qualities of Four Rooms Using Questionnaires" (paper presented at the Acoustical Society of America meeting, Washington D.C., May 1995).

21. Harold C. Schonberg, "Music: Good Acoustics," *New York Times*, 12 September 1966, 34.

22. Ada Louise Huxtable, *New York Times*, 17 September 1966, 17.

23. Schonberg, "Music: Good Acoustics," 36.

24. Ibid.

25. Cyril M. Harris, Oral History Interview, December 21, 1990, conducted by Sharon Zane. Lincoln Center for the Performing Arts, Inc. Funded in part by a grant from the National Endowment for the Humanities.

26. Beranek, *Concert and Opera Halls*.

27. Harold C. Schonberg, "The Verdict on Fisher Hall: Sounds of Unparalleled Clarity," *New York Times*, 24 October 1976.

28. Margaret Barnett, "An Art in Acoustics," *Sky*. (June 1990): 32–40.

29. "New Tool Invented by Bose Corporation Revolutionizes Sound Engineering and Acoustic Design in Public Places," News release of the Bose Corporation, Framingham, Mass., April 27, 1995

30. Anastasia Toufexis, "Now Hear This—If You Can," *Time*, 5 August 1991, 50.

31 Suter, "Hearing Conservation," 5.

32. See the classic by R. D. Berendt, C. B. Burroughs, and G. E. Winger, *A Guide to Airborne, Impact and Structure-Borne Noise in Multifamily Dwellings* (Washington, D.C.: GPO, 1967). Information on comprehensive treatments of noise control problems can also be found in Cyril M. Harris, ed., *Handbook of Acoustical Measurements and Noise Control* (New York: McGraw-Hill, 1991).

33. Jones and Cohen, "Noise as a Health Hazard at Work, in the Community, and in the Home," *Public Health Reports* 83 (July 1968): 535.

34. Dougherty and Welsh, "Community Noise and Hearing Loss," 761.

35. Samuel Rosen et al., College of Physicians and Surgeons, Columbia University, as quoted by *New York Times*, 19 March 1967, 42.

36. Samuel Rosen et al., "Presbycusis Study of a Relatively Noise-Free Population in the Sudan," *Annals of Otology, Rhinology and Laryngology* 71, no. 3: 732−733.

37. Ibid. See also Samuel Rosen et al., "Relation of Hearing Loss to Cardiovascular Disease," *Transactions of the American Academy of Opthamology and Otolaryngology* (May–June 1964): 433−444; and Samuel Rosen and Pekka Olin, "Hearing Loss and Coronary Heart Disease," *Archives of Otolaryngology* 82 (September 1965): 236−243.

38. Rosen et al., "Relation of Hearing Loss," p 436−437.

39. Ibid.

40. Rosen and Olin, "Hearing Loss," 236.

41. R. Skelton, "The Sky's the Limit?" *Amicus Journal* (Summer 1996): 31−35.

42. Mary Ann Grasser and Kerry Moss, "The Sounds of Silence," *Sound and Vibration* 26, no. 2 (February 1992): 24−26.

43. See Andrew D. Hosey and Charles H. Powell, eds., *Industrial Noise: A Guide to Its Evaluation and Control*, and Alexander Cohen, *Location-Design Noise Control of Transportation Systems*, both from U.S. Department of Health, Education and Welfare, Washington, D.C., 1967.

Chapter 7

1. Stewart Brand, *How Buildings Learn: What Happens After They're Built* (New York: Penguin Books, 1994), 13.

2. Francis Duffy, "Measuring Building Performance," Facilities (May 1990): 17; cited in Brand, *How Buildings Learn*, 1994.

3. Raymond G. Studer, "The Dynamics of Behavior-Contingent Physical Systems," in Proceedings of the Symposium on Design Methods (Portsmouth, England: Portsmouth College of Technology, December 1967.

4. James J. Gibson, *The Senses Considered as Perceptual Systems* (Boston: Houghton Mifflin, 1966), 111.

5. Winston Churchill, in 1943, before Parliament requesting that the bomb-damaged parliament building be rebuilt exactly as it was before. In 1924 he had made a similar statement at an awards ceremony for the Architectural Association. "There is no doubt whatever about the influence of architecture and structure upon human character and action. We make our buildings and afterwards they make us. They regulate the course of our lives." Cited in Brand, *How Buildings Learn*, 3.

6. Christopher Alexander, *Notes on the Synthesis of Form* (Cambridge: Harvard University Press, 1964), 3.

7. D. A. Norman, "Designing the Future," *Scientific American*, (September 1995) 197−198.

8. C.E.A. Winslow and L. P. Herrington, *Temperature and Human Life* (Princeton, N.J.: Princeton University Press, 1949).

9. Jane Brody, *Jane Brody's Nutrition Book* (New York: Bantam Books, 1987), 280−283.

10. George Constable, *Fitness, Health and Nutrition: Setting Your Weight—A Complete Program* (Alexandria, Va.: Time-Life Books, 1988), 32−33.

11. C.E.A. Winslow and L. P. Herrington, *Temperature and Human Life*, 178.

12. Samuel H. Bartley and Eloise Chute, *Fatigue and Impairment in Man* (New York: McGraw Hill, 1947), 39.

13. T. Cox and A. Griffiths, "Work-Related Stress: Nature and Assessment," in *Stress and Mistake Making in the Operational Workplace—Hazard Forum*. (London: Institute of Electrical Engineers, 1995).

14. Alvin Toffler and Heidi Toffler, *Creating a New Civilization: The Politics of the Third Wave* (Atlanta: Turner Publishing, 1994), 57.

15. Hans Selye, *The Stress of Life* (New York: McGraw-Hill, 1956).

16. Robert M. Sapolsky, "Stress in the Wild," *Scientific American* (January 1990), 116.

17. J. Horowitz, "Health: Crippled by Computers," *Time*, 12 October 1992, 70.

18. W. Leary, "Feeling Tired and Run Down? It Could Be the Lights," *New York Times*, 8 February 1996, A18. (Also, Brigham and Women's Hospital study as published in February 1996 issue of *Nature*).

19. Tillisch and Walsch, in Samuel H. Bartley and Eloise Chute, *Fatigue and Impairment* 39.

20. P. Adler, "Capitalizing on New Manufacturing Technologies: Current Problems and Emergent Trends in U.S. Industry," in *People and Technology in the Workplace* (Washington D.C.: National Academy Press, 1991), 59–88.

21. Toffler and Toffler, *Creating a New Civilization*.

22. R. Kanter, "Improving the Development, Acceptance and Use of New Technology: Organizational and Interorganizational Challenges," in *People and Technology in the Workplace* (Washington, D.C.: National Academy Press, 1991), 15–56.

23. D.R. Kenshalo, The Skin Senses (Springfield, Ill: Thomas, 1966).

24. The literature, especially in periodical form, is vast and increasing. No brief summary is possible. Even bibliographies quickly become obsolete. An early and influential collection of papers of special significance to contemporaneous architects and planners is *Environmental Psychology: Man and His Physical Setting*, edited by Harold M. Proshansky, William H. Ittelson, and Leanne G. Rivlin (New York: Holt, Rinehart and Winston, 1970).

25. Stanley Schacter et al., *Social Pressures in Informal Groups* (Berkeley: University of California Press, 1962).

26. Hall, *The Hidden Dimension* (New York: Doubleday, 1966).

27. Robert Sommer, "The Ecology of Privacy," *Library Quarterly*, 36 (July 1966): 236.

28. Ibid., 248.

29. Ibid., 244.

30. Humphry Osmond, "The Relationship Between Architect and Psychiatrist," in *Psychiatric Architecture* (Washington, D.C.: American Psychiatric Association, 1949).

31. Humphry Osmond, "The Psychological Dimension of Architectural Space," *Progressive Architecture* 46 (April 1965): 160.

32. Christopher Day, *Places of the Soul: Architecture and Environmental Design as a Healing Art* (San Francisco: HarperCollins, Thorsons, 1995), 174.

33. Alexander Kira, *The Bathroom* (New York: Grosset and Dunlap, 1967), 202.

34. W.T. Dempster, "The Anthropometry of Body Action," *Annals of the New York Academy of Sciences*, 63 (1955), 564–565.

35. "Materials Handling: Paving the Way to Better Ergonomics," *Modern Materials Handling* 50 no. 4 (April 1995) 29.

36. F.J. Kiesler, "On Correalism and Biotechnique: A Definition and Test of a New Approach to Building Design," *Architectural Record* 86 (September 1939), 60–75.

37. Kira, *The Bathroom*, 12.

Chapter 8

1. A lucid exposition of modern structural theory is found in Mario Salvadori and Robert Heller, *Structure in Architecture* (New York: Prentice-Hall, 1964). For information on the origins of structures and the theory of tensile structures and domes see Horst Berger, *Light Structures— Structures of Light* (Boston: Birkhauser Verlag, 1996).

2. John R. Hall, Jr., *U.S. Experience with Sprinklers: Who Has Them? How Well Do They Work?* (Quincy, Mass.: National Fire Protection Association, August 1996), 4.

3. Ibid.

4. Ibid, 17.

5. See "The Golden Leap: The Palace, The Bridge and the Tower" in James Marston Fitch, *American Building: The Historical Forces That Shape It* (Boston: Houghton Mifflin Company, 1966), 140.

6. R. A Sedjo, "Forests: Conflicting Signals," in Ronald Baily, ed., *The True State of the Planet* (New York: Free Press, 1995), 188–190.

7. Cheri Sugal, "Labeling Wood," *Worldwatch* (September/October 1996): 20–34.

8. Horst Berger, *Light Structures—Structures of Light*. (Boston: Birkhauser Verlag, 1996).

Chapter 9

1. E. R. Biel, "Microclimate, Bioclimatology and Notes on Comparable Dynamic Climatology," *American Scientist* 49, no. 3 (1961): 330.

2. Cited by Helmut Landsberg in "Microclimatogy," *Architectural Forum* 86 (March 1947): 115.

3. Abel Wolman, "Metabolism of Cities," *Scientific American* 213 (September 1965): 179–190.

4. The noted German microclimatologist Rudolph Geiger published many actual measurements of such variations in his epochal study, *The Climate of the Air Layer Nearest the Ground* (Munich, 1929). This study was last reprinted by Harvard University Press in 1980. A more recent classic is *Boundary Layer Climates* by T. R. Oke (London and New York: Methuen, 1987).

5. James Marston Fitch with Daniel Branch, "Primitive Architecture," *Scientific American* 203, (December 1960): 133–144.

6. James Marston Fitch, "The Aesthetics of Function," *Annals of the New York Academy of Sciences* 128 (1965): 706–714.

7. Paul A. Siple, "Regional Climate Analysis and Design Data," Bulletin of the American Institute of Architects, September 1949, 17.

8. Rudolph Geiger, *The Climate Near the Ground* (Cambridge: Harvard University Press, 1959).

9. Charles F. Brooks, "Parade-Ground Temperatures at College Station, Texas," *Monthly Weather Bureau* (November 1919): 801.

10. Geiger, *The Climate near the Ground*, 213.

11. Jeffrey Aronin, *Climate and Architecture* (New York: Reinhold, 1943).

12. See Bernard Rudofsky, *Architecture Without Architects* (New York: Museum of Modern Art, 1964), figs. 15–18.

13. Climate Control Project of *House Beautiful*. The meteorological data and architectural performance analyses were published in monograph form by the *Bulletin of the American Institute of Architects* between the years 1949 and 1953.

14. Aladar and Victor Olgyay, *Solar Control and Shading Devices* (Princeton, N.J.; Princeton University Press, 1963).

15. Ralph Knowles, "Form and Stability," and *Owens Valley Study: A Natural Ecological Framework for Settlement* (Los Angeles: University of Southern California, 1969).

16. Rudofsky, *Architecture Without Architects*; Ernest Schweibert, "The Significance of Primitive Architecture" (Ph.D diss., Princeton University, 1965).

17. Knowles, "Derivation of Surface Responses to Selected Environmental Forces," *California Arts and Architecture* (June 1964): 21–23; Ralph Erskine, "Building in the Arctic," *Architectural Design* 30 (May 1960): 194–197; "Two Lectures," *Journal, Royal Institute of Canadian Architects* 41 (January 1964): 194–197; "Indigenous Architecture: Building in the Sub-Arctic Region," *Perspecta* 8: 59–62; "Construire dans le Nord," *Architecture d'aujourd'hui* 38, no. 134 (October–November 1967): 96–97; "Restructuration de Kiruna, Ville de Laponie," *Architecture d'aujourd'hui* 38, no. 134 (October–November 1967): 98–99; "Turistation i Borgafjall," *Byggmasparen Arkitekture* 3 (March 5, 1955): 82–86.

18. Christopher Alexander, *Notes on the Synthesis of Form* (Cambridge: Harvard University Press, 1964).

19. Knowles, "Derivation of Surface Responses," 21.

20. Hassan Fathy, *Gourna: A Tale of Two Villages* (Cairo: Ministry of Culture, 1969).

21. "Ecological Architecture: Planning the Organic Environment," *Progressive Architecture* (May 1966) 120–137.

22. Donald Canty, "The Sea Ranch, California: Lawrence Halprin, MLTW, Joseph Esherick, Charles W. Moore, Donlyn Lyndon, William Turnbull, and Others," *Progressive Architecture* (February 1993): 84–99.

23. Geiger, *The Climate Near the Ground*, 377.

24. Canty, "The Sea Ranch."

25. Wolman, "Metabolism of Cities," 180.

26. Ibid., 179.

27. Ibid., 190.

Chapter 10

1. John Ruskin, *Seven Lamps of Architecture* (New York: John W. Lovell, 1885), 17.

2. This classification is adapted from that originally set forth by K. Lonberg-Holm and C. Theodore Larson in their pioneering study, *Planning for Productivity* (New York: International Industrial Relations Institute, 1940).

3. G. Ahluwalia and M. Carliner, National Association of Homebuilders, G. Fulton, Fulton Research, Inc., and Housing Guides of America, *What Today's Home Buyers Want*, 1996.

4. Jane Jacobs, *The Death and Life of Great American Cities* (New York: Random House, 1959).

5. Louis Winnick, "The Economic Functions of the City, Today and Tomorrow," in Thomas P. Peardon, ed., *Urban Problems*, 28th Proceedings of the Academy of Political Science (New York: Academy of Political Science, 29 April 1960), 12–13.

6. Jane Jacobs, *The Economy of Cities* (New York: Random House, 1969).

7. Ibid., 13.

8. Christopher Alexander, "A City Is Not a Tree," parts 1 and 2, *Architectural Forum* (April 1965); (May 1965).

9. Ada Louise Huxtable, *The Unreal America: Architecture and Illusion* (New York: New Press, 1997).

10. Fourth Congress for the New Urbanism, New Urbanism Charter signed at Charleston, S.C., May 1996, reprinted in *Environmental Building News*, September/October 1996, 6.

11. "Neotraditional Neighborhoods Funded for Inner Cities," *New Urban News* 2, no. 3 (May–June 1997): 1.

12. Alex Wilson, "Dewees Island: More Than Just a Green Development," *Environmental Building News* 6, no. 2 (February 1997): 5–7. Also literature provided by Dewees Island Real Estate, Inc., Isle of Palms, S.C.

13. Paul Kerlinger, *How Birds Migrate* (Mechanicsburg, Pa.: Stackpole Books, 1995).

14. Alexander, "A City Is Not a Tree," *Architectural Forum*, part 2, 61.

15. Ibid., 58.

16. Alexander, "A City Is Not a Tree," part 1, 60.

17. Ibid., 62.

18. Kenneth T. Jackson, "Why America Has Gone Suburban," *New York Times*, 9 June 1996, sec. 4, 15.

19. Michael Crosbie, "Critique: The Vatican of Consumption?" *Progressive Architecture* (March 1994): 70.

20. Blair Kamin, "Can Public Housing Be Reinvented?" *Architectural Record* (February 1997): 84.

21. Christine Killory, cited in Kamin, "Can Public Housing Be Reinvented?" 89.

22. Jackson, "Why America Has Gone Suburban," 15.

23. F. Pearce, "Megacities: Bane or Boon?" *World Press Review* (August 1996): 8–13.

24. Robert W. Kates, "Sustaining Life on the Earth," *Scientific American* (October 1994): 114–122.

Chapter 11

1. For background information on the theory and practice of the American preservation movements, see these two works published by the University Press of Virginia, Charlottesville, Virginia: *Preservation Comes of Age: From Williamsburg to the National Trust* by Charles B. Hossner Jr. (1981), and *Historic Preservation: Curatorial Management of the Built World* by James Marston Fitch. (1982).

2. U.S. Energy Information Administration, Commercial Building Characteristics (1994) as cited in American Institute of Architects, *Environmental Resource Guide* (New York: John Wiley & Sons, 1997), Project Report 2, 10.

3. "New York City Establishes 'Green' Building Program," *Building Design and Construction* (April 1997): 14.

4. Associated Press, "Nuclear Waste Dilemma—Home Sought for Three Mile Island Reactor Debris," *Herald Statesman* 2 February 1997, 6B.

5. Lester Brown, Christopher Flavin and Hal Kane, *Vital Signs 1996: The Trends That Are Shaping Our Future*. A Worldwatch Institute report. (New York: W.W. Norton, 1996), 54.

6. American Institute of Architects, *Environmental Resource Guide*.

7. American Society for Testing Materials, ASTM E-50.06 Subcommittee on Green Buildings, "Standard E-50.06.1, Standard Practice for 'Green Buildings,'" Draft Document 4.01, December 7, 1993.

8. Alan Durning, *How Much Is Enough? The Consumer Society and the Future of the Earth*, The Worldwatch Environmental Alert Series (New York: W. W. Norton, 1992).

9. Promotional brochure for the Environmental Studies Center of Oberlin College, Oberlin, Ohio. Prepared by William McDonough + Partners Architects, 1997.

Credits for Illustrations

Fig. 1–1   German Pavilion, Barcelona Exposition, Barcelona, Spain, 1929. Ludwig Mies van der Rohe, architect. Photograph courtesy Museum of Modern Art, New York, N.Y.

Fig. 1–2   "Falling Water" Bear Run, Pennsylvania, 1936. Frank Lloyd Wright, architect. From Edgar Kaufmann Jr., and Bruno Zevi, *La Casa sulla Cascata* (Milan: Etas Kompass, 1965), p. 50.

Fig. 1–3   Haj Terminal, Jeddah International Airport, Jeddah, Saudi Arabia, 1981. Skidmore Owings & Merrill, architects. From Horst Berger, *Light Structures - Structures of Light: The Art and Engineering of Tensile Architecture* (Basil, Switzerland: Birkhäuser Verlag, 1996), pp. 90–91.

Fig. 1–4   Diagram by James Marston Fitch.

Fig. 1–5   From George E. Ruff, "Psychological Stress," *Program*, Journal of the School of Architecture of Columbia University (Spring 1962), p. 67.

Fig. 1–6   From Duane P. Schultz, *Sensory Restriction: Effects on Behavior* (New York: Academic Press, 1965), p. 71.

Fig. 1–7   Diagram by James Marston Fitch.

Fig. 1–8   Hospital for Special Surgery, Major Modernization Project, New York, N.Y., 1996. Architecture for Health Science & Commerce, PC, architects. Photograph by Peter Mauss/Esto.

Fig. 1–9   The Arnold Center for Radiation Oncology, The New York Hospital Medical Center of Queens, New York, N.Y., 1995. Architecture for Health Science & Commerce, PC, architects. Photograph by Peter Mauss/ESTO.

Fig. 2–1   Diagram by James Marston Fitch.

Fig. 2–2   Example of universal design provided by the American Association of Retired Persons (AARP) Connections for Independent Living.

Fig. 2–3   Excerpted from U.S. Department of Housing and Urban Development, Fair Housing Act Design Manual.

Fig. 3–1   Based on Victor Olgyay, *Design with Climate* (Princeton, N.J.: Princeton University Press, 1963), p. 19.

Fig. 3–2   Kresge Dining Hall, Harvard University Business School.

Figs. 3–3–3–6   Diagrams by James Marston Fitch.

Fig. 3–7   Diagram by William Bobenhausen.

Fig. 3–8   Photograph by William Bobenhausen.

Fig. 3–9   Occidental Petroleum building, Niagara Falls, N.Y., 1979. Cannon Design, architects. Photographs courtesy Cannon Design.

Fig. 3–10   Mart Library and Computer Center, Bethlehem, Pennsylvania. Warner, Burns, Toan & Lunde, architects. Photographs by William Bobenhausen.

Fig. 3–11   Hypothetical study in surface response by Ralph Knowles assisted by R. R. Biggers, J. B. Coykendall, D. E. Egger, B. L. Hagler, J. T. Regan and W. T. Savage. Photograph courtesy Professor Knowles.

Fig. 3–12   From Lester R. Brown, Christopher Flavin, and Hal Kane, *Vital Signs 1996: The Trends That are Shaping Our Future*. The Worldwatch Institute (New York: W. W. Norton & Company), p. 49.

Fig. 3–13   Brookhaven (Laboratory) House, Brookhaven, N.Y. Photograph by William Bobenhausen.

Fig. 3–14   Based on William Bobenhausen, *Simplified Design of HVAC Systems* (New York: John Wiley & Sons, Inc., 1994), p. 193.

Fig. 3–15   Environmental Education Center, Milford, Pennsylvania, 1982. Douglas Kelbaugh, architect. Photographs by Donald Prowler.

Fig. 3–16   Girl Scout Building, Philadelphia, Pennsylvania, 1983. Bohlin, Cywinski & Johnson, architects. Photographs by Donald Prowler.

Fig. 3–17   Screen captures from *ENERGY-10* program.

Fig. 3–18   Photovoltaic arrays at National Renewable Energy Laboratory, Golden, Colorado, 1996. Photograph by William Bobenhausen.

Fig. 4–1   Hopewell, Virginia. Photograph by Earl Dotter, photojournalist.

Fig. 4–2   Photograph by William Bobenhausen.

Fig. 4–3   Bolivar County, Mississippi. Aerial pesticide application. Photograph by Earl Dotter, photojournalist.

Fig. 4–4   *Forge à Canons* (project), 1804. Claude Nicholas Ledoux, architect. From Ledoux, *Architecture Considérée sous le Rapport de l'Art*, vol. 1 (Paris: 1847), p. 98.

Fig. 4–5   Lower East Side, New York, N.Y., 1968. Photograph by Earl Dotter, photojournalist.

Fig. 4–6   Global average temperature. From Lester Brown et al., *State of the World 1997: A Worldwatch Institute Report on Progress Toward a Sustainable Society*. The Worldwatch Institute (New York: W. W. Norton & Company, Inc.), p. 79.

Fig. 4–7   World carbon emissions from fossil fuel. From Lester Brown et al., *State of the World 1997: A Worldwatch Institute Report on Progress Toward a Sustainable Society*. The Worldwatch Institute (New York: W. W. Norton & Company, Inc.), p. 10.

Fig. 4–8   World production of chlorofluorocarbons. From Lester Brown et al., *State of the World 1997: A Worldwatch Institute Report on Progress Toward a Sustainable Society*. The Worldwatch Institute (New York: W. W. Norton & Company, Inc.), p. 152.

Fig. 4–9   Screen captures of computational fluid dynamics (CFD) modeling results provided by Steven Winter Associates, Inc.

Fig. 4–10   Nineteenth-century masking device, designed by Richard Bridgens, engraved by S. Porter.

Fig. 5–1   Mud-walled huts in Ethiopia. Photograph by Diane Serber.

Fig. 5–2   Millowners' Association Building, Ahmedabad, India. Le Corbusier, architect. Photographs by Donald Prowler.

Fig. 5–3   From *Light and Color*, Technical Publication No. 119, General Electric Corporation, Nela Park, Ohio, 1967, p. 10.

Fig. 5–4   From S. K. Guth, "Light and Comfort," *Industrial Medicine and Surgery*, vol. 27 (November 1958), p. 575.

Fig. 5–5   Diagram by James Marston Fitch.

Fig. 5–6   From S. K. Guth, "A Review of Research in Seeing," *Light* (July/September 1958), p. 3.

Fig. 5–7   Rosemont Railway Station near O'Hare International Airport, Chicago, Illinois. Photograph by William Bobenhausen.

Fig. 5–8   House at Stony Point, N.Y. James Marston Fitch, architect.

Fig. 5–9   Diagram by Henry Wright from "Microclimatology," *Architectural Forum* (March 1947), p. 117.

Fig. 5–10   Daylighting scenarios. From Donald Prowler, *Modest Mansions: Design Ideas for Luxurious Living in Less Space*. (Emmaus, Penn.: Rodale Press, 1985), p. 137.

Fig. 5–11   Sacramento Municipal Utility District (SMUD) offices, Sacramento, California. Photographs courtesy SMUD.

Fig. 5–12 National Education Association Headquarters, Washington, D.C., 1990. Geier Brown Renfrow, architects. Photograph courtesy of Andrew Lautman.

Fig. 5–13 Photograph by Ben Rose, courtesy *Scientific American*.

Fig. 5–14 John Hancock Tower, Boston, Massachusetts, 1973. I. M. Pei & Partners, architect. Photographs by William Bobenhausen.

Fig. 5–15 Bell Telephone Laboratories, Holmdel, New Jersey. Eero Saarinen and Associates, architects. Photographs courtey *Scientific American*.

Fig. 5–16 Lighting fixtures in the Library at the College of Staten Island, New York. Photograph by William Bobenhausen.

Fig. 5–17 Daylighting and use of lighting fixtures. Photograph by William Bobenhausen.

Fig. 5–18 Overglazed skylight in atrium. Photograph by William Bobenhausen.

Fig. 5–19 United Airlines, Terminal 1, O'Hare International Airport, Chicago, Illinois, 1988. Murphy/Jahn, architects. Photograph by William Bobenhausen.

Fig. 5–20 Data excerpted from Joseph, J. Romm (U.S. Department of Energy) and William D. Browning (Rocky Mountain Institute), *Greening the Building and the Bottom Line*, (Snowmass, Col.: Rocky Mountain Institute), 1994.

Figs. 5–21, Diagrams by James Marston Fitch.
5–22

Fig. 5–23 House at Stony Point, N.Y. James Marston Fitch, architect. Photographs courtesy *House Beautiful*.

Figs. 5–24 Photograph courtesy French Cultural Services.

Fig. 5–25 House at Fox River, Illinois. Ludwig Mies van der Rohe, architect. Photograph above courtesy Museum of Modern Art; below, photograph by James Marston Fitch.

Fig. 5–26 From the RADIANCE program, Lawrence Berkeley National Laboratory.

Fig. 6–1 Diagram by James Marston Fitch.

Fig. 6–2 Typical impulse response from concert hall. Courtesy Siebein Associates, Inc.

Fig. 6–3 General view. Theater, Epidaurus, Greece, fifth century B.C. Foto Marburg/Art Resource, N.Y., S0093615, 134406, B&W Print.

Fig. 6–4 Margrave's Opera House, Bayreuth, 1748. Giuseppe Galli Bibiena, architect. From Gunther Beyer and Georg Mielke, *German Baroque* (Leipzig: Veb Edition, 1962), p. 96.

Figs. 6–5– Avery Fisher Hall (formerly Philharmonic Hall), Lincoln Center, New York, N.Y., completed 1962.
6–12 Harrison and Abramowitz, architects. Rendering and photographs for the years 1962 through 1997 provided by Lincoln Center for the Performing Arts Archives.

Fig. 6–13 Segerstrom Hall, 1983. CRS Sirrine, architects. Courtesy Siebein Associates, Inc.

Fig. 6–14 Meyerson-McDermott Concert Hall, Dallas, Texas, 1989. I.M. Pei, architect. Courtesy Siebein Associates, Inc.

Fig. 6–15 Evangeline Atwood Concert Hall, Anchorage, AK, 1989. Hardy Holzman and Pfeiffer Associates, architect. Photograph by Chris Little, courtesy Hardy Holzman and Pfeiffer Associates.

Fig. 6–16 Auditioner' station. Photograph courtesy the Bose Corporation.

Fig. 6–17 From Samuel Rosen, Dietrich Plester, Ali El-Mofty, Helen V. Rosen, "Relation of Hearing Loss to Cardiovascular Disease," *Transactions of the American Academy of Opthamology and Otolaryngology* (May-June 1964), p. 436.

Fig. 6–18 From Samuel Rosen and Pekka Olin, "Hearing Loss and Coronary Heart Disease," Archives of Otolaryngology, vol. 82 (September 1965), p. 238.

Fig 7–1 Photographs courtesy *Scientific American*.

Fig. 7–2 U.S. Dept. of Agriculture clerk at computer keyboard, Rosslyn, Virginia, 1997. Photograph by Earl Dotter, photojournalist.

Fig. 7–3 Yale School of Architecture, New Haven, Connecticut, 1964. Paul Rudolph, architect. Photograph by William Bobenhausen.

Fig. 7–4 Vancouver Public Library—Central Branch at Library Square, Vancouver, BC, Canada, 1995. Moshe Safdie and Associates and Downs Archambault and Partners, architects. Photograph by William Bobenhausen.

Fig. 7–5   Formulated by William Bobenhausen.

Fig. 7–6   From Frederick Kiesler, "Cor-realism and Biotechnique," *Architectural Record*, vol. 866 (September 1939), pp. 60–75.

Fig. 7–7   Clarendon Branch, Brooklyn Public Library. Photograph by Louise Harpman.

Figs. 7–8,   From Alexander Kira, *The Bathroom*. Copyright 1966 by Cornell University, Ithaca, N.Y. By permission
7–9   of Bantam Books, Inc.

Fig. 7–10   Excerpted from U.S. Department of Housing and Urban Development, Fair Housing Act Design Manual. Designed and developed by Barrier Free Environments, Inc., Raleigh, North Carolina, 1996.

Fig. 8–1   Detail from the inner sanctum, Temple of Hera II, Paestum, Italy. Alinari/Art Resource, N.Y., S012642, AN24933, B&W Print.

Fig. 8–2   Hall of Rites, Kamingano, Japan. From Werner Blaser, *Tempel and Teehaus in Japan* (Lausanne: Urs Graf Verlag, 1955), p. 153.

Fig. 8–3   Temple of Venus, Horti Sallustiani, Rome. Painting by A. F. Harper (1725–1806) from Sigfried Gideon, *Architecture and the Phenomenon of Transition* (Cambridge: Harvard University Press, 1971), p. 199.

Fig. 8–4   Entrance hall, house at Telč, Czechoslovakia. Photograph courtesy Czechoslovak Ministry of Culture.

Fig. 8–5   Diagram by James Marston Fitch.

Table 8–1   Formulated by James Marston Fitch.

Fig. 8–6   San Francisco Main Library, San Francisco, California, 1996. Pei Cobb Freed & Partners and Simon Martin-Vegue Winkelstein Moris Associated Architects. Photographs by Anthony Bernheim of Simon Martin-Vegue Winkelstein Moris.

Fig. 8–7   John Hancock Tower, Chicago, Illinois, 1970. Skidmore, Owings and Merrill, architects. Slide Library of the School of Architecture, CCNY.

Fig. 8–8   Cable-suspended roof, Utica, N.Y. Photograph courtesy Lev Zetlin and Associates, engineers. Descriptive diagram from Horst Berger, *Light Structures—Structures of Light: The Art and Engineering of Tensile Architecture* (Basil, Switzerland: Birkhäuser Verlag, 1996), p. 29.

Fig. 8–9   Madison Square Garden, New York, N.Y., 1962. Severud Associates, structural engineers. Berger, *Light Structures*, pp. 160 and 36.

Fig. 8–10a.   Yale Hockey Rink, New Haven, Conn., 1958. Eero Saarinen, architect. Slide Library of the School of Architecture, CCNY.

Fig. 8–10b.   Olympic National Stadiums, Tokyo, Japan, 1964. Kenzo Tange, architect. Berger, p. 31.

Fig. 8–11a.   Convention Center, New York, N.Y., 1988. I.M. Pei & Partners, architect. Photograph by William Bobenhausen.

Fig. 8–11b.   Baltimore-Washington Airport, Main Terminal Building, 1979. Peterson & Brickbauer, architect. Photograph by William Bobenhausen.

Fig. 8–12a.   One Liberty Plaza, New York, N.Y., 1972. Skidmore Owings and Merrill, architect. Photograph by William Bobenhausen.

Fig. 8–12b.   Flame shielding. Adapted from David Guise, *Design and Technology in Architecture* (New York: John Wiley & Sons, 1985), p. 74.

Fig. 8–13   Figure depicting design of Swiss engineer Robert Maillart's bridges formulated by Horst Berger.

Fig. 8–14   Marina City, Chicago, Illinois, Bertrand Goldberg, architect.

Figs. 8–15a.   Trans World Airlines (TWA) Terminal, John F. Kennedy International Airport, Queens, N.Y., 1962. Eero Saarinen, architect. Slide Library of the School of Architecture, CCNY.

Fig. 8–15b.   Main Terminal Building, Dulles Airport, Chantilly, Virginia, 1962. Eero Saarinen, architect. Slide Library of the School of Architecture, CCNY.

Fig. 8–15c.   Terminal Building, Newark International Airport, Newark, N.J., 1973. The Port Authority of New York and New Jersey. Photograph by William Bobenhausen.

Fig. 8–16   Thorncrown Chapel, Eureka Springs, Arkansas, 1980. Fay Jones & Associates. Courtesy Fay Jones & Associates.

Fig. 8–17   Timber frame house, Bucks County, Pennsylvania. Donald Prowler and Associates, architect. Photographs courtesy Donald Prowler.

Fig. 8–18   U.S. Pavilion, Expo '70, Osaka, Japan. Davis, Brody and Associates, architects; David Geiger and Horst Berger, engineers. Photograph courtesy Davis, Brody and Associates.

Fig. 8–19   Pontiac Stadium (the Silverdome), Detroit, Michigan, 1975. Berger, *Light Structures*, p. 161.

Fig. 8–20   Main Terminal of the Denver International Airport, Denver, Colorado, 1994. W. C. Fentress, J. H. Bradburn & Associates, architects, Severud Associates, structural engineer, Horst Berger, principal consultant. Berger, Light Structures, pp. 144, 145, 155, and 156.

Fig. 8–21   Garden Exhibition, Mannheim, Germany, 1967. Frei Otto, architect, Ted Happold, engineer. Berger, *Light Structures*, p. 15.

Fig. 9–1   Diagram from Victor Olgyay, "The Temperate House," *Architectural Forum*, vol. 94 (March 1951), p. 183.

Figs. 9–2– Formulated by James Marston Fitch.
     9–9

Fig. 9–10   Adapted from Helmut Landsberg as cited in "Microclimatology," *Architectural Forum*, vol. 86 (March 1947), p. 115.

Fig. 9–11   Images including those from CITYgreen™ software courtesy American Forests.

Fig. 9–12   Charts from *AIA Bulletins* (Washington: American Institute of Architects). No. 12: Portland, Oregon area, July 1951, pp. 4–5; no. 4: Arid Southwest area, March 1950, pp. 36–37; no. 3: South Florida-Miami area, January 1950, pp. 40–41; no. 8: Twin Cities areas, November 1950, pp. 14–15. AIA Bulletins copyright 1950, 1951 by The American Institute of Architects.

Fig. 9–13   Adapted from Victor Olgyay, *Design with Climate* (Princeton, N.J.: Princeton University Press, 1963), p. 19.

Fig. 9–14   CITYgreen™ software images courtesy American Forests.

Fig. 9–15   From Helmut Landsberg, as cited in "Microclimatology," *Architectural Forum*, vol. 86 (March 1947), p. 119.

Fig. 9–16   Adapted from Victor Olgyay, *Design with Climate* (Princeton, N.J.: Princeton University Press, 1963), p. 99.

Fig. 9–17   From W. Knochenhauer as cited by Jeffrey Aronin, *Climate and Architecture* (New York: Reinhold, 1943), p. 144.

Fig. 9–18   Hunan Province, China. Photo by Norman F. Carver, Jr.

Fig. 9–19   Photo from Norman F. Carver, Jr., *North African Villages* (Kalamazoo, Mich.: Documan Press), p. 31.

Fig. 9–20   From James Marston Fitch and Daniel P. Branch, "Primitive Architecture," *Scientific American*, vol. 203 (December 1960), pp. 138, 140.

Fig. 9–21   Fitch and Branch, pp. 139, 142.

Fig. 9–22   San Francisco de Asis Church, Ranchos de Taos, New Mexico, 1755. Photograph by William Bobenhausen.

Fig. 9–23   Roof wind scoops in Pakistan. Photograph by Donald Prowler.

Fig. 9–24   New Town, Cumbernauld, Scotland. Photographs courtesy Cumbernauld Corporation.

Fig. 9–25   Gourna, Egypt. Plans and photographs courtesy the architect, Hassan Fathy.

Fig. 9–26   Sea Ranch, Sea Ranch, California, 1966. Moore Lyndon Turnbull Whitaker, architect; Lawrence Halprin and Associates, landscape architect. Photograph by Donald Prowler. Photographs courtesy of the planners and landscape architects, Lawrence Halprin and Associates.

Table 9–1   Input-output energy ratios of cities. From Abel Wolman, "Metabolism of Cities," *Scientific American*, vol. 213 (September 1965), p. 189.

Table 10–1 Classification of plan types. From K. Lönberg-Holm and C. Theodore Larson, *Planning for Productivity* (New York: International Industrial Relations Institute, 1940), p. 23.

Fig. 10–1   Liberty Science Center, Jersey City, N. J. Photograph courtesy Liberty Science Center.

Fig. 10–2   Chan Centre for the Performing Arts, University of British Columbia, Vancouver, Canada. Bing Thom, architects. Photograph by Dori Clarke.

Fig. 10–3   Seaside, Florida. Andres Duany and Elizabeth Plater-Zyberk, Architects, Inc., designers. Photographs by Donald Prowler.

Fig. 10–4   View of Atlantic City from Brigantine National Wildlife Refuge. Photograph by William Bobenhausen.

Fig. 10–5   Aerial view of conventional subdivision. Slide Library of the School of Architecture, CCNY.

Fig. 10–6   South Street Seaport, New York, N.Y. Photographs courtesy South Street Seaport.

Fig. 10–7   Baltimore's Inner Harbor, Baltimore, Maryland. Photograph by William Bobenhausen.

Fig. 10–8   New Haven, Connecticut, low-income housing renovation. Photograph by Earl Dotter, photojournalist.

Fig. 11−1   Lower Broadway, New York, N.Y. From David W. Dunlap, *On Broadway* (New York: Rizzoli, 1990), p. 4.

Fig. 11−2   Schermerhorn building, New York, NY, 1891. George Browne Post, architect. Photographs by William Bobenhausen.

Fig. 11−3   Construction debris. Photograph by Ferdinand Mehlinger.

Fig. 11−4   Natural Resources Defense Council offices, Washington, D.C. Photograph courtesy National Resources Defense Council.

Fig. 11−5   The Environmental Studies Center, Oberlin College, Oberlin, OH, completion date 1998. William McDonough + Partners, architect. Rendering courtesy William McDonough + Partners.

Fig. 11−6   The SCJ World Wide Commercial Markets Division Headquarters Building, Racine, WI, completion date 1997. Hellmuth Obata Kassabaum Architects, the Zimmerman Design Group and Flad Associates, design team. Photograph courtesy Hellmuth Obata Kassabaum.

Fig. 11−7   C.K. Choi Building for the Institute of Asian Research and the Centres for China, Japan, Korea, India and South Asia, and Southeast Asia Research, University of British Columbia, Vancouver, Canada, 1994. Matsuzaki Wright Architects, architect. Photograph by William Bobenhausen.

Fig. 11−8   Nuclear reactor starts. Worldwatch Database Disk, The Worldwatch Institute, 1997.

Fig. 11−9   U.S. generating capacity. Worldwatch Database Disk, The Worldwatch Institute, 1997.

Fig. 11−10   Wind turbines of Northern State Power, Lake Benton, MN. Photograph courtesy Wind Energy Association.

Fig. 11−11   Graphical rating scale and categories. From American Institute of Architects' *Environmental Resource Guide* (New York: John Wiley & Sons, Inc., 1997).

Fig. 11−12   Photovoltaic prices. Worldwatch Database Disk, The Worldwatch Institute, 1997.

Fig. 11−13   Building-integrated photovoltaics. Photographs courtesy Solar Design Associates.

Fig. 11−14   U.S. population growth and rate of consumption. Worldwatch Database Disk, The Worldwatch Institute, 1997.

Fig. 11−15   Energy-efficient refrigerators. Worldwatch Database Disk, The Worldwatch Institute, 1997.

Fig. 11−16   The Gateway Arch, St. Louis, Missouri, 1965. Eero Saarinen, architect. Photograph by William Bobenhausen.

Index

Note: Page numbers in *italics* refer to illustrations or tables.

accessibility, *29, 30*
accidents, relationship to spatial configurations, 186–87
acid rain, 83–85
acoustics (*see also* sound): Alaska Center for the
    Performing Arts, Evangeline Atwood Concert Hall,
    Anchorage, Alaska, 173–74, *174;* banners for sound
    reflection, 159; computer modeling, 159;
    Concertgebouw, Amsterdam, Netherlands, 153; design-
    ing for acoustical intimacy, 152; Lincoln Center for the
    Performing Arts, New York City, 163–70, *164–66, 168,
    169–70;* Morton H. Meyerson Symphony Center,
    McDermott Concert Hall, Dallas, Texas, 172; Orange
    County Performing Arts Center, Segerstrom Hall, Costa
    Mesa, California, 170–71; seating capacity and, 167;
    sonic control, 149; substandard performance in mod-
    ern theaters, 162; Symphony Hall, Boston,
    Massachusetts, 153; theater, Epidauros, Greece, *157*
adaptability: in the human body, 9–10; in modern build-
    ings, 305–7
Addams, Jane, 310
adhesives, recycling materials with, *335*
adobe structures, 287
advocate planning, 326–27
agriculture, ability to change climatic conditions, 270
air-conditioning, 43–45, 49
air-pollution, 69, 297; acid rain, 83–85; allergies and,
    71–72; asthma, 31, 34, 71–72; attempts to control, 82;
    chlorofluorocarbons (CFCs), 86–88; filtration, 90–93;
    global warming, 85–86; plants air filtering functions,
    71; plants as sources of, 68–69; results of industrial-
    ism, *78, 79;* role of automobiles in, 34, 82–83; smog,
    79–82
air-pressurization, U.S. Pavilion, Expo '70, *251*
airports: Denver International Airport, *254, 255;* Dulles
    Airport, Main Terminal Building, *245;* Haj Terminal,
Jeddah International Airport, *7;* John F. Kennedy
    International Airport, TWA terminal, *245;* as a source
    of sonic pollution, 176, 179
Alaska Center for the Performing Arts, Evangeline
    Atwood Concert Hall, Anchorage, Alaska, 173, *174*
aldehydes, in auto emissions, 34
Alexander, Christopher, 187, 312–13, 317
Alice Tully Hall, Lincoln Center for the Performing Arts,
    New York City, 163, 167
allergies, air quality and, 71–72
Altamont Pass, California, *341*
altitude, *263, 265,* 267–68
aluminum, replacing steel, 240
ambient temperatures, in thermal habitat, *40*
amenities, city, 322–23
American Building: The Historical Forces That Shape It
    (Fitch), 350
American Institute of Architects (AIA), energy standards, 60
American National Standards Institute (ANSI), 211
American Optometric Association (AOA), 111
American Society for Testing Materials (ASTM), 346
American Society of Heating Refrigerating and Air-
    Conditioning Engineers (ASHRAE), 60
Americans with Disabilities Act (ADA), 30, *216*
Ames, Amyas, 168
amplitude, defined, 153
Andres Duany and Elizabeth Plater-Zyberk, Architects
    Inc., Seaside, Florida, *315*
anechoic environments, 159n
annual fuel utilization efficiency (AFUE), 49
anthropometry, 185, 200–206
arc lamps, 131
architects: backgrounds of, 324, 355; lack of qualified pro-
    fessionals, 349–50; perspectives of, 355–56
Architectural Barriers Act, 30
"Architecture and Energy," (Stein) *Architectural Forum,*
    58–59

Architecture for Health Science & Commerce, PC: Arnold
    Center for Radiation Oncology, 23; Hospital for Special
    Surgery, 21
Architecture Without Architects (Rudofsky), 289
Arendt, Hannah, 16
Arnold Center for Radiation Oncology, Queens, New York, 23
Aronin, Jeffrey, 278
arsenic, in auto emissions, 34
articulated structures: characteristics of, 253–56; stick
    structures compared to steel cage, 240; Temple of Hera
    II, 222
artificial light. See illumination
artisans, decreased need for, 357–58
arts, compared to architecture, 4–5
ASHRAE 90-1975 standard, 60
asphyxiation, from faulty heater design, 28
Association of Safe and Accessible Products (ASAP), 27
asthma: connection with smog, 34; prevalence of, 71; rela-
    tionship to thermal stress, 43; statistics for metropoli-
    tan areas, 31
atmosphere, 68–101 (see also air-pollution): airborne
    microorganisms and health, 71–74; alteration of, 78;
    effect of insect control on quality, 75–77; effect of
    wood on quality, 334; filtration, 91–92; movement of,
    40, 95; pressure, 70, 77; suspended impurities, 68–69,
    70–71
audition. See hearing
Auditioner acoustical system, Bose Corporation, 174, 175
automobiles, pollution issues, 34–35, 82–83
Avery Fisher Hall, Lincoln Center for the Performing Arts,
    New York City, 164, 166, 167–70, 168–70. See also
    Philharmonic Hall, Lincoln Center for the Performing
    Arts, New York City

balance in exogenous and endogenous forces, 354
Balcomb, J. Douglas, 61, 62–67, 279
Ball State University, Muncie, Indiana, College of
    Architecture and Planning, 359
Baltimore-Washington Airport, Main Terminal Building,
    239
Baltimore's Inner Harbor, Maryland, 322
banners, for sound reflection, 173
Barcelona Exposition, German Pavilion, Spain, 5
Baroque theaters of Northern Europe, 157
barriers: privacy barriers, 209; wind barriers, 277
basal metabolic rate (BMR), 189
bathrooms: bathtub design, 27; bidets, 217n; designing
    optimal personal hygiene tools, 217–20; designs for
    persons with disabilities, 220; safety issues, 26; sink
    design, 218; toilet design, 219
Bayreuth Opera (Margrave's Court Theater), Germany, 157
BC TEL Studio Theatre, 309
bedding, optimal, 212
behavior: factors affecting, 206, 323–24; structures' influ-
    ence on, 186–87
Bellamy, Edward, 107
Beranek, L.L., 152, 162
Berger, Horst, 254, 255, 256, 290
Bernardo, Jose, 188
Bernecker, Craig A., 114
Bertrand Goldberg, Marina City, 244
Bhopal, India, 89

bidets, 217n
bioclimatic chart, 40, 40
birds, migratory, Brigantine National Wildlife Refuge, 316
Blackwell, H. R., 129–30
Bohlin, Cywinski & Jackson, architects, Girl Scout
    Building, Philadelphia, Pennsylvania, 65
bombing, New York's World Trade Center, 232
bookcase, optimal design, 214, 215–17
boredom, 13–14
Bose, Amar G., 174
Brainard, George C., 114
Brand, Stewart, 184
Brazil, air-pollution in, 83
Bridgens, Richard, gilding factory mask design, 97
bridges, 232–35, 243
Brigantine National Wildlife Refuge, Oceanville, New
    Jersey, 316
brightness: balancing illumination, 133; defined, 113
Brill, Michael, 199, 218
brise-soleils, 55, 121–23
British thermal units (Btus), 329
Broadacre City, 310
Brookhaven National Laboratory, 60, 61
Brooklyn Bridge, New York, 232–34, 235
Brooklyn Public Library, Clarendon Branch, New York,
    216
brownfield sites, 320
Btus (British thermal units), 329
Building Energy Performance Standards (BEPS), 60
building materials: as an exogenous architectural force,
    353; chosen for environmental control reasons, 281;
    concrete, 203, 242–45, 243, 244, 245; embodied energy
    equivalents for common, 333; environmental stresses
    on, 224–25; masonry, 249–50; parallels between form
    and, 253; photothermal properties for thermal control,
    55; steel, 232–41, 233, 235, 236–39, 241; sustainability
    issues, 333, 334, 335, 341–48; synthetic strings and
    membranes, 250–53, 251, 252, 254, 255; wood, 223,
    246, 246–49, 248
buildings: abandoned, 319; environmental stresses on,
    223–24; relationship between, 323; role of, 8, 10,
    18–19; two components of, 228; types of, 22
Burnham, Daniel, 310

cable-net tensile structures, steel cables used in, 238
California Air Resources Board, 82
calories/Calories, defined, 189
Calthorpe, Peter, 313
Cannon, Walter B., 9
Cannon Design, Occidental Petroleum Building, 56
canopies, sound-reflecting, 173
capillary thermal systems, 54
capitalism, effect of on esthetics, 352–53
carbon dioxide emissions, 34, 86
carbon monoxide emissions, 34
carcinogens, air pollutants, 82
Carlisle House, Carlisle, Massachusetts, 344
carpal tunnel syndrome. See repetitive strain injury
Carson, Rachel, 77
CAT scans, spaces designed for, 23
Centers for Disease Control (CDC), 32
Centres for China, Japan, Korea, India, and South Asia,

and Southeast Asia Research, University of British Columbia, Vancouver, British Columbia, Canada, *338*

ceramic. *See* masonry

CFCs, decreasing use of in buildings, 86–88, 334

Chan Centre for the Performing Arts, University of British Columbia, Vancouver, Canada, *308*

charrettes in urban planning, 327

Château de Chambord, France, *143*

chemical induced immune dysfunction, 90

chemicophysical stress on structures, 223–24

Chernobyl nuclear power plant, pollution issues, 89

chlorofluorocarbons (CFCs), 86–88, 334

choice, as a benefit of cities, 311–12

chronic fatigue syndrome, 19–20

cities (*see also* plans and planning): amenities, 322–23; artificial, 312–13; diversity, 318–19; downtowns, 319; ecologies of, 34; economies of, 312; immigrants preference for suburban environments, 327; input-output mechanisms, *297;* interrelationship of buildings, 323; natural *versus* artificial, 317–18; New Urbanism, 313–14; rural population compared to, 327; sprawl as evidence of lack of qualified architects, 350; tree analogy, 317–18; as works of art, 311

"A City Is Not a Tree" (Alexander), 313

CITYgreen™ software, 275, *275*

C.K. Choi Building, Vancouver, British Columbia, Canada, *338, 339*

classification of plan types, 300–303

classrooms, 18–19

Clean Air Act Amendments of 1990, 84

clients: as an exogenous architectural force, 353; contributions to the planning process, 325–27; relationship to architect, 354–55, 358–59

climates: as an exogenous architectural force, 353; architects' underestimation of, 282–83; design considerations, 204–5; effect of urbanization on, *269, 269–70, 270;* effects of meteorological and geographical influences, *268;* energy conservation, 61–62; environmental factors of, 260; four major cities compared, *272–74;* microclimates in structures, 293; orographic uplifts, *265;* thermal and visual comfort in hot climates, 121; variations in, 266–71

clothing, to regulate temperature, 10

clouds (reflectors) in a concert hall for acoustical intimacy, *164, 165, 166*

Cocoanut Grove nightclub, Boston, Massachusetts, 230

collectors, energy, 59–60

College of Staten Island Library, New York, New York, *132*

color, 104, 139–41

communication, 156–59, 353

communities (*see also* cities): contributing to the planning process, 326–27; "new towns," 313–14; systematic development of, 301

compact fluorescent lamps (CFLs), described, 132

composites, replacing steel, 240

compression, *versus* efficiency, 305–7

computational fluid dynamics (CFD) modeling, *95*

computers: ability to quantify energy in Btus, 329–30; in accounting for environmental variables, 290; in acoustical science, 158, 159, 163, 174, *175;* in architectural design, 6–8; business implications, 196–99; designing thermal environments, 45; detrimental phys-

iological effects of, 111, 194; effect of on the conventional wisdom of the field, 357–58; in evaluating structural alternatives, 256

concert halls, 162–75 (*see also* acoustics): theaters; asymmetry in, 170; "concert hall of the twenty-first century" (Johnson), 158; late nineteenth century, 158; performances and seating quality, 154

Concertgebouw, Amsterdam, Netherlands, 153

concrete, *203,* 242–45; compared to steel, 243; luminous *versus* thermal characteristics, *105;* Marina City, Chicago, Illinois, *244*

conduction, 40

consciousness, sensory perception regulated by, 15

continuous dimming control, used with natural lumination, 135

convection, 40, 50

cooling. *See* air conditioning

cooling towers, 73

Cor-Ten, corrosion resistant alloyed steel, 240

corrosion and exposed steel, 240

cost effectiveness, as a consideration in selecting building materials, 333

costs, computing, 330

cotton, use of pesticides on, 76

Crabgrass Frontier: The Suburbanization of the United States (Jackson), 318

creativity in architecture, 191

critics and criticism: and architecture, 350–51; Avery Fisher Hall of the Lincoln Center of the Performing Arts, Inc., 169; music critics compared to architectural critics, 164–67; Philharmonic Hall of the Lincoln Center of the Performing Arts, Inc., 164–67

cross-pollution, 97

Croxton Collaborative, 333

CRS Sirrine, Segerstrom Hall, Orange County Performing Arts Center, 170–71

Crumlish & Sporleder and Associates, Ball State University, College of Architecture and Planning, *359*

Crutzen, Paul, 87

Crystal Palace, 225, 232

culture: influence on design, 217n; relation to esthetics, 15; sensitivity to diversity in planning, 311, 327

Cumbernauld, Scotland, "new town" design, 292, *293*

curtains, *139, 140*

Darwin, Charles, 71

Davis Brody and Associates, U.S. Pavilion, Expo '70, *251*

Day, Christopher, 210

dead load, as a vertical stress, 228

Death and Life of Great American Cities (Jacobs), 311

deaths: air-pollution related, 79–81, 82n; design related, 28; fire related, 231; infectious diseases related, 32; thermal stress related, 38–39, 42–43

decibels (dB), 147n

declination, 261

defecation, natural postures for, *219*

demolition, recycling from, *335, 342*

density, optimal population, 210

Denver International Airport, Denver, Colorado, *254, 255*

Department of Housing and Urban Development (HUD), *29,* 91, 314 design (*see also* plans and planning): accounting for climate variations, 269; adopting a defensive posture in, 258; failings of, 187; isolation of in post-industrialization, 354; office furniture, 197; optimal tools for tasks, 213–17, 218; range of motion, *218;* reliance on visual perspective *versus* polydimensional realities, 3–8; thermal control, 53–58; walls, 53

Dewees Island, as an example of New Urbanism, 314–16

direct sound, a component of impulse response, 154

disabled users, design considerations for, 29, 30, *220*

discontinuity, as a quality of natural light, 104–6

disease: air-pollution related, 90; airborne, 71, 75; buildings and, 31–32; digestive disease and availability of plumbing, 32; effect of cold on influenza incidence, 43–44; effect of heat on incidence of, 43

distance, types and effects of, 207–8

domes: Liberty Science Center geodesic dome, *304;* U.S. Pavilion, Expo '70, Osaka, Japan, *251*

Donora, Pennsylvania, disastrous smog of, 80

Doric temple, *222*

Downs Archambault and Partners, Vancouver Public Library, *205*

downtowns, 319

drive-in movies, technical compromises of, 161

Duany, Andres, 313

Duany Plater-Zyberk, 327

Dubos, Rene, 78

Duffy, Frank, 184

Dulles Airport, Main Terminal Building, Chantilly, Virginia, *245*

durability *versus* performance in primitive buildings, 284

dust, plants ability to reduce, 278

dust mites, as a source of allergens, 71

Eagle Mountain Landfill, 89

early field system, 173

early sound reflections, a component of impulse response, 155

Earth in the Balance (Gore), 78

earthquakes, San Francisco Main Library's adaptation to, *233*

echo, defined, 155

ecological systems: architects' need for understanding, 260; of cities, 34

"Economic Functions of the City Today and Tomorrow" (Winnick), 311

economics: effect of lighting on, 145–46; effects on building types and usage, 306–7; environmental zoning and, 279–80

economists, in city planning, 310

The Economy of Cities (Jacobs), 312

EcoVillage, Ithaca, New York, as an example of New Urbanism, 316

efficiency: in planning, 306–7; in production methods, 195; progression toward, 253

Eiffel Tower, Paris, France, and strength-weight ratio, 232

electric cars, 82

electrochromic glazing of glass, 129

electrostatic precipitation, 92

elevation, effect on climate, 265

embodied energy, 329–30, 333, *333,* 339

enclosure, 230

endogenous forces in architecture, 353

endoskeletal structural systems, 225n, 230, 234, 253–56

energy (*see also* photovoltaics): ability to quantify in Btus, 329–30; amount required for contemporary buildings, 289; architects response to the energy crisis, 58–59; buildings that export, 339; codes and standards, 288; conservation, 329–48; as a cost of building conservation, 330; difference between structure and equipment, 228; effect of 1973 energy crisis, 134; James Bay hydropower plans, *341;* and lumination, *117;* natural lighting, *134;* nuclear power plants, *340;* software for planning systems, 62–67, *66;* utilities and independent producers of, *340;* from wind, *341*

ENERGY-10 software, 62–67, *66*

energy efficiency: achieved with a small budget, *337;* Ball State University an advocate of, *359;* buildings designed for, 56, *61, 64, 65;* increased levels of, 104; natural illumination and, 135; Natural Resources Defense Council, Washington, D.C., *336;* savings from energy efficient products, 347

energy exporter, Environmental Studies Center, Oberlin College, *336*

entertainment, home, 303

entrepreneurs, influence on architecture, 354–55

environmental control, difficulty of achieving optimal, 257

Environmental Education Center, Milford Pennsylvania, *64*

environmental fit, dimensions of, 184–87

Environmental Resource Guide (ERG) (American Institute of Architects), *333,* 341–46, *342*

Environmental Studies Center, Oberlin College, 335–37, *336*

environments: architects' tendency to underestimate natural forces, 259–60; interaction between organisms and, *16;* six Ss of, 184

EPA, development of principles for material selection, 335

Epidauros, Greece, fifth century B.C. theater., *157*

equilibrium, requirement of architectural space, 189

equipment: defined in building terms, 228; plants role as, 278

ergonomics, 197; considered in equipment design, 213; defined, 185; standards for, 211

error, minimizing through design, 187

Erskine, Ralph, 290–91

esthetics: aristocratic leanings of modern architects, 355–56; in city planning, 323; culture-based standards, 15; effect of the production method on, 351–53; emphasis on, 33; experiential *versus* visual priorities, 163; as the goal of city planning, 311–12; *versus* health considerations, 22; historical perspective on, 310; relative nature of, 15; role of in architecture, 350–51; society's effect on, 360; theory, 3–4; visual richness as a byproduct of solving environmental problems, 103

evaluating effectiveness of buildings, 24

Evangeline Atwood Concert Hall, Alaska Center for the Performing Arts, Anchorage, Alaska, 173, *174*

evaporation, 40

exogenous forces in architecture, summarized, 353

exoskeletal structural systems, 230, 253–56

experience, influence on perception, 15

experiential requirements, 163, 323

exteriors. *See* skin

eyes: as data receivers and encoders, *108;* light modulation abilities, 110; near vision, 106, 114

fabric structures, Haj Terminal, Jeddah International Airport, 7
factories, *78,* 301, 319
failures in architectural design, 22–23
Fair Housing Accessibility Guidelines, 30
Fair Housing Amendments Act (FHA), 91
Falling Water, Bear Run, Pennsylvania, *6,* 243
Farnsworth House, Fox River, Illinois, *144*
Fathy, Hassan, New Gourna Egypt, 292, *294, 295*
fatigue: designing environments to combat, 194–95; effect of artificial light on circadian rhythms, 194; effect on production, 193; sleep and, 212–13; stress and, 191–95; work environments and, 19–20, 192–95
Fay Jones & Associates, Thorncrown Chapel, *246*
fc (foot candles), 109
fenestration. *See* windows
field of vision, stimulating middle and far fields, 116
fire: advances in prevention of, *233;* concrete's fireproof properties, 242; as a force of structural attrition, 230–32; as a limitation on exposed steel, 240
fireplaces, inefficiency of, *46*
Fischer, Ernst, 23
Fitch, James Marston: kinesthetic research on stair climbing, *188;* light-filtering glasses, *126;* structural orientation and environment, *118;* windows and illumination, *140*
Fladd Associates, SCJ World Wide Commercial Markets Division Headquarters, *337*
flame-shielding, One Liberty Plaza, New York, 240, *241*
flat plate collectors, 59–60
flexibility, as a characteristic of modern buildings, 305, 307
flexible membranes, 253
flooring, Mayo Institutes recommendations for allergies, 72
floors, tactile-haptic properties of, 202
fluorescent lamps, described, 131
folk arts, 351–52
foot-candles, 109
foot-lamberts, 110
Ford, Henry, 88
Ford Motor Company, 83
Forge à Canons, 78
form: *versus* function, 22; parallels between building materials and, 253
frame house, Bucks County Pennsylvania, *248*
Franklin, Benjamin, 47
Freilich, Jerry, 89
freon, 86
frequency, defined, 152
Fresh Kills Landfill, New York, 89
function: difference between structure and equipment, 228; *versus* form, 22
functional distance, 207
fungi, toxin-producing molds, 74
furniture: influence of arrangement, 209; Mayo Institutes recommendations for allergies, 72; office, 211; thermal considerations, 212; as a tool for relieving stresses on the body, 211–12

Garden Exhibition, Mannheim, Germany, *256*
gaseous composition, air, 70

Gateway Arch, St. Louis, Missouri, 347, *348*
Geier Brown Renfrow, National Education Association Headquarters, *123*
Geiger, Rudolph, 276–78
Geiger-Berger Associates, Pontiac Stadium (the Silverdome), Detroit, Michigan, 252
General Electric, "Real Life" demonstration kitchen, 28
generalization, limited opportunity for professional, 358
geodesic dome, Liberty Science Center, *304*
geography, 260
geology, architects' underestimation of, 282–83
Georgetown University, Intercultural Building, Washington D.C., *344*
Gerard, Robert M., 141–42
German Pavilion, Barcelona Exposition, Spain, 5
germicidal lamps, 92
Gibson, J. J., 186
Girl Scout Building, Philadelphia, Pennsylvania, *65*
Givoni, Baruch, 278
glare: controlling for, 121; importance of avoiding, 133; plants ability to eliminate, 278
glass: controlling luminance with, 124–25; designed for filtration of the visible band, *126;* glazing, 55, 127, 129; luminous disequilibrium after dark, *140;* optical behavior of, *138;* photochromic, 127; reflective, *127, 128;* spectrally selective, *54;* thermal comfort and, *139, 139;* thermal control with, *127;* transparency of, 104
glazes, 55, 127, 129
global warming, *85, 85–*86
Goldberg, Bertrand, Marina City, *244*
Gore, Al, 78
grass: effects of on temperature, 276–77; as a thermal modifier, 278
green architecture, 35–36
Green Buildings: ASTM Standard E-50.06.I, 346
greenfield sites, 320
greenhouse gas, in auto emissions, 34
Gropius, Walter, 3
Grosser Musikvereinsaal, Vienna, Austria, 153
Guggenheim Museum, New York City, 186, 243

habitats: defined, 182–84; manipulating to achieve an optimal fit, 183–84; need for active acquisition, *316;* personal, 11
Haj Terminal, Jeddah International Airport, 7
Hall, Edward, 12, 207–8
Hall, Jane, 82n
Hall of Rites, Kamingano, Japan, *223*
Halprin, Lawrence, 292–95
Hannover Principles, 35–36
Hardy Holtzman and Pfeiffer Associates, Inc., Evangeline Atwood Concert Hall, Alaska Center for the Performing Arts, 173, *174*
Harris, Cyril M., 168
Harrison and Abramowitz, Philharmonic Hall, Lincoln Center for the Performing Arts, 164, *164–*66
Harvard Business School, Kresge Dining Hall, *41*
Haussmann, Baron Georges Eugène, 310
health, 24–36; air pollution, 78–79; architects' responsibilities, 35–36; buildings as a source of disease, 31–32; evaluating buildings performance based on, 33–36; planning that emphasizes, 299–300; safety issues and buildings, 25–30

hearing: acuity of Mabaan tribesmen, Sudan, 177–78, *178;* auditory system, 150–51; auditory thresholds, 147–48, *148;* aural habitat, 11, 18, 147; aural simulations, 159, 161–62; noise pollution and hearing loss, 148–49, 175–77; supplemented with visual cues, 151–52

heat and heating, 41; achieving optimal thermal fit, *259;* blocking with applied glazes, 334; effect of plants on, 276–77; furniture and thermal considerations, 212; generated by human bodies, 38, 189; history of appliances for, 47–49; igloos' prevention of loss of, 284; installation types compared, *47;* pavement's absorption and retention of, 205; primitive structures, 290; structures to mediate, 6; traditional methods, *46*

heat islands, caused by urbanization, 270

HEPA filters, in fighting allergies, 72

Herrington, L.P., 189, 190

Heschang, Lisa, Brookhaven (Laboratory) House, *61*

high-intensity discharge (HID) lamps, described, 132–33

highways, as a source of sonic pollution, 176

historical buildings, preservation and development, *331*

HOK Architects, SCJ World Wide Commercial Markets Division Headquarters, *337*

Holden, Mark, 174

Holtzman, Hardy, 173

home, safety issues, 26–30

homeostasis, 9, 38, 52–53

Hooker Chemical Company Building, Niagara Falls, New York, *56*

Hospital for Special Surgery, Major Modernization Project, *21*

hospitals, design considerations for, 20–22

House at Bear Run, Pennsylvania, *6*

Housing and Urban Development, Department of (HUD), 29, 91, 314

Human Factors Society (HFS), 211

humidifiers, effect on air quality, 74

humidity, in thermal habitat, *40*

Hunan Province settlements, China, *280*

Huse, Brian, 89

Huxtable, Ada Louise, 314

HVAC systems. *See* air-conditioning; thermal control

Hyde, Jerald R., 170

hydrocarbons, in auto emissions, 34

HydroQuebec, James Bay, 341

hyperbaric chambers, 21, 77

hypercars, alternative fuels, 82

hypersensitivity, chemical or environmental, 90

iconoscope, vision compared to, 108

igloos, thermal performance of, 284, *285*

illness: associated with cities, 34–35; buildings as a source of, 31–32

Illuminating Engineering Society of North American (IESNA), 113

illuminating engineers, working with architects, 116

illumination: artificial light, 104–6, 130–34, *134,* 142–46; behavioral effects, 106, 111–12, *112,* 136, 137, 142; controlling, 114, 121, 123–25; defined, 109–10; design considerations, 104, 113, 116–24, *117, 118,* 135, 145–46; economic considerations, 123–24; and industrial technology, 107; laws of, 133; luminous disequilibrium after dark, *138,* 138n, *140;* mood lighting, 137n; natur-

al lighting, 116–21, *118, 119,* 334; physiological effects, 28, 110–11, 142–43, 194; software for planning lighting, *145;* thermal considerations, 37, *104, 134, 135*

I.M. Pei: McDermott Concert Hall, Meyerson Symphony Center, *172,* 172–73

I.M. Pei & Partners: Jacob Javits Convention Center, *239;* John Hancock Tower, *127*

impulse response in concert hall design, 153–55, *154*

incandescent lamps, 131

Industrial Revolution, effect of the development of a scientific theory of structure, 221

industrialization: effect of on design and fabrication, 352–53; role of artificial light in, 107

inflated structures, developing field of, 77

infrared radiation, 52, *54*

injuries: in the home, 26–30; job related, 213

insects, airborne, 75–77

insolation: controlling for with wall extensions, 124; and global air circulation, 261; retained in urban areas, 269–70

Institute of Asian Research, University of British Columbia, Vancouver, Canada, *338*

insulation: avoiding CFC-based materials, 334; thermal, *46*

internships, need for in current architectural education, 359–60

inversions resulting in smog, 79–81

Irminger, J.O.V., 95

iron, strength-weight ratio of structures made of, 233

irradiation, 92–93

Isler, Heinz, 244

isotropism, 234

J. de Saint-Pierre, Margrave's Court Theater, *157*

Jackson, Kenneth, 318

Jacob Javits Convention Center, New York, New York, *239*

Jacobs, Jane, 311–12, 317

Jaffe Acoustics, Inc., 173–74

James Bay, HydroQuebec, 341

Jefferson, Thomas, 353

John Hancock Tower, Boston, Massachusetts, *127*

John Hancock Tower, Chicago, Illinois, *235*

Johnson, Russell, 158, 172

Johnson/Burgee, Lincoln Center for the Performing Arts, *169–70*

Jones, Fay, Thorncrown Chapel, *246*

Joshua Tree National Park, California, 89

Kates, Robert, 327

Kelbaugh & Lee, Environmental Education Center, Milford Pennsylvania, *64*

Kennedy Space Center, use of light-opaque walls, 123

Kernot, W.C., 95

Kidwell, John, 162

Kiesler, Frederick J., 213–17, *214*

Killory, Christine, 326

kinesthesis, 186, 206

Kira, Alexander, 211, 217

kitchens: designs and functionality, 306–7; safety issues, 27–28, 30

Kivett & Myers, Pontiac Stadium (the Silverdome), Detroit, Michigan, 252

Knowles, Ralph, 287, 290; metabolic response to surrounding

environmental forces, 282; orientation and design in solar heat control, 56–58, *58,* 124
Kuching, Malaysia, air-pollution in, 83

La Salle Hotel, Chicago, Illinois, 230
labor: compared to work, 16–18; as a cost of conservation, 330; "mind workers," 198; new theory of, 198; productivity and environmental considerations, 106, 114, 115, 136, 212, 335
Laguna West, example of a "new town," 313
lamination, benefits of, 247
land masses, thermal behaviors of, 263
landscape architecture, 275–79
Larson, C. Theodore, *302–3*
late field system, 173
latitude, *261, 262, 262,* 267–68
lawns, air filter functions of, 71
Lawrence, Charles, Segerstrom Hall, Orange County Performing Arts Center, 170–71
Lawrence Halprin and Associates, Sea Ranch, California, *296*
Lawrence Livermore National Laboratory, 95
laziness, 185
Le Corbusier, 310
Le Corbusier, Millowners' Association Building, *105*
lead poisoning, 32
Ledoux, Charles Nicholas, *78*
Legionnaires' disease, 72
Lenôtre, André, 310
Leonardo da Vinci, 4
Lev Zetlin and Associates, Utica Municipal Auditorium, *236*
Liberty Science Center, Jersey City, New Jersey, 304, *304*
libraries, Kiesler's prototype for, *214,* 215–17, *216*
licensing, history of in architecture, 357
life-cycle assessment (LCA), ERG methodology, 345
life expectancy, role of architecture in, 25–26
life sciences, relationship of architecture to, 8
light shelves, *120,* 121, *122*
*Light Structures—Structures of Light (*Berger), 256
lighting. *See* illumination
lighting components, 130
Lighting Handbook of the Illuminating Engineering Society of North American, 113
Lincoln Center for the Performing Arts, Inc., New York City, 18, 163–70
linearity, 5
literacy, role of luminance in, 106
live load, as a vertical stress, 228
load collector ratio (LCR), 61, *62*
Lonberg-Holm, Knud, *302–3*
London, England, problems with smog, 34–35, 81
Looking Backward (Bellamy), 107
Los Alamos National Laboratory, 61
Los Angeles, California, problems with smog, 34, 81–82
loudness, early sound reflections contributing to, 155
louvers: for luminance control, *123;* for thermal efficiency, 55–56, *56, 57*
Ludwig Mies van der Rohe: Farnsworth House, *144;* German Pavilion, Barcelona Exposition, 5
luminance. *See* illumination
Lyndon, Donlyn, 295

Mabaan tribesmen, Sudan, 177–78
macrocosmic habitats, defined, 182
macroenvironment, 258
Madison Square Garden, New York City, 237
Maillart, Robert, Schwandbach bridge design, 242–44, *243*
malaria, fear of, 71
Malaysian Department of Environment, 83
malls, proliferation of, 319
Margrave's Court Theater, Bayreuth, Germany, *157*
Marina City, Chicago, Illinois, *244*
market research, as the guide to design, 358
Marshall Day Acoustics, 170
Mart Library and Computer Center, Bethlehem, Pennsylvania, 57
Martin County Courthouse, Florida, 73
masonry, as a building material, 249–50
mass transit, city planning issues, 313
material consumption and population, *345*
math, analysis of structural efficiency, 232–34
Matsuzaki Wright Architects, C.K. Choi Building, *338*
Mayo Clinic, 31, 72
McDermott Concert Hall, Morton H. Meyerson Symphony Center, Dallas, Texas, 172, *172*
McDonough, William, 35, 347
McMillan Commission, 310
mechanical stress on structures, 223–24
mechanization, as a characteristic of modern buildings, 305, 308–9
megacities, increasing number of, 327
megastructures, 291–92
membranes, 229, 250–53
mesocosmic habitats, defined, 182
mesoenvironment, defined, 10
metabolism: of cities, 297; cities as organisms with, 270; effect of work upon, *189;* existence on the level of, 10; habitats of, 11–12; inefficiency of, 38; interrelated functions for feedback, 8
meteorology, 260
Metropolitan Opera, Lincoln Center for the Performing Arts, New York City, 164–67
Meuse Valley, Belgium, disastrous smog of, 79
Meyerson Hall, Dallas, Texas, 159. *See also* McDermott Concert Hall
MGM Grand Hotel, Las Vegas, Nevada, 231
microclimates, *264,* 266–74, *268*
microcosmic habitats, defined, 182
microenvironments, defined, 8
Millowners' Association Building, Ahmedabad, India, *105*
minorities: air quality in minority communities, 81, 82n; thermal stress in minority communities, 43
mirrors, one-way, used to limit structural heat gain, 125
Mojave Desert, 89
mold in water damaged buildings, 74
Molina, Mario, 86
Monadnock Building, Chicago, Illinois, 234
Monier, Joseph, 242
Montreal Protocol on Substances That Deplete the Ozone Layer, 87
mood lighting, 137n
Moore Lyndon Turnbull Whitaker, Sea Ranch, 292–95
Moshe Safdie and Associates, Vancouver Public Library, *205*

motivation, required to overcome resistance, 323
MRIs, spaces designed for, 23
Mt. Sinai Hospital, New York, 240
mud masonry, 286, 287; application of, 294, 295; limited
    role of illumination in, 104; megastructures in the
    Moroccan desert, 281; performance in thermal stress,
    284–87; thermal performance of, 286
multilayer polarizers, 129–30
multiple chemical sensitivity (MCS), 90
Murphy/Jahn, United Airlines, Terminal I, O'Hare
    International Airport, 136
musculoskeletal injuries, 213

NASA, Langley Research Center, 96
Nashville, Tennessee, Smoky Joe smog research, 81
natatorium of the 1996 Olympics, Atlanta, Georgia, 344
National Association of Home Builders, 28
National Audubon Society headquarters, 331–35, 332
National Center for Health Statistics, 34
National Education Association Headquarters,
    Washington, D.C., 123
National Fire Protection Association (NFPA), 231
National Renewable Energy Laboratory, Golden, Colorado,
    62–67, 66
Natural Resources Defense Council, Washington, D.C., 336
nature, influence on structural design, 258
near vision, 106, 114
neon vapor lamps, described, 133
New Gourna, Egypt, 292, 294, 295
New Urbanism, 282, 313–14
New York City: preservation and development of build-
    ings, 331; smog, 80, 81
New York Hospital Medical Center of Queens, Arnold
    Center for Radiation Oncology, 23
New York State Theater, Lincoln Center for the Performing
    Arts, New York City, 163
New York Times, criticism of the Lincoln Center of the
    Performing Arts, 164–67, 169
Newark International Airport, Newark, New Jersey, 245
nitrogen oxides, in auto emissions, 34
Nobel Prize in chemistry, 87
noise (see also sound): court rulings on, 179; level of
    annoyance, 151–52; as a measurement of sonic pollu-
    tion, 149; noise-free communities, 177; physiological
    consequences of, 148–49, 175–78, 179; plants effect on,
    276, 278; sources of, 176
nongaseous aerosols, 70
normal, stress patterns, 229
Norman, Donald, 187
nuclear power, 339–41, 340

Oberlin College, Environmental Studies Center, 335–37,
    336
obsolescence, designing to delay, 305–9
Occidental Petroleum Building, Niagara Falls, New York,
    56
O'Dell/Hewlett & Luckenbach, Inc., Pontiac Stadium (the
    Silverdome), 252
odors, controlling through architectural means, 100–101
offgassing, minimizing, 334
offices: designing workspaces for increased productivity,
    199–200; increasing necessity to cool, 44

O'Hare International Airport, United Airlines, Terminal I,
    Chicago Illinois, 115, 136
oil, price of, 59
olfaction, 96–100; air as the habitat of, 69–70; habitat of,
    11; sensitivity of, 98
Olgyay, Aladar, 282
Olgyay, Victor, 259, 282
Olmsted, Frederick Law, 310
Olympic National Stadiums, Tokyo, Japan, 238
One Liberty Plaza, New York City, 240, 241
one-way mirrors, use to limit heat gain, 125
open plan, affect on olfaction, 96
orchestra pits, 158
organism and environment, 182–83
orientation, 58, 116–23, 118
oriented strand board (OSB), 247
orographic uplift, 265, 265
Osmond, Humphry, 209
Otto, Frei, Garden Exhibition, 256
oxygen depletion sensor (ODS), 28
ozone, 81, 86

Pacific Gas and Electric Energy Center, San Francisco,
    California, 125
Panama Canal, construction of, 71
panels, sound-reflecting, 171, 171
Paoletti Associates, Inc., 170
parasitic diseases, connection with availability of plumb-
    ing, 32
parking in "new towns," 313–14
particulates, 79, 276–78
partitions, preserving privacy in crowded areas, 209
pavement, heat absorption and retention properties, 205
paving materials, resilience of, 203
pedestrians: behavior of, 203–4, 323–24; city planning
    issues, 313; designs to encourage walking in Seaside,
    Florida, 315
Pei, I.M. See I.M. Pei: McDermott Concert Hall, Morton H.
    Meyerson Symphony Center
Pei Cobb Freed & Partners, San Francisco Main Library,
    233
perception: existence on the level of, 10; thresholds of, 14
performance versus durability in primitive buildings,
    284
performing arts centers, designed for flexibility of use,
    309
period, defined, 152
peroxyacetyl nitrate (PAN), production of, 81
Perry Dean Rogers, College of Staten Island Library, 132
Persian Gulf War, pollution issues of, 89
persistent organic pollutants (POPs), 77
pesticides, environmental effects of, 76–77
Peterson, Mary Jo, 28
Peterson & Brickbauer, Baltimore-Washington Airport,
    Main Terminal Building, 239
Pheiffer Associates, Inc., Architects, 173
Philharmonic Hall, Lincoln Center for the Performing
    Arts, New York City, 163–64, 164–66. See also Avery
    Fisher Hall, Lincoln Center for the Performing Arts,
    New York City
photochemical smog, production of, 81
photochromic glass, 127–29

photography, affect on architectural appreciation, 5
photovoltaics, *66, 342, 343, 344. See also* solar energy
physical distance, 207
physiology: analogy with architecture, 9; consequences of noise, *179;* effect of temperature on ability to work, 190; sensory trauma, 14
Piazza San Marco, Venice, Italy, 205
planners, traditional backgrounds of, 324
plans and planning, *293, 294, 295,* 299–328, 309–22; advocate planners, 326–27; architectural *versus* urbanistic, 301; building types, 22, 300–303, 305; cities and towns, *293, 294, 295,* 309–22; cities as works of art, 310; implementation of, 317; need for comprehensive strategy, 324; New Urbanism movement, 313–14; Seaside, Florida, *315*
plants: air filtering functions of, 71; ecological impact studied with computer software, *275;* effect on pollution, *276;* heat reducing properties, 205; sources of air pollution, 68–69; as thermal modifiers, *278;* used in environmental control, 278–79, 281
plastic, as a building material, *224*
plastic bag collectors, 60
Plater-Zyberk, Elizabeth, 313
plazas, weather inhibiting usefulness, 204
plumbing, relation to health issues, 32
plywoods, 247
pneumatic structures, 250–53, *252, 254, 255*
policy, need for environmental, 297
pollution (*see also* air pollution): from cities, 34–37; Clean Air Act Amendments of 1990, 84; effect of plants on, *276;* particulate, 88; plants as sources of air pollution, 68–69; sources of sonic, 176
Pontiac fever, infection from airborne microorganisms, 72
Pontiac Stadium (the Silverdome), Detroit, Michigan, *252*
population density, *209, 210,* 223
Post, George Browne, Schermerhorn Building, *332, 334*
precipitation, changes due to orographic uplift, *265*
precision, strength achieved through, 233
predictability, as a benefit of cities, 311–12
preservation of structures, 329
primitive cultures, building practices of, 283–90, *286*
prismatic glass blocks, 124
privacy: issues, 143–45; reflective glass, *128;* trees and, *276*
production, esthetics and, 351–53
productive sound, 149
productivity: designing environments for optimal, 190–92, 299–300, 335; environmental variety, 44–45; length of work week and, 195; reducing injury, 213
professionalism, development of in the field, 357
proprioception, 9
Prowler, Donald, frame house, Bucks County Pennsylvania, *248*
proxemics, defined, 185
proximity, as a benefit of cities, 311–12
psychoacoustics, 153
public housing, 324–26, *325*

quadratic residue sound-diffusing surfaces (QRDs), 171
quality, 195, 358–59

radial cable system, *237*
RADIANCE lighting design software, *145*

radiant temperature control, *40, 46,* 50–52
radiation oncology center, 23
recommended practices (RP) of the Illuminating Engineering Society of North America, 113
recordings, compared to live performance, 161–62
recycling, 334–37, *335, 338*
Reed, Walter, 71
reflection: as a physical phenomenon of sound, 155; reflectors in concert halls, *164, 165, 166*
refraction, as a physical phenomena of sound, 155
refrigerants, 87–88
Rehabilitation Act of 1977–78, 30
relationships, role in the planning process, 300
renovation: of historic Baltimore waterfront, *322;* low-income housing, 324–25, *325*
repetitive strain injury, 194, *198,* 213
residences, evolution in, 305–6
resonance, as a physical phenomena of sound, 155
respiratory infections: in Brazil, 83; effect of cold on incidence of, 43–44; from molds, 74; from smog, 79–81; statistics for metropolitan areas, 31
respiratory system, air as the habitat of, 69–70
restoration, Schermerhorn Building, New York City, 331–35
reverberation: chambers, 159; electronic sound systems, 173; reverberant sound fields, 155; with sound-reflecting panels, 171
Richardson, H.H., 306
Riverwalk, San Antonio, Texas, 320–22
Roebling, John Augustus, 235, 251n
rotating buildings: for luminance control, 121; for thermal control, 53–55
Rowland, Sherwood, 86
Rudofsky, Bernard, 289–90
Rudolph, Paul, Yale School of Architecture, *203*
rural population compared to cities, 327
Ruskin, John, 195, 300

Saarinen, Eero: Dulles Air Terminal, John F. Kennedy International Airport, *243, 245;* Gateway Arch, *348;* Yale Hockey Rink, *238*
Sacramento Municipal Utility District (SMUD), Sacramento, California, *122*
safety, in the home, 26–30
Saint-Pierre, J. de, Bayreuth Opera (Margrave's Court Theater), 157
Salt River Project, 84
San Francisco de Asis Church, Ranchos de Taos, New Mexico, *287*
San Francisco Main Library, California, *233*
sanitariums, an obsolescent plan type, 305
sanitation facilities, digestive diseases and, 32
São Paulo, Brazil, air-pollution in, 83
scale, limitations of large models with small, 324
Schermerhorn Building, New York City, 331–35, *332*
Schermerhorn Row, New York City, *321*
Schonberg, Harold C., 167, 169
Schwandbach bridge design, *243*
Schweibert, Ernest, 289
science centers, Liberty Science Center, *304*
SCJ World Wide Commercial Markets Division Headquarters, Racine, Wisconsin, *337,* 337–39

screens, for shading, 55
Sea Ranch, California, 292–95, *296*
Seaside, Florida, *315*
seating quality and concert hall performances, 154
secondary light sources, as modifiers and retransmitters of light, *108*
Segerstrom Hall, Orange County Performing Arts Center, Costa Mesa, California, 170, *171*
Seldes, Gilbert, 161–62
Selye, Hans, 185, 191
senses: and building performance, 33; habitat of, 11; optimal environments for, 190; role of, 8–9; sensory deprivation/overload, 12–14, *14*; tactile perception, 200–202; trauma, 12–15; visual perception, 102–3; visual perspective *versus* polydimensional realities, 3–8
Severud Associates: Denver International Airport, *254, 255*; Madison Square Garden, *237*
sewage, in cities, 34
shading: for paved surfaces and buildings, 278; for thermal control, 55
sick building syndrome (SBS), 90
The Significance of Primitive Architecture (Schweibert), 289
signs, esthetic dilemma of, 142
Silent Spring (Carson), 77
Simon Martin-Vegue Winkelstein Moris Associated Architects, San Francisco Main Library, *233*
skeleton: as the structural frame, 225; task of, 229
Skidmore, Owings and Merrill: John Hancock Tower, Chicago, Illinois, *235*; One Liberty Plaza, *241*
skin, structural, 53, 225
skyscrapers, 235–40
slab: an element of structure, 229; principle of surface continuity, 253
slab-edge insulation, *46*
smog, 34–35, 79–82, *80*
smoke alarms, absence of in MGM Grand Hotel, 231
social activists, influence on cities of, 310
social architecture, shift toward, 355
social processes, buildings as settings for, 210–11, *302–3*
social scientists, in city planning, 310
socialization of architecture, 356
society: conflicts in expressed in architecture, 360; and esthetics, 350–51; influence on planning, 301
software: Auditioner™, used in acoustical simulations, 174, *175*; CITYgreen™, used to analyze ecological impacts, 275, *275*; ENERGY-10, used to evaluate energy strategies, 62–67, *66*; RADIANCE, used in lighting design, *145*
Solar Design Associates: Carlisle House, *344*; Olympic Natatorium, *344*
solar energy: buildings blocking access to natural light, 279; cells for electricity production, *344*; comparative passive solar performance, *63*; controlling for surpluses and deficiencies, 288; double envelope design, 60; effect of on temperatures, *261*; heating, 60–61, *62, 63*; orientation, *58*, 116–23, *318*; popularity resurgence, 59; solar savings fraction (SSF), *62*; solar screens, 121
solar radiation, 271n
Solar Radiation Data Manual for Buildings, National Renewable Energy Laboratory, Golden, Colorado, 271n
solar screens, for luminance control, 121–23

Solarex & Hughes, Georgetown University, Intercultural Building, *344*
Solarex Manufacturing Plant, Frederick, Maryland, *344*
solid waste, 89
Sommer, Robert, 208–9
son-et-lumière, 143, *143*
sound (*see also* noise): barriers inhibiting, 156; humans skills of discrimination, 150; level of annoyance, 151–52; measuring, 152–53; noise free communities, 177; productive *vs.* counterproductive, 149; social implications of, 180–81; supplementing with visual cues, 151; trees' effect on airborne sound, 276; types and behaviors of waves, 152–55
South Coast Air Quality Management District (SCAQMD), 82n
South Street Seaport, Manhattan, New York, *321*
Southeast Asia, decreasing air-quality, 83
space: described in visual terms, 103; multiple uses of, 305–7; personal, 207–8; in photography, 5
space frames, steel, *239*
spatial organization, effects of, 12, 207
speaking, decreasing reverberation with banners for, 173
specialization, in production and design, 351–53
sport-utility vehicles, 82–83
sprinkler systems, 231–32
St. Gaudens, Augustus, 310
St. Louis, smog issues, 34
stadiums, Pontiac Stadium (the Silverdome), 252
stair-climbing analysis, *188*
steel: applications of, 235–39; cables, 235, 236–38; cage, 235–40; isotropic properties of, 234; limitations of, 240; optimal application of, 240; used in reinforcing concrete, 242
Steelcase Corporate Development Center, Grand Rapids, Michigan, 199
Stein, Clarence, 310
Stein, Richard, 58–59
stereo systems, 155
Stern, Robert, 313
stick, an element of structure, 229, 253
stone. *See* masonry
stoves, as heat source, *46*
Stramit International, wall system, *336*
street lamps, social significance of, 107
strength-weight ratio, 232
stress, physiological: cumulative effects, 193; in hospital environment, 20–22; as a result of unnatural behaviors, 15; role of architecture to in reducing, 3, 191–92; sensory overload/deprivation, 12–14; types of environmental, 223–24
stresses, structural, 228–29
string, an element of structure, 229, 253
structural insulated panels (SIPs), *248, 249*
structures and structural systems: four primary elements of, 229; function of, 224, 228–32; morphogenetic classification of, *226*; structural theory, 221–22, 225, 227
Studer, Raymond G., 184–85
studio apartments, economies of, 306
subterranean housing, as an environmental response to thermal stress, 280
suburban growth, immigrants contributing to, 327
suction, as a horizontal stress, 228

sulfur, in auto emissions, 34
sulfur dioxide, air pollution, 79
sulfur lamps, described, 133
sunspaces, 60, *61*
Superfund law (Comprehensive Environmental Response, Compensation, and Liability Act), 320
support, 230
surfaces: continuity, 253–56; tactile-haptic properties of, 202–3; weather and outdoor, 203–4
surgical suites, design considerations for, 21
surround-sound audio systems, 155
suspension bridges, 235, 251n
sustainability, 329–60; Ball State University an advocate of, *359;* building materials, *333,* 341–46; embodied energy concepts, 329–30, 333, 339; preservation, 329; renovation, *322,* 324–25, *325;* restoration, 331–35
"Sustaining Life of the Earth" (Kates), 327–28
Symphony Hall, Boston, Massachusetts, 153
synthetic strings, 250
systems, social, 301
Szell, George, 168

Tacoma Narrows suspension bridge, failure of, 229n
tactility, 11–12, *201,* 202; role of in design, 200–202; types of information transmitted by, *201*
Tange, Kenzo, Olympic National Stadiums, *238*
tangent, stress patterns, 229
technology: devices to eliminate physical injury, 213; effect on personal interaction, 208; effect on preindustrial exogenous limitations, 354; pace of, 349
technology, reliance upon, 282
Telc, Czech Republic, 225
telecommuting, 200
television, experiential compromises of, 161
temperature: altitude and, *263;* controlling, 21, 277, 334; correlation with work and physical condition, *190;* effect of latitude on, *261, 262;* effect of solar exposure, *264;* effect of temperature on body processes, *190;* global, *85;* orographic uplifts and, *265;* plants ability to affect, 276–78, *278;* size of land mass, *264;* stratification in rooms, 50; structures suited to variations in, 6, *280, 281, 286;* in Toronto, Canada, *269*
Temple of Hera II, Paestum, Italy, *222*
Temple of Venus, Horti Sallustiani, Rome, Italy, *224*
Tennessee Valley Authority system of locks and dams, use of reinforced concrete in, 242
tensile structures, 250–52
tent structures, 250–52
terpenes, source of air pollution, 68–69
theaters, *157 (see also* concert halls): acoustics in modern structures, 162; dynamic nature of their role, 160; economies of, 306; Greek theaters, 18, 160; Lincoln Center for the Performing Arts, Inc., 18; live performance compared to simulations, 161; societal roles of, 160
Theatre Projects Consultants of London, BC TEL Studio Theatre, 309
theory, need for in the field of architecture, 349
thermal control systems, 50–52; animal analogies, 52–53; common characteristics of, 47; components of, *48*
thermal environment, 37–67; asymmetry of in freestanding buildings, *54;* balance of, 38–42; control of, *259;* factors of, 39; industrial requirements, 44; stabilizing, 45–52

thermal habitat, 39, *40*
thermal storage walls, 60, *64, 65*
thermal stress: controlling with architecture, 270–71; disasters involving, 42; physiological reactions to, 38–39; primitive attempts at controlling, 283–84; relationship with disease, 43–44; responding to via clothing, 10; social consequences of, 43
thermochromic glazing of glass, 129
third environment, 10, 15–16
Thom, Bing, Chan Centre for the Performing Arts, *308*
Thoreau, Henry David, 90
Thorncrown Chapel, Eureka Springs, Arkansas, *246*
Three Mile Island nuclear reactor, Harrisburg, Pennsylvania, 339–41
time, in photography, 5
tissue fatigue, 194
TNDs. *See* traditional neighborhood developments (TNDs)
Today and Tomorrow (Ford), 88
Toffler, Alvin, 198
Toffler, Heidi, 198
toilets, 32, *219*
Tokyo, smog issues, 34
tools: designing optimal equipment for users, *214, 216, 218, 218, 219, 220;* development of optimal, 213–18
Top of the Mark, San Francisco, California, 124
topography, 202, 260
Total Environment Action (TEA), Brookhaven (Laboratory) House, *61*
touch. *See* tactility
town planning. *See* plans and planning
toxins, as a product of molds, 74
traditional neighborhood developments (TNDs), 313–14
training: apprenticeship, 356–57; emphasis on esthetic priorities, 324–25; need for internships in architectural education, 359–60; professional licensing, 357
Trans World Airlines (TWA) Terminal, John F. Kennedy International Airport, Queens, New York, 245
transparent walls, as a means of controlling luminance, 124–25
transportation: as an exogenous architectural force, 353; influence on structural advance, 234–35
Tredgold, Thomas, 47
trees, benefits of summarized, 276
tuberculosis, statistics for metropolitan areas, 31
twentieth-century disease, 90

Union Carbide plant, Bhopal, India, 88–89
universal design, 27, 28
University of British Columbia, Chan Centre for the Performing Arts, Vancouver, Canada, *308*
University of California at Berkeley, 359
University of California at Davis, 95
University of Virginia in Charlottesville, 35
urban design, 275
urbanization, climatic changes due to, 269–70
U.S. Department of Housing and Urban Development (HUD), 32
U.S. Department of Transportation, 83
U.S. Environmental Protection Agency (EPA), 83
U.S. Fair Housing Act, 220
U.S. Pavilion, Expo '70, Osaka, Japan, 251, *251*
U.S. Public Health Service, statistics on digestive disease, 32

U.S. Steel, Pittsburgh, Pennsylvania, 240
Utica Municipal Auditorium, New York, *236*
utilities, growth of, *340*
UV lamps, for air filtration, 92

Vancouver Public Library, Central Branch, British
   Columbia, Canada, *205*
vapor retarders, fungi contamination, 73–74
vaulting, late Gothic, *225*
ventilation, 287, *288*
Venturi, Robert, 313
vibration, effects of, 229n
Victorian entrepreneurs, responsible for revolution in
   architecture, 354–55
virtual reality, 162
viruses, airborne, 74–75
vision: attrition of visual acuity, 109n; boundary of, 11;
   computer vision syndrome, 111; habitat of, 11, 18;
   health considerations, 107; and illumination, 133; optimal conditions, 114–15; role of visual perception in
   design, 102–4; society wide changes in, 106–7; spatial
   parameters of, *109;* strain, *112;* theories of, 108; visible
   spectrum, 109–10, *110*
"Vital Signs" workshop, University of California at
   Berkeley, 359
Vivian Beaumont Theater, Lincoln Center for the
   Performing Arts, New York City, 163, 167
Voeux, Harold Antoine Des, 79

W. C. Fentress, J. H. Bradburn & Associates, Denver
   International Airport, *254, 255*
Wagner, Richard, 158
wall paper, as a vapor retarder, 74
walls: as barriers, 229; decreasing structural significance
   of, 234; load bearing *versus* environmental control
   functions, *227;* made of compressed wheat straw, *336;*
   significance of in design, 53
warmth system, for low frequency sound reflections, 173
Warner, Burns, Toan & Lunde, Mart Library and
   Computer Center, 57
waste, 34, 297, *297*
water: conservation, 297–98; heat-holding capacity,
   262–63; mold growth in water damaged buildings, 74
waterfronts, revitalization of, 320
wavelength, defined, 152
weather, 260. *See also* wind; affected by urban development, 269–70; designing outdoor spaces considering,

203–4; effect of sun on, *261;* measured in macroscopic
   scales, 266; patterns, *261*
weight, as a vertical stress, 228
Wendt, Fritz, 68–69
Weston, H. C., 110–11
Whitaker, Charles Harris, 310
wildlife refuge, Oceanville, New Jersey, *316*
William McDonough + Partners, architects, *336*
wind: accounting for architecturally, 292–95; aerodynam-
   ics of buildings, 93–96; affect of buildings on, 94;
   architectural adaptation to, *296;* construction suited to
   combat, *280;* as a horizontal stress, 228; as a power
   generator, *341;* rooftop wind scoops as seen in the
   Middle East, *288;* tunnels used in research, 94–96;
   windbreaks, 277
windows: allowing for natural daylight, 334; difficulty of
   controlling structural luminance with, 138–39; and
   luminance, 118–19; and optimal natural luminance,
   114; psychological effects of, 116; radiant effects of, *40;*
   windowless buildings and worker dissatisfaction,
   115–16
Winnick, Louis, 311–12
Winslow, C. E. A., 43, 189, 190
Wolman, Abel, 297–98
wood: and air quality, 334; behavior of, 247; as a building
   material, 246–49; environmental concerns, 247, 249;
   fires in structures made of, 231; frame house, *248;* Hall
   of Rites, Kamingano, Japan, *223;* transition to steel,
   234
Wood, Edith Elmer, 310
work: correlation with temperature and physical condition, 190; effect of on metabolism, *189;* environments
   of, 19, 44–45, 189–200; nature of, 16–18; work-fatigue-
   rest-recovery cycle, 25
World Trade Center, New York, bombing of, 232
World's Fair, Hannover, Germany ???, 35
Wright, Franklin Lloyd, *6,* 243, 310
Wright, Henry, 310

Yale Hockey Rink, New Haven, Connecticut, *238*
Yale University, New Haven, Connecticut: School of
   Architecture, 202n, *203*
Yost, William A., 151

Zimmerman Design Group, SCJ World Wide Commercial
   Markets Division Headquarters, *337*
zoning, environmental, 279–80